DATE DUE

JUN 7 1989			
NOV 20 1993			
AUG 10 1994			
AUG 28 1995			
JUN 3 0 1998			

Restructuring the Automobile Industry

COLUMBIA STUDIES IN BUSINESS, GOVERNMENT, AND SOCIETY
ELI NOAM, GENERAL EDITOR

Restructuring
the Automobile Industry

A Study of Firms and States
in Modern Capitalism

DENNIS PATRICK QUINN, JR.

New York   COLUMBIA UNIVERSITY PRESS   1988

Library of Congress Cataloging-in-Publication Data
Quinn, Dennis Patrick, 1955-
Restructuring the automobile industry.

(Columbia studies in business, government, and
society)
Bibliography: p.
Includes index.
1. Automobile industry and trade—United States.
2. Automobile industry and trade—Great Britain.
3. Industry and state—United States. 4. Industry
and state—Great Britain. I. Title. II. Series.
HD9710.U52Q56   1988   338.4'76292'0941   87-15919
ISBN 0-231-06524-8

Columbia University Press
New York   Guildford, Surrey

*Clothbound Columbia University Press editions are Smyth-sewn
and printed on permanent and durable acid-free paper*

TO
K. S. A.
and
to my parents,
Joan and Dennis Quinn.

COLUMBIA STUDIES IN BUSINESS, GOVERNMENT, AND SOCIETY
Eli M. Noam, GENERAL EDITOR

CONTENTS

List of Illustrations

List of Tables

ACKNOWLEDGMENTS

THE WRITING OF A BOOK is ultimately a social process, and I am pleased to be able to thank publicly my colleagues who invested labor in my academic projects - a small reward, I know. My academic career and interests were intimately shaped by my association, first as a student and then as a teacher, with people connected to Columbia University and its Political Science Department. My deepest academic debt is to Doug Chalmers, the chairman of the Department, a tolerant and humane teacher who forbore my frequent forays from the fold with good humor. Many of my less tenable arguments fell victim to his critical eye. I am also indebted to Mark Kesselman, who read and commented on my work with similar tolerance, and Eli Noam, who encourage the transformation of a dissertation into a book. Stefanie Lenway (University of Minnesota) and Tom Jones (University of Washington) read the complete manuscript, and each made many helpful suggestions. Many others have read and commented on parts of the manuscript (sometimes in earlier forms). These included: John Ruggie, James Shenton (History), Glen Adler, Robert Amdur, Kathleen Andersen (SUNY—Stony Brook), Stanley Aronowitz (CUNY—Sociology), John Delaney (Columbia—Business), Randell Dodd (Columbia—Economics), James Douglas (Northwestern), Wyn Grant (Warwick), Gary Hansen (University of Washington), Peter Kane (Trades Union Congress), Joel Krieger (Wellesley), Fritz Kratockwil, Ian Maitland (Minnesota—School of Management), Rita Moore, Alex Motyl, Phil Oldenberg, Robert Parmele, Paul Peretz (University of Washington), Thomas Pogge (Columbia—Philosophy), Don Redfoot (Duke—Sociology), Craig Robinson, Tom Roehl (University of Washington—International Business), Don Scarfe, Eric Smith (California—Santa Barbara), and Robert Y. Shapiro. Robert Jacobson (University of Washington) patiently taught me econometrics, and provided many crucial suggestions for the section on corporate taxation. The manuscript would not have been completed without the help of the many trade union officials, corporate executives, and civil servants (in Britain, Canada, and the United States) who spent hours answering my questions.

Ms. Margaret Freund provided many different forms of logistical support, as did Columbia College (most notably in the form of a semester-long sabbatical). Research funds and grants toward completing the book were provided by the Business Schools at the University of Washington and Columbia University, and the Center for Research in Management of the University of California. Research assistance was provided by Nancy Eiselt, Gail Morton, Jeff Terry, and Dennis Zacharopolous. Even though I typed the bulk of the manuscript, Ms. Andersen and Harpreet Mahajan provided crucial editorial (and, in Ms. Andersen's case, some typing) assistance. Mr. James Pickrel proofread the manuscript and prepared the index. Mr. Leslie Bialler of Columbia University Press edited the manuscript with great care and precision. Ms. Kate Wittenberg, Executive Editor for Political Science at Columbia University Press, shepherded my manuscript through the review and editorial process at Columbia; I am particularly grateful to her for her persistence. I also thank the anonymous referees for Columbia University Press.

My research was done in the following libraries: Lehman and Business Libraries (Columbia), the British and the Science and Technology Libraries (British Museum), Baker Library (Harvard), New York Public Library, London School of Economics and Social Science Library, the archives of the Society of Motor Manufacturers and Traders (SMMT—London), Library of Congress, the Library of the University of Maryland (Europe), and Americanishe Häus—Munich and Nuremberg. To the librarians of these institutions, I owe my thanks. To those Canadians who spent much time educating me about the politics of their economy, my apologies for the omission of the Canadian section of the manuscript.

Illustration Credits

Table 2.6, Table 4.11, and 4.15 reprinted with permission from the *Financial Times* (London). Table 2.2 and Table 3.1 reprinted from P. J. S. Dunnett, *The Decline of the British Motor Industry*, with permission from Croom Helm, Ltd. Table 2.3 reprinted from Krish Bhaskar, *The Future of the World Motor Industry*, with permission from Kogan Page, Ltd. Table 3.3 reprinted from Jeffrey Allen Hunker, *Structural Change in the U.S. Automobile Industry*, with permission from D.C. Heath, Inc. Table 3.7 reprinted from Ronald Fox, *Managing Business Government Relations*, with permission from Richard D. Irwin, Inc. Table 3.8 reprinted from Murray L. Weidenbaum, *Business, Government and the Public*, with permission from *Chilton's Automotive Industries*.

Restructuring the Automobile Industry

1.
OVERVIEW

IN ENTITLING MY BOOK *Restructuring the Automobile Industry* I run the risk of being accused of false advertising; it is not about the automobile industry per se. Instead, I examine the restructuring of the auto industries of Great Britain and the United States in light of our understandings of comparative public policy and of the state in modern capitalism. Marx, Rawls, and pluralism receive as much line space here as do Ford, GM, and economies of scale. My interests in writing this book are: to argue that capitalist governments of larger countries demonstrate common patterns of public policy toward their private firms, but only under conditions of economic decline; to help to develop a "mid-range" theory of the state, one that understands the state as being more than the captive agent of societal and economic interests; and to explore the implications for democratic societies when states advance their interests in public policy. The automobile industry afforded me a platform from which I reconnoitered a small patch of the terrain of politics and policy. The theoretical issues raised in analyzing the auto industry are essential to the purpose of the book.

I have two central themes—the conditions under which market societies exhibit similar patterns of public policy toward private firms, and the interests of the welfare state.

Similar Public Policies Toward Firms

Do democratic capitalist governments have similar public policies toward their private sectors? The extent of similarities in the substance and timing of public policies among Western governments has been an important question for comparative politics and sociology; Marx and Weber, among others, advanced convergence arguments. With respect to similar industrial policies, the general view among academics, journalists and politicians is clear—No. Some governments, in addition to macroeconomic intervention, engage in microeconomic planning, other governments rely on market forces, and still others mix and match markets and planning. Industry structures, world market positions, domestic interests, and institutions of government all differ among capitalist countries. We therefore see fundamental differences in form and substance of public policies among Western governments. This is the conventional answer, and there is much evidence to recommend this view.

The primary purpose of the first part of this book is to test for similarities in public policies among Western governments toward their private firms and, if similarities are found, account for the timing of these policies. I use a comparison study of government policies in the United States and Great Britain to examine this problem. From this study, I derive several hypotheses that I test using regression techniques borrowed from econometrics. I conclude that we do find similar public policies toward private firms among four Western governments: those of the United States, West Germany, Japan, and Great Britain. The common pattern is that these countries have, since 1978, subsidized the capital investments of their domestic firms, but only during periods of economic downturn.

Theories of the State

The "state,"

> is a more fundamental concept than government, because it is not merely the specific regime in power at any one moment—the governing coalition of political leaders—but also the basis for a regime's authority, legality, and claim for popular support.[1]

The three generic theories of the state are the pluralist, elite (sometimes referred to as managerial), and Marxist perspectives. Each of these perspectives has some analytic utility, though, as Alford and Friedland note, pluralism remains the dominant perspective among political scientists in the United States. In understanding comparative public policies toward firms, what are the circumstances under which each is useful?

I argue that the best explanation for this common pattern of public policies among countries requires an understanding of the perceived "interests of the welfare state," and of the theories about economics that inform these perceptions. The "similar" public policies among these countries are those that attempt to minimize costs to state and national accounts while promoting "public welfare" through policies of "economic efficiency." Subsidizing the investments of private firms while preventing the failures of large firms is the substance of these policies. In a sense, the development of policy similarity among some Western countries is the consequence of a dilemma described by Joseph Schumpeter in 1942. My findings also indicate that the "state interest" explanation has analytic utility only in circumstances of declining economic activity. Some implications for democratic societies follow from states advancing their own interests, and the last chapter comprises a discussion of these.

Method

I undertook a comparison of the auto industries of the United States and Great Britain as one way of grounding some theoretical questions about public policy and political theory. The auto industry provided all the attributes of political economy I found to be necessary for an analysis of the state in modern capitalism: strong actors (firms, unions, governments), wide geographic dispersion, well developed international trade, extreme fluctuations in demand, rapidly changing production processes, strong consumer preferences, great economic importance, and, most importantly, winners and losers in market competition where the stakes mattered to governments, firms, and unions. From the comparison, I developed several hypotheses about the general pattern of public policy toward firms in market societies. I next collected a new body of data, one unrelated to the automobile case study: corporate taxation returns in four major economies (U.S., U.K., Japan, Germany). I then proceeded to test these hypotheses using statistical methods. I found statistically significant associations that confirmed most of my hypotheses.

From these results, I developed an argument on behalf of the explanatory power of a "state interest" theory of the state. The standard that I used in assessing the adequacy of various theories is "best fit" in light of falsifiability. Although my conclusions about the adequacy of a "state interest" theory of the state are interpretive, my argument is not normative. The argument is capable of disconfirmation: it is not a "language of description."[2] Because of the "falsifiability" of this explanation, "state interests" has a narrower focus and a more limited utility than do broader explanations. By way of contrast, many other theories of the state are capable of describing and understanding virtually any state action. The "interests of the welfare state" as used here, on the other hand, would not be useful in understanding, for instance, the many instances where government policy resulted directly from societal pressures.

In this limitation I find virtue. Because I take it as a given that each of the generic theories of the state has some analytic utility, but not complete utility, the question becomes *when* does a theory have utility. Hence, a discussion of state theories needs to be grounded in the specifics of cases and data. The reader will not then be surprised that I believe the main problem with much of the literature on the theory of the state, particularly that done from the neo-Marxist perspective, is that rarely is it grounded in anything approaching data. Public policy analysis, on the other hand, has tended toward the reverse direction from the theories of the state literature—lots of data, little theory.[3] Only sometimes done comparatively, rarely done in order to address broader issues in political science, public policy analysis has largely told us who did what to whom when—important questions, crucial questions, but not usually grounded in theory. In this book, each is embedded in the other.

The research design of this book is one not commonly used in comparative politics. The historical, interpretive method is more usual. Peter Katzenstein's *Small States in World Markets: Industrial Policy in Europe* is one of the best representatives of this tradition in political science. As Professor Katzenstein notes:

> Although I use numbers in this book where relevant, I deliberately differ from statistically inclined investigations that seek to enhance our understanding by correlating small size with a broad range of economic, social, and political outcomes. In method of analysis I accord pride of place to historically informed comparisons rather than to statistical investigations.[4]

Professor Katzenstein instead, through use of secondary as well as primary sources, provides a highly persuasive, synthetic analysis of the politics of European industrial policy. This model of appropriate evidence is an older and, of course, valid one—employed more in history than in economics.[5] Fortunately, political science as a discipline enjoys a healthy heterodoxy of research models and standards of appropriate evidence.

As I explain in chapter 4, my own research design is something of a hybrid. The form of research used—the generation of hypotheses through a comparison study, the testing of these hypotheses using statistical techniques on data different from the original material, drawing both positive and normative inferences concerning theory from the data analyses—is, nonetheless, accepted as being appropriate in the field of political science. Of course, I need not have chosen this model of research. I considered adding more countries to my study, and conducting many more interviews with corporate, government, and union leaders than I actually did in lieu of directing my energies to data collection and quantitative analysis. My choice was partly dictated by my desire to reach (and be persuasive to) an audience in which the accepted rules of inference work against using case-study–based comparisons to advance general arguments. For an argument to be thought to have explanatory power, some claim that the rules of deduction require of the argument that it be generalizable to a context different from that in which it was derived. Economists, for instance, tend not to accept much less than the formal testing of hypotheses.[6]

Although I do not subscribe to the necessity of using this form of modeling and testing in the study of political economy, I concluded that my arguments would be more persuasive with some effort at quantitative analysis. Though I am, of course, pleased that this analysis supports the argument made in light of the U.S./U.K. comparison, I would have remained confident of the analysis of the auto industry study, even if the hypotheses had been disconfirmed by the quantitative analysis used in the study of corporate taxation. My overall point is that in political economy, one's choice of audiences is in part a choice of methods—a mixed constituency, which is my aim, breeds mixed methods!

Background

Those who study industrial policy/competition policy know that all Western governments (the U.S. included) have encroached into the domain of (more or less) free trade and market competition that has characterized Western economies since the Second World War: the United States already has an elaborate and expensive industrial policy, we hear *sotto voce*.

Much like the debates over the "crisis of democracy," "overloaded institutions," and the fiscal crisis of the cities, the subject of the already extensive government intervention in the American economy has gone out of academic fashion and been shunted aside; considerations of the consequences of government intervention on economic performance dominate. Only a handful of "structuralists" (e.g. neo-Marxists) continue to talk about the common "structural imperatives" imposed on Western governments by the "necessities of capitalism."[7]

Public attention has instead focused on the merits of two models, public interventionism (or "statism") vs. the "free market" or liberal arrangements, as the alternative solutions to problems in growth and distribution.[8] We look past the existing American industrial policies, assuming that what the United States currently has is a free market strategy. This assumption is clearly unsound. Nevertheless, despite all the evidence to the contrary, the assumption underlies the current debate in Congress and the popular press as to whether the United States would be better off or worse off it it no longer fully played the role of the neutral state, and adopted an industrial policy, including trade restraints.

In the current political climate, the free market model of the neutral state has had the better of the public debate. The argument on its behalf is more or less as follows. The underlying rationale for Western governments to adopt freer trade and market competition as the public regime is simple in the extreme—economic growth is best promoted by unrestrained factor markets.[9] Public intervention distorts market signals, protects inefficient producers, drains resources from the general public to special interest groups, provides subsidies to foreign consumers of sheltered firms, and is held to be largely unable to "pick winners" in promoting economic growth: this is the liturgical litany of the neoclassically liberal literati. We might sum the credo of much economic analysis by paraphrasing and reversing Keynes:

> public interventionism, in the hands of which we found ourselves after the war, is not a success. It is not intelligent, it is not beautiful, it is not just, it is not virtuous—and it doesn't deliver the goods.[10]

We do find nuances in this analysis; some forms of public intervention overcome collective action problems in the provision of public goods (e.g., the business cycle, negative externalities) and therefore promote economic efficiency, at least in the short-term. On balance, however, public intervention is not seen to promote society's welfare, and the political parties of the Western democracies have substantially changed tack to catch the winds of the new climate of public opinion, one increasingly sympathetic to market solutions to problems of distribution. By 1983, even the Socialist government of France had adopted profitability as its overall criterion toward its noncompetitive nationalized firms in autos and steel.[11]

The beliefs of economists and the ideological disposition of politicians are not the only elements promoting the free market solution to problems of economic growth and distribution; the institutions of the international free trade regime (GATT, EC, IMF), the general legitimacy of economic liberalism, and the interests of the "hegemon," the U.S., in free trade, reinforce this tendency.[12]

This analysis on behalf of the neutral state is not without its anomalies. Japan and France successfully used a variety of selective incentives toward domestic firms and of nontariff barriers toward foreign firms in achieving higher than average rates of economic growth.[13] A second anomaly has emerged from new models of trade, which suggest that, although cumulative global welfare might not be advanced by forms of protectionism, the welfare of individual nations might be. These recent models of intra-industry trade and technological competition suggest that the incentives for governments to provide protection for some industries, particularly high-tech industries, might be strong.[14]

Neoclassical economists generally consider these anomalies as outliers in the otherwise strong linear correlation between free markets and economic growth. We do find political pressure on governments to employ defenses to protect industries, and not necessarily "infant industries." The political facts of life, however, do not refute the argument on behalf of the economic benefits of the nonintervention-ist state. Economists generally regard "rent-seeking" activity as an inevitable, though regrettable, feature of democratic practices.[15] Firms, farmers, and the federations of labor learned long ago the politics of pluralist protectionism.

Proponents of the statist tradition, however, are usually neither members nor defenders of rent-seeking interest groups. Neither are they necessarily poorly educated in microeconomic theory. Instead, Reich, Thurow, and others point to the undeniable fact of the relative economic decline of the United States and Great Britain. The free market model, its intellectual rigors notwithstanding, is forced to confront the declining industrial competitiveness of these two countries, which have espoused the liberal model of economic activity.[16] Work by the French economist Jacques Mistral provides evidence for the claim that the United States and Great Britain are in the midst of a long-term deterioration in industrial competitiveness. As a measure of this phenomenon, Mistral has used the demand elasticity of a country's imports divided by the demand elasticity for its exports. That is, $E^M \div E^X = T$.[17] He argues that the ratio in the United States has moved from .5 in the 1870s to 2 in the 1970s. The ratio for the United Kingdom has remained at 2 for most of the past 120 years. This implies a steady erosion of both the terms of trade in manufacturing and a loss of home markets as foreign firms sell into once isolated markets.[18] The auto industry, my case study, is thus a specific case of a general trend. From the evidence of economic decline has come a search for other models of resource allocation, models drawn from countries that apparently are not infected by economic "slugitis."

In addition to these questions of industrial competitiveness, the adherents of the free market model are confronted with the modern welfare state. Like it or not, almost all Western nations are concerned with economic growth and public welfare; these items are embedded in the state's agenda. The question confronting governments is what sort of strategies for promoting public welfare should they chose, not whether governments should have such strategies. The free market vs. the interventionist state debate in the industrial policy literature is thus something of a smokescreen.

The free market vs. the interventionist state are nonetheless the proffered choices in the public debates in the United States and the larger Western European countries. We would therefore be justified in expecting the conclusion to this background discussion to be that, as we review the public policies of Western governments in the late 1970s and 1980s, one of two characterizations of public policy will be true. Either we shall find national public policies to be divergent (as they clearly were in the 1950s through the mid-1970s) as some nations follow market solutions and others adopt *dirigisme*; or, should we find similarity, we shall find governments adopting competition policies that, following from the assumptions of neoclassical economics, "seek to ensure the efficient allocation of resources by means of open and competitive markets."[19]

Neither description is adequate. Owing to the "interests of the welfare state," I will argue that, under circumstances of economic decline, governments have adopted roughly similar policies—policies designed primarily to prevent the failure of large firms.

General Outline of the Book

Chapter 2 begins with a brief review of the economic and political history of the automobile industry. The purpose of this section is to provide a brief discussion of important processes, policies, and persons in its development. The next section of chapter two focuses on automobile firms, the factors of production important in the industry (such as economies of scale), and the range of choices available to firms. The chapter concludes with a discussion of the state's interests, and their relationship to the firm's interests. Particular attention is devoted throughout chapter 2 to a discussion of the rationale for the internationalization of production. Those readers who have little prior knowledge of either industrial issues or corporate strategy might find this section an important prerequisite for later discussions of why governments have relatively few choices when negotiating with automotive firms.

In chapter 3, the problems of the American and British auto industries are introduced, and the differences in their structures are highlighted. Their industries are different in size, in products, and in general financial conditions. Government policies from the 1940s through the mid-1970s were also different. The British were more concerned with economy-wide demand stimulation, regional development, and sterling's value than with any particular strategy for the motor vehicle industry. The American Government, when involved at all, focused on antitrust, safety, and environmental regulations. Chapter 3 demonstrates the general absence of similarity between these two nations in industry and public policy, and makes the case that development of policy congruence from such different material and political conditions is unexpected.

Chapter 4 outlines, first, the policy similarities, and secondly, the sources of similarity. In this chapter the argument about the substance and forms of policy similarity is developed. I advance here one of the central arguments of this work. The United States and Great Britain developed a policy similarity with regard to their automobile industries, which consisted in the altering of the cost structures of production in order to produce a commercially viable industry. The governments did this by limiting the access of foreign competitors to domestic markets, and by absorbing much of the cost necessary to restructure the industry.

In the last part of chapter 4, several hypotheses are tested. I conclude that public policy similarity has developed among four Western nations since 1978 with regard to investment subsidies to private corporations, though this similarity is still limited to periods of downturn in the economy of each nation.

The fifth chapter begins with a brief review of the argument to that point; thereafter, the chapter examines explanations for policy similarity. I discuss four generic explanations for why states intervene: societal pressures, ideology, common crises in the political economy, and state interest. I argue that the best explanation for similarity is an interests-of-the-welfare-state argument. Specifically, the governments' policies can be understood as a strategy to minimize long-term costs to their treasuries and to their national accounts while promoting economic growth. I conclude that the state-interest argument is the best explanation on the grounds that it is the only falsifiable argument consistent with the facts of the case. Neither a state-interest argument nor any other theory of the state, however, is a universal political explanation. My argument, for instance, is of little use in understanding instances of public policy divergence.

The final chapter begins with an overview of the arguments that I have made. Following this, the bulk of the chapter is devoted to a discussion of two implications stemming from a state-interest argument. The first issue is, what are the consequences for private interests of state interests influencing policy? The second issue is a more normative one. What justifications and normative assumptions underpin policies based upon state interests being defined in terms of economic efficiency?; are there alternative bases for public policies?

2.

THE WORLD AUTO INDUSTRY

THE WORLD AUTO INDUSTRY is not a declining industry. In the past fifty years, no new products have been developed that are likely to replace the automobile as the primary means of transportation in the developed world. The value of the sales of automobiles products totaled over $500 billion worldwide in 1982, and it will continue to rise.[1] The image of decline associated with the industry is a nationally biased one; only some nations, and only some auto companies, have suffered employment, trade and profit opportunity losses.

Neither is the industry a static or slowly changing one. Automobile sales and production are cyclical; the demand for automobiles rises and falls in first world countries in four to six year intervals. The industry has also undergone a twenty-year period of what can be described as structural change during which time the capacity of the world industry to produce cars has both expanded in volume and diversified in location.

The quality and methods of production have changed as well. Innovation in automobile production processes, both technological and social, has advanced far beyond Henry Ford's conveyor belt. Japanese and other manufacturers have combined the large-scale use of industrial robots with the "kanban," or "just-in-time" system of inventory, to achieve both substantial production cost advantages over less innovative manufacturers and a highly diversified range of products. Over half of the world's industrial robots are employed in automotive assembly.

The imagery of decline, which was used to described these structural changes in the world auto industry, was reinforced in 1979 and 1980 as the world economy and its auto industry endured one of their periodic downturns in the business cycle. This particular downturn, during which time the supply of automobiles substantially exceeded demand, led in some companies to reductions in auto production of 20 to 40 percent and in turn to the consequent temporary layoffs of up to 30 percent of the American auto work force. This combination of a structural shift in world production and a cyclical downturn in demand nearly drove several auto manufacturers into bankruptcy; even the industry leaders, Ford and GM, lost hundreds of millions of dollars.

The United States and Great Britain were the two nations most affected by the combined effects of cyclical and structural change. The governments of both countries substantially surrendered longstanding public policies toward the industries, and developed similar (though not identical) strategies to revive them. The development of policy similarity, and the explanations for it, are the subject of this book.

In this chapter, some background information will be provided. I will begin with a review of past events in the auto industry, and from this recounting isolate and discuss the chief influences on the modern industry. These are the importance of scale economies and of government-firm relations. Because of them, the auto industry has become both international and concentrated.

A Brief Review of Past Events in the Auto Industry

Automobile manufacturing on a small scale began in the 1890s more or less simultaneously in Europe and North America. The large-scale assembly of cars on moving conveyor belts with each worker being assigned to a specific narrow task was developed first by Ford in the United States during the early 1900s. The key features of American automotive assembly—mass production (Fordism) and huge business combinations—have come to characterize all the major auto producers.

Even though the production process was similar for most auto firms, the end product frequently was not. The automobile markets of the various producing countries differ in terms of consumer preferences (the demand profile of a market) and, in consequence, the product sold in various countries had unique characteristics. American automobiles, for instance, tended to be volume cars, of indifferent mechanical quality, with a low sales price and an emphasis on comfort and large size. European-manufactured cars, on the other hand, tended to be more fuel efficient, and to be of better mechanical quality. At least part of these differences resulted from the higher per capita income in the U.S. during most of this century; European cars were necessarily produced for a narrower, wealthier clientele than were American cars. When American manufacturers invested in Europe, they also produced European-style cars.[2] These national traditions persisted long after the underlying economic circumstances began to converge. In the post-War European market, substantial levels of product differentiation continued, even when European automobile manufacturers adopted Ford-style production techniques to take advantage of their growing mass markets.[3]

In addition to similar production processes, almost all auto industries evolved in the by now familiar pattern of new consumer industries: increasing barriers to entry by new firms, managerialism, and economies of scale. The early industries of the U.S., Britain, France, and Germany each had many companies (over 30 in the U.S. in the 1910s) producing a nonstandard product; many of the early cars were in fact powered by steam. Most companies were operated by inventor/owner/managers, men whose inventing skills usually exceeded their managerial skills. Most of these early firms (e.g. Buick, Maxwell, Hudson, Chalmers) either went into receivership during the periodic business cycle downturns, or were consolidated into larger firms. The larger firms also endured boom and bust cycles; Ford Motor Company had a net loss after taxes for the period between

1927 and 1937.[4] General Motors was saved from bankruptcy after its owner/manager, William Durant, was finally ousted in 1920 and replaced by Alfred Sloan.

The Sloan era at GM saw the development of a more "scientific" management, with managers replacing owners, and marketing and close fiscal control replacing product innovation as management's chief focus. Sloan's success in reorganizing GM manifested itself when in 1927 GM passed Ford as the world's leading auto manufacturer, a position it has held since.[5] Though Henry Ford resisted GM's decentralized system of management, the GM-Dupont management practices were widely adopted by many other firms in the auto industry and beyond.

As American firms were the first to introduce mass production and modern management techniques, they dominated the world auto market. By the end of the 1930s, 80 percent of the automobiles in use were in the United States, even though European governments had made the establishment of domestic automotive industries a priority after the First World War.[6]

Part of European government policy toward the auto industry was aimed at excluding cheap imports of automobiles and trucks from the United States in order to promote domestic auto production. Some nations—Britain, France and Germany among them—were willing to permit foreign auto manufacturers to establish domestic subsidiaries. Ford and General Motors were quick to do so during the 1920s and 1930s, largely to avoid tariff barriers.[7]

These and other government development policies were adopted by many European and Latin American nations, and were largely responsible, in combination with the economic growth of the post-World War II period, for the diversification of location for auto production. Over 45 nations have used trade restriction or domestic content requirements or both to induce multinational firm investments or to protect local industries.[8]

This shift in the location of production is probably the most salient change in the world auto industry, and it occurred largely in consequence of the strategies of governments. The most striking success

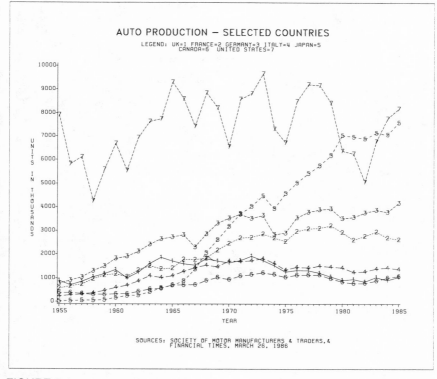

AUTO PRODUCTION — SELECTED COUNTRIES

FIGURE 2.1

of government strategy is Japan's postwar creation of an auto industry and its capture of export markets, an event which has transformed the production process, marketing arrangements, and investment policies in the world industry.[9] Japan has, through government/industry cooperation, developed from a negligible producer in the 1960s to the world's largest producer and exporter in the early 1980s (see fig. 2.1). Other nations, such as Brazil, Korea, and Spain, have also developed substantial motor vehicle production industries (see fig. 2.2).

Two primary methods for creating an auto industry are used by

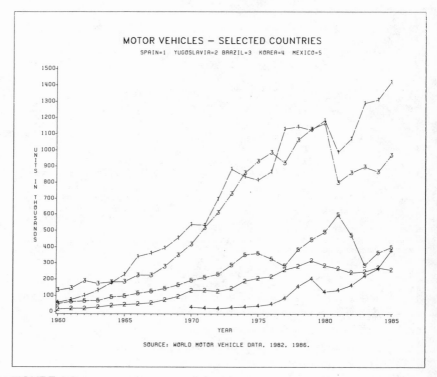

FIGURE 2.2

governments: inviting (sometimes coercing) multinational corporations to invest within a country, and establishing an infant industry
behind tariff and other entry barriers. These methods, we should
note, are not unique to the auto industry. Governments concerned
with employment, trade balances, and industrialization have employed these and other quasimercantilist policies of stimulating investment for much of the twentieth century.

Excepting Japan, the usual method of developing a motor industry
has been for governments to induce or allow multinational corporations to establish production facilities within a given country, as
table 2.1 demonstrates. The multinational corporation (MNC) is not

TABLE 2.1
1980 Auto production of MNCs
Selected Countries

	Argentina	Belgium[a]	Brazil[a]	Spain
Ford	71,555	224,901	164,974	266,005
GM	—	304,535	231,557	65,756
Renault	58,126	173,428	—	324,680
VW	27,771	110,108	514,237	—
Other MNCs	61,064	116,033	248,040	84,680
Domestic	—	—	5,917	293,536[b]
Total	218,516	929,005	1,164,725	1,034,657
MNC as % of total	100%	100%	99.5%	61.5%[b]

Source: Society of Motor Manufacturers and Traders.
[a]Figures for Belgium and Brazil include commercial vehicles.
[b]SEAT of Spain (293,536) was jointly owned by FIAT and the Spanish government in 1980: Volkswagen purchased majority ownership of SEAT in 1986. SEAT's figures could reasonably be put in the MNC category.

only faced with the choice of producing in the country or losing access to the country's markets, but also is often required to purchase local goods and services (domestic content), and occasionally to export auto products—usually to subdivisions in other countries. Consequently, the major American and European auto companies have production footholds in most first and third world markets. In 1979, almost 22 percent of the world's motor vehicle output was produced by subsidiary companies of the MNCs. Further, world trade in auto components was worth $25 billion in 1978, much of it intrafirm.[10]

Mercantilist government policies are not universally successful. The success of governments in inducing MNCs to invest has been largely limited to major first world markets. The third world does receive 5 to 10 percent of worldwide auto investment (perhaps $10 to 20 billion), but three quarters of this goes to Brazil, Argentina, and Mexico. Smaller nations, owing to limited effective demand, are not in a position to adopt this method.[11]

A second consequence of these government policies is that most non-MNC domestic producers are either weak or nonexistent, or are in junior positions in joint production agreements with the MNCs. Few small firms can compete in the same national markets with the MNCs, unless they produce specialty cars (e.g. BMW).

The main alternative method of developing an auto industry is for a nation to create an industry behind tariff barriers while excluding MNC investment. The Japanese were successful in developing and rationalizing their indigenous infant industry behind barriers that prevented both substantial auto imports and MNC investments or takeovers. Ironically enough, the pre-World War II auto market in Japan was dominated by Ford and GM, with a combined share of 90 percent of the market in 1934.[12] After the war, many Japanese economists argued against the establishment by the government of a domestic auto industry. Hisato Ichimada, the former governor of the Bank of Japan, is now remembered mostly for his famous quote arguing against this policy: "Efforts to foster an automobile industry in Japan are meaningless. This is a period of international specialization. Since America can produce cheap, high quality cars, why should we not depend on America for automobiles?"[13]

The Ministry of International Trade and Industry (MITI) nonetheless developed an import substitution industrialization strategy for autos, so that Japan by the 1960s had a consolidated industry, grouped around Toyota and Nissan (excepting Mitsubishi). Japan imported virtually no cars. Though the restrictions on foreign capital investments were ultimately broken in 1971 by Mitsubishi's aggressive development of links with a non-Japanese firm (i.e. Chrysler), the restrictions survived long enough for Japan to develop a competitive industry.[14]

The Japanese model is difficult to duplicate successfully (though Korea's Hyundai Motor Company has enjoyed spectacular success in the Canadian and American markets[15]). The presence of a dozen competing MNCs in the world auto industry makes the establishment of a national industry patterned after the Japanese extremely problematic. For instance, the Canadian government concluded that Canada could not sustain a Canadian-owned new producer. Canada is a rich industrial nation with a Gross Domestic Product of C$420 billion (in 1984) and a car market with a strong demand for cars and trucks—more than 1.5 million unit sales.[16] Even so, a small market relative to the U.S. and the European Community (EC), heavy investment costs, difficulties in attracting private investors, and the low costs to the government of permitting MNCs to produce cars in Canada were among the cited reasons for not establishing a Canadian owned automobile firm. Several nations that have tried to duplicate Japan's success either produce low volumes of expensive, unreliable cars (e.g. India), or have found some export markets partly blocked by tariffs, quotas, or Japanese competition (e.g. Korea). The Japanese strategy is probably viable only in the relatively rare circumstances of expanding markets, high growth, and relatively free trade—and even then only if the domestic market is large or the country's firms have access to other large markets.[17]

The net effect of the auto industrialization strategies of various governments, in addition to producing new loci of auto manufacturing, was to create a "surplus capacity" in the industry by the late 1970s. Auto industries in 1980 were estimated to be operating at slightly below 60 percent of capacity in the United States and at approximately 79 percent in Western Europe.[18] Automotive sales recovered with the overall economy in 1983 through 1985; production as a percentage of capacity rose to 90 percent in the American market, but estimates are that rates will fall to the 80 percent level between 1988 and 1990.[19]

By 1980, the basic features of the world auto industry included a growing convergence of world consumer preferences for small, fuel-efficient cars, and a surplus capacity both of autos (3 million unsold units) and of the capacity to produce them. The industry had a high concentration ratio; eight companies accounted for 73 percent of world production.[20] Total direct and indirect worldwide vehicle manufacturing employment was estimated to be somewhere between 28 and 35 million, and world production was estimated to be more than 30 million units.[21] Over 39 percent of those vehicles produced were said to be exported; the value of these cars accounted for approximately 5.5 percent of the value of world trade.[22] In sum, the world automotive sector was both economically important and rapidly changing.

Also characterizing the world automotive industry by 1980 were government strategies designed to either protect their fair share of the market or to increase exports of cars and components. More than 45 nations produced or assembled autos, and nearly all who did not produce them imported them; autos are valuable in an economy both as incentive goods and as infrastructural assets.[23] Auto production is associated with high sales and employment in collateral industries like steel, rubber, and more recently robotics, as well as in auto assembly. Domestic auto production therefore means higher employment, a lessening of a sectoral drain on the visible balance of payments, and for some nations, a source of export earnings. In consequence, governments have, individually and in regional associations (e.g. the EC), tried to set the conditions of world production and trade.

The auto industry, then, is dominated by two considerations: the imperative of production imposed on firms by market structures, and government-firm relationships. I will address both topics in turn.

Market Structure and Firm Choice

An assumption made in the "Theory of the Firm" literature is that firms are profit "satisficing," if not profit maximizing, institutions. In the automotive industry, profitability is a function of process (of production), product preferences, and politics. Processes and preferences are not standardized throughout the industry, however. We find two distinct markets, the mass market and the specialist market.[24] Firm behavior regarding production processes and product choices will vary between these markets.

The Production Process—the Routes to Profitability

Every firm seeks to reduce the per unit cost of producing a product. In a competitive market of standardized products—the mass market—the firm with the largest productions runs will usually be the most profitable as it will benefit from scale economies. These larger production runs increase the returns to scale, thereby lowering the per unit cost of a product, and producing a higher rate of profit. More simply, a larger manufacturer can afford greater specialization of labor and can purchase machinery suitable to a narrower task, all because large production runs avoid leaving men and machines idle. A smaller producer frequently must purchase general purpose machinery, assign workers to many tasks, and buy component parts of automobiles from an outside supplier instead of manufacturing the products itself. The cost advantage per per car of the larger firm is attributable to these economies of scale. Larger companies are therefore usually more profitable.[25] Part of the increased capacity to produce automobiles is thus the result of strategies by automobile firms to develop larger production runs.

Economies of scale are particularly important for the automobile industry—perhaps more so here than for almost any other consumer durable goods industry—because auto production is capital intensive. That is, the costs of durable goods (fixed capital) such as machinery and buildings, plus the costs of raw materials and components, constitute the majority of the costs of production, approximately 70 to 80 percent in the U.S. Because these costs are mostly fixed, and therefore must be paid, the larger the production run, the lower will be the cost of these fixed charges as a percentage of the cost of each unit. For instance, most of the cost to GM of its plants and machinery will come due whether GM produces 2 million or 3 million cars. Hence, at 3 million units, the capital cost per unit is a third less than at 2 million units.

The usual threshold measurement for economies of scale is the Minimum Efficient Size (MES).[26] Firms whose production level falls below the MES for cars and their component parts operate at a per unit cost disadvantage to companies whose production runs exceed the MES. The MES is not an exact measure—analysts frequently disagree—and the MES varies among the elements of a car: hence, the following figures should be read with caution. Among the larger

MES estimates are over 1 million units per year (upy) for engines and transmissions, 4 million upy for auto body pressings, 2 million upy for foundry work, and 5 million upy each for automotive sales networks (including advertising) and for research and development. Many analysts suggest that production of 2 million cars per year is the probable minimum overall standard for efficient auto production, a standard consistently exceeded in recent years by only 5 of the 21 major Western auto producers.[27] Others (OECD, Jones) have argued that the plant-size MES might decrease owing to increased use of computers and robots, though the capital intensive production that results will have roughly the same effects on competition as MES.

The Minimum Efficient Size of auto firms increased steadily after the Second World War, as table 2.2 demonstrates. As profitability in the mass market is linked to increasing economies of scale, auto firms have had an incentive to increase production capacity and sales. Table 2.3 gives some indication of the increase in capacity, though it measures (through 1985) only the number of automobiles actually produced.

Increasing the size of production runs to benefit from economies of scale is not the only route to profitability for firms. Labor costs, work rules, and labor productivity are significant contributors to the overall cost structures of firms, even though wages, salaries, and related costs generally average between 20 and 30 percent of an auto firm's operating costs.[28] Wage costs paid by firms vary substantially among nations (as table 2.4 indicates), though—thanks to unionization—rarely within nations. These hourly wage cost differentials, despite much attention by the American news media during the 1980–1982 recession, are not necessarily a true measure of the costs to the firm of the work force, especially as comparative wage evaluations are in part skewed by fluctuations in currency values and inflation rates in various countries, and firms have different procurement policies regarding automotive components.

Of greater interest to a firm is the per unit wage cost of production, a figure influenced not only by wages, but also by plant work rules, labor stoppages, work culture, and other issues in labor productivity.

TABLE 2.2

**Minimum Efficient Scale of Production,[a] Selected Years
(with reference to British data)**

Year	Largest Firm's Share[b]	Total Market	Estimate[c] of Biggest Firm's Production	MES	MES Est.
1947	21%	287,000	60,000	150,000	.4
1954	38%	769,000	292,000	600,000	.5
1960	36%	1,352,000	486,000	750,000	.6
1967	45%	1,552,000	700,000	1,000,000	.7
1974	48%	1,543,000	740,000	1,250,000	.6
1977	49%	1,315,000	651,000	2,000,000	.3

Source: Dunnett, The Decline of the British Motor Industry, p. 23.
[a]MES and the "Break-even point" are not identical for a firm. The BEP includes the MES for the firm's functions plus capital and wage costs.
[b]For years: 1947, Nuffield; 1954, BMC; 1960, BMC; 1967, BMH; 1974, BL; 1978, BL.
[c]Actual production figures not available.

A famous illustration of this point has been made by comparing the nearly identical Ford plants of Saarlouis in West Germany and Halewood in Great Britain. Table 2.5 illustrates the point that worker productivity is measured poorly if one examines only wage rates.

TABLE 2.3
**World Capacity for Auto Production, in millions
(until 1985, defined as actual production or assembly)**

	1960	1970	1973–8	1980	1985	1990
N. America[a]	7.0	7.5	10.9	9.2	9.1	11–13
W. Europe	5.1	10.4	11.5	11.3	11.2	11–13
Japan	.2	3.2	5.8	5.7	7.5	7–9
1st World Total	12.3	21.1	28.3	26.2	27.8	29–35
others	.6	1.9	4.2	5.0	6	7–10
Grand total	12.9	23.0	32.5	31.2	33.8[b]	36–45

Source: Bhaskar, p. 354; Financial Times, January 3, 1986 & September 5, 1985; Ford Motor Company, Annual Report, 1985.
[a]includes U.S. and Canada
[b]Several sources report different figures for 1985. Ford, in its 1985 annual report, gives 29.2 million as the figure for total world automotive sales.

TABLE 2.4
Hourly Wage Rates of Auto Workers
(Selected Countries)^a

	1975		1977		1979	
U.S.	$9.60	100	$11.61	100	$13.72	100
Germany	7.50	80	9.67	83	14.05	102
Belgium	7.58	79	9.51	82	13.06	95
Canada	7.50	78	9.13	79	9.46	69
France	5.22	54	6.12	53	8.97	65
Italy	5.11	53	5.59	48	7.90	58
Britain	3.95	41	3.91	34	6.36	46
Japan^b	3.56	37	4.82	42	6.85	50
Mexico	2.95	31	2.92	25	3.91	28
Brazil	1.59	17	2.06	18	2.53	18
Korea	.50	5	1.01	9	1.58	12

Source: CBO, p. 37.
^{a}$U.S. = 100
^{b}Japanese data include bonuses.

Despite Halewood's lower wage rates, Ford Escorts produced in Germany and shipped to Britain cost Ford $1000 less than do Ford Escorts produced at Halewood. Even though some productivity gains were made in Ford's British plants in the subsequent five years, Ford estimated in 1986 that its U.K. plants still operated at two thirds of the productivity of its German plants.[29] More restrictive work rules and poor management-labor relations are usually credited with accounting for these differences.

Since per unit labor costs are a crucial consideration for profitability, auto makers are attempting to implement nonconfrontational, corporatist forms of management–labor relations.[30] This approach is thought to improve the the general tenor of labor relations, work organization, and worker's commitment by providing workers with nonmaterial incentives (as well as new material incentives like profit sharing) for better quality work. At least in the case of the United States and Great Britain, the recognition by managers that quality and efficiency are strongly influenced by the labor force is a by-product of the internationalization of competition. That is, nations

TABLE 2.5
Two Identical Ford Plants Compared:
Productivity at Halewood and Saarlouis—1981

	Halewood	Saarlouis
Daily Auto Output	800	1,200
Employment	10,040	7,762
Man Hours per Car	40	21
Strikes—1981	20	0
Average Hourly Wage	$8.25	$13.50

Source: *International Herald Tribune*, October 15, 1981. p. 7.

and firms with cooperative or incorporated work forces have a competitive advantage over those countries and firms with poor management–labor relations. Table 2.6 provides one measure of the range of national differences in work relations—Industrial stoppages.

The automobile industry is the prototypical Taylorist industrial production process—with deskilled, highly routinized work, the pace of which is set by the pace of the assembly line. In industries with standardized products and production processes, a certain degree of industrial hierarchy and routinized work is probably inevitable. Cars may be produced with varying technologies and varying methods of organizing work, but if a firm adopts Fordist practices of assembly, then some form of hierarchy follows. But within these hierarchical work practices, we find major differences in the incentives offered to workers, and in the degree of incorporation of the work force. Traditional Taylorist practices assume that workers find work painful, and that some coercion/compensation incentive structure will motivate workers to an acceptable level. While few firms openly adopt the Taylorist model—research has shown that people are motivated by nonmaterial as well as material incentives—American and British auto firms most closely approximate it among the major producers. Proposals for reform (by, say, increasing the productivity and motivation of American and British workers) tend to center on giving workers a broader financial stake in the success of the firm, rather than on giving workers voice in the production process.[31]

WORLD AUTO INDUSTRY

TABLE 2.6
Industrial Stoppages[a]
(working days lost per 1,000 employees)

	US	UK	West Germany	Japan	Canada
1975	990	540	10	390	2810
1976	1190	300	40	150	2550
1977	1070	840	—[b]	70	830
1978	1070	840	370	60	1930
1979	890	2430	40	40	1660
1980	830	1180	10	50	1530
1981	590	310	—[b]	20	1790

Source: Financial Times, March 14, 1983. p. 3.
[a]In mining, manufacturing, construction, & transport industries.
[b]less than 5.

Automobile firms in East Asia and, to a lesser extent, Western Europe have adopted forms of corporatism—a reluctance to layoff workers, bonus incentives, less rigid forms of hierarchy, consultative practices. In response to the success of Japanese firms in particular, American firms are experimenting with more cooperative forms of management. The Saturn project, for example, is said to be patterned after Volvo's work practices, with a limited no-layoff program for most workers.

The success of American firms in adopting cooperative work practices is likely to be limited by the strategies these firms are following with regard to automation and multinational production. Why should Chrysler's workers cooperate with a firm that is replacing Chrysler workers by establishing low-wage maquiladoras in Mexico to provide components for Chrysler cars? Why would GM's workers accept the imports of cars by GM from GM's Korean allies? Why should Ford's workers cooperate with the replacement of labor by capital equipment? The success of Japanese firms in inducing cooperation from their work force is partly the consequence of the alliance of interests between firm and workforce, an alliance made possible by prosperity and by home-country production. The American firms did not start in the early 1980s with conditions of prosperity and exclusively domestic production. Cooperative labor relations are difficult to introduce in the absence of these conditions.

Cooperative management–labor relations are influenced as well by the type of product the firm produces, the mix of skills used in producing the product, and by the degree of competition in a firm's chosen market. Assume, for the purposes of this discussion, a regime of free trade. A firm in the specialty market whose production competency is a byproduct of the skills of its labor force is likely to develop cooperative work relations, and is less likely to be vulnerable to other firms' strategies to take its markets. Imagine another firm with a relatively capital intensive production process using unskilled labor and whose products are sold in the standardized or mass market. This firm will compete with other firms on the basis of the product's price; the wages paid to its workforce are then a threat to a firm's profitability. Firms can overcome this zero-sum situation by increasing the capital intensity of their production process, thereby increasing its productivity, though usually at the expense of overall levels of employment if not per capita wages. But, in a situation in which many firms have comparable capital endowments in the production process, wage levels are the basis of competition; increasing the capital intensity of production might only defer wage reductions for employees. Cooperative relations depend then on the degree of competition in the mass market. For those firms unfortunate enough to produce a standardized product using labor intensive methods of production in a situation of intense interfirm competition, cooperative management–labor relations are highly unlikely.[32]

Figure 2.3 is a representation of the relationship between product and production process. Assuming still a regime of free trade, cooperative relations are most likely for firms in or approaching block I, least likely for firms in block II. The relations between management and labor for firms in blocks III and IV will depend on the competitive circumstances; the conditions for compromise will not always be present.

A system of production known as "flexible production" is credited with arranging machines and labor so that wage costs are substan-

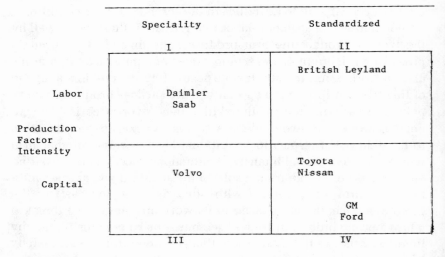

FIGURE 2.3

tially reduced by increasing productivity without cutting the wages of the individual worker. This method of production offers the possibility for capital intensive, specialty products. Flexible production has been defined as

> consist[ing] of a line of machine tools and transfer machinery which can easily be reprogrammed to manufacture several types of components, or the same type of component to different specifications. The emphasis here is on the "system" so that the different components operate as a whole.[33]

In one instance, General Motors, in its Saturn project, is attempting to implement a form of flexible production in which labor flexibility, a cooperative style of labor–management relations, salaried (not hourly) workers, and a no-layoff system of work will combine with new equipment to reduce the number of man hours per car by 75 percent. GM plans to install 20,000 industrial robots by 1990, many of these in its Spring Hill, Tennessee plant. The flexible production system generally results in an increase in the capital–labor ratio of production, though the labor component tends to be more highly skilled than is the case with more traditional assembly line work. The OECD has argued that flexible production may reduce the Minimum Efficient Size of production of a given type of a specific product; for instance, four-cylinder, fuel injected engines displacing 1800cc. Even if this were true, a broader notion of economies of scale—that is, encompassing the production of many types of engines on the same assembly line using the same machinery and workers— still would be an important consideration in reducing production costs.

In general, economies of scale are of greater importance in achieving a low cost product than are lower wage rates, a point illustrated by the experience of multinational auto firms in third world countries, where wage rates are extremely low but per unit production costs are usually high. The elements needed in achieving economies of scale—concentrations of plants, machinery, highly developed infrastructures, research facilities, component suppliers, and skilled labor—are generally available only in the developed world. As a result, substantial movement of auto production from the developed world to the underdeveloped world (save Brazil and Mexico) is considered highly unlikely through the end of the century.[34] Even when low wages are found in the auto industry of an industralized nation, this is not enough to ensure the firm's profitability.[35]

Achieving Scale Economies

Auto firms, as we have seen, have an incentive to achieve economies of scale, especially as the development of similar market demands in North America, Japan, Western Europe created a sales market of 25 million new cars per year in 1985. Three strategic decisions confront firms as they attempt to achieve economies of

TABLE 2.7
Auto Firms—Total Production, 1980
(in units of thousands)

Firm	world-wide production	foreign production	foreign as % of total	% of world production
GM	6,712	1,959	29.2	19.2
Ford	4,183	2,294	54.9	12.0
Toyotā	3,801	—	—	10.9
Nissan	3,118	—	—	8.9
VW	2,531	899	35.5	7.3
Renault	2,137	424	19.8	6.1
Peugeot	2,019	372	18.4	5.8
Fiat	1,569	219	14.0	4.5
Toyo-Kogyo	1,121	—	—	3.2
Mitsubishi	1,195	—	—	3.2
Chrysler[a]	1,009	251	24.9	2.9
Honda	957	—	—	2.7
Daimler-Benz	707	80	11.3	2.0
BL	597	71	12.0	1.7
Isuzu	472	—	—	1.4
Suzuki	469	—	—	1.4
All firms	34,877	6,073	19.2	100

Source: United Nations, p. 41.
[a]includes Latin American subsidiaries, but not European.

scale (hereafter, e.o.s.). These choices concern plant location, degree of vertical integration, and the extent to which one firm will cooperate with other firms in developing and sharing products.

The location choices are to concentrate all the factors of production in a central location or to disperse auto production among foreign subsidiaries—each of which may specialize in one aspect of auto production (e.g. engines). Until recently, firms from Japan tended to concentrate production in Japan, whereas American and European companies have adopted the multinational production model, as table 2.7 reveals.[36]

The Japanese in the late 1970s and early 1980s achieved extraordinary success by concentrating production of autos and their components in integrated complexes. Japanese companies, and their suppliers, are usually located in close proximity, as in Toyota City. By way of contrast, in traditional American production systems, plants are geographically disbursed, and products are shipped to an assembly point; for instance, GM's new Hamtramck assembly plant is 200 miles from the nearest stamping plant.[37] This integration between assembly and supply of parts allows Japanese companies to dispense with dual sourcing (purchasing from more than one supplier per part) as well as much of the costs of storage. Crucial to the success of this system has been the development by Japanese auto firms of a network of dependent supplier firms. These firms pay lower wages than do the automobile manufacturers (20 to 30 percent lower), and they absorb some of the risk associated with product development.[38] Along with quality control systems and other productivity measures, this integrated production system is said to account for 80 percent of the cost advantage Japanese companies enjoy over their American counterparts. In 1983, Japanese production costs were sufficiently low that, even with the costs of transoceanic shipping added to the price, Japanese cars were approximately $1500–$1700 per car cheaper than similar American cars, and had a 20 to 30 percent advantage over similar European cars.[39]

The major alternative method of achieving profitable economies of scale is for a firm to invest in assembly operations in each of its primary markets. From the firm's perspective, this alternative is less desirable than to concentrate production in its home country. Problems of currency adjustments, political changes, and variable work force cultures increase the risks of investments. And, until the advent of the European Community Common Market and the U.S.–Canada Automotive Agreement, investment outside of the U.S. took place in relatively small markets that did not have a market demand substantial enough to allow firms to benefit from contemporary e.o.s.

The impetus behind the decisions of Ford, GM, and other multinational producers to invest outside their home market was the tariff barriers and other export entry requirements that governments have imposed on would-be exporting auto firms. These barriers change the export profit calculations of firms. Tariff barriers can be quite expensive for an exporting firm. For instance, in 1960 France, Britain, and Japan had tariffs on car imports of between 30 and 40 percent. The uniform tariff of 10.9 percent on cars imported from outside the European Community is still substantial. Some countries (e.g. Brazil, India, and Korea) do not permit auto imports at all.[40]

Other non-tariff barriers are often imposed on firms by governments. Twenty-seven countries, including all the major Latin American producer-nations, have domestic content laws, which require varying percentages of the total value of the car to be produced within the country. Eighteen nations, again including the Latin American countries, also impose export requirements on auto firms.[41] Other forms of trade restriction include quota arrangements as well as different taxation rates and safety and pollution standards for imported cars. These limit the ability of concentrated firms to profit from their economies of scale through the export of cars.

Given these government policies (and the threat of future restrictions on imported cars), most firms (including the Japanese) will become increasingly transnational in operations, especially those companies most dependent on foreign sales.[42] For instance, Honda, a company which exports 40 percent of its production to the U.S. in the form of two models, was the first to establish an American assembly plant. Toyota, which exports only a fifth of its products (but many more models) to the U.S., only recently announced plans to create an independent subsidiary in the U.S. By 1990, Japanese auto manufacturers will have the capacity to produce 1.3 million cars inside the United States.[43]

Multinational auto firms have differed in the tactics that they have used to invest in foreign countries. General Motors purchased existing companies (e.g., Opel, Vauxhall), which operated more or less independently from each other until the late 1970s. Ford, on the other hand, established its own subsidiaries, usually by raising capital within the proposed subsidiary's market. Ford's operations have been largely integrated on a world-wide scale since the 1960s, and its European operations have consequentially proven to be profitable.

Ford, UK lent Ford, USA £656 million in 1981 and £961 million in 1982.[44]

Nevertheless, the outlines of foreign investment strategies remain roughly similar for the major transnational firms. The majority of capital investment takes place within a firm's home market; GM will invest $8 billion, or 20 percent of its total, abroad, and Ford will invest approximately $2 billion (a third of its total) abroad.[45] Firms will attempt to balance intrafirm trade among countries so as to avoid being a contributor to a nation's balance of trade deficit.[46] The usual method of balancing trade is for subsidiaries to specialize in a component (say engines) or a model line, and to exchange this for the rest of a firm's products. For instance, all of the LTDs that Ford sold in North America in 1982 were manufactured in Ontario, as were all of Chrysler's intermediate-size rear-wheel drive cars.[47] The increasing specialization by the subsidiaries of transnational firms is what helps the firm as a whole achieve the economies of scale necessary for profitability, while avoiding the cost penalties which result from tariffs and other government imposed restraints. And, perhaps most importantly, the firm can then produce a fairly uniform "world" car, though based largely on common parts rather than common exteriors. Ford's Escort, VW's Rabbit, GM's "J" car, and the Renault-AMC Alliance are examples of such cars.

Related to the choices of location for production is the decision by firms regarding their desired degree of vertical integration (the extent to which a firm will produce all the products needed for the end product). For instance, a completely integrated auto producer would mine coal, iron, and alumina ores, would produce steel, plastics, and aluminum, would manufacture all the component parts of the car, and assemble the components. No auto manufacturer is completely integrated, but the integration ratios (value-added to the end product produced intrafirm as a percentage of the total value of the product) varies from 20 to 80%.

In theory, vertical integration offers a firm both benefits and costs. Vertical integration allows firms to internalize markets, and to control the quality of the components of the end product with some degree of certainty regarding costs.[48] For multinational producers, vertical integration through component plant dispersion permits them to overcome some of the quality, price, and currency fluctuation disadvantages associated with international production. If they produce components internally, they can control quality and, through transfer pricing policies, can control to some extent the costs of components. Vertical integration also offers the prospect of shaping the technological advances in other fields to the specific needs of the main firm. GM produces many of its own robots, has imposed a standard machine assembly protocol on its many robots and computers, and has purchased Electronic Data Systems (EDS) to reduce production costs by harnessing new technological developments. Daimler-Benz's aquisition of AEG and the efforts by Ford and Chrysler to find suitable hi-tech partners are versions of this strategy of vertical integration.

The disadvantages of vertical integration can be substantial, however. Since the auto business is subject to severe business cycle fluctuations, a fully integrated producer would find much of its capacity idle during economic downturns. By purchasing at least some of its components from suppliers, the assembling firm can pass on part of the risk of downturn to the suppliers—the assembling firm simply reduces purchases when necessary, and the supplying firms will bear the cost of idle labor and equipment. Furthermore, assuming a competitive supplier market, the assembling firms can enforce what amount to monopsony contracts. Chrysler's recent profitability, as well as much of the success of the Japanese auto industry, results from its ability to cut costs through "disintegration."

Table 2.8 gives us a proxy measure for the degree of a firm's vertical integration. Although we need to exercise caution in interpreting this table (Toyota's employees were not five times more efficient than were GM's in 1985), the table measures the differences in integration between the major Japanese auto producers and the major American auto producers. GM supplies more of its components internally; therefore, GM will have more employees and a "lower ve-

TABLE 2.8
Worker Productivity as a Measure of Vertical Integration

Firms	Motor Vehicles Produced[a]	Number of Employees[b]	Vehicles per Employee
1981			
Toyota	3,254,942	48,757	66.76
Nissan	2,617,899	56,284	46.51
Ford	4,402,462	411,202	10.17
General Motors	6,762,000	741,000	9.13
British Leyland	525,000	126,000	4.17
1985			
Toyota	3,535,495	61,665	57.33
Nissan	2,463,982	58,925	41.82
Ford	5,634,348	369,314	15.26
General Motors	9,305,000	811,000	11.47
British Leyland	542,000	78,000	6.95

Sources: Annual Reports, various companies, various years.
[a]includes trucks and vans as well as automobiles.
[b]worldwide employees in all cases.

hicle per employee" ratio. (British Leyland, however, purchases approximately 70 percent of its components. Its numbers are not promising.) The strategic choices that American firms have made regarding component production are not necessarily unwise; as Japanese firms diversify their production locations, their "cars per employee" ratio will fall.

As the reader can probably surmise, the choice concerning the degree of vertical integration is closely related now to choices concerning plant location. If a firm produces the great majority of its products within one market, then vertical disintegration is an appealing choice, provided that a constellation of supplier firms is capable of providing good quality products. Chrysler and the Japanese producers now manufacture overwhelmingly in one market, and these firms each acquire 70 to 80 percent of the car's final "value added" externally, though Cusumano notes that, when allied supplier firms are included in the calculation of integration, the figure for the Japanese industry rises. Ford and General Motors, in contrast, are highly integrated firms, with 70 percent of the car's value-added produced internally, though Ford is seeking to reduce its internal production.[49] These producers are also multinational, and a high degree of vertical integration is thought to be a rational choice under those circumstances. Most analysts expect that, as Japanese producers begin to manufacture in foreign markets, the cost advantages they derived from their supplier networks will diminish, and that these companies will increase their degree of vertical integration.

The third method of achieving profitable economies of scale is for firms to establish linkages among themselves. The instruments of linkages vary. One common form of arrangement involves equity exchanges or the creation of a jointly held corporation. For instance, the Mitsubishi-Chrysler agreement foresaw Chrysler's acquiring a third of Mitsubishi's automotive division, and for Chrysler to import a Mitsubishi built car, the Dodge Colt. Ford owns approximately 25 percent of Mazda's equity, and GM has substantial equity stakes in Isuzu, Suzuki, Daewoo (Korea), and Lotus. Other forms of cooperation include joint production agreements. Among the many illustrations are the Honda-BL agreement on joint production of the Acclaim, and the GM-Toyota agreement to manufacture a small car in the U.S. Nearly a score of other agreements are in effect. The final major form of firm linkage is for a firm to purchase auto components from other firms, frequently those with whom the firm has equity ties.

The benefits of these links can be substantial. First, in joint production agreements, the risk of failure is shared, as the costs of development and production are not borne by one company. Second, joint production agreements allow North American and European companies access to Japanese technology and production techniques. The Japanese companies benefit because these agreements are a way of skirting quotas; the BL Acclaim is counted as being of British, not Japanese, manufacture.[50] The importation of cars and parts produced by other firms but sold by the home company has also proven to be profitable; these "captive imports" give a company access to a model line far more cheaply than it could develop on its own. Chrysler's importing of Mitsubishi cars is one example. Finally, many firms are purchasing components from component suppliers in low-wage third world countries. This form of linkage allows importing firms to decrease both vertical integration and costs.

These avenues of cooperation seem to have limitations, however. GM's plan to import cars from one of its Japanese allies, Isuzu, was partly blocked by the U.S.–Japanese quota agreements; the Isuzu imports are to be counted against Japan's overall total, a total that initially discriminated against new entrants.[51]

The linkages among auto firms are likely to grow, especially as smaller firms confront the choice between being forced out of markets and developing product and cost sharing agreements.[52]

Product Choices

The decisions that firms make regarding their production processes are partly determined by the range and quality of the automobiles they seek to sell. Two strategies are widely employed by auto manufacturers. The first is to produce a full spectrum of cars, ranging from subcompact to standard-sized luxury cars; the second is to make and sell a limited range of cars, usually in the luxury car market. A variation found among mass producers and some specialist producers occurs when firms use common components or body types for similar market niches in different countries, or employ common components in different market lines. Most mass automobile producers produce a full line of cars, regardless of whether a firm's production is located in one market or in many. The prototypical examples are Ford and General Motors. Examples of specialist producers include companies ranging in size from Daimler-Benz (with luxury car sales of more than half a million world-wide) to Aston Martin, whose sales are counted in the hundreds.

American car makers have historically offered a full range of cars—Chevys and Pintos to Cadillacs and Lincolns. Success in the mass market has depended (and still does) upon reducing production costs, since the consumers in the mass market tended in their purchasing patterns to be sensitive to changes in a product's price. Consumers in the luxury section of the market, on the other hand, tended to be sensitive to quality and status. Success in this market has depended (and still does) on product differentiation, consumer satisfaction, and status appeal.[53] Although the sale of a luxury car is more profitable than that of a mass car, the auto companies are reluctant to surrender the lower price market, feeling that this market will eventually promote the sale of the more expensive cars when their consumers acquire enough money to buy more expensive cars. The mass market is thus an investment in customer loyalty.

Offering a full range of products, however, can impose inefficiencies in production on a firm. In the manufacturing of a range of cars of varying quality, an auto maker will lose some of the advantages of economies of scale.[54] This problem can be compounded in the case of multinational producers if the nations served by the firm have markets with different demand profiles. In that case, many different product lines, with many different production lines, may be needed. The solution arrived upon in the 1970s by Ford, General Motors, Volkswagen, and Renault was first to use common components and body types in many different sales lines, and second to sell comparable cars in different markets. The Ford Escort is sold, with minor modifications, in both the North American and Western European markets, as is the VW GTI, Renault's Alliance, and GM's J cars. Producing a world car cuts manufacturing costs.

GM and other firms have discovered that this strategy is in contradiction to the market differentiation strategy. The difficulty is that, by producing common components and line types, the differences among the product lines begin to erode. Rational consumers might well wonder why they should pay two times as much for a Cadillac Cimarron as for a Chevy Cavalier (both are J body cars with but minor modifications), or 60 percent more for a Buick Century than a Chevy Celebrity (both are A cars). In order to compete at the bottom end of the market, the multinational producers have standardized production, but lost product differentiation at the upper end of the market.

With their cost advantages in production, the Japanese manufacturers are able to remain profitable even if they do not achieve full e.o.s. Toyota, for instance, which produces more than 20 models in its home markets, has been able to offer a full range of cars, produce them with little e.o.s. disadvantage, and maintain product differentiation. Japanese firms do not rely on the world car, as do American firms, in producing a full range of cars.[55]

The alternative strategy has been for a firm to produce a narrow range of higher quality automotive products. Scale economies are still achieved through the use of skilled labor and specialized machinery, though the greater value of the end product means that production costs are less important than consumer satisfaction. Volvo, for instance, prides itself both on its reputation for safety and on its non-assembly-line method of production (a method which GM is said to be copying in part at its Saturn plant). BMW and Porsche rely upon their reputations for high performance (e.g., speed and handling). The combined North American/Western European market for these expensive, specialist cars is estimated to be around 2.3 million in 1986, less than 10 percent of the total market, but this is by far the most lucrative part. Of the American luxury market, four German producers (Daimler-Benz, BMW, Audi, and Porsche) have a market share of between and third and a half of the total market.[56]

In practice, the major auto firms are adopting converging strategies: both specialization and mass production. Volkswagen has had for many years a specialist division (Audi) as has FIAT (Lancia), and GM and Ford have each sought to purchase one. GM's efforts to purchase Jaguar in 1984 failed, as did Ford's efforts to buy Alfa Romeo (like Jaguar a state-owned company), but these attempts demonstrate the willingness of the U.S. manufacturers to adopt specialization as a complementary strategy to the world car approach. Ford has, in the meanwhile, opted to import Sierras made by Fordwerke in West Germany, and market them as "Merkurs." GM purchased Lotus, a British auto firm, and negotiated a design contract with an Italian design house, Pinninfarina. Chrysler formed an agreement with Maserati. Honda has created both a specialist division and a separate dealer network for its "upmarket" car, the Accura. Nissan has its "Z" cars, and Mazda its "Rx" cars. These illustrate the point that the strategy of mass production of many lines, sometimes on a world car basis, and the strategy of market specialization, are not mutually exclusive.

Consumer Demand—Market Saturation and Market Share

Understanding the design and production strategies of the suppliers of cars is necessary in forecasting events in the automobile industry. Nonetheless, the demand for cars, while influenced by the sales and marketing strategies of firms, is substantially beyond the manufacturers' control. The key components of demand are (1) the average size of households and the labor participation rate of the household members, (2) the expected income of the household, (3) the policies of governments regarding highway construction and mass transit alternatives, (4) the "scrapping rate" of cars, and (5) the price of new cars.[57] The first two components, labor force participation rates and expected income, are closely related (in a mature economy) to changes in the macroeconomic conditions of a nation's economy. That is, movements in the business cycle of a nation are the best predictor of the demand for new cars. Government policies regarding automobiles and mass transit will vary from country to country, and are generally not easily influenced by firms (but, see Yago's study of GM and mass transit). The scrapping rate of cars generally will determine the replacement demand; car owners usually buy another car when they dispose of their current one. In the mature car markets of North America and Western Europe, the scrapping rate is important for automobile sales as the car replacement market is roughly 85 percent of the total new car market. Finally, consumers in the mass market are sensitive to changes in the price of new cars, though, surprisingly, not much to the changes in the cost of operating a car (e.g., oil prices).[58]

The automobile markets of the industralized nations are often referred to as being near to saturation. In other words, these markets will grow much less quickly than they grew in the past, and less quickly than the markets of less developed countries. The OECD estimated in 1981 that the demand for new cars would average an annual increase of no more than 2 percent in all the major car markets, and much less in some cases; the growth rates in Canada, Britain, and Western Germany are estimated to be below 1 percent. By the mid-1980s, these projections appeared to have been somewhat optimistic. For instance, the sales of new cars in the major automotive markets approached record levels in 1985—a boom year. In 1981, the OECD estimated that 1985 new car sales in the United States would be 11.3 million; in Western Europe, 11.2 million; and in Japan, 4.4 million. The actual sales fell short of the OECD's estimate: the U.S. 11 million; Western Europe, 10.7 million; and in Japan, 3.1 million.[59] The limited increase in market demand likely means that, during the next business cycle downturn, many automobile firms will be in financial trouble.

An analysis of the financial results and market shares of the Western European and the U.S. markets in 1984 and 1985 provides a proxy measure of this market saturation, the 1984 and 1985 booms notwithstanding. The new car sales market in Europe is both competitive, with six producers capturing between 10.7 percent and 12.9 percent of new car sales, and large, with sales of 10.7 million in 1985, nearly matching the record sales year of 1978.[60] Despite near record sales, three of the six major producers (General Motors, Renault, and Peugeot) lost substantial sums of money, almost $1.5 billion (10.9 billion FFrancs) in the case of Renault. Ford, Europe earned $326 million in Europe, a return on sales of only 3.4 percent.[61] These losses occurred even though the Japanese manufacturers have been more or less completely excluded from the French and Italian car markets, and operate within quota systems in Britain and West Germany. To complicate matters for the major auto producers, Nissan and Honda intend to begin assembly operations in the EC, thereby circumventing some of the quota restrictions. Given that the European market is thought to have an overcapacity of roughly 2.5 million cars per year before the Japanese establish assembly operations, the prognosis for the European companies, as the economies of Europe begin to slow, is not good.

Capacity reduction is unlikely to occur through bankruptcy. The two weakest major firms, Renault and Peugeot, will not be permitted by the French government to go out of business, we may safely say. The two most European companies are Ford and General Motors, with major production and component assembly plants in most major markets. Though Ford and GM have no protected national market in Europe that guarantees them a minimum sales volume, these companies are unlikely to withdraw from Europe. VW and FIAT remain profitable. Hence, the usual method of reducing spare capacity in an industry, bankruptcy, is unlikely to occur in Europe. Barring an unforeseen increase in market demand, the European mass producers will likely remain unprofitable for the near future.

The combined profits of General Motors, Ford, and Chrysler were $9.8 billion in 1984 and $8.1 billion in 1985. These net income figures seem to indicate that the substantial investments in products and production processes had successfully restored the American automobile industry to prosperity. "We're all the way back, America!" as Lee Iacocca says on TV.

A careful analysis of the sources of the Big Three's prosperity reveals a less sanguine picture. First, much of the success of the Detroit firms results directly from U.S. government subsidies or trade barriers. Seventeen percent (or $1.6 billion) of the net income of these firms came directly from investment tax credits in 1984, and 14 percent (or $1.2 billion) of net income in 1985.[62] More important to the success of the auto firms has been the "voluntary" quota system imposed by the Japanese government on Japanese firms. The quota system, extended through April 1988, has restrained the number of Japanese-produced cars in the United States to less than 2.3 million cars per year. The International Trade Commission estimated that, without any trade restraints, in 1984 the Japanese producers would have been able to sell one million more cars in the United States than they did, thereby reducing the sales of American firms by 10 to 15 percent.[63] Second, despite these quotas, American firms did not recapture market share from the Japanese producers. The share of the total car market held by GM, Ford, and Chrysler (excluding Mitsubishi-assembled cars) fell to 71 percent of the domestic market, which is the market share these firms held in 1981, when the quota system was first introduced.[64] These quotas soon will be less effective in protecting American firms from Japanese competition; I noted earlier that, by 1990, Japanese producers will have the capacity to produce 1.3 million cars in the United States. Finally, both the European specialist producers and Japanese car makers are targeting the luxury car market, and are expected to take half of this market in 1988. Consumer demand in this market is a function of quality and prestige, and less of price. The bad news for the American producers in this market is that consumers do not believe that U.S. made cars are comparable in quality with foreign cars.[65]

Yet another measure of the problems facing the U.S. auto makers is to be found in the stock market's valuation of the equity issues of the Big Three. As the price/earnings ratio of a firm is the stock price divided by the annual dividends of a firm, the stock price will measure the expected future earnings of a firm. The average price/earnings ratio on the New York Stock Exchange was roughly 12–14, during the summer of 1986. The p/e ratios for Chrysler, Ford, and GM (common) were 5, 6, and 6 respectively.[66] The expectations of stock analysts were that earnings for the Big Three would fall soon.

In Europe and in the United States, the indications are that, despite substantial government protection from Japanese producers, the next economic downturn will confront those firms selling to the mass market with problems of overcapacity.

In reviewing market structures and the choices of firms, we see that a dilemma confronts auto firms. In order to achieve profitable economies of scale, they must either expand production or reduce production costs or both. But the firms must do so at a time when the auto markets of the developed world have approached saturation. And, as most of the major producers are expanding capacity and cutting costs at roughly the same time, the cumulative capacity of the world auto industry will increase far beyond current demand.

One potential solution to this problem is for governments to arrange a cartelization agreement amongst themselves to manage this surplus capacity, a tactic which has been employed in other sectors.[67] Because governments too have an interest in capacity expansion, we find no multinational agreements.

The newly created productive capacity generates capital costs that must be paid, production or no. (See the previous discussion of fixed costs.) Given the likely future world shortfall in demand, those auto firms that are in serious financial trouble might not survive. Even GM and Ford, the largest firms in the world, are expected to face difficult times. GM's long-term debt as a percentage of long-term capital has tripled since 1971 to 17.7 percent (1981); Ford's figure was 26.9 percent, also in 1981.[68] For weaker firms like Chrysler and BL, their recent gains in reducing production costs only succeed in preventing the economies of scale gap between them and the most efficient producers from widening further; Japanese companies continue to install more labor saving devices. The competitive pressure is such that the Economist Intelligence Unit estimated in 1980 "that, by 1990, the global volume car industry will be heavily concentrated around perhaps eight of these [15 or so] world companies, of which four are expected to be European owned."[69] This prognosis now appears in 1986 to have been too pessimistic. Governments generally have been unwilling to permit large firms to collapse or smaller national firms to merge with other (multinational) producers. No major auto firms have filed for bankruptcy recently, and only SEAT of Spain has merged with a stronger multinational producer (VW). Nonetheless, the next economic downturn will brush aside the mist obscuring the tenuous competitive position of many of the world's automotive firms.

Auto firms confront a set of contradictions: expansion of capacity when sectoral rationalizations are needed; increased firm cooperation at a time of intense competition; pressure from home governments to maintain production and from importing countries to begin production. Some firms will fail.

Balance of Interests—Firm and State

Charles Wilson, former chairman of GM, became famous for saying "What's good for America is good for G.M., and vice versa." To a degree, as governments have increasingly become involved in the management of the economy, industry and government in capitalist societies do have some common interests in economic growth and in corporate profitability. Postwar Western governments are "welfare" states—welfare in the sense of promoting the public "good."

The responsibility for the welfare of a nation's citizens creates an ironic paradox for Western politicians—they are often evaluated by the electorate on the performance of the economy, even though much of the success of the economy depends on the actions of private firms. Governments depend on private enterprise to provide investment and employment, except in the rare cases where governments manage the bulk of investment directly or indirectly. Because investment funds are a relatively scarce and highly mobile resource, firms, banks, and other sources of investment funds have some leverage (perhaps the decisive leverage) on Western governments. In consequence, the promotion of "business confidence" and business investment guides much of government policy, regardless of the political ideology of the party in power.[70]

In the case of the auto industry, the commonality of interests between a government and domestic firms is substantial. High levels of domestic production, at a minimum, reduce the auto imports and the consequent balance of payments costs. For some nations, autobiles are an important export item; Japan earned $75 billion between 1976 and 1980 through the export of autos. For other nations, the importation of autos made by foreign firms constitutes a substantial cost; one third of the $50 billion trade deficit that the United States had with Japan in 1985 is attributable to the importing of Japanese cars.[71]

In some cases, benefits to a nation represent costs to a firm. For instance, the European auto industry (including component producers), employed directly 2 million workers (more than 5 percent) of the total EC employment in 1981), and provided employment indirectly to perhaps an additional 4 million workers. The industry uses 20 percent of all community steel production and machine tools, and substantial portions of the glass, rubber, and plastic industries' final products.[72] These wages and purchases represent costs, and the firm does have an interest in reducing wage and other factor costs. This is not to say that employment and the domestic content of automobiles are always points of contradictory interest between firm and state. As we have seen, firms can reduce costs only within constraints imposed upon them by the structure of production, as well as those imposed by government policies and union strength.

Employment is a particularly important issue for governments. Since the Depression and the Second World War, Western democracies have assumed some responsibility for the management of their economies, and have established social "safety nets" to cushion their populations from sudden firm or sectoral failures. In all the main OECD (Organization for Economic Cooperation and Development— 25 Industrial Nations) countries, aid to those individuals who have suffered job and income losses attributable to market or other failures is determined by income thresholds and other categorical grants, which are automatic in the sense that government funding is nondiscretionary. That is, funding levels of programs are determined not by direct legislation, but by the need levels of individuals. Approximately 80 percent of the American budget is nondiscretionary, even though the U.S. is among the OECD countries with the lowest levels of social spending.[73] Therefore, as workers are laid off, state expenses rise automatically. In addition, one consequence of concentrated auto production is that some regions (e.g. Michigan) are more dependent on auto production than are others. When auto employment falls, the impact is deeper in these regions. Reductions in production and employment are then costly to governments in terms of state expenses, regional policies, national accounts, and (less directly) the public welfare. Even considering the cost of employment, firm and government interests are clearly reconcilable under conditions of high auto production. In a declining market, however, state interests and firm interests usually will diverge.

In the case of a few countries, most notably the United States, this partial commonality of interests seems to have extended, at least until recent years, to direct foreign investment by their home firms into foreign markets. This may seem to be something of a paradox; overseas investment is usually thought to replace at least some domestic investment, so why would governments acquiesce in the transferring of production abroad? In the case of the auto industry, however, investment in foreign markets is almost always defensive; that is, firms are confronted with the choice of investing in a foreign market or losing access to that market.[74] In consequence, overseas investment is not necessarily "lost" investment to the home economy.

Overseas investment can also return fairly high profits to the investors. Ford, Europe, for example, was much more profitable in the late 1970s and early 1980s than was Ford, USA, and the loans and remitted profits made to Ford, USA by its European subsidiaries helped Ford survive billion-dollar losses in 1980 and 1981. The investment by companies also, in theory, benefits the home economy. For instance, Britain's net earnings from direct foreign investments (excluding those from oil investments) between 1977 and 1982 totaled £17 billion, a figure which (on average) translated into between 1 and 2 percent of British GDP for the period.[75]

Some analysts have argued that, in the American case, policymakers have seen foreign direct investment by firms as in some sense furthering American interests by extending American hegemony to so-called peripheral countries.[76] Even when foreign investment occasions a decrease in home investment, again at least for the United States, the commonality of interests may continue between firm and state as "power," "influence," or some other asset valuable in the international arena may accrue to the state as its return on the investment bargain.

In recent years, the premise of the commonality of interests between the firm and the state on the issue of direct foreign investment

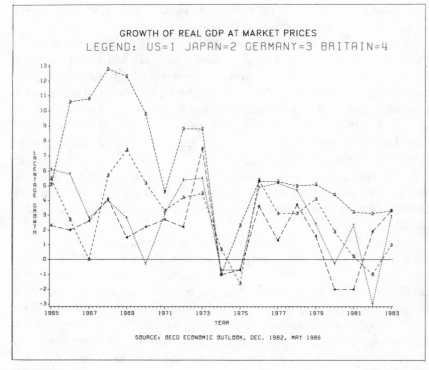

FIGURE 2.4

has been undermined by the comparatively low growth in countries like the U.S. and Great Britain (see fig. 2.4), where outward foreign investment and other capital flows are large and relatively unimpeded. This disparity between the U.S. and British growth rates and those of the other major OECD countries has been matched by an investment gap (see fig. 2.5).

Some commentators have seen these phenomena as causally linked; lower rates of investment produce lower rates of growth. Though this hypothesis is not proven (and probably not provable), the link is plausible enough so that proposed solutions to the problem of this investment lag have included restrictions on the export of

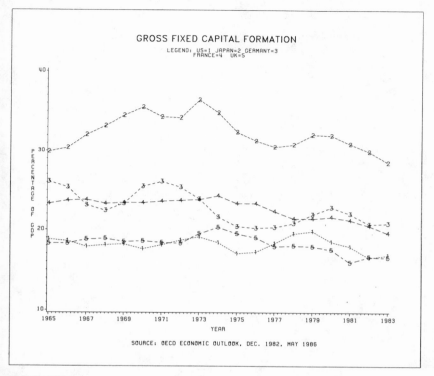

GROSS FIXED CAPITAL FORMATION

LEGEND: US=1 JAPAN=2 GERMANY=3
FRANCE=4 UK=5

SOURCE: OECD ECONOMIC OUTLOOK, DEC. 1982, MAY 1986

FIGURE 2.5

capital for investment.[77] Britain, through exchange controls, did attempt to regulate capital flows (largely to protect sterling's value) in late 1970s, and achieved a rough "parity" in investments. After the removal of exchange controls in 1979, the balance of investments swung against Britain by over £20 billion. (See fig. 2.6) In fact, large capital movements seem to be associated with lower rates of growth, though again, no causal link has been proven. On one item, most analysts agree. In situations of low or declining growth, as in most of the auto industry of 1979–82, countries with extensive domestic production do not benefit from home firms investing in other nations; the interests are not reconcilable.[78]

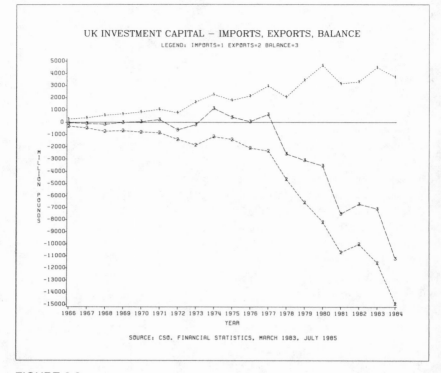

FIGURE 2.6

Governments generally have relatively few tools for resolving these conflicts of interest in their favor. Militating against government dominance of privately owned auto firms is the difficulty of structuring customer preferences. Consumers purchase many varieties of automobiles, and often develop strong brand loyalties, loyalties only marginally influenced by state policies. Further, as a result of international agreements like the European Common Market, the North American Automotive Pact, and the Tokyo Round of the General Agreements on Trade and Tariffs, governments have surrendered a certain range of policy options. The British government, for example, cannot legally discriminate against Fords made in Germany. This loss of some freedom of action is buttressed by the ethos of what John Ruggie calls "the normative framework of embedded liberalism" or a commitment to multilateral trade and domestic stability, commitments generated by the social upheavals caused by rising tariffs, a depression, and war.[79] By agreeing not to deny to imports from treaty-participant nations, the North American and West European states have yielded some of their most potent weapons of control over multinational auto producers.

An increase in the multinational corporation's leverage over governments in making plant investment decisions is among the unintended consequences of this internationalization of the trade markets. For instance, GM can as well supply the British market from Belgium and Spain (now that Spain has entered the EC) as from Britain. The British government must therefore induce GM to increase production in Britain (or rely on union pressure) as Britain can no longer deny GM's EEC-produced products access to Britain's market.[80] European governments have recently engaged in bidding wars for auto firm investments reminiscent of those among American state and Canadian provinces. The auto firms have utilized these competitive situations to gain tax and other economic advantages from the "winners."[81]

Another consequence of the internationalization of the auto industry is that the ability of governments to foster their own profitable domestic "national champions" has sharply diminished. Smaller mass producers, BL and SEAT of Spain for instance, operate largely within one protected market, but do not have sufficient volume of production and sales to profitably compete with the multinational corporations, even in that protected market. The Spanish government under the Socialists chose in 1986 to sell its interests in SEAT to Volkswagen, citing in part the British experience with British Leyland for avoiding the government maintenance of small mass producer. The British government ultimately rebuffed Ford's attempt to acquire BL (Rover), apparently in the hope that BL's links to Honda will prevent the complete foreign takeover of Britain's (mass) automotive production. Puegeot and Renault are much larger companies than are SEAT and BL, but they remain financially troubled, despite much French government assistance. FIAT of Italy is something of the exception to the rule; it has withdrawn from a number of markets in order to concentrate on its (protected) Italian market while maintaining its profitability. In general, the reliance by governments on a national champion has not been a successful strategy in the automotive industry.

Governments also face internal constraints on their power vis-à-vis firms, though the dimensions of these internal constraints vary considerably. The parameters that limit the domain of state actions are many. Among the most important are the institutional arrangements of the state. Such arrangements include the degree of incorporation of producer groups (e.g. unions, business associations) into policymaking, the relations among the branches of the government, the strength of political parties and bureaucratic elites, the extent of political centralization and so on. These institutional arrangements are the results of past political battles and power struggles among political groups. For instance, the social safety nets of the Western democracies are generally the result of the political struggles of organized labor and ther political allies, during and after the Great Depression, for protection against the consequences of market failure. Though such arrangements are not set in concrete, and are potentially changeable by current contenders for power, they influence a government's ability to achieve desired political ends (as well as helping to define those desired ends). For instance, the American Courts and Congress are institutionally stronger vis-à-vis the Executive branch, though more open to societal pressure groups, than are their French counterparts. In consequence, the French Executive has has greater capacity to act vis-à-vis its own society than does the American. Other important variables in assessing state capacity include a nation's international market position in the world economy, the perceived interests of societal pressure groups, and their capacity to mobilize political resources, and the dominant ideological strains within a country. As these vary among nations, so too will the general capacity of states to act vis-à-vis firms.[82]

These relative capacities are important in understanding the leverage governments can bring to bear on firms. The French and the Japanese governments, for instance, have among the institutional capacities of their states effective control over the financial system and corporate access to it.[83] This dramatically increases state leverage, especially when firms already have substantial investment within the country or when firms develop financial difficulties. The American government, in contrast, has no such arrangements, and the Chrysler bailout was possible only through the very public and contentious creation of an ad hoc rescue agency, the Chrysler Loan Guarantee Board.[84] Other states have substantial discretionary authority to make outright grants; Section 8 of the Industry Acts of 1972, 1975, 1980 and 1982 (called the Industrial Development Act) allows the British government to provide grants to virtually any transnational firm in return for investing in Britain.

Nonetheless, even with the inducements of industrial policies and the possibility of restricting access to markets, state power with regard to firms is vulnerable to broad changes in the economy, changes over which governments have little immediate control. For instance, the American dollar was said to be overvalued in relation to the Japanese yen by 15 percent for much of the early 1980s, which strongly reduced the incentive for Japanese firms to invest in the United States.[85]

Conclusion

The world auto industry is structured by scale economies, consumer preferences, and government-firm relations. The consequence has been a concentrated industry, with 27 companies producing 97 percent of all non-East bloc autos. The mass market industry will likely become more concentrated yet, as the Minimum Efficient Size below which a firm is at a competitive disadvantage has increased to at least 2 million cars per years, a size exceeded in recent years by only five firms. Government strategies that promote auto industrialization have often required or induced firms to establish foreign subsidiaries, though the effectiveness of some policy tools available to governments has diminished in recent years. The effect on firms of the need to achieve scale economies while satisfying government policies is that firms have increased the capacity to produce autos even though the developed world's markets are near saturation. During the last business downturn (1979–82), several major firms nearly failed.

The relationship between governments and auto firms is guided by the balance of interests between them, and the assets each brings to the bargaining process. Firms and governments have some common interests, especially in conditions of high or steady economic growth. But, during cyclical economic downturns, this commonality of interests vanishes over issues like employment and foreign investment. The pattern of bargaining between firm and government is not a universal one, as the various states of the Western world have differing capacities to act, and those firms near to bankruptcy are often in need of public support. But in general, the balance of power in bargaining rests with the firm: firms control investment and employment levels, have unmatchable technical expertise, operate within a (relatively) free trade regime, have much discretion about the location of future investment, and produce a consumer durable good not easily replaceable by substitutes. Governments do influence the shape of the automotive market through the tax code and through environmental and safety regulation. Government leverage on firms, however, has been eroded by the free trade regime, though some states have financial and other capacities with which to influence firm behavior. In general, firms are in the better bargaining positions.

3.

THE AMERICAN AND BRITISH INDUSTRIES: PROSPERITY AND DECLINE IN THE 1970s

THE UNITED STATES and Great Britain are the two nations whose automobile production levels in the early 1980s decreased both absolutely and in percentage of total world production from the early 1970s (fig. 3.1). The production and sales decrease, and the resulting employment layoffs, stood in contrast to the relative prosperity of the previous 10 years.

In the 1970s, production of autos by the domestic industries was at its high point: 8–9.5 million cars were produced in the U.S. by 800,000 workers, another 2 million in the U.K. by 300,000 employees. Prosperous times were forecast: *Ward's Automotive Yearbook* predicted in 1973 (before the oil embargo) that the American market would grow to 16 million cars sold by 1980.[1] (Auto sales diminished in both markets, and production fell by a third.) The industries had, and still have, a broad impact on their home economies. Apart from direct employment, the British industry in the early 1970s indirectly employed an additional 1 million workers (more than 5 percent of the labor force) and was the nation's leading exporter.[2] Including the multiplier effects (but excluding retail jobs), approximately 10 percent of the British work force was provided with jobs thanks to the motor industry.[3] The American industry had a similar impact; the

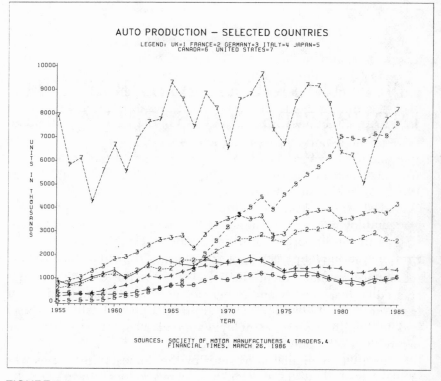

FIGURE 3.1

total net sales of the American industry in 1971 was $53 billion, or approximately 5% of the total of the American Gross National Product of that year.[4]

The reversal of fortunes from the prosperity of the 1970s for the auto industries can be seen in the production figures from figs. 2.2–2.3, which show that production in both markets fell by a third. Falling sales were attributable not only to changing (cyclical) macroeconomic conditions. In addition, imports into the United States increased by 150 percent, and into Britain by almost 300 percent for the 1970s.

These symptoms of lost competitiveness are to be found in the manufacturing sectors of both countries; the auto industries of Britain and the U.S. were not the only industries to suffer a loss of production, profits, and employment. Each country has endured a relative decline of its manufacturing sector in relation to the other major sectors, a decline masked by the general prosperity of most OECD countries during the 1950s and 1960s.[5] The relative decline in industrial production is especially acute for Great Britain. Britain's share of the exports of the main manufacturing countries' share of manufactured exports has fallen steadily since the Second World War: 26.7 percent in 1950, 15.9 in 1960, 10.1 in 1970, and 8.2 in 1979.[6] For both countries, the symptoms of this relative decline included slow increases in national productivity, large shifts away from employment in the manufacturing sectors, and substantial increases in the imports of finished products. This relative decline, amplified in the late 1970s by a downturn in the domestic business cycles, became a political issue in the United States and Great Britain, especially as the so-called basic industries of steel, ship building, and, of course, automobiles each suffered an absolute decline. The automobile industry is therefore only one example of this problem, albeit the largest example.

We would expect that as the economic circumstances of the auto industry have changed, so too would the public policies of the American and British governments toward it. I will argue, in the next chapter, that the states' policies have changed so that these policies are now substantially similar in intent and in substance. Here, however, the discussion of traditional public policies in Britain and the United States will focus on the essential differences between these countries in the form, content, and substance of industry policy.

The argument that American and British public policies were highly dissimilar, until the mid 1970s, is hardly new or surprising.[7] Even now, elements of these policy differences remain. The American style of policy through adversary and litigation procedures and the British style of policy through consensus both continue, though in a more limited fashion. Institutions and bureaucratic habits are rarely transformed easily or quickly, especially when groups, whose interests and agendas are reflected by existing institutions, are able to mobilize political resources to defend these agendas. Ecological, safety, and employment issues have important supporters within each political system. So, not surprisingly, important remnants of the policy concerns of the 1960s and 1970s in each country are visible and account for much of the remaining policy differences between them.

This chapter will focus on two aspects of the American and British auto industry: the traditional industry structures of each country, and the traditional government policies towards the industry. The time frame of the discussion will encompass the period from the Second World War until early 1975.

Industry Structure

The American and British motor industries historically have been relatively dissimilar with regard to industry concentration, market size, firm competition, auto products, export policies, and labor organization despite the presence in the British market (at one point) of all three American auto firms. Though the range of differences has been narrowed, the industry structures of the U.S. and Britain remain largely dissimilar.

Great Britain

In Britain, the "specialist automakers" like Jaguar and Rolls-Royce survived in large numbers; 30 remained in the early 1950s. The process of industry consolidation, thought to be necessary if the British companies were to achieve competitive economies of scale, reduced the number of major firms to four, as table 3.1 indicates.

This process of consolidation occurred much later in Britain than in other producer countries for a number of reasons. First, though the process of industry consolidation has been encouraged by the government in recent years, this was not so during the 1940s and

TABLE 3.1
Shares of UK Car Production by UK Manufacturers in Percentages, for Selected Years

			1947	1954	1960	1974	1978	1985
Morris	} BMC		20.9	38.0	36.5			
Austin			19.2					
Jaguar		} BMH	1.6	1.5	1.7			
		> BL				48.2	50.0	44.4
Standard	} Leyland		13.2	11.0	8.0			
Rover			2.7	1.7	1.6			
Rootes	} Chrysler		10.9	11.0	10.6	10.9	16.1	6.4
Singer			2.1					
GM/Vauxhall			11.2	9.0	10.7	8.9	6.9	14.6
Ford			15.4	27.0	30.0	25.0	26.5	30.3

Sources: Dunnett, Decline of the British Motor Industry, p. 20; SMMT, quoted in Financial Times, February 17, 1986.

early 1950s. Postwar quotas on steel deliveries guaranteed that smaller companies received a share of steel, and that larger companies could not increase auto production. The British government also required that, at a time when supply in Britain was already low and the demand great in Europe's markets, up to two-thirds of auto production be exported. This meant that even overpriced and poorly made British products were salable.[8] Finally, the British industry has never been particularly integrated vertically. That is, British auto companies produce comparatively few of the components of a car, preferring to contract with one of Britain's many component makers. The presence of numerous component producers, some of whom (like Lucas and GKN) are large enough to achieve their own economies of scale, allowed smaller companies to survive at lower than "scale" production (really assembly) levels.[9]

In consequence, more efficient and profitable firms were unable to exploit economies of scale, and thereby put smaller firms at a competitive disadvantage, until the late 1960s. The general conditions of postwar prosperity, and a seller's market for industrial products in the 1950s and 1960s, masked the structural weakness resulting from the fragmentation of the British industry.[10]

Even when industry consolidation did occur in the 1960s, the resulting industry structure was such that not even British Leyland (now called BL), the largest firm, achieved suitable economies of scale. (See table 2.2.) The resulting company was poorly integrated, and had too many plants producing too many models relative to the volume of production: in 1967, BL produced 13 basic models and more than 800,000 cars. In comparison, General Motors produced 4 million cars in the U.S. at the same time, but had only eight basic models.[11]

In addition to fragmented production, the company inherited some archaic management practices. For example, the British Motor Company (BMC), one of the companies merged into British Leyland, reportedly "disdained formal education" among its managerial employees; it hired one college graduate in 1967.[12] Pay was based on "piece rate" work, and lines of segmentation (between management and labor, between skilled workers and unskilled workers) were sharply drawn.

Not surprisingly, the firms in the British motor industry lost money, Ford excepted. In addition to BL's losses, Chrysler/Peugeot-Talbot lost money for 18 of the 22 years between 1963 and 1985, and Vauxhall (GM's subsidiary) lost money in all but one year between 1972 and 1985.[13] Even during the relatively prosperous years of 1970 through 1973, the profitability of British firms (as measured by the percentage return on shareholders' funds) was low: Chrysler, U.K., −9.6%; Vauxhall, −8.4%; BL, 5.6%; and Ford, U.K., 5.9%. In contrast, the figures for some of the world's more profitable companies (for the same period) were: Toyota, 15.4%; Nissan, 15.5%; Ford, West Germany, 17.9%; Peugeot, 18.4%; and Opel (GM, West Germany), 19.1%.[14] As the reader can see, profitability seems to be location specific. That is, the same companies, Ford and GM, are in both West Germany and Britain, using similar products and management styles in each. Yet the German subsidiaries are very profitable, but the British are not.

One important feature of British industry structure is that three of the four remaining companies are foreign subsidiaries of multinational firms, though the largest producer remains BL. (See figure 3.2.) These multinational firms have produced ambivalent reactions in the British political elite. On the one hand, investment in Britain has generated substantial employment, and has contributed to the balance of trade through exports. Britain has received the bulk of both U.S. and Japanese investment in the E.C. More than 14.1 percent of all employment and 16 percent of salaries in Britain are attributable to foreign investment.[15] American investment is especially important. For instance, over 650,000 British workers are employed by subsidiaries of American corporations.[16] On the other hand, multinational firms in Britain—especially in the auto industry—have loyalties more divided than do "British" firms. Issues such as "captive imports," production levels, and "foreign sourcing" of production have become issues of negotiation among the multinational auto producers, the Trades Union Congress, and the Thatcher government.[17] The opposition in 1986 to Ford's takeover of Austin-Morris, and to GM's proposed purchase of Bedford and Rover, seems to have revolved around whether these companies would be good "corporate citizens" as measured by levels of production and employment. Mrs. Thatcher notwithstanding, the Conservative Party judged not.

The ambivalence concerning multinational investment in Britain is rooted not just in the fear of a loss of British government influence to decisionmakers in other countries; especially in the automotive sector, some fear was expressed that multinational companies were entering industries in which British firms were unconsolidated and not producing at world competitive levels. For instance, the Labour government in 1967 initially balked at Chrysler's request to purchase majority shares in Rootes, a company in which Chrysler already had a substantial equity stake. Anthony Wedgwood Benn, the Minister of Technology (the former Viscount Stansgate) said at the time,

Our doubts about this did not arise from anti-American feeling, but from the anxiety that Britain, looking ahead over a period of years,

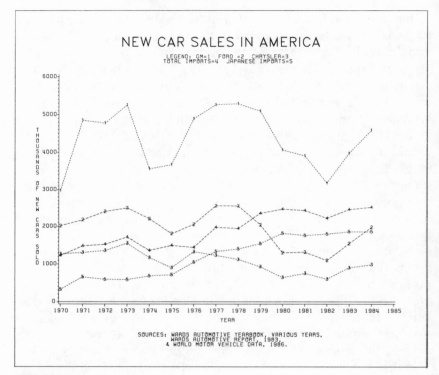

FIGURE 3.2

might not be able to sustain three large American Corporations and a British corporation when the United States which is three times our size and has a much larger output can only sustain three corporations.[18]

This fear has proven to be well founded. A British government report in 1975 said that "three out of the four British car manufacturers are not now viable and are caught in the vicious downward spiral created when profits are inadequate to finance the investment necessary to introduce new models at the same rate as the competition."[19] In 1986, only Ford earned a profit.

TABLE 3.2
Minimum Efficient Scale of Production, Selected Years
(with reference to American data)

	Largest Firm's Share[a]	Total Market	Biggest Firm's Production	MES	MES Est.
Year					
1947	40%	3,558,000	1,438,000	150,000	9.5
1954	52%	5,559,000	2,874,000	600,000	4.8
1960	48%	6,696,000	3,193,000	750,000	4.2
1967	56%	7,707,000	4,118,000	1,000,000	4.1
1974	49%	7,290,000	3,557,000	1,250,000	2.8
1977	57%	9,211,000	5,262,000	2,000,000	2.6

Sources: Data from Ward's Automotive Report various years.
[a]GM in all cases

America

The structure of the American industry is substantially different from the British. The market is much larger, allowing for scale economy production, as Table 3.2 shows. The worldwide production of each included, all three American firms in the 1970s met or exceeded the Minimum Efficient Size.

The American Industry also consolidated much earlier; by 1935, General Motors, Chrysler and Ford accounted for 90 percent of American automotive production.[20] The remaining four "minors,"—Packard, Studebaker, Nash, and Hudson—did survive in their original form through the 1950s. (Nash and Hudson in some sense still exist. They merged to form American Motors, a company which survived largely as an American assembler for the French company, Renault before it was purchased by Chrysler.) The three largest firms have produced over 95% of the cars for more than 30 years.

The two largest firms, Ford and GM, are also substantially integrated. For instance, Ford's River Rouge plant produced most of the steel needed for auto assembly, and did so with coal from Ford's mines. Both companies produce a line of component parts for use both as original equipment and replacement parts (e.g., Delco, Motorcraft).[21]

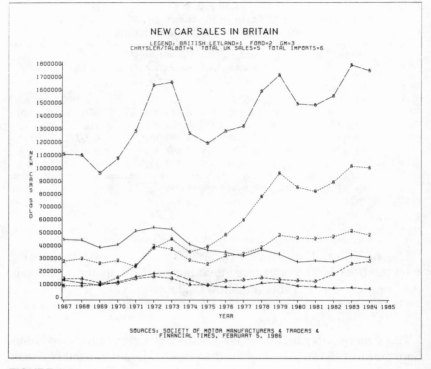

FIGURE 3.3

The American auto industry, unlike Britain's, was both profitable and highly competitive for much of the postwar era, as table 3.3 demonstrates.

The competition among American firms was not confined to the U.S. Chrysler's expansion into Europe during the 1960s was largely an attempt to expand the range upon which it could compete with Ford and GM. Even today, GM's recent emphasis on its European operations is partly aimed at overtaking Ford's position in Europe.[22]

TABLE 3.3
U.S. After-Tax Return of
Stockholder's Equity, 1965–1976

	U.S. Automobile Industry	All Manufacturing
1965	21.0	13.0
1966	16.8	13.4
1967	11.6	11.6
1968	15.7	12.1
1969	13.2	11.5
1970[a]	6.0	9.3
1971	14.2	9.7
1972	16.1	10.6
1973	16.4	12.8
1974	5.9	14.9
1975	5.8	11.5
1976[b]	22.2	14.4

Source: Hunker, Structural Change in the U.S. Automobile Industry, p. 22
[a]strike at GM
[b]first six months of 1976 annualized, but not seasonally adjusted.

Exports

The overseas expansion of American firms highlights another of the central differences between the American and British industry structures. For the American industry, the export of automobiles, save to Canada, has been of peripheral interest since the Second World War. The American firms have instead become multinational firms. British firms, including the American subsidiaries, have been major exporters.

Throughout the 1970s, approximately 35 to 45 percent of British auto production was exported, with the United States taking the largest share of the value of the exports. It averaged £150 million a year in British auto imports during the late 1970s.[23] Twice as valuable as the export of cars to the British economy has been the export of auto parts and accessories. In 1981, the value of this trade exceeded £2 billion, and in 1984 and 1985, component exports returned more than £3 billion each year to the British economy.[24] In 1980, even after British auto production had fallen to 46% of its all-time high in 1972, the 3rd, 4th, 10th, 22nd, and 31st leading British exporters were auto and auto part manufacturers, with a total export value of over £2.7 billion. Only the petroleum sector exported more.[25] The British auto sector is heavily reliant on foreign sales. Foreign sales are important to the subsidiaries of American firms, but not to the American domestic industry as such.

Labor Organization

Another important area of difference between the industries concerns the organization of labor, though we do find some important areas of similarity. The differences revolve around union organization; the similarity involves traditions of distrust.

The auto industry is in some ways the prototype of the industrial bureaucracy, with its rigid industrial norms and practices. Authority relations in an auto plant are arranged so that a large labor force, mostly semi-skilled or unskilled, works in synchrony at a pace set by the line speed of the conveyor belt. Individual initiative among assembly workers in completing their work assignments is not encouraged. Authority relations are sharply defined. The industry is also characterized by substantial role conflicts among senior management, line officers and foremen, staff employees, and line workers. Such conflict is reinforced by the subcultural and the social caste differences among the groups. As a result of these tensions, an "us versus them" attitude is prevalent in American and British industry. This has led to the development of trade unions in the American and British auto industries.[26]

The auto industries of the U.S. and Britain are nearly totally unionized, though Nissan and Honda are exceptions in the United States. Full industry unionization occurred in both countries during the late 1930s and early 1940s, frequently as a result of government intervention, and usually with the deep hostility of management. This tradition of hostility is rooted not only in the wage/cost relationship

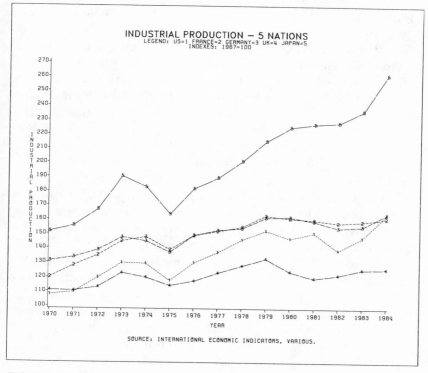

FIGURE 3.4

of labor and management, but also in the Taylorist style of industrial organization, which is characteristic of the extreme division of labor in an auto assembly line. To a large extent, assembly line production of mass consumer goods results inevitably in boring, repetitive work and, at least among the Western working class, some degree of alienation. Thus, the gulf between management and labor is rooted in authority relations, wage/cost relations, and social caste relations. In consequence, their relationship has often been seen as a zero-sum game. Complaints about poor workmanship and sabotage, seasonal layoffs and rapid redundancies, poor communications and hostile cultures are part of the legacy of Anglo-American auto manufacturing.[27]

The differences between the American and British auto work forces are nonetheless substantial. British workers in the auto industry are organized along craft lines, with as many as seventeen separate unions present within each plant, though the largest union, the TWGU, represents approximately 60 percent of the automotive labor force. The unions are far from united on issues like pay and shop seniority, while substantial pay differentials divide categories of jobs. Infighting among these unions is common.[28]

In many cases, the basic unit of labor organization in the industry is the plantwide shop stewards committee, composed of the elected representatives of the various craft unions. Paradoxically, these committees have no formal standing with the companies in negotiations (or, for that matter, with the union hierarchies), even though the shop steward committee exerts much power due partly to its strategic position in the factories as well as to a unique feature of British labor law.

Labor contracts historically have not been binding in Britain. A union thus was not financially responsible for a wildcat or any other authorized or unauthorized strike during the terms of a labor contract. As a result, local committees during the 1970s and early 1980s sponsored many walkouts over local issues, frequently without the authorization of the umbrella organization of the unions, the Trades Union Congress (TUC). For instance, recent auto work stoppages included a month-long walkout in 1983 against Ford over the attempted dismissal of a worker who allegedly vandalized a 86p ($1.15) bracket, a "washing-up" strike roughly at the same time at BL over a three-minute addition to the working time at the end of the shift, and a "swearing" strike at BL's Cowley plant in November 1982.[29]

The issues over which disputes occur are frequently those over job definition and work rules. For instance, Chrysler and BL moved away from the piece rate method of payment (payment by results, or PBR) in the early 1970s, to an hourly rate (Measured Day Work, or MDW), a change which seems at face value to be a more equitable

TABLE 3.4
Work Stoppages & Strikes, BL—1977–1981

	1977	1978	1979	1980	1981
Man-hours (millions) Lost					
Internal	14.8	10.0	13.5	3.5	0.9
External	12.2	0.5	1.3	0	0
Total	27.0	10.5	4.8	3.5	0.9
As % of Available Time	5.9	3.5	5.1	1.4	0.5
Vehicles Lost in Strikes, 000s					
Internal	192.9	117.9	113.0	51.0	n.a.
External	58.6	13.4	10.8	0.7	n.a.

Sources: House of Commons (U.K.), Industry and Trade Committee, BL Limited, 1981–83, and House of Commons (U.K.), Industry and Trade Committee, BL PLC, 1982–83.

method of dividing salaries and wages. The unions did not see this change as innocuous. The ICW study claimed that:

> In contrast to piecework, where the speed of the work is to some extent under the control of the gang, the principle of MDW is that management makes the assignments, management determines line speed and production quotas, management allocates the workers to the tasks it deems suitable. The history of MDW is the attempt by management to make this principle a reality—to break down the resistance of the work force.[30]

One complication in management–labor relations is that work stoppages occasionally are caused by issues over which neither management nor labor has control. Table 3.4 gives some indication of this problem. In 1977, almost half of the hours lost as a result of work stoppages came as a result of work stoppages external to BL (e.g., among BL's component suppliers.) The plants closed when shortages of parts developed. Another problem is that strikes are occasionally aimed at the government. The 1969 Ford strike was in response to the government's wage and price controls under which Ford had tendered its offer.[31]

The motor industry in Britain is more prone to industrial disputes

TABLE 3.5
**Days Lost in the United Kingdom through Industrial Action
(per 1,000 workers)**

	British Motor Industry	All British Manufacturing
1969	3,100	484
1970	2,150	729
1971	6,100	816
1972	2,631	1,013
1973	4,027	741
1974	3,442	981

Source: Central Policy Review Staff, The Future of the British Car Industry, p. 98.

than is the industrial economy as a whole (see table 3.5). In both the motor industry and in the manufacturing sector, we find wide variability concerning the frequency of disputes. The level of work stoppages seems to vary with the general economic conditions; those unionized industries most affected by import replacement seem particularly strike-prone, especially as an economy enters into a recession.[32]

Management-labor strife has influenced firm strategies in sometimes subtle ways. S. J. Prais argues that the relatively small size of factories in the British automobile industry prevents British firms from achieving world competitive economies of scale. Small factories are a deliberate choice of management in the British industry, despite the e.o.s. penalties, because "strike-proneness in Britain rises strongly with plant-size."[33] Smaller factories are therefore a rational response by management to problems of labor instability. Poor labor–management relations then, have underlying effects on the industry structure and on British competitiveness even in situations where industrial relations play no apparent role.

Most analysts agree that labor troubles are a significant, though perhaps not the most significant, cause of the British motor vehicle industry's decline.[34] The list of potential villains for labor troubles is long: a hostile (sometimes incompetent) managerial class, residues

of Britain's class structure, union fragmentation and rivalry, Trotsky-
ite shop stewards, industrial alienation, poor communications, capitalist greed and underinvestment, government policies, a shift from
distributing surpluses to issues involving income and job losses, and
so on. The consensus is that industrial relations are poor in the
industry.[35]

The American auto industry's labor force is organized differently.
The auto industry was unionized by a unit of the Congress of Industrial Organizations (CIO): the United Auto Workers (UAW). The
American Federation of Labor (AFL) tried unsuccessfully to organize
the industry along craft lines. Hence, in practice, one union represents all auto workers. The UAW is centralized and not especially
prone to strikes by its locals. This tendency reinforced by American
law, which holds unions liable for breaches in the contract. As a
result, local work stoppages due to shop floor grievances or to the
grievances of a particular craft group are much rarer in the American
industry than in the British.

Also adding to the relative labor peace in the industry is the bargaining strategy of the UAW. Auto industry contracts are usually
three years in duration, and until the Chrysler "givebacks" of 1980–
82 were uniform throughout the industry. Previously, the UAW
would, during the third year of a contract, target one of the Big Three
companies for a strike, and the resulting labor contract would set
the standards for the rest of the industry. For instance, Ford was the
"strike target" in 1967, GM in 1970. The 1970 strike against GM
lasted over 65 days, and the terms of that contract were quickly
agreed to by Ford and Chrysler.[36] On average, 0.95 percent less than
1 percent of total American auto work days were lost due to strikes
during the 1950s and 1960s, with the peak strike years occurring at
the end of the three-year contracts.[37] In contrast, BL lost between 3
and 5 percent of its total work days during the late 1960s and early
1970s.[38] The ability of the UAW to successfully target one auto company and force it to terms resided in part in the competition among
the auto firms, and in part in the resources of the UAW. In 1981,

despite substantial long-term layoffs, the UAW strike fund contained liquid assets of more than $388 million. The UAW's net worth was more than $500 million.[39] The UAW could (and still can) partially compensate striking workers for lost wages.

In recent years, the UAW has suffered some reverses as auto employment has declined. UAW membership fell from 1.53 million in 1979 to slightly under 1 million in 1983. The UAW must also contend with the resistance to unionization of Honda and Nissan, which have invested in the U.S. The UAW was also forced by Chrysler's weakened position and by the terms of the government bailout into making wage concessions—concessions that GM tried, but failed, to gain also.[40]

At least in terms of union membership, the UAW's problems will continue as firms replace unskilled labor with machinery, and as firms import car components from lower-wage countries like Mexico and Korea. For instance, GM is planning to introduce up to 14,000 robots in its plants by 1990; it employed 1200 robots in 1981. Furthermore, 400,000 additional workers may be displaced by robotization in the auto industry, mostly in the welding, assembling, and machining functions. The cost advantage to firms of replacing workers with machines is said to be substantial (if one assumes that job classifications are rigid and that wages will continue to increase); one estimate is that the application of robots to auto assembly can reduce costs by a third.[41] The same process is underway in the British industry; BL's Cowley and Longbridge plants have nearly doubled car output per worker thanks in part to new industrial robots.

In general, American and British labor relations in the auto industries have been characterized by substantial hostilities between management and labor, though, owing to union fragmentation, work stoppages have been more common in the British industry.[42] Though these troubles did not help the industry's long-run future, as long as the American and British markets remained relatively isolated from foreign competition, the costs of bad labor relations, high wages, and and periodic work stoppages could be passed on to auto buyers with only minor repercussions.[43]

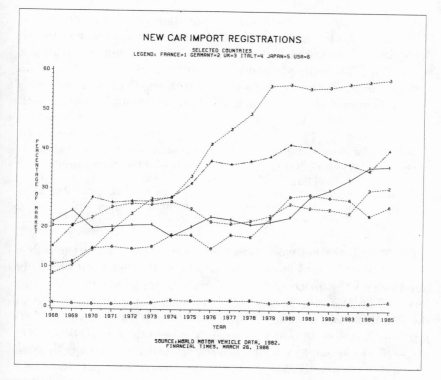

FIGURE 3.5

Market Isolation

In one respect, the American and British industries were similar. Relative isolation from foreign competitors characterized the postwar auto industries of both countries until the mid-1970s, as figure 3.5 shows. This relative isolation enabled the British and American industries to ignore the competitive pressures from industries like the Japanese and the German until the mid-1970s. In both cases, the market isolation was the result of barriers to entry of foreign products. These barriers, however, were different for the American and British markets.

British market isolation resulted from state policies regarding infrastructure, trade, and taxation. Central among the barriers to imports was the nature of British roads, which "tended to follow the rights of way determined by medieval institutions."[44] Britain had no highway or *autobahn* system in postwar years. British automobiles were of course designed for such a lack, and imported cars were not. The autos

> suitable for these conditions were ones which would trundle along easily in top gear at twenty miles an hour with sufficient engine torque to accelerate to forty or fifty miles an hour when the opportunity to pass slow traffic arose.... Thus, British cars tended to emphasize maneuverability, light steering and good engine torque, and to deemphasize high-speed cruising ability.[45]

The British market was also protected by tariff barriers to entry. During the 1950s and most of the 1960s, tariffs were approximately one-third of the price of a car, though Commonwealth countries received preferential treatment.[46] Even after the tariff reductions of the Kennedy Round of the GATT talks, the non-Commonwealth tariff rate was between 11 and 22 percent depending on the class of vehicles.[47] These two factors, high tariff barriers and a unique market demand for low-idling, highly maneuverable cars effectively shielded the British market from much of foreign competition.

The American market was also partly shielded, but not by tariff barriers; American tariff barriers on automobiles have ranged from a high of 10 percent (from the 1930s, 1940s, and early 1950s) to the current 3 percent.[48] Instead, the American auto market was characterized by a consumer demand for large, fuel inefficient cars for which product differentiation was established not through quality improvements but through styling changes. American cars as a whole have much larger engines than do foreign cars. In 1975, the average American domestic car engine displaced 5,400 cubic centimeters (329 cubic inches) and nearly three-fourth had eight cylinders.[49]

In contrast, British auto engines were on average under 2500 cubic centimeters (150 cubic inches) and had only four cylinders. The

American car was also heavy; the 1975 model averaged just under two short tons. Not surprisingly, American autos averaged 14.7 miles per (U.S.) gallon for the 1975 model year. American fuel economy as a whole was much lower than for European cars; some models (e.g., Lincoln Continentals) averaged as little as 7 mpg.

The central reason for these fuel inefficiencies was the extremely low cost of gasoline to the American consumer. In 1971, gas prices were as low as 29 cents per gallon. In Europe, thanks to gasoline taxes, importation costs, and monopolistic pricing by national oil companies, prices were at least three times higher.

A demand for smaller economy cars (10 to 20 percent of the market) did exist in the United States during the 1950s, 1960s, and early 1970s, but the American auto manufacturers did not choose to produce enough economy car lines to meet this demand.[50] Given the production constraints of the time, bypassing the subcompact market appeared to be a rational, profit-maximizing strategy. The American auto industry frequently operated at full capacity, so in order to produce another product line, existing products would need to be discontinued or new investment undertaken. Sales of larger cars are more profitable than those of smaller cars, so a one to one sales swap of small cars for big cars would reduce a company's profit margins.[51] The American auto companies also had an alternative source of smaller cars. Their European subsidiaries produced fuel efficient cars like the Capri and the Opel. American firms imported several hundred thousand cars a year from their European subsidiaries ("captive imports") in the early 1970s, accounting for an eighth of all imported cars. The cars were originally imported from England, then Germany, and in recent years from Japan.[52]

Foreign auto manufacturers did export some European-style autos into the American market, earning over 10 percent of the total auto market in 1958, and from 1968 on. In the 1950s and 1960s, Volkswagen, with its famous Beetle, was the leading importer. VW exported 568,000 autos into the U.S. during its best year (1970), but its market position in the U.S. was already being undermined by the increasing sales of Japanese cars.[53] Nonetheless, sales of economy

cars were a small part of the total market, and no foreign firms produced large volumes of American-style cars. The American market
was therefore partly protected from foreign competition.

In summary, the American and British auto industry structures
were relatively dissimilar. The American industry was characterized
by three dominant firms, which each achieved competitive economies of scale. The British had four firms, three of which were foreign
subsidiaries of multinational firms, in a market 20 percent of the size
of America's. None of the firms achieved competitive scale economies, and only Ford was considered viable in the long term. The
American industry was substantially integrated; the British was not.
The British industry was export dependent; the American was not.
Both industries had a long tradition of tempestuous industrial relations, but Britain's work force was not organized in a single union,
which added to industrial turmoil. The major similarity was in the
relative isolation of each market from foreign competition. But the
barriers to entry were different: Britain—poor highways and high
tariff barriers; American—cheap gas and large cars. Given the differences in industry structure, we should not be surprised to discover
that American and British government policies have also been largely
dissimilar.

Government Industrial Policies—Traditional Differences

Great Britain and the United States were the first industrial nations.
In both countries, private entrepreneurs created factory organizations
based around specialization, labor discipline, and, sometimes, new
technological innovations. Both economies had substantial markets
to sustain the production of the first products, light consumer-goods
like textiles. The second stage of industrialization, in the late nineteenth century, was based on the production of capital goods like
coal, iron, and the railroads; it too was undertaken by private entrepreneurs. By this time both the mechanisms of finance and the man-

agement of these industrial firms had changed, producing the joint stock company with some professional staff or management.[54]

Though private entrepreneurs were the agents of industrialization, government intervention in both economies was substantial, especially in the first half of the nineteenth century. Mercantilist policies and the expansion of the boundaries of political control (e.g. imperialism, "manifest destiny") meant in practice substantial tariff or preference duties on a variety of imports, government expenditures on the economy's infrastructure, and substantial government purchases for military-related goods. Nonetheless, the formal ideology of both political economies by the end of the nineteenth century was economic liberalism, or, according to John Stuart Mill, the belief that

> ... in all the more advanced communities, the great majority of things are worse done by the intervention of government, than the individuals most interested in the matter would do them, or cause them to be done, if left to themselves.... people understand their own business and their own interests better, and care for them more, than the government does or can be expected to do.... Laisser-faire, in short, should be the general practice: every departure from it, unless required by some great good, is a certain evil.[55]

This "myth of the inevitable obtuseness of government officials," as Andrew Shonfield has called it, meant that even though government intervention, especially in the United States, was substantial, it lacked legitimacy in the political metaphors of the period.[56]

The legacy of this ideological hostility to government intervention in the economy is still visible in the political life of modern Britain and America. Both Prime Minister Thatcher and President Reagan are committed to a disengagement of the government from much of economic life, a disengagement based upon the inherent efficiency and fairness of markets. This has drawn much public support, particularly in America. There is some irony in this, as "the conventional view of a[n] [American] business community with a zero margin of tolerance for public intervention is false. Historically, American capitalism in its formative period was much readier to

accept intervention by public authority than British capitalism." [57]
The irony is, of course, that from the 1930s on it was the British who
constructed a substantial state apparatus for both large-scale (macro)
and selective (micro) intervention in their economy, while Americans have generally relied on the regulatory process as the preferred
tool for government policy.[58]

British Policies

In Britain, the substantial break with economic liberalism came,
not with the election of Labour and Clement Atlee in 1945, but with
the Conservatives in the 1930s. For an American audience, this may
be paradoxical, but the British Conservatives were not the traditional
advocates of economic liberalism; the Liberal Party was.

The Conservatives have a tradition of collectivism and hostility to
market forces, just as does the Labor Party (though the policy conclusions each party draws from this differ).[59] The abandonment of
free trade and the gold standard, and the beginnings of government
rationalization of the industrial and agricultural sectors, date from
1931 and the National Government.[59]

The wartime experiences of course deepened British government
involvement in the economy, so that

> By 1948 the basic elements of modern planning were present in Britain
> as in no other major Western country. In addition to the Development
> Councils, which seemed to offer the means for the systematic assertion
> of governmental influence in private industry, there was by then a
> large nationalized sector which was responsible for a substantial part
> of the country's investment. The nation's finances had also apparently
> been brought under tight central control. The Bank of England, now
> nationalized, could no longer claim the formal independence of gov-
> ernment policy it had possessed previously, and much more important,
> the introduction of modern budgeting methods provided the British
> Chancellor of the Exchequer with the means of exercising a sophis-
> ticated form of control over the economy as a whole.[60]

In fact, the French, in searching for a planning model with which
to rebuild their postwar economy, believed that Britain's planning

devices were substantially suited for the French economy, and adopted many. Nonetheless, not until the 1960s did the British Government undertake any attempts at long-term planning.[61]

Government intervention in the economy might not have been planned in the French sense of the word, but British government in the economy was far from minimal. The Labour Government of 1945–51 nationalized "the commanding heights" of the economy (e.g. the steel industry), and created the National Health Service and other agencies of the Welfare State. Even though the Conservative Governments from 1951 on reversed several Labour policies (e.g. steel nationalization), they continued to exhibit many of the same macro-policy concerns. These included concern for the balance of payments, for the value of sterling, and for regional development, all more or less at the same time, and all more or less uncoordinated.

The microeconomic consequences to Britain's industries of these policies, we can now see from a vantage point 20 years later, were "short-term wise, long-term foolish." For instance, industrial investment in both the private and public sectors was cut at various times during the 1950s and 1960s as a way of relieving Britain's chronic balance of payments problems, a solution not in the interests of long-term economic growth. Another policy response to the problems of balance of payments deficits/value of sterling was to reduce domestic demand for goods (especially consumer goods), thereby reducing the demand for imports. This policy tool, when applied frequently and then reversed (the "stop-go" cycles of the 1950s and 1960s) makes domestic corporate planning and investment difficult (though having minimal impact on foreign producers), and handicaps home industries. The sacrifice of the domestic industry in the interests of sterling's value and external commitments has been identified in a number of studies as an important contributor to Britain's industrial decline.[62]

When the British Government did attempt the process of long-term economic planning, the Conservative Party was again in power, and ironically the French model of planning, with important differences, was adopted. The centerpiece was the National Economic Development Council (founded in 1962) to bring together producer groups and the government in order to exchange information in the manner of French indicative planning. This neocorporatist institutional arrangement never achieved the degree of success of its French counterpart, largely because the NEDC was designed as an advisory council, not as a planning agency, and it had no coercive power; Shonfield wrote that "the NEDC system depends ultimately on moral pressure."[63]

The Labour Government of Harold Wilson attempted in 1964 to advance the planning process, first by introducing a National Plan (1965), and then followed by a series of new agencies with economic growth as their foci (e.g. the Industrial Reorganization Corporation—1966–1970; the Ministry of Technology; the Department of Economic Affairs.) The National Plan was unsuccessful for a number of reasons: overambitious growth targets; poorly coordinated industry goals; and, according to Stuart Holland, the active opposition to planning and selective intervention by Britain's capitalist class. After 1966, the Government instead gradually introduced policies usually referred to as those of selective intervention, though the tools upon which the Government relied were still those of macroeconomic (Keynesean) demand management.[64]

Because of the relative openness of the British economy and the weakening of sterling's role as a reserve currency, these tools of demand management were ineffectual in promoting economic growth. As demand increased, so too did imports. But, stagnating demand meant lower British investment and employment. This dilemma effectively blunted the Labour Government's industrial policies, especially as the Wilson Government (and all subsequent British governments, save possibly Labour in 1974–75) sought to preserve the commercial autonomy of Britain's private and public firms.[65]

Following the Conservative Party victory in 1970, something of a shift in policy occurred. Though the Conservative Party has had a "collectivist" or "corporatist" aura for much of the twentieth century, the party has developed an ideological undertone based on economic liberalism (or the "social market" strategy). This "new right" strategy came to dominate Conservative Party circles in the late 1960s, and was linked to populist appeals based upon such themes as "law and order," immigration restrictions, and anti-union sentiment. Though Edward Heath, the Conservative Prime Minister in the early 1970s, can hardly be considered a member of the "new right," his government announced a series of governmental "disengagements" from the economy. Some government grant programs were ended, the Industrial Reorganization Corporation was abolished, and a policy of privatization was undertaken. Following a series of clashes with the trade union movement—and the near bankruptcy of several firms, among them Rolls-Royce—in 1972 the Heath government undertook its famous "U-turn."[66]

The central legislative act of the period was the Industry Act of 1972, which gave substantial authority to the Government in order to provide financial inducements to firms for regional development, technological, or almost any other policy aims of the Government's choice. The relevant sections are 7 (regional assistance) and 8 (general assistance). The key wording of section 7 is:

> [T]he Secretary of State may, with the consent of the Treasury, provide financial assistance where, in his opinion—
> (a) the financial assistance is likely to provide, maintain or safeguard employment in any part of the assisted areas, and
> (b) the undertakings for which the assistance is provided are or will be wholly or mainly in the assisted areas.

That of Section 8 is:

> [T]he Secretary of State may, with the consent of the Treasury, provide financial assistance where, in his opinion—
> (a) the financial assistance is likely to benefit the economy of the United Kingdom, or of any part or area of the United Kingdom, and
> (b) it is in the national interest that the financial assistance should be provided on the scale, and in the form and manner, proposed, and
> (c) the financial assistance cannot, or cannot appropriately, be so provided otherwise by the Secretary of State.[67]

As the reader can see, section 8 is vague enough in its description of national interest so as to provide the Government almost unlimited discretion. One consequence of the Act was the provision to offer selective assistance to firms and sectors threatened with stagnation or failure, though the political rhetoric of the time was that this assistance was meant for the growth sectors of the economy ("picking winners").[68]

The Labour Government of 1974–79 continued these microeconomic policies of selective intervention. The government retained Sections 7 and 8, and it also broadened the state's capacity to intervene with the 1975 Industry Act. On paper, the 1975 Act dramatically increased the government's leverage over firms. Foreign takeovers of British manufacturing firms could be prevented, firms could be forced to disclose to the government (and to the unions) information on the firm's capital and sales structures, and a framework under which planning agreements with firms might be negotiated was established.[69]

In practice, these provisions were hardly ever used (the Chrysler planning agreement being the major exception) as the Wilson-Callaghan Governments continued to rely on the 1972 Act. The only major practical innovations were expansion of the National Economic Development Council (NEDC) and creation of the National Enterprise Board. The Sector Working Parties and Economic Development Councils (47 separate committees) extended the NEDC "tripartism" process into individual sectors (e.g. the pump and valve sector) in the hopes of achieving intra-industry coordination vaguely like the French and Japanese intra-industry committees.[70]

The National Enterprise Board (NEB) was originally intended to be a state holding company, which would gradually increase the public sector by buying into or funding corporations, especially those in need of venture capital and those that would generate new jobs in depressed areas.[71]

The NEB did, in fact, take equity in a number of venture firms, but is largely known for its rescue of such "lame ducks" as British Ley-

land. The NEB was designed to be more than an instrument of selective intervention, but like most of Labour's innovations in
government intervention, the NEB was in practice a further extension
of the spirit of the Industry Act of 1972.

By the mid-1970s, the British Government had a wide range of
general and selective tools with which to influence industrial growth
and development. The traditional policy concerns (balance of payments, value of sterling, regional development) continued to guide
much of British policy, but economic growth, rather more than distributional policies, had become a policy focus by the 1970s. To that
end, microeconomic (or selective) interventions in firms and sectors
had become the order of the day, with the government providing
inducements for firms to behave in ways thought to advance national
growth.[72]

Government industrial policy toward the auto industry generally
paralleled these overall industrial policies. In fact, the auto industry
was frequently used by governments as a vehicle to achieve government aims in regional, sterling, and demand management policies,
tactics which did little for the prosperity of the industry itself. (Many
analysts blame these government policies for the poor financial condition of the industry.)[73]

For instance, as part of a larger regional policy, the Tory government in 1960 denied "industrial development certificates" to auto
firms, which they needed to expand investment. These certificates
were granted only if the investments were to take place in depressed
or underdeveloped regions of the country (e.g., Linwood in Scotland).[74] Even now, the Thatcher government provides subsidies and
grants for development in designated regions, though substantial
doubts remain as to the effectiveness of these policies in promoting
employment.[75] Ford, for instance, received at least £7 million in the
third quarter of 1982 in regional assistance alone, and Nissan is said
to have received more than £100 million in various government
grants for its investment in Northeast England. Ford in particular
has received substantial regional grants. Ford's Bridgend engine

plant in Wales (designed to produce 500,000 engines a year for British and Continental cars) was built with £73 million in regional development grants and £75 million under section 7.[76]

More than any single set of policies, the government's direction of the economy through its macroeconomic policies had a great impact on the structure of the industry. As part of its sterling defense and demand management policies, various governments between 1952 and 1982 altered 24 times the consumer credit arrangement known as "hire-purchase" (see table 3.6) These changes in consumer downpayment requirements translated into an increase or a decrease in aggregate demand. The "stop-go" impact of these policies was especially devastating to the credit-sensitive auto industry since the time frame from planning and development of a car to production is usually three to five years. This instability in demand contributed to the cancellation of £400 million of investment in the British industry.[77] In consequence, imports, especially captive imports of the American MNCs (often manufactured in Germany), filled whatever shortfall in supply the U.K. industry was unable to meet. Further, as a side consequence of the protection of sterling's value, the U.K.'s cost advantage in producing autos evaporated as sterling appreciated.[78]

The increased microeconomic intervention by the government in the economy was also reflected in the auto sector. For instance, as part of its policies of mergers and acquisitions, the now defunct Industrial Reorganization Corporation of the government sponsored (with loans) the merger between BMC and Leyland in 1967. The government also prevented Chrysler's complete takeover of Rootes in 1964, though Chrysler was permitted in 1967 to assume control as the only viable alternative to bankruptcy. When Chrysler, U.K. was in danger of closing in 1975–76, the Labour Government intervened by providing up to £72.5 million in loans and grants to Chrysler in order to induce Chrysler to continue production in Britain. The Government also negotiated a Planning Agreement (one of only two ever) with Chrysler.[79]

The more substantial government intervention was in the rescue

TABLE 3.6
Hire Purchase Restrictions on Motor Vehicles
United Kingdom—1952–1982

Types of Vehicles Affected	Dates and Nature of Changes		Minimum Deposit (percent)	Maximum Repayment period
Cars & CVs	Feb. 1952	Restrictions Added	33.3	18
	Feb. 1954	Restrictions Dropped		
Cars	Feb. 1954	Restrictions Added	15	24
	July 1955	Deposit Increased	33.3	24
Cars & CVs	Feb. 1956	Restrictions Added	50	24
Cars	Dec. 1956	Restrictions Eased	20	24
Cars & CVs	May 1957	Restrictions Increased	33.3	24
Cars	Oct. 1958	Restrictions Removed		
	April 1960	Restrictions Added	20	24
	Jan. 1961	Period Increased	20	36
	June 1965	Deposit Increased	25	36
	July 1965	Period Reduced	25	30
	Feb. 1966	Period Reduced	25	27
	July 1966	Restrictions Added	40	24
	June 1967	Restrictions Eased	30	30
	July 1967	Restrictions Eased	25	36
	Nov. 1967	Restrictions Added	33.3	27
	Nov. 1968	Restrictions Added	40	24
	July 1971	Restrictions Dropped		
	Dec. 1973	Restrictions Added	40	24
	June 1977	Restrictions Dropped for Company Cars, not for private buyers		
	July 1982	Restrictions Dropped		

Source: Society of Motor Manufacturers and Traders.

of British Leyland from 1975 on. The basis for the rescue was a report by a team led by Donald Ryder: hence the Ryder Report.[80]

The NEB was to be the device used to oversee the rescue (and restructuring), and £1.5 billion was to be provided through long-term government loans (mostly changed into equity grants), a new equity issue (with the Government as the purchaser), a buyout of existing shareholders, and new bank loans. Though the institution used to intervene in BL (the NEB) was different from that used in the case of British Steel and British Shipbuilding, the policy content was similar. Weak firms were prevented from going into bankruptcy by selective government intervention.[81]

In general, British Government policies helped to undermine the auto industry's competitive position. The macroeconomic policies employed by the British Government in the 1950s and 1960s used the auto industry to achieve policy goals in regional, sterling, and export areas without much regard for the consequences to the industry. The subsequent microeconomic interventions did have the auto industry as their focus, but these policies (at least in the early to mid-1970s) did little to produce a commercially viable industry. For instance, BL's strategy, both during the late 1960s and during the mid-1970s, did not include plant closings and consolidations despite BL's uncompetitive scale economies.[82] Further, the Chrysler rescue avoided a reduction in industry capacity at a time when a number of reports (e.g. CPRS) were calling for a reduction in U.K. auto capacity. In fact, the Government's rescues of both Chrysler and BL were seen by some as incompatible and weakening more competitive parts of the industry, such as Ford. In general, government policy seemed to be driven more by "social accountancy" than by commercial viability.

American Policies

The American industrial policies during the 1950s and 1960s were different from those of Britain's in both style and substance. In Britain, the idea of state planning was part of the political rhetoric of both parties. The American political tradition, by way of contrast, has been hostile to the idea of state direction of the economy. As Shonfield pointed out, "the principle of anti-planning (has been) deliberately elevated into a way of life."[83] The American state has little institutional capacity for the planned microinterventions common to other industrial nations. When the Federal Government has intervened on behalf of bankrupt institutions, it has had to do so in a public and very contentious way, and then only with ad hoc institutions like the Chrysler Loan Guarantee Board. The American government has no National Enterprise Board.[84]

Part of the American incapacity to plan is institutional. The federal system of shared sovereignty and the shared power among the branches of government (including the bureaucracy) mean in practice two things: interest groups have many points of access into the political process, and policy initiatives need the approval of more and varied political actors than in almost any other Western democracy. Business interests in particular exercise an effective veto power over anything but incremental change.[85]

Shonfield, in contrasting American and British approaches to planning, said that "the basic prerequisites for planning therefore exist in Britain—even though the administrative habits required to make a success of the planner's task have not yet been much cultivated. In America, there is no reason why the competing centers of power concerned with different aspects of economic policy should ever agree."[86]

The general premise in the U.S. concerning government involvement in the economy has been that market competition will best achieve the public good, and that government intervention is justified only in the instances of market failure.[87] American industrial strategy has followed rather directly from that premise. For instance, the United States, unlike most industrial nations (including Britain), has not placed restrictions on the flow of investment capital in and out of the country.[88] The United States has also been (at least in its public pronouncements) an initiator and supporter of the General Agreement on Trade and Tariffs (GATT) process, a process which in theory expands the range of international markets and, ipso facto, the world's welfare.

The most prominent market "failures"—or at least those that have been used to justify public sector intervention—are those relating to income distribution, externalities (such as pollution and safety), and antitrust.

The distribution of personal income in America income becomes an issue for us in the study of the auto industry because the distribution of income will affect the consumer demand for cars. A relatively equitable distribution of income will produce a demand for standardized, price-competitive cars, whereas a less equitable distribution of income will promote the development of the specialist or luxury market.

The distribution of income has been the object of numerous policies and programs. The progressive income tax, in which the marginal tax rate increases with income levels, is the centerpiece of government redistributionary policies, while such income supplement programs as Social Security and Aid to Dependent Children were developed following the "discovery" of poverty and the underprivileged in America. These "welfare" programs have had some impact on distribution of income (but almost none on distribution of wealth.)[89] Nevertheless, income distribution in the United States remains very skewed. In the early 1970s, the top 10% of American income earners received approximately 28 perent of the total revenue; the bottom 10% received 0.8%. By way of comparison, in Brazil, a country with an exceptionally high Gini Index of Inequality, the respective figures were 49% and 0.9%. For East Germany, a country with a low inequality index figure, the 1970 figures were 17% and 4%.[90] Tax rates and income redistribution have been the subject of enormous political debate in the United States, especially that area of public policy referred to as "welfare."[91]

We would then expect that, should the incomes of wealthier households increase, the firms producing a luxury or specialist car will prosper. The marginal income of the consumers will shape the profile of consumer demand.

Two aspects of taxation policy do have a more direct impact on industry. The first is the Corporate Income Tax, the rate at which profits are taxed. In the United States, as in most other industrial countries (including Britain), the corporate tax is progressive; that is, the marginal tax rate increases with the rate of profit. As an incentive to investment, the United States and most OECD countries permit capital (or depreciation) allowances. Some or all of the costs of capital investments may be deducted from a firm's tax liability. The second aspect is the presumed link between the money available to the upper class and the levels of investment in the economy. The upper class has a higher marginal propensity to save; hence, the argument is made that economic growth will follow from inequitable income distributions.

The second area of market failure and government intervention concerns externalities, or when a person or a group's consumption or production has an impact on someone else. The essence of externalities, "whether in production or consumption, is that their costs or benefits are not reflected in market prices, and so the decision of the consumer or firm creating the externalities on the scale of the externality–creating activity generally does not take its effect into account."[92]

Among the major recent concerns have been equal opportunity, pollution, safety, and energy conservation, though each area has become a federal policy area only recently. The primary method that the American government has used to address the problem of externalities has been to establish regulatory agencies or commissions, which enforce Congressional mandates and issue their own administrative rules. Some agencies like the Nuclear Regulatory Commission (1975), have an independent status. Others are subunits within cabinet departments. The Occupational Safety and Health Administration (OSHA—1971) is part of the Labor Department. Still others, like the Environmental Protection Agency (1970), are executive branch agencies. The Congress and these agencies set the conditions under which regulated industries in the United States operate. The theory has been that by changing the terms of market competition, the regulatory process can correct both specific evils (e.g., asbestosis) and general social problems (e.g., child labor).

The regulatory process has provoked strong opposition, largely on the grounds that government regulations impede economic growth.[93] In addition to the numerous horror stories of federal red tape, some commentators seem to also fear that the expanding regulatory process threatens free enterprise. Murray Weidenbaum wrote that,

> If we step back and assess the long-term impacts on the private enterprise system of the rapidly growing host of government inspections, regulations, reviews, and subsidies, we find that the entire business–government relationship is being changed in the process. To be sure, the process is far from complete—and it proceeds unevenly in its various phases—but the results to date are clear enough: The government increasingly is participating in and often controlling the internal decisions of business enterprise, which are at the heart of the capitalist system.[94]

Despite these complaints, the regulatory process, in conjunction with the tax code, is by far the most common form of public sector intervention in the American economy.

Antitrust policy has been an important component of American industrial strategy during the twentieth century. Monopolies have generally been regarded as a form of evil in the United States (and by most economists), a perversion of market competition.[95] This policy marks the U.S. off sharply from the practices of the West Europeans and the Japanese, where intra-industry consultations have frequently been institutionalized, and where governments have encouraged industrial consolidations.[96]

In the United States monopolies were seen not only as a source of economic inefficiency but as a threat to political liberties as well. Richard Hofstader, writing about the Progressive movement at the end of the nineteenth century, said that economic efficiency was not the driving force behind the antitrust movement: "Still more widely felt was a fear founded in political realities—the fear that the great business combinations, being the only centers of wealth and power, would be able to lord it over all other interest and thus to put an end to traditional American democracy."[97]

TABLE 3.7
Summary of Antitrust Laws

1. *Sherman Act, Section 1—1890*
Prohibits all contracts, conspiracies, and combinations, that restrain trade.

2. *Sherman Act, Section 2—1890*
Prohibits monopolizing or attempting to monopolize.

3. *Clayton Act, Section 7–1914*
Prohibits acquisitions or mergers that may lessen competition substantially or tend to create a monopoly.

4. *Federal Trade Commission Act—1914*
Outlaws "unfair methods of competition" and "unfair deceptive acts or practices."

5. *Robinson-Patman Act—1936*
Prohibits price discrimination in the sale of a commodity where the effect may be to lessen competition or tend toward monopoly.

Source: Fox, *Managing Business-Government Relations*, pp. 79–80.

The American legal framework for anti-trust policy is summarized in table 3.7. Several agencies have responsibility for antitrust policy. Both the Justice Department and Federal Trade Commission can bring charges against companies or cartels, as can affected parties. The importance of this field, however, is not measurable by the number of complaints filed by the Justice Department. Because much of the enforcement of the law is left to the courts, and because private parties who feel that their interests have been harmed by anticompetitive behavior have an incentive (i.e., the award by the courts of damages) to sue firms that engage in such behavior, firms are generally self-regulating, and seek to avoid even the appearance of collusion or of price fixing.[98]

Antitrust policy highlights a unique feature of American politics—the role of the judiciary and the adversary nature of American politics. The American courts are politically powerful, perhaps more so now than ever. When President Truman, during the Korean War, seized a portion of the U.S. steel industry to ensure the production of needed war materials, the Supreme Court ruled his actions unconstitutional, and Truman obeyed the court ruling. Thus, even should the Congress and Executive Branch evolve an industrial policy of government intervention along European lines, the Judiciary might not permit the policy to stand.[99]

The courts (and American politics) were designed to operate as an adversarial system. In constructing the American political system, a major grounding assumption seems to have been made; this was of the "ordinary depravity of human nature" (Hamilton, Federalist 79) which required that "Ambition must be made to counteract ambition" (Madison, Federalist 51). Not only were the branches of government provided with shared powers (thus generating institutional conflict of interests), but private interests also (factions) were to be brought into conflict through the device of the national government and through generous public access to the courts. In consequence, the United States is easily the most litigious society in the world. Not only do private parties freely bring suit against each other, but almost every major decision by a government agency concerning a regulated industry is sure to be challenged through the courts either by the industry or by the recently emerged consumer movement.[100]

In summation, American public policy has generally assumed that market operations will advance the public good. In instances of market failure (assumed to be the deviant cases), the government has intervened, usually in the form of public regulation. Sometimes, as in the case of antitrust policy, government intervention is aimed at restoring market competition. In other cases, pollution and other externalities, the government intervention has been to change the cost incentives by taxing or subsidizing firms' activities. In general, American public policy has not sought to replace market operations, or to extend the range of government–business cooperation.

American government policies toward the auto industry have been similar in style and substance to the broader American policies. The government has not directly interfered with operations of firms, preferring instead—through the regulatory process—to impose standards on the industry while leaving to the industry the task of meeting them. The major regulatory concerns have been over such issues as safety, pollution, and fuel economy.[101]

Governmental concern for vehicular safety is usually dated from the publication of Ralph Nader's *Unsafe at Any Speed* and the passage by Congress of the National Traffic and Motor Vehicle Act in 1966. (Congress in fact first asked for regulatory standards on some aspect of motor vehicles—hydraulic brake fluid—in 1962.)[102] The issuing of standards by an executive agency (the National Highway Traffic Safety Administration [NHTSA] since 1970; the Department of Commerce before), was authorized by the 1966 act. Among the standards that have been set by the NHTSA (though not necessarily enforced) have been those for seat belts, air bags, 5 mph impact bumpers, "shatterproof" glass, and other elements of the car, all with the intention of making cars more "crash-resistant." No standards for driver training or operator use have been issued.

The issue of environmental pollution, to which automobile exhausts have been a significant contributor, received much political attention in the United States, especially as a social movement has formed to address the problem. Congress passed a number of acts to set standards for auto emissions, among them the Motor Vehicle Air Pollution Act of 1965 and the Clean Air Act of 1970.[103] The basic principle is that auto manufacturers are to reduce most pollutants from emissions by 95 percent of uncontrolled (i.e., pre-1968) levels or face a $1000 fine per vehicle sold.[104] To meet these standards, a number of changes in the "burn" system and the exhaust system—such as unleaded gas and catalytic converters—have been introduced.

Following the energy crisis of 1973–74, the Federal Government sought to find new sources of energy to reduce U.S. dependence on Persian Gulf oil, and to reduce oil consumption. The auto industry was a natural focus of public energy policy—motor vehicles consume more than a third of the nation's oil—and improvements in the fuel efficiency of autos (measured by miles per gallon) seemed to be achievable, and likely to reduce overall oil consumption by 15 to 20 percent.[105] Congress, after all, was aware that all three major auto manufacturers were producing more fuel efficient cars in Europe. In part to induce the manufacturers to produce and sell more fuel efficient cars in America, Congress passed in 1975 The Energy Policy and Conservation Act, which mandated that the Corporate Average Fuel Economy (CAFE) of each of the corporations selling in the United States be at least 27.5 miles per gallon by 1985. Each company was obliged to meet the following schedule (in mpg): 18, 1978; 19, 1979; 20, 1980; 22, 1981; 24, 1982; 26, 1983; and 27, 1984. A fine of up to $5 per car per 0.1 mpg averaged over the total sales was to be imposed for failure to meet these standards.[106]

The Federal regulations with regard to safety, pollution, and energy did impose costs on the auto manufacturers (and the consumers). Table 3.8 gives some indication of the cost of safety and pollution regulations. The fuel improvements were particularly expensive since, as Ward's said in 1978, "The [Congressional] mandates require revolutionary product downsizing and new materials utilization and technology, all of which do not exist today."[107] Further, these standards were not made in reference to each other; hence, reducing the weight of the car to improve fuel efficiency might make the car less safe.

The standards met much opposition from the industry, an industry whose managers traditionally exercised great autonomy vis-à-vis the external environment. In a typical complaint, Ward's Automotive Yearbook, 1974 said that "the Federal Government had just about taken control of the motor vehicle industry with its endless legislation dictating emissions control hardware, seat belts, warning buzzers, starter-interlock systems, side-door beams, roof-intrusion protection, impact bumpers and wage and price controls, plus antiskid systems and noise levels for trucks."[108] In another such comment, Henry Ford II said that "Our strategy in the U.S. is plain and simple. It's dictated by government regulation.[109]

The resistance by the auto companies varied from court suits to block (so far successfully) airbags, to successfully lobbying Congress for the delay of implementation of standards, to outright re-

Table 3.8
Increase in the Retail Price of Autos Due to Federal Regulations
(in 1978 dollars)

Year	Action	Estimated Regulation Cost
1968	Seat and shoulder belts, standards exhaust emissions	48
1968–9	Windshield defrosting and defogging systems, door latches and hinge systems, lamps, reflective devices, & associated equipment	15
1968–70	Theft protection devices	13
1969	Head restraints	27
1969–73	Improved side door strength	21
1970	Reflective devices and further emissions standards	15
1971	Fuel evaporative systems	28
1972	Improved exhaust emissions; seat belt warning system and locking systems on retractors	
1972–3	Exterior (rust) protection	95
1973	Flame resistant materials; controls improvement	9
1974	Improved exhaust emissions	133
1975	Safety features; catalytic device	147
1976	Hydraulic brakes; improved bumpers	42
1977	Leak resistant fuel system	21
1978	Redesigned emission controls	10

Source: Murray L. Weidenbaum, Business, Government, and the Public, Englewood Cliffs: Prentice-Hall, 1981. p. 34.

fusal by the industry to meet emissions standards and CAFE mandates on time. As Lawrence White has pointed out, the size and importance of the auto industry ensures that the industry will not be shut down if it fails to meet standards. The industry has incentives for collusion in "foot-dragging" and "brinksmanship" with the Federal Government, a strategy that has been at least partially successful.[110]

In fact, despite industry complaints, the American auto makers at the time never faced federal influence on direction of production, employment, and investment (domestic or overseas) planning. Unlike their British counterparts, the managers of U.S. producers had far fewer of their prerogatives restricted by the state.

Conclusion

The aim of this chapter has been to demonstrate that the American and British industries were different in organization and structure, and that the American and British government's policies toward their auto industries were different up to the early 1970s. The British industry is much smaller, export dependent, and more fragmented, with no firm having achieved competitive scale economies. The American industry was the world's largest, with all three firms achieving (in their worldwide operations) competitive scale economies. Both industries had a history of labor troubles, but the British labor force was fragmented and poorly coordinated. British government policies involved extensive government intervention in the industry in order to achieve policy ends in regional, demand management, trade, and sterling policies. The tools employed included both those of macro and selective intervention. The American government's strategy has been to maintain market competition, intervening only in the case of market failures (such as pollution and safety), and then only by the use of regulatory procedures.

4.

POLICY SIMILARITY

B Y THE END OF the 1970s, each country had established a new
agenda for its auto industry. Safety, pollution, and demand management were not the preeminent concerns. Firm survival was. The
once very different policies of the American and British governments
toward their industries had developed a remarkable similarity. Each
nation withdrew from its previous strategies: the U.S. and the "neutral" market; the U.K. and macro- and micro-economic interventions
aimed at achieving high employment, regional growth and a surplus
on visible trade. This similarity of public policies did not end state
involvement in the industries, thereby permitting market forces to
operate. Instead, the free market was supplanted as the similarity
was in the direction of a series of bargains struck among firms, unions
and governments in the U.S., U.K. and Japan over (a) access to markets and (b) the distribution of the costs of restructuring the auto
industry. Though these negotiations preserved the form of market
competition, the agreements altered the terms under which firms
competed by replacing the market in some trade and investment
decision areas. Nonetheless, the aim of the policies was to create a
commercially viable industry capable of withstanding market
competition.

I will argue that important aspects of similarity in industrial policy
were limited neither to the auto industries nor to the United States
and Great Britain. In one crucial area, corporate taxation and investment subsidies, the governments of the Japan, West Germany,

as well as the United States and Great Britain, have exhibited substantial policy similarity, though only during periods of economic downturn.

This chapter begins with an overview of several issues in the study of comparative politics and comparative public policy; I discuss my work in light of these. "Sources of similarity" is followed by "The components of similarity." "Sources" precedes substance because, as I have already argued, industry structures and government policies historically have been different between the countries. Therefore, a change to similar policies requires a search for changing root circumstances. A description of the policies, I believe, will be more meaningful against the backdrop of changing features of the business and political environment in each country. In the second part of the chapter, the components of similarity are explored, and several hypotheses derived from this study are tested in light of new data.

THE SOURCES OF SIMILARITY

A Note on Comparative Public Policy and Business/ Government Studies

Comparative public policy is a subspecies of comparative politics, but the boundaries separating policy studies from other subspecies are porous. Comparative public policy studies the "outputs" of governments, the "inputs" of government, and the institutional and environmental context of policy—in short, comparative politics, but with a more pronounced emphasis on government per se.

As with comparative politics, comparison in public policy implies a methodological approach to politics, as much as it does a subject area.[1] Comparison, the foundation of analysis, allows us to examine the relationships among variables of our choice in different settings so as to give us some foundation for accepting generalizations. Even in those curious cases where comparative politics and comparative public policy is not done comparatively—single-country case studies are still commonly undertaken—comparison is implicit, at least in the minds of readers.[2]

In practice, comparative public policy usually has come to mean a study of government policies in advanced industrial nations.[3] Advanced industrial nations all have industries and bureaucracies, public or private or both, plus other apparatuses of the modern welfare state. Narrowing the range of form and function seems to be a preliminary step in comparative public policy analysis, Przeworski and Teune's injunctions on behalf of the "method of greatest difference" notwithstanding.[4]

Comparative political economy and comparative business and public policy studies are the sub-subfield within the subfield of comparative politics in which my work is situated.[5] With few exceptions, the authors in these subfields are not plagued by the methodological doubts found among the group of comparativists as a whole. Because the state per se is rarely taken as the unit of analysis, the problems of sample size are diminished. Attributes of states and of capitalism (environmental regulation, firm behavior, etc.) are found everywhere among us, in sufficient quantities to allow for statistical reasoning if the analyst is so inclined. And, because many of the analysts in the field are trained as economists, formal modeling or quantitative analysis, which each breeds its own peculiar form of self-confidence, are frequently employed. Methodological doubts are also limited because the concepts used in political economics are well defined (in the sense that we all know (more or less) what, e.g., net income is). The central institution of capitalism, the business firm, operates under much the same profit/loss rules everywhere. Economic activity produces externalities everywhere. Governments intervene to overcome externalities everywhere. In short, the problems of equivalence and of concept definition, though far from solved, are less severe in comparative political economy and in business and public policy than in other fields.

Three problems in the relations between business and government have captured most of the scholarly attention. The consequences of government intervention in the economy and its effects on comparative economic growth rates may well be receiving, as subjects of academic and political controversy, more column space in university publications and in the popular press than any other subject in the social sciences.[6] This is likely to continue. Economists dissent among themselves as to the origins and concomitants of economic growth, and in many ways the debate over the sources of economic growth is less value-laden and and less wide-ranging than are the debates concerning equity, distribution, the role of social values in resource allocation, and the costs and benefits of various forms of regulation.

Business's influence in government or, if the reader prefers, the state's autonomy from capitalism (its associations, its interests) is equally controversial in academic circles.[7] (*Time, Newsweek, Business Week,* et al. have shown less interest in the "state in capitalism" debate.) I find it hard to summarize this literature because the participants do not agree on the definition of the debates (capitalism or business), the units of analysis (class, interest groups, firms), the levels of analysis (institutions of government, political action committees, lobbying, the "structure of power," hegemonic ideology), or of the relevant theoretical perspectives (pluralism, neopluralism, neo-Marxism, public choice economics). Part of the controversy stems from the limited view of the elephant had by each of the observers.[8]

The third topic—the convergence–divergence debate or the development of common trends or patterns among Western industrial nations—is of greatest concern in this book. Do we find a common set of variables present in industrial or market societies—technology, market capitalism, bureaucracies, the welfare state, progressive rationality—such that governments respond in similar ways to these problems?

As with much of the social sciences, the convergence–divergence debate has its roots in Marx and Weber.[9] Convergence was used in the 1960s and 1970s to refer to debate about the perceived growing similarities of market and nonmarket societies.[10] Lindblom's *Politics and Markets* strongly argued that market and nonmarket societies both demonstrate fundamental differences in methods of resource allocation, but Lindblom does envision convergence among market societies, a convergence premised on the "privileged position of business" in capitalist societies.[11] Arguments on behalf of varying degrees of policy convergence among market societies continue to be advanced (Michael Moran, *The Politics of Banking*, Macmillan, 1984) and challenged (David Vogel, *National Styles of Regulation*, Cornell, 1986). A modified form of the convergence among market societies is my thesis here.

I have avoided using the word "convergence" in this book in part because it has meant so many different things to different writers. Convergence, if it has any objective meaning at all, is most often used to describes a situation in which the bureaucratic mechanisms or legal devices used by countries are identical—for instance, the "national champions" found in Western Europe and described by Raymond Vernon in *Big Business and the State*. I am using the word "similarity" to refer to a situation in which Western governments adopt public policies that serve the same goal. When applied to government policies, policy similarity means that the course of action adopted by two or more governments is in correspondence in terms of the goals of the governments, and that broadly congruent methods—that is, functionally equivalent—are employed to reach these goals. The analogy I think appropriate is that of a pair of geometrically similar triangles. These have corresponding angles and, hence, shapes, but they remain separate. I do not mean convergence in the above sense; American and British policies are not moving toward an identity or uniformity. The scale of the problem is different, as are the industries, so policies can only come close, not converge.

The substance of this similarity is that Western governments have adopted policies aimed at promoting competitive firms; policy similarity among governments could have had (and has had) a different content. Divergence means that we see no similar policies.

Sources of Similarity

The American and British auto firms, and ultimately their central governments, were confronted by a number of structural problems common to both countries during the late 1970s and early 1980s. These problems were such that, despite all the differences between the industries enumerated in the previous chapter, the central governments resorted to similar public policies. These structural problems were an end to home market isolation, the emergence of efficient competitor firms, a shortage of investment capital, and the severe financial costs to governments when large firms declared bankruptcy.

End of Market Isolation

Firms will, as a rule, develop products and processes well suited for their home markets; firms and nations have fields of competency and expertise that are grounded in the characteristics of their domestic markets. Not surprisingly, therefore, American firms were well suited to produce and sell American-style cars, and British firms were well suited to produce and sell British-style cars. Within national markets, firms will choose market "niches" and develop productive and sales competency in this niche. For instance, BMC, one of the firms merged to form British Leyland, manufactured the Mini, a tiny car with a one liter engine that pioneered front wheel drive.

The American and British auto industry each evolved in markets with consumer preferences different from those in the rest of the world's market. As we saw in the third chapter, a variety of government policies in each country contributed to these differences in the demand profiles of the market, though these differences were not always directly the result of state policies. For instance, the American consumers preferred the large, fuel-inefficient, relatively low performance autos produced by Detroit. As a rough proxy for measuring national differences, we might say that the domestic British motor industry specialized in cars with engines between 800cc and 1300cc (50 cubic inches to 85 cubic inches), whereas the American industry

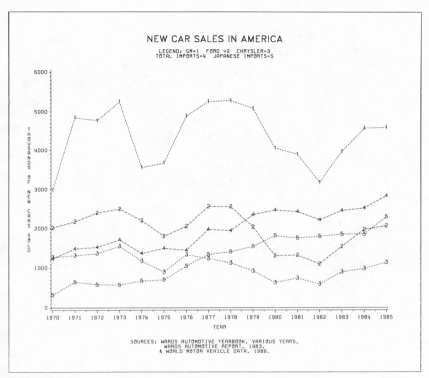

NEW CAR SALES IN AMERICA

LEGEND: GM=1 FORD =2 CHRYSLER=3
TOTAL IMPORTS=4 JAPANESE IMPORTS=5

SOURCES: WARDS AUTOMOTIVE YEARBOOK, VARIOUS YEARS.
WARDS AUTOMOTIVE REPORT, 1983.
& WORLD MOTOR VEHICLE DATA, 1986.

FIGURE 4.1

specialized in cars with engines of six or eight cylinders and engine
capacities of from 170 cubic inches (roughly 3 liters) to 305 cubic
inches or larger (roughly 5 liters).[12]

As a result of these national differences in consumer preferences,
American and British firms were sheltered from international competition in their home markets until the mid-1970s (see figs. 4.1 and
4.2). This sheltering produced the benefits of high profits and high
wages, at least in the short run, for those in the industry. But, these
national differences, and the resulting (limitations on) firm competencies, did have disadvantages. For one, the American and British
industries were "pinned" in their home markets; exporting "do-

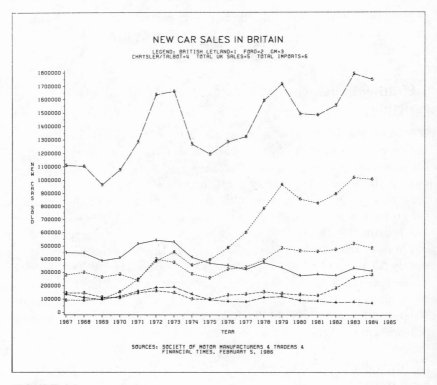

FIGURE 4.2

mestic" American and British products to foreign countries was difficult.[13] Not too many Italians needed a 2-ton Mercury Montego with
a 356" V-8 Windsor engine that got 11 miles to the gallon. When
consumer preferences changed in Britain and the United States to
more nearly resemble those in the rest of the world, American and
British firms discovered a second disadvantage of sheltered markets.
Foreign firms, German and Japanese firms in particular, had already
developed competencies in producing and selling cars with the features now demanded by American and British consumers.

Whatever the origins of these barriers to entry, as they diminished,
the American and British industries were forced into a radical re-

organization of their products and processes. The reorganization proved to be impossible without state aid for Chrysler and British Leyland.

Shifting Preferences and the End of American Market Isolation

1973 was the biggest boom year for Detroit: Nearly 10 million vehicles were produced, and 57 percent of them were large or intermediate cars (as opposed to over 36 percent in early 1980).[14] Almost half of the small cars sold in America were foreign imports; these took 15.1 percent of the total U.S. market.[15] Imports of these small cars were not a major concern for the American industry as the auto makers operated at full capacity that year, producing the more profitable large cars. In fact, Detroit was one of the largest car importers; nearly 13 percent of all imports were "captive-imports" of the Big Three (see fig. 4.3). Despite several predictions about the possibility of an energy crisis, the industry had no plans for major revisions of its products, even though, to take the prototypical case, General Motors' cars for the 1974 model year averaged only 12.0 miles per gallon.[16]

The Arab oil embargo in 1973, and the Iranian Revolution in 1979, were watershed events in twentieth-century economic history. They created shortages of petroleum supplies, which allowed oil producers both within and without the Organization of Petroleum Exporting Countries (OPEC) to raise prices on crude oil. American consumers suffered a quadrupling of prices, long waiting lines and occasional shortages, despite being partly sheltered from the full financial impact (owing to price controls on American-produced oil). With the increase in oil prices came a shift in consumer demand away from large cars (see table 4.1).

This shift, however, came in two waves, producing a strategic problem for Detroit. In 1974 and 1975, smaller fuel efficient cars were much in demand, and Detroit developed new products on the premise that consumer demand had permanently shifted. Chrysler

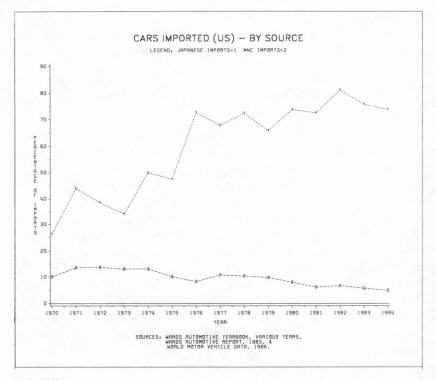

CARS IMPORTED (US) — BY SOURCE
LEGEND: JAPANESE IMPORTS=1   MNC IMPORTS=2

SOURCES: WARDS AUTOMOTIVE YEARBOOK, VARIOUS YEARS,
WARDS AUTOMOTIVE REPORT, 1983, &
WORLD MOTOR VEHICLE DATA, 1986.

FIGURE 4.3

began what was to be a virtual withdrawal from the large car market. From 1976 to mid-1979, demand for the larger cars increased, largely in response to the decrease in the price of oil (in real terms). This reversed the trend toward smaller cars, and raised the question in senior management's minds that perhaps the 1973–75 period was only a short-term disruption in the American preference for larger cars. This delayed Detroit's downsizing so that in 1979 and 1980, the auto makers had relatively few products available in the compact and, especially, subcompact ranges. As a result, imports of fuel efficient Japanese and European cars grew, especially in important markets like California where 52 percent of new car sales in 1980

TABLE 4.1
Size of New Cars Sold
U.S., 1967–1985
(in percent)

Year	Compacts	Mid-Size	Full-Size/Luxury
1967	25	23	51
1968	25	26	49
1969	27	25	48
1970	38	22	40
1971	39	20	41
1972	39	22	39
1973	43	22	35
1974	48	25	27
1975	54	24	23
1976	48	27	25
1977	47	28	25
1978	48	28	24
1979	56	32	21
1980	62	21	17
1981	64	20	16
1982	62	19	19
1983	54	27	19
1984	54	26	20
1985	55	27	18

Sources: CBO, p. 11; Hunker, p. 18; Ward's Automotive Yearbook.

were imports (see fig. 4.4).[17] American auto production declined by nearly 3 million units from 1973 to 1975, returned to 9 million units in 1977 and 8 million in 1978, then bottomed out to 5.5 million in 1982.

Fuel economy was not the only rationale for the growth in imports. Some foreign imports were cheaper than were comparable American cars, often by $1000 to $1500. Further, many consumers believed them to be of higher quality.[18]

In a sense, the Federal Government's regulatory policies, much maligned by the auto industry, helped prevent a deeper erosion in the domestic industry's market share. The American industry was pushed into reorganization as much by government policies as by consumer demand for fuel efficient cars. Following the first oil crisis,

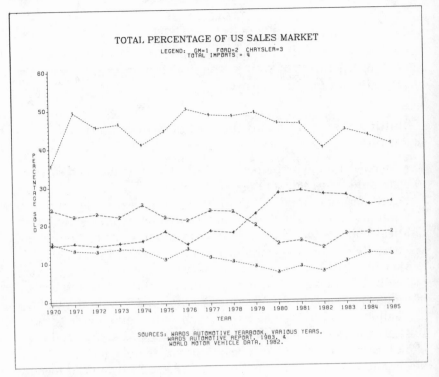

FIGURE 4.4

Congress mandated that the cars produced in the United States average 27.5 miles per gallon by 1985.[19] This compelled the industry to begin downsizing the cars even though consumer demand for compact cars decreased in 1976 and 1977. In consequence, when the second oil crisis happened in 1979, the industry had a four-year start on retooling.

Despite this governmentally enforced head start in retooling, foreign imports increased their market share until 1981. A particularly ominous sign for the auto industry was the extent of import penetrations in selected growth markets. In 1981, more than 30 percent of all cars on the road in California and Oregon were imports.[20] This implied that importers were capable of achieving high sales in other markets, perhaps including those of Michigan and Ohio, where imports account currently for under 10 percent of the vehicles on the road. A restructuring of both products and production process was clearly in order for the industry.

Shifting Preferences and the End of British Market Isolation

The increased foreign competition in Britain was more closely tied to state policies—trade and taxation policies.

Regarding trade policies, the British entrance into the European Community and the end of the Commonwealth Preference Area were political choices that were intended to produce a prosperous and industrially competitive Britain. The idea was that by enlarging the market for British products, British industry would become more specialized, achieve scale economies in more industries, and become more prosperous. The elimination of duties on E.C. products, however, allowed multinational corporations in the automotive sector to shift production out of Britain into countries with more productive work forces, and to produce cheaper products in factories that were newer and more modern than those in Britain. Ford and GM together imported 21 percent of the new car market in Britain in 1985; 36 percent of all imports were the captive imports of these two firms.[21]

This feature of the British auto market has been largely superseded by the hoopla concerning Japanese imports. Before the 1980s, few had noted that Ford, G.M. and Talbot (Chrysler/Peugeot) have imported more cars from their Continental factories than all the Japanese companies put together have exported to the U.K. (see Fig 4.5). (Japanese firms accounted for 11 percent of the 1985 new car market.) This development is directly tied to the end of duties in 1975 on cars from Germany and Belgium, and represents the single largest factor in the decline of Britain as a producer (see fig. 4.6). This has enabled Ford and GM to expand market shares (see fig. 4.7) even as they reduced production in Britain (see fig. 3.3).

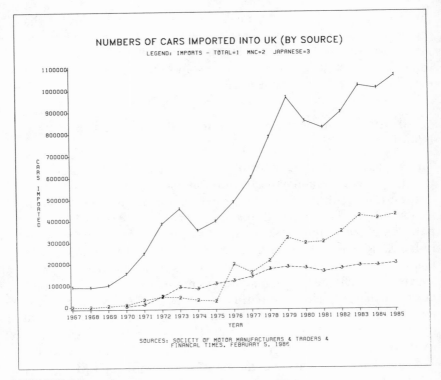

FIGURE 4.5

Some idea as to why the multinationals should have shifted production from Britain to the Continent can be gained from comparing
Britain's industrial and economic performance with those of its European competitors. I have already discussed Britain's labor difficulties in some detail, and made specific reference to Ford's
experiences at Halewood and Saarlouis. Of perhaps more significance has been the greater general price and wage increases in Britain
in contrast to its main competitors. See tables 4.2 and 4.3.

The implication of these figures is that Britain has suffered a substantial loss in general price competitiveness with its major trading
partners. Britain's market was fully opened to EC members just as

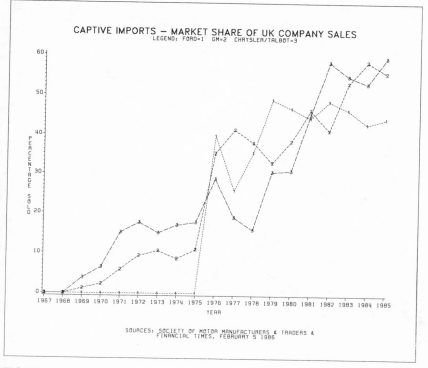

FIGURE 4.6

it was going through one of its worst ever bouts of inflation (1974–1977). The normal mechanism for adjusting national deviations from world norms in inflation and trade matters—a change in the nation's exchange rates—was made less effective in Britain's case, first by exchange controls, and then by the "petro" pound following the discovery of North Sea Oil.[22]

In the auto sector and most other oligopolistic sectors in Britain, both real prices and real costs (per unit) relative to Germany and France did not fall, but rose. Firms then had an incentive—substantial short-term profits—to produce cars in Germany or Belgium at lower real costs, and then import and sell them at British prices,

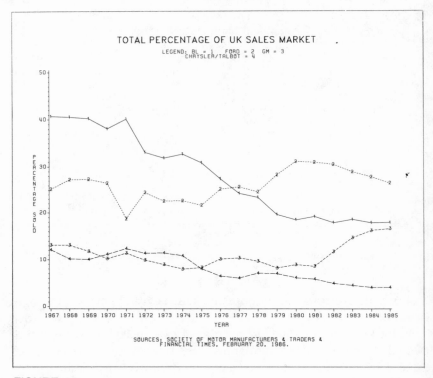

FIGURE 4.7

thereby gaining £1000 to £2000 (on average) per car. This they have done. They have also greatly diminished their exports from Britain (see fig. 4.8). In fact, as the costs of production in Britain have risen, long-term investment has fallen as industrialists have engaged in something of an investment strike against Britain.[23] The paradox of Britain's entry into the Common Market is that, at least in the short run, the Government has hastened Britain's manufacturing decline.[24]

Nonetheless, the multinationals will limit the transfer of production from Britain; apart from a sizable investment in Britain, Britain is among the most profitable new-car sales markets in the world. Nevertheless, unless the British government restricts access, the

TABLE 4.2
Earnings/Wages per capita in Manufacturing Indices—1970 = 100

	Britain	France	Germany	U.S.	Japan
1970	100	100	100	100	100
1971	111	110	113	106	114
1972	126	121	123	113	132
1973	142	136	135	121	163
1974	166	159	151	131	205
1975	209	184	165	143	229
1976	244	211	174	154	258
1977	269	236	187	168	282
1978[a]	308	267	199	183	295
1979[a]	356	302	206	199	316
1980[a]	419	347	218	216	339
1981[a]	477	393	231	235	360

Sources: Trade and Industry, September 8, 1978, p. 555; British Business (April 1983) 3: 411–12.
[a]data from 1978 on recalculated from data which took 1975 as the base year. The formula used was x/y*z where x = 1975 data in 1970 terms, y = 100, and z = discrete data from each year of the 1975 series from 1978 on.

MNCs will continue to import substantial numbers of cars into Britain.

As for taxation, in 1964, 17 percent of cars in Britain were either owned or subsidized by companies.[25] By 1985, somewhere between 40 and 60 percent of new car sales in Britain were purchased by businesses.[26] High marginal tax rates on income gave an incentive to companies for providing cars to employees in lieu of salary, a practice that continues despite lower marginal tax rates on income under the Conservatives.[27] The shift from a market in which more than 80 percent of the consumers were unsubsidized individuals to a company car market clearly benefited Ford and, to a lesser extent, General Motors—companies that focused on sales to business customers. British Leyland (and its ancestors) and Chrysler/Peugeot/Citroen (and its ancestors, most notably, Rootes) relied on sales to individual customers to a greater extent, and these firms lost much of their market.

Williams, in his study of the decline of British Leyland, argues that the shift from individual consumers to fleets had the effect of

TABLE 4.3
Consumer Price Index—5 Countries
Indices—1970 = 100

	Britain	France	Germany	U.S.	Japan
1970	100	100	100	100	100
1971	109	105	105	104	106
1972	117	112	111	108	111
1973	128	120	119	114	124
1974	148	136	127	127	154
1975	184	152	135	139	172
1976	215	169	141	147	188
1977	249	183	146	156	204
1978[a]	269	199	150	168	211
1979[a]	305	220	157	188	218
1980[a]	361	251	165	213	236
1981[a]	403	284	176	235	248
1982[a]	438	316	184	249	256

Sources: Trade and Industry, September 8, 1978, p. 555; British Business (April 1983,) 3: 411–12.
[a]data from 1978 on recalculated from data which took 1975 as the base year. The formula used was x/y*z where x = 1975 data in 1970 terms, y = 100, and z = discrete data from each year of the 1975 series from 1978 on.

undermining the traditional market of British Leyland in two ways. First, Ford had established a dealer and service network geared specifically to business markets even before the increase in fleet demand. British Leyland (and its ancestors) serviced the individual consumer market, and did not have the dealer network to compete with Ford. Secondly, the producers that became British Leyland (and Chrysler) specialized in small cars (with thin profit margins) like the Mini (and the Hillman/Chrysler Imp). The purchasers of company cars prefer medium or large cars: 1400–2000cc. In 1964, cars with engines under 1100cc accounted for 45 percent of total British car sales, and these sales were overwhelmingly to individual consumers. By 1979, 1100cc cars captured only 14 percent of the new car market. Market shares of cars in the 1600–2000cc category and in the 1100–1300 category roughly doubled between 1964 and 1979—from 10 percent to 20 percent and from 14 percent to 29 percent respectively.[28]

The domestic British producer, British Leyland, saw the market in

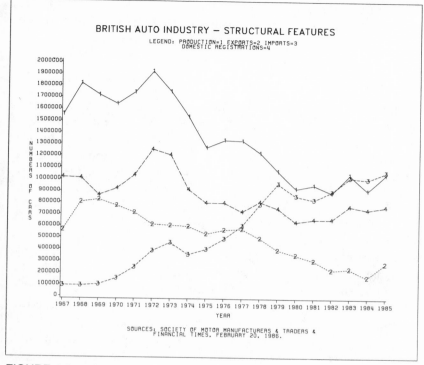

FIGURE 4.8

which it had established its traditional competency erode. BL was forced to begin to compete in markets in which other firms had established competencies. The fleet market was and is dominated by Ford, with General Motors (Vauxhall) attempting to gain market share in this sector. Both companies chose to manufacture elsewhere 40 to 60 percent of their cars sold in Britain. The consumer market meanwhile developed a preference for cars in the 1100–1600cc range, the range at which Japanese producers had developed an extraordinary comparative advantage in terms of price and quality. Nissan, for example, took 6 percent of the total British car market in 1978— eight years before it had almost none—and almost all of the increase came in the shrinking individual consumers market. The preferences of Britain's consumers changed just as trade barriers with the European community ended.

Efficient Competition

Efficiency is not a thing in and of itself; "efficient in terms of what" is always a necessary question. American and British auto manufacturers did, after all, have product sectors in which they were relatively efficient (i.e. profitable) in producing a certain type of car. If the world demanded Lincoln Continentals, Chrysler New Yorkers and Olds 88s circa 1973, Ford, General Motors, and Chrysler would possibly dominate world markets. But, markets—or more correctly the consumers within these markets—changed preferences. Hence, American and British producers were inefficient relative to foreign firms given these new consumer preferences and given the prevailing exchange rates and other macroeconomic factors. Efficiency in production is therefore a contingent measurement.[29]

The adoption and application of technological innovation to production processes and products is also contingent in its effects on efficiency and competition. In markets with relatively stable consumer preferences ("mature markets" as Abernathy would say), technological innovation tends to have a "conservative effect" that "allows a company to do better what it currently does, not to do something entirely different."[30] In the context of changing consumer demand ("de-maturity" in Abernathy's words), relatively minor innovations in production process and work organization can change the basis of firm competition. It is not technology, and the social organization of work built around it, that determines per se what is and what is not "efficient." Rather, innovation's effect on efficiency and competition is also meaningful only in light of changing consumer preferences and macroeconomic conditions.[31]

If consumer preferences matter in understanding relative firm efficiencies, we then should analyze firm efficiency in light of the two major types of automotive markets—the mass market and the specialist market. I will conclude the discussion of "efficient competition" with a discussion of the organization of work.

The Mass Market

The end of the auto market isolation in America and Great Britain confronted government, labor, and industry with the fact of a huge Japanese competitive advantage in the mass market for automobiles. Even Volkswagen—a firm widely praised for innovative engineering leading to a good-quality, reasonably cheap automobile—lost much of its market in the United States to Japanese imports: from 6 percent of the car market in 1970 to 3 percent in 1975. Estimates vary, but many observers believed that, for 1982, production costs (including shipping) were between $1000 and $1500 cheaper in Japan than in America (assuming ¥/$ = 249/1), and as much as £1500 cheaper than in Britain (assuming ¥/£ = 435/1). Since Japanese companies have installed the capacity to produce nearly 3 million more vehicles than they do now, unrestricted competition would bankrupt many existing producers given those exchange rates.[32]

In countries that permit a more or less free market in cars (Belgium and Denmark for instance) Japanese competition drove prices on cars (in 1983) from £1000 to £3000 lower than those of identical cars sold in Britain. In Belgium and Denmark, Japanese companies have captured much larger market shares than in the protected markets of France, Italy, Germany, and Britain. If Japanese imports were permitted to rise to their "natural" levels, the auto industries of the large EC nations would be much more pressed than they are now.

The origin of this competitive advantage in autos (and in other industries) has been the subject of much media and academic attention; proposals abound for an industrial policy (based on government, labor, and management cooperation) to match Japan's.[33] Probably the most complete estimate of the sources of Japanese advantage was printed by the DOT, here reprinted in table 4.4.[34] In accounting for the price disparity, most attention is usually focused first on the scale economies possible in integrated complexes like

TABLE 4.4
Summary of Japanese Production Cost Advantages
Over American Producers
(for a sub-compact car)

Technology	$ 73
Management Systems & Techniques	
Quality Control Systems	$ 329
Just-in-Time Production	$ 550
Material Handling & Engineering	$ 41
Productivity Improvements (Quality circles, etc.)	$ 478
Union-Management Relations	
Unscheduled Absenteeism	$ 81
Relief Systems	$ 89
Union Representatives	$ 12
Wage Costs and Fringe Benefits	$ 550
Manufacturing Cost Advantage	$2,203
Minus Shipping Costs	−485
Net Japanese Cost Advantage	$1,718

Source: Department of Transportation, *The U.S. Automobile Industry 1981*, p. 15. Originally printed in *Analysis of Japanese Landed Cost Advantage for the Manufacture of Sub-Compact Cars*. Berkley, Michigan: Harbour and Associates.

Toyota City, and second on the cooperative relations between industry, government, and labor. Very little evidence is available to support the claim that the advantages in production enjoyed by the Japanese are the consequence either of newer technology or of greater "capital intensity" in production.[35]

Japanese automotive companies have attempted to concentrate production in complexes not unlike those established by Henry Ford in the United States. But Japanese manufacturing is not a carbon copy of Fordism—with its vertical integration and tight control of the division of labor. The Japanese firms developed a concern for quality control that was more broadly defined than the American approach of product inspection.[36] The Japanese automotive industry also developed unique institutional arrangements. For instance, the "Kanban" ("just in time") system of production requires close collaboration between the producer of a car component (be it a separate company or a division of the auto company) and the production line. As only small stocks of supplies are kept (reducing storage and maintenance costs), any interruption of supplies quickly halts the production process. This interruption is apparently rare in integrated Japanese production centers like Toyota City. As Cusumano and others have noted, underlying the kanban system is a dependent-affiliation relationship between the suppliers of parts and the automotive manufacturer. (The features of this relationship were discussed in chapter 2, in the section entitled "achieving scale economies.") Concentrating all the factors of production in one complex has long been regarded being as more cost effective than the recent American approach of plant dispersion. The emphasis on quality and the just-in-time system of supply by Japanese companies have added to this advantage.

The cooperative labor–management relations said to characterize Japanese industry, and the resulting productivity, is often credited with Japan's economic success. At least in the automobile industry, this claim seems to be borne out by productivity figures. Japan's 665,000 auto workers produced more than 9 million cars in 1978. In 1979, the U.S. produced 11.5 million cars with 2.2 million workers, and the European Community 11.5 million cars with 2 million workers.[37]

Japanese government policies of selective intervention, which protected and then rationalized the industry after it emerged from World War II, is also sometimes cited as an explanation for Japan's current development.[38] Loans at low rates and high tariff barriers were among the policy tools used. As a result, Japan's growing auto market was used by the state to establish efficient domestic producers. The American multinationals were prevented from establishing production facilities, even though they had been dominant in Japan before the war. These policies toward the automotive industry reflected the approach of the Japanese state to industrialization. Selective intervention by the Japanese state in the area of firm finance was widespread, particularly during the early stages of import substitution industrialization. In recent years, however, the Japanese auto companies have become largely self-financing.

Direct Japanese government rationalization of the industry ended in the early 1970s. First Mitsubishi, then Honda, broke with the Ministry of International Trade and Industry over its attempt to build the industry into two producer groups (based on Toyota and Nissan); Honda and Mitsubishi became major producers themselves.[39] The ability of the Japanese Government to restrict foreign investment in the auto sector had been weakened before Mitsubishi announced its ties with Chrysler. Japan's entry into both GATT (1963) and the OECD (1964) precluded formal investment barriers.[40] Further, an easing of those barriers was one of the major demands of the American government in trade negotiations with Japan.[41] The U.S. industry now owns equity in Japanese companies; GM owns 34.2 percent of Isuzu, Ford 25 percent of Toyo Kogyo, and Chrysler 15 percent of Mitsubishi. The government still has influence in the industry; it was MITI that organized the Japanese auto producers' export quotas to the U.S. But government influence is relatively limited in the automotive sector.

Though the development of Japanese industry in general was undoubtedly fostered by Japanese industrial policies, the current success of the Japanese automotive industry cannot be directly attributed to Japanese industrial policy.

In accounting for Japan's price advantage in autos, more attention should be paid to Japan's yen policy, since a 20 percent rise in the yen's 1981 value had, by 1986, eliminated their price advantage in the production of automobiles.[42] For example, Abernathy et al. list the final delivered cost of a small 1981 Mazda (Toyo Kogyo) car at $4928; a comparable 1981 Ford cost $6498. In 1981, the average ¥/ $ exchange rate was 220.5.[43] During the fourth week of September 1986, the average ¥/$ exchange rate was 155.[44] All other things being equal, the Mazda would, with the 1986 exchange rate, cost roughly $7000.

Japan maintained a current account surplus of approximately $22 billion with the world from 1967 to 1980, the only industrial country (excepting Germany) to do so. Yet, the Japanese currency appreciated only 27.3% against the U.S. dollar in the 12-year period beginning in 1970.[45] Many observers believe that the Japanese currency was substantially undervalued (until 1985) as a result of the policies of the Japanese government. At least part of the explanation for this situation is to be found in Japan's Direct Investment Capital Flows. Between 1977 and the third quarter of 1982, direct investment outflows from Japan totaled nearly $19 billion, a figure slightly larger than France's and smaller than Germany's. In the same period, direct investment inflows totaled only $1.2 billion, by far the smallest total for any major industrial country. By comparison, capital inflows in the U.S. were more than $70 billion during the same period. Because direct investment in Japan has been discouraged, the demand for yen (and foreign control over the Japanese economy) was lessened. Japan's policies were aimed at preventing the yen from becoming a world reserve currency.[46]

The Japanese "liberalized" their financial dealings with the other Western nations in 1983 and 1984, events greeted with much enthusiasm in the United States. In one major reform, the 20 percent withholding tax imposed on Japanese citizens who raised yen on the Euroyen market was repealed. To date, however, these liberalizations seem to have had effects comparable to those of previous Japanese liberalizations in other markets. In 1984, less than 2 percent of the value of the $1.02 billion Eurocurrency market was denominated in yen; nearly 75 percent of the total value of transactions was in dollars.[47]

In summary, the ability of the Japanese producers to provide a cheaper, more fuel efficient, better quality car into the American and British markets was a function of production arrangements—concentrated plants, well coordinated work systems, cooperative labor arrangements—and a relatively "cheap" yen from 1970 to 1986.

The "Luxury" or Specialist Market

As I noted in chapter 2, the specialist or luxury market accounts for approximately 10 percent of new car sales in Western countries, but the "profits per car sold" are much higher in this sector of the market. Engineering, quality, and prestige factors are thought to be of greater influence on buyers in this market than is price. As of yet, the Japanese auto-manufactures sell relatively few luxury cars.[48] European firms, especially those of Germany and Sweden, dominate this market.

The comparative advantage of the European specialist firms rests neither in greater efficiency of productive technology per se nor in a more capital intensive production.[49] Rather, the products themselves are endowed with safety and performance features that embody such new technological developments as anti-skid braking systems and fuel injection. Product technology is perhaps the decisive factor in competition among European specialist firms, and this vesting of the product itself with distinguishing attributes makes these firms relatively invulnerable to price competition from Japanese firms.[50] Product quality and brand loyalty, not necessarily economies of scale or other measures of efficiency in production, matter in this luxury market.

The West German auto industry is the world's third largest, with 1985's production volume of 4.17 million cars exceeded only by that of the United States and Japan.[51] (German mass producers—VW, Fordwerke, Opel [GM]—are among the few profitable firms in the intensely competitive European car market.) Germany's specialist or luxury market approaches one quarter of total German car sales. Between 1970 and 1985, production for all four specialist firms steadily increased: Porsche, a 294 percent increase (1985 production, 49,400); BMW, 277 percent (439,500); Daimler-Benz, 190 percent (533,500); and Audi, 125 percent (395,700)[52] These firms are the major competitors for the specialist "branches" of the American and British industries—mainly Cadillac, Lincoln, and Jaguar.

The luxury market has expanded substantially in both Britain and the United States, (though the definitions of the comprising features of luxury vary somewhat between the markets). In the British market of 1964, the year I used above as a point of reference, the sales of cars with engines 2 liters or larger (a very rough proxy for luxury sales) was 7 percent of the total market; in 1979, the percentage was 11.5.[53] In the United States, 3.7 percent of the car sold (375,000) were described by *Automotive News*, as "luxury;" in 1985, 9 percent (or 1 million cars) of cars sold were such luxury cars.[54] In both markets, much of the growth in sales has gone to German and Swedish firms.

The growth in the luxury market is influenced by government policies and by changing demographics and income distribution. In the case of Great Britain, the subsidizing of "business" cars has encouraged the purchases of luxury cars: BMW estimates that two-thirds of its sales in Britain are to businesses. In the case of the United States, changing patterns of income distribution away from the middle class and toward the upper class are credited with increasing the demand for luxury cars.[55] The *New York Times*, citing J. D. Power & Associates, a well known marketing research firm that specializes in the auto industry, reported on March 3, 1986 that "the number of households with incomes of $50,000 or more is expected to double over the next 10 years, from 9.5 million this year [1986], to 18.8 million in 1995." With the doubling of wealthy households, the American luxury market in cars is estimated to grow to 1.8 million cars by 1990.

In the American market, the imports of European luxury cars expanded rapidly after 1977. At that time, the major European specialist producers exported 83,000 cars—0.7 percent of the total American market for new cars. In 1980, the Europeans captured 2 percent of the market with sales of 175,000. In 1985, European sales reached 450,000, for 4 percent of the total U.S. market. The four largest German specialist firms (Daimer-Benz, BMW, Audi, Porsche) accounted for one-third of U.S. luxury sales in 1985, and were expected to capture one half of the market by 1990.[56]

In Britain, the success of European specialist firms is mirrored by the dramatic decline of British Leyland's specialist branches—Jaguar/

Rover/Triumph—in the decade of the 1970s. In 1970, BL's specialist firms produced 200,771 cars; in 1980, they produced 80,779—a 60 percent decrease in production at a time when the specialist producers of other nations generally doubled production. The remaining two British producers of luxury cars are Jaguar (privatized during 1984–85) and Rolls-Royce, but both companies export most of their products, and have relatively small market shares of the British market—0.4% and 0.04% respectively. Volvo (3.3% of the U.K. market), BMW (1.8%), Daimler/Mercedes (1%), and Saab (0.5%) each have larger shares of the British market than do Jaguar or Rolls-Royce. The rates of growth of the sales of the German specialist producers in the British market has been substantial—30% from 1984 to 1985 for BMW, and 25% in the same period for Daimler/Mercedes.[57]

Given that product differentiation is important to sales in the luxury market, the 1973–1982 strategies of Ford, General Motors, and BL in producing a full range of cars with many common components while seeking to expand luxury sales were contradictory. Many consumers were for example reluctant to pay a premium price for a Cadillac Cimarron, which is only a fancy Chevy Cavalier with power "everything." Jaguar did not share components with the Mini, but nonetheless suffered from its association with British Leyland, though its privatization should help its product differentiation and, hence, its sales.

In neither the United States nor Great Britain did the penetration of the luxury market by overseas competitors have any simple solution for domestic firms. Unlike the mass market, where more productive process technology offers the hope of a more price-competitive product, the currency of the specialist market was and is product differentiation, quality, and customer loyalty. Competency in these areas is not quickly developed.

The Organization of Work

In chapter 2 I argued that the hourly wage paid to auto workers was not per se a crucial consideration for a firm's profitability. Far more important is the per unit labor cost, which is determined by the general tenor of labor relations, by the history of authority relations, by work organization, and by worker commitment. Product quality and productive efficiency are strongly influenced by the relations between management and the labor force.

Why do German and Japanese workers exhibit greater productivity and work commitment than do their American and British counterparts? Cultural explanations of the Protestant ethic–Tokugawa ethic sort are by themselves inadequate; in previous decades, the Japanese and German working classes were far from acquiescent.[58] Both the German Social Democratic Party and the Japanese Socialist Party (and the unions associated with them) periodically have been models of socialist militancy. Furthermore, in Germany at least, the "guest workers" labor alongside their German counterparts without their "Turkishness" or "Portugueseness" or "Italianness" impeding "German" efficiency. Another explanation, "peasants to workers" "poverty to comparative wealth," suggests that late-developing countries, or nations with workforces that have recently migrated from poor areas, might enjoy a cooperative workforce, at least for a period of time.[59] Hence, the Turks in Germany might even be more cooperative than their German comrades. The movement in the United States of assembly plants to Appalachia and the mid-South, beginning with VW (New Stanton, Pa.) and continuing with Nissan, GM, and Toyota, gives evidence that firm managers put some credence in this theory. But, the German and Japanese work forces have also become less strike-prone than they once were, and American and British factories organized in "corporatist" forms have been productive by Japanese standards, even when using workers socialized under a "Taylorist" regime (e.g. GM–Toyota's Freemont, California plant).

In their organization of work, firms in both Germany and Japan demonstrate a form of "welfare corporatism" in which the workers and their unions are drawn into the organizational life of the firm to a much greater degree than in the "market individualist" organizations of American and British firms.[60] The differences between the German and Japanese forms of corporatism are substantial: German corporatism is imposed through the State as part of the postwar social contract; Japanese corporatism is firm based—"enterprise welfare," to use Dore's phrase. But the common element in these organizational forms is that they act as nonmaterial incentives to supplement material incentives as a method for motivating employees. The effects of corporatist organization of work are not universally applauded, but higher rates of productivity and commitment are thought to follow from adoption of these methods.[61]

German corporatism in the workplace results from the imposition by the federal Government of worker rights legislation in the period between 1949 and 1976. Betriebsrats (workers' councils) were authorized throughout German industry to govern the conditions of work and employment. Mitbestimmung (codetermination) granted German unions a supervisory role in the governance of corporations, though it was restricted (until 1976) to "heavy" industry. Germany's unions are organized into a hierarchical association (the Deutscher Gewerkschaftsbund—DGB) that has been broadly incorporated into government decisionmaking, especially during those years in which its political ally, the German Social Democratic Party, governed. The consequence has been labor peace with few interruptions: 1978 and 1984 were years with extensive strike activity. The influence of trade unions has manifested itself in German industrial policy, which tends to focus on manpower policies, and not on firm- or sector-specific policies.[62]

Japanese corporatism is company-specific, and is in many ways a "total institution." One's personal life is said to be subsumed within one's company life.[63] Peer pressure is added to managerial control as a method of inducing high levels of commitment from employees. As in Germany, workers' organizations are said to be consulted prior to the undertaking of new ventures and new innovations.[64] Unlike Germany, employees generally are organized into company unions, rather than industry-wide unions.[65] Company unions provide management with advantages over an industry-wide union. The lower wages paid to employees in the subcontracting—supplier sector are possible because supplier workers are not organized by the unions of the main companies. Further, company unions in the Japanese automobile sector have been willing to cooperate in the introduction of labor-saving technology and quality control programs. These corporatist institutions are not without benefit for those employees who work for "core" firms: lifetime employment and a bonus-based system of profit sharing. The average wage paid to each Japanese worker is lower than that paid to the autoworker in America, but employment is less cyclical, and authority relations in factories are said to be less Taylorist.[66]

For whatever reasons, the Japanese and German workforces in the automobile industry are more productive, less prone to work disruptions, and more accepting of technological innovation and changing job classifications than are their American and British counterparts. American and British managers in the auto industry recognize the advantage that cooperative management–labor relations have conferred on German and Japanese firms. American and British managers are adopting a "softer" style of management, but to date neither group of managers is willing to grant to workers the related benefits of corporatism.

Sources of Financing

Another source of congruence lies in the limited ability or willingness of the American and British financial systems to fund the retooling of the auto industry to match Japanese productivity and costs.

The saving/consumption behavior of the citizens of Japan and Germany is credited with contributing to their economic success relative to other nations.[67] Japanese long-term investment in plant and machinery was over three times that of the United States during the 1970s (see table 4.5). Certainly heavy investment (and productivity growth) were key to expansion of the Japanese auto industry. If the American and British auto industries were to survive, they needed

TABLE 4.5
Comparison of Capital Formation in 6 Countries, 1971–80

Country	Net Fixed Investment[a]	Growth Rate, Output per Man-hour
Japan	19.5%	7.4%
France	12.2	4.8
Germany	11.8	4.9
Italy	10.7	4.9
Britain	8.1	2.9
United States	6.6	2.5

[a]*Investment as percentage of gross domestic product*
Source: Organization for Economic Cooperation and Development.

to restructure and reinvest in their industries, a task which the governments have partly borne. Why has American and British investment lagged behind Japan's and Germany's?

I will first review some of the general issues involved in the application of financial analysis to the study of industrial restructuring, and then return to a discussion of the auto industries.

A General Review of Financial Markets

The problem of financing long-term investment is not one limited to the auto industries. A number of analysts have argued that several features of financial markets (as well as the general management education that "informs" corporate officers) have produced a short-term profitability orientation among American and British managers, and this orientation has played a role in the comparatively low rates of American and British capital investment.[68]

The argument goes roughly as follows. In evaluating two or more proposed investments, even if of different time frames, managers, bankers and stock analysts have several statistical tools available with which to assess the merit (i.e. the real rates of return) of competing proposals. These tools are generally variants of discounted cashflow techniques; the most commonly used is the Net Present Value (NPV) standard.[69]

These discount methods employ as grounding concepts the opportunity costs of capital (the discount or interest rate), uncertainty, and the future stream of income. A number of axioms follow from use of NPV. These are

• the best project from a company's perspective is one that maximizes the NPV of a firm's assets given the above factors[70]
• any investment a firm undertakes should pay back more than the best prevailing "safe" rate of return[71]
• "all securities in an equivalent risk class are priced to offer the same expected rate of return"[72]
• firms that undertake investments that do not maximize NPV will find that the company's stock value will decline, thereby reducing the shareholders' wealth and (in theory) management's autonomy.[73]

The standard of NPV (and its axioms) does have real world consequences. First, Copeland and Weston estimated that, by 1978, more than over 80 percent of major corporations adopted one or another of the discounted cash flow measures as their major evaluation tool in capital allocation (i.e., investment).[74] Second, the use of these measures by outside stock analysts places substantial pressure on American (and British) management to maintain high dividends, even if at the expense of retained income and future investments—especially those investments with a long payback period and low initial cash flows. The undertaking of long-term investments is particularly discouraged if the interest rate is high ($r > 10\%$) as this thereby reduces the value of investments undertaken when investment rates were lower. If high nominal interest rates are combined with inflation, the replacement cost of current equipment is often higher than is the value of operating this equipment.[75] Firms then have an incentive not to invest in new plant and equipment; rather, raiding other companies or buying their assets is a "better"—that is, more efficient—allocation of capital. The recent trend towards mergers and the proliferation of hostile takeover bids make more sense in light of the NPV standard (and its axioms) of capital allocation.

For American and British companies, the high rates of interest ($r >$

20% at their peak), in conjunction with high rates of inflation made much long-term investment during the late 1970s and early 1980s unwise, given other available investment opportunities (like under-valued companies and government bonds). Japanese and German companies, on the other hand, operated in environments where the prevailing rates of interest and inflation were much lower. This made economical investments that would be rejected for NPV reasons if one presumed American or British interest rates.

What then are the general features of each of these financial markets?

Japan. The Japanese financial system, through its stabilization of the economy and its allocation of capital, is often credited with much of the success of the Japanese economy in the postwar era. While Japanese firms often competed fiercely within an industry, the Japanese government, by tightly regulating the banking industry (and providing cheap, rationed credit), remained the final arbiter of success into the 1970s. Some public control over firm investment was thought to prevent "wasteful" competition, and this control was effected by an interest-rate-based industrial policy. Favored firms received subsidized credit, a subsidy made possible by the high rate of saving of Japanese consumers in conjunction with the very restricted financial instruments offered to consumers. Consumers would ultimately benefit through higher real wages paid by successful firms, rather than from interest or dividend income.[76]

Until the 1970s, firms had few choices but to coordinate their economic decisions with the government—few other sources of capital were available. As late as 1972, the equity and bond markets accounted for less than 10 percent of the funds raised by corporate businesses in Japan (as opposed to 43 percent in the United States.)[77] Another possible source of capital, borrowing overseas sources, required prior government approval.

The Japanese government's control over corporate decisions is no longer monolithic: the profitability of Japanese firms allows many to be self-financing, the equity market has developed more fully, Japanese firms have begun production of goods in foreign markets, and an offshore, Euroyen market has developed.[78] Very wealthy consumers and firms also have more choices in terms of savings instruments—a CD market (though of large denominations—¥300 Million [$1.5 Million]) has existed since 1979 and the postal system now offers longer term, higher interest rate deposits. The financial instruments available to the corporate and banking sector now more or less approximate in rate of return those prevailing in a free market (i.e. the Euromarket.) Individual savers, however, still face many regulatory restrictions both on the saving instruments available to them and on the interest rates paid on these instruments. The Japanese government continues to regulate the Japanese financial industry and, through its interest rate policies, the Japanese economy. Japanese firms continue to be able to pay lower rates of return to Japanese investors than American firms pay to American investors.[79]

The Federal Republic of Germany.[80] West Germany's financial system is characterized by a relatively small equity market and by a "universal" banking system. German banks offer a full range of financial services, and they own or control much of the equity in German firms. Several sources report that banks own or control 70 percent of the voting stock of the largest 425 German corporations. Ellsworth reprints a table that reveals that banks are majority stockholders in 30 of the 62 largest publicly traded German companies, and own between 25 and 50 percent of 11 of the remaining 32 companies. In addition to owning or controlling voting stock, German banks have provided much of the capital necessary for the investment of German firms—the debt to equity ratio of German firms averaged approximately 3 for the 1966–1982 period.[81] German banks are intimately involved in the ownership and control of German firms in a fashion precluded by law in the United States and by tradition in Great Britain. Many analysts (Shonfield, Ellsworth, Medley, Zysman) have argued that the dominance of firm finance by banks allows firms the luxury a "long-term perspective," as they are insulated from the "rate of return" pressure assumed to follow from well-developed equity markets. Even the banks are partly insulated from investor pressure; they own stock in each other.

The German government (including the *Bundesbank*, for the purposes of this discussion) apparently does not directly control the interest rates banks charge to firms in Germany. The government, however, has "profound" influence in the direction of the German economy, though most analysts agree that this influence is the result of incentives rather regulation.[82] First, successive governments have followed macroeconomic policies aimed at maintaining low rates of inflation—inflation averaged 4.1 percent for the 1960–1982 period, the lowest figure for any OECD country.[83] Second, the Bundesbank sets three interest rates; the Discount rate, the Lombard rate, and Treasury paper rate (Medley, pp. 103–6). The main features of the Discount rate are that banks are permitted to borrow money at below interbank rates, but only for three months, and only up to the quota amount set for each bank. This provides the Bundesbank with substantial discretionary authority over banks, and indirectly, the firms that borrow from them. Third, the government has the capacity to influence the D-Mark dealing of firms and banks on foreign financial markets.[84] These restraints prevented neither the early development of the D-Mark Euromarket (active from the early 1960s on) nor the emergence of the D-Mark as the "second" currency in the Euromarket, but the restraints do exist.[85] Fourth, the government and the managers of the large banks are said to have a "well-developed system of highly discreet, ad hoc communication." (Soindler, p. 13). Finally, the German government has given itself greater discretionary stabilization and planning powers (1967 *Stabilisationsgesetze*, 1978 *Finanzplan*) over the German economy, though German industrial policy of the microeconomic sort seen in other countries is not substantial.[86]

In summary, the German financial system consists of a set of unique and subtle relations among the government, banks, and firms. Banks are universal agents with strong controlling interests in German firms; these firms hence have access to sources of capital at lower costs than do firms raising money on equity markets. Banks are in turn strongly influenced through direct and indirect means by the German authorities. Scholars seem to agree that, while the Federal Republic has a formal commitment to a "social market strategy" with markets setting prices, the German government has the capacity (and, occasionally, the desire) to intervene to set prices.

The United Kingdom.[87] Britain's financial industry is characterized by a well-developed and funded equity market, and by banking institutions with limited ties or loans to industry. British banking institutions are generally categorized as either merchant banks or commercial banks. Merchant banks originally traded in commodities and bills of exchange, in addition to providing finance for trade. Commercial banks are deposit institutions that provide credit and overdraft facilities, and other short-term loans. The distinctions between these banking institutions is now based more on tradition than regulation. Since 1971, the commercial banks have been active in the wholesale banking activities that once were the preserve of merchant bankers. Since 1986, the legal boundaries among different types of financial institutions have been eliminated.[88]

The relationship between Britain's financial industry and its manufacturing sector has been a subject of some political and academic controversy, with Britain's government occasionally standing accused of "betraying" industrial Britain through the promotion of financial Britain. British firms historically have relied on raising funds from equity and debenture (bond) issues rather than from bank loans, though Williams suggests that retained income was far more important in industry's finance than either equity or loans. These instruments are more expensive for firms in terms of cost of capital than are bank loans. As with French banks, British financial institutions did not develop close financial or equity ties to industry. Unlike the French case, the British state did not develop effective public substitutes for providing investment capital for private firms.[89]

The British government did attempt, before Margaret Thatcher's election, to fashion an effective industrial policy. Occasionally, it would use credit controls and other financial restraints. The British government, in the 1960s and 1970s, employed capital controls in the hopes of providing both industrial investment credit to firms and direction as to which sectors and to what ends banks would lend money. Both formal guidelines and "moral suasion" were employed.[90] (The Government also established such agencies as the National Enterprise Board through which funds were to be provided to support investment.) The ability of the British authorities to direct economic activity by restricting financial markets was limited, however, by several factors. These included a series of sterling crises (culminating in IMF help to the British economy) and the development of "offshore" trading in London, a market over which the British authorities exercised little control. In any case, financial controls were quickly lifted by the Thatcher Government shortly after its election in May of 1979. The Conservatives have continued to press for the deregulation of Britain's financial markets, with final deregulation of all securities markets occuring in October of 1986.

The United States. The American financial industry is highly segmented and relatively unconcentrated, with sharp divisions between and among the functions and services offered by various banking institutions. This segmentation and lack of concentration are usually attributed to a populist political culture hostile to a concentrated banking and financial industry, and the fragmented nature of American banking regulation (State vs. Federal interests; divided Federal powers).

The American financial industry is, in some ways, one of the most regulated in the industrial world. The existing regulations are aimed at banking solvency and industry concentration, and not at providing cheap investment credit to firms. As is generally true with American public policy, these regulations are neither coordinated among regulatory institutions nor especially coherent. Overlapping federal and state jurisdictions, disagreements among agencies and regulators, state and regional boundaries, and Congressional indecision characterized financial regulatory policy.[91]

The relationship between the financial industry and the financing of corporate investment has been shaped both by regulatory restrictions and by the traditions of financial practices. First, American banks do not own (directly) stock in American corporations: the Glass-Steagall provisions of the 1933 Bankruptcy Act prohibit this. Second, American firms have traditionally preferred to raise capital internally or through the equity market.[92] The debt/equity ratio of American firms has averaged well below 1 for the postwar era. The overall market equity capitalization in the United States was slightly below $2 trillion in 1985.[93] New firms, or those with new products or new processes, are often successful in raising equity funds through "venture" markets. The United States has a well-established "venture capital" market; the *Financial Times* estimated that, in 1984, $16 billion had been assembled in "venture pools," though little more than $3 billion had actually been invested.[94] Third, institutional investors dominate trading on the securities markets; institutions (e.g., pension fund managers, insurance companies) are estimated to account for 60 to 65 percent of the volume of transactions on Wall Street, and Wall Street "houses" account for another 25 to 30 percent of the volume of trade, though the stock ownership of most companies remains highly dispersed.[95] These institutions have shown a marked interest in quarterly, short-term profits. The much-discussed owner–manager conflict, raised first by Berle and Means in the 1930s, seems to have come down to pension-fund managers demanding high quarterly profits. American firms thus prefer to finance investment through equity and retained income, American commercial banks have been precluded from developing equity stakes in American companies, and the American securities markets are both huge in terms of capitalization, and characterized by a short-term orientation. As Ellsworth has demonstrated, the cost of capital to American firms is, as a result, higher than the costs for either Japanese or German firms.

In summary, Japanese and German financial markets are structured so that Japanese and German firms have been able to successfully raise capital more cheaply than have American and British firms. Lower rates of investment in the United States and Great Britain result.

American and British firms in general have confronted this problem of lower rates of investment; capital intensive industries faced particular difficulty. The restructuring of auto products and processes (in light of the changes in market demand) strained the resources of American and British auto manufacturers. The reluctance of auto firms in 1975–1980 to undertake the sorts of investment needed to compete with Japanese producers is understandable given the features of financial markets discussed above. Chrysler and British Leyland "failed" before this pressure.

Finance and the auto industries

The costs of industrial restructuring for the auto industries are enormous. An outside analyst for Paine Weber estimated that GM would need to raise up to $50 billion between 1980 and 1984, and that Ford's capital needs would equal $22 billion for that same period. Estimates indicated that the capital needs of the auto industry and its finance companies exceeded that of American Telephone and Telegraph Company.[96]

To give some idea of the size of the financial undertaking, one needs to consider that all nonfinancial institutions in the U.S. raised only $35 billion in long-term loans in 1981, and the shares market suffered net divestment. In fact, the American (and British) structure of saving and investment were skewed away from long-term industrial investments. Analysts believed that investors in both markets were uncertain about long-term interest rates and the depth of the 1980–83 recession. As a result, investors showed a strong preference for short-term financial instruments (see above). Money market funds ($107 billion), short-term loans ($136 billion), and government bonds ($146 billion) dominated the American markets in 1981.[97]

The British market showed much the same pattern. BL required £990 million in capital from the British government in 1981. All of the nonfinancial industries in the country raised only £1.9 billion in long-term loans for that year. Short-term securities, loans and other deposits totaled more than £100 billion.[98]

Given the difficulty for nonfinancial enterprises in raising long-term loans, corporations interested in expansion have several options, including internal generation of capital, sale of shares or assets, or both. Internal generation of capital is feasible for a company with a large revenue stream (and passive shareholders) through dividend cuts, income depreciation, and amortization. Most of the funds GM and Ford raised came from these sources. Even so, they needed an additional $17 billion.[99]

The other option is to raise equity funds. General Motors raised nearly $10 billion by 1985 through this method. For corporations like General Motors, with a debt to equity ratio of 4.6 percent in 1979, or Ford (12.2% in 1979) expansion was not difficult.[100]

But for Chrysler (40% in 1979) or British Leyland (40% in 1975), the additional funding was not forthcoming, especially since more solvent companies, such as General Motors, were in the same borrowing or equity market. Chrysler was able to raise over $600 million in capital by selling such assets as a tank manufacturing division; but these transactions are one-time cash fixes. Smaller companies like Chrysler and BL, already uncompetitive in products and processes, face the classic problem of small producers in an oligopolistic market. Any changes in the market environment (e.g. government demands for fuel economy, Japanese producers) fall equally on all firms. GM has to upgrade its fuel efficiency just as does Chrysler. But the resources of the major producers (Ford, GM, Renault, Fiat, Volkswagen) are much greater than are Chrysler's or BL's. Hence, the requisite expenditures to meet these changes have a greater impact on firms with weaker financial bases. This also implies that weaker firms must pay higher returns to would-be investors to induce them to lend capital; long-term investment becomes more difficult for these firms, since money must then be rolled over more often.[101]

Chrysler and BL proved unable to continue to attract investment

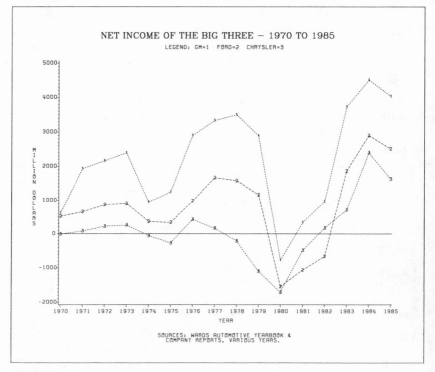

FIGURE 4.9

as their losses deepened (see figures 4.9 and 4.10). Only when the central governments agreed to underwrite the costs were the companies able to avoid bankruptcy.

Chrysler was "rescued" by both the British and American governments. Chrysler had expanded its production network into Europe in the 1960s in order to compete with Ford and GM, but at a much later date than did either Ford or GM. Rather than investing in "greenfield" sites, Chrysler chose to purchase small and not very efficient producers like Rootes and Simca. Unlike Ford, Chrysler was not able to establish a European-wide production system. Hence, when the Japanese commenced their export drive, and when the world auto

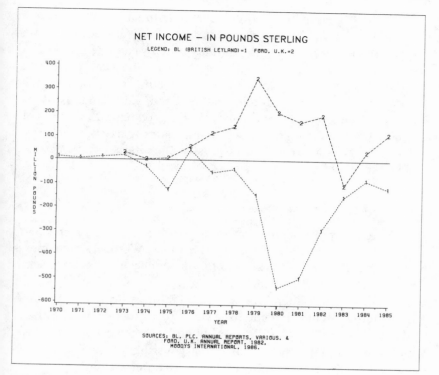

NET INCOME — IN POUNDS STERLING
LEGEND: BL (BRITISH LEYLAND) =1   FORD, U.K. =2

SOURCES: BL, PLC. ANNUAL REPORTS, VARIOUS, &
FORD, U.K. ANNUAL REPORT, 1982,
MOODYS INTERNATIONAL, 1986.

FIGURE 4.10

markets contracted in 1974 and 1975, Chrysler was left producing too few cars in out-of-date plants. Chrysler's withdrawal from Britain was staved off for a few years by government commitments totaling £160 million in 1975 and 1976, but in 1979 the company finally departed, selling what is now called Talbot to Peugeot. In fact, Chrysler's withdrawal from most of its world involvement was linked to its problems in the U.S. Chrysler lost over $3 billion between 1979 and 1982. Bankruptcy was averted when Congress imposed conditions on lenders, management, and workers in return for federal loan guarantees up to $1.5 billion. This gave Chrysler renewed access to lending markets.[102]

The British government's involvement with BL has been deeper and more expensive. BL is in an even worse market position than is Chrysler; Chrysler produces three times as many cars as BL. Counting all sorts of aid, BL has drained over £2.34 billion from the central treasury. In return, BL's losses have been cut, new products have been introduced, and production rationalized; yet the company has not made a trading profit, and Tory plans to privatize BL are probably unrealizable. Nonetheless, no sentiment seems to exist for eliminating all state aid for BL. As with Chrysler, the alternative to state aid was bankruptcy.[103]

Financial Cost to the State

At the root of policy similarity are the welfare costs to governments associated with firm failures. Since the 1930s, Western democracies have assumed some responsibility for the management of their economies, and have established social "safety nets" to cushion their populations from sudden firm or sectoral failures. Aid to individuals who suffered job and income losses due to market or other failures is determined by income thresholds and other categorical grants, which are automatic in the sense that government funding is nondiscretionary. That is, funding levels of programs are determined not by direct legislation, but the needs of individuals.

As a result, when an important production sector suffers an economic downturn, several types of losses accrue to state accounts, the most important of which is that workers, once taxpayers, are now receiving food stamps or welfare. The absolute value of this tax payment–welfare receipt swing can be large. In 1980, the Congressional Budget Office estimated that "a 1 percent increase in general unemployment (more than 1 million workers) reduces tax revenues by about $20 billion annually and increases spending for unemployment related programs by $5 to $7 billion.[104] The swing in Britain is also large as unemployment cost the Treasury an estimated £15 billion in 1982 (or $27 billion at the 1982 average exchange rate.)[105] The impact on the economy is also broad. A reduction of employment

TABLE 4.6
Earnings Losses of Displaced Workers, US
Average Annual Percentage Loss

	Selected Industries first 2 years	subsequent 4 years
automobiles	43.4	15.8
steel	46.6	12.6
meat packing	23.9	18.1
aerospace	23.6	14.8
petroleum refining	12.4	12.5
women's clothes	13.3	2.1
electronic components	8.3	4.1
shoes	11.3	1.5

Source: U.S. Senate. Committee on Labor and Human Resources. Subcommittee on Employment and Productivity. Employment and the American Automobile Industry, 1982. Statement of Roland Droitsch, January 12, 1982. page 209.

levels by 1 percent reduces the GNP by 2 or 3 percent.[106] National income is further reduced by this swing, as the multiplier impact of transfer payments is lower than is the impact of equivalent wages. Consumption decreases, as does aggregate demand, producing a deeper downturn and further treasury losses.[107] Governments also lose corporate tax revenues, though this swing is less substantial. Ford, Chrysler, and GM paid a total of $2.5 billion in corporate taxes in 1978 and claimed $3 billion in tax credits in 1980; the swing cost the treasury accounts over $5 billion.[108]

For the unemployed and the governments, the problems are compounded during industry layoffs if other sectors of the economy are in recession, as was the case during the 1979–1983 downturn. The unemployed workers in the "basic" industries are particularly hurt by the loss of high-wage, semiskilled, or unskilled labor, as the composition of the workforce has changed, so that those new jobs being created, are found primarily in the service sector. Even when the unemployed of the basic industries do find work, the jobs they find pay much less well, and their income losses are sustained over many years. As we can see from table 4.6, the income loss is visible for at least six years. From the perspective of the treasuries, the losses of forfeited tax revenues continue, even after a displaced worker finds a new job and the losses from transfer payments cease.

If an industry decline occurs as a result of a downturn in the business cycle and a structural shift in the composition of production and trade (due to consumer preferences), another set of direct and indirect costs to the treasuries emerges. One problem is that production and unemployment may not reach the levels of past peak years even when a recession ends. Given the difficulties unskilled workers have in finding new well-paying work, some part of the negative tax receipt–welfare payment swing costs will remain permanent.

A related problem is that, at least in the short to medium term (5 to 8 years), the imports of a major product may contribute to trans-border payments deficits. As we can see from figure 4.11, the U.S., Britain, and Japan have each suffered dramatic shifts in their Current Accounts Balance of Payments.[109]

Nations generally seek to avoid either major surpluses or deficits in their current balances. They have several reasons for doing so. The main reason is that changes in the absolute value of the national balance usually produces changes in the value of a nation's currency.[110] An increase in the value of a nation's currency can price that nation's exports out of competitive foreign markets. A decrease in currency values causes that nation to run the risk of "importing inflation" (as the price of foreign goods and services rises) thereby contracting domestic demand. In either case, too rapid a shift in currency values produces economic dislocations and at least a short-term reduction in domestic production and aggregate demand. Such a reduction translates into reduction of national incomes, the nation's tax-base, and its Treasury accounts.[111]

A second reason for avoiding major deficits is that such deficits can diminish a nation's range of public policy choices—its room for maneuver. Should the current accounts deficit reach the equivalent of 2 or 3 percent of GDP, as happened to Britain and Italy in 1973–75, the government might loss some degree of national policy autonomy, as external creditors such as the International Monetary

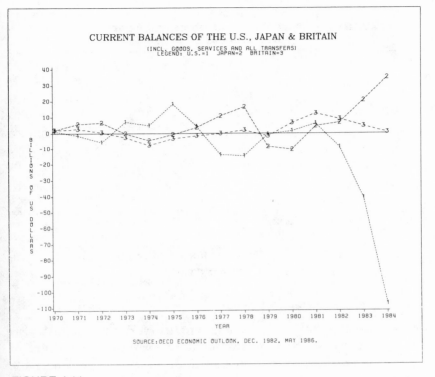

CURRENT BALANCES OF THE U.S., JAPAN & BRITAIN

(INCL. GOODS, SERVICES AND ALL TRANSFERS)
LEGEND: U.S.=1   JAPAN=2   BRITAIN=3

SOURCE: OECD ECONOMIC OUTLOOK, DEC. 1982, MAY 1986.

FIGURE 4.11

Fund (IMF) impose conditions on state policies before access to hard currency loans is granted.

The decline of the American and British auto industries during the 1970s produced the twin effects of treasury and payments losses. The industries were confronted with two cyclical downturns in consumption (1974–76 and 1979–83), a structural shift in production (mainly to Japanese and German firms), and worldwide production overcapacity. Several firms nearly failed, and auto production in both countries shrank by almost 50 percent during the ten years between 1972 and 1982. The direct consequences of these changes to the state

TABLE 4.7
American Employment in Automobiles and Related Industries
(1978, business cycle peak)

Direct:	Motor Vehicles & Parts	950,000
	Supplier Industries	1,400,000
	Total Direct Employment	2,350,000
Secondary:	Dealers, Purchasers, etc.	2,310,000
Total:	Direct & Secondary	4,660,000
U.S. Manufacturing Employment:		21,000,000
Auto Related Employment as %:		22.2%
U.S. Total Employment:		98,280,000
Auto Related Employment as %:		4.7%

Source: Department of Transportation, The U.S. Industry, 1980, p. 84.

accounts of each country was substantial, though much conjecture surrounds estimates of the indirect costs.

Costs to the American Treasury

In the United States, the automobile industry, during its peak year of 1978, was the single most important private sector industry in terms of employment and value-added. As we can see from table 4.7, the direct and indirect employment of the industry was enormous, even discounting the multiplier impact of high employment on the rest of the economy.

When the economic downturn of the 1979–1982 period deepened, and Japanese imports increased, industry layoffs followed. Even with a work force base already substantially below the 1978 peak, the industry had indefinite layoffs of between 25 and 32 percent of its unionized workforce in 1980 and 1981.

The raw direct cost in 1979 to the Federal Treasury per unemployed worker can be seen in table 4.8.

In 1980, with 250,000 autoworkers, 350,000 supplier workers, and 100,000 dealer employees unemployed, total federal costs exceeded $26 billion in 1980 and 1981.[112]

TABLE 4.8
Governmental Transfer Payments to Unemployed Auto Workers
Automotive and Supplier Industry Employees
(Average Cost per worker in 1979 dollars)

Federal Costs	Auto Worker	Supplier Worker
Lost Tax Revenues	5,000	2,000
Unemployment Insurance	4,400	3,300
Trade Adjustment Assistance	4,700	—
Welfare, Food Stamps, etc.	—	3,750
	$14,100	$9,050
State Government Costs		
Lost Tax Revenues	600	250
Medicaid & Welfare	—	50
	$600	$300
Total Government Costs	$14,700	$9,350

Source: Department of Transportation, *The U.S. Automotive Industry*, 1980, p. 98.

The American balance of trade was also negatively affected by the structural changes in the auto industry. As figure 4.12 demonstrates, the negative balance in the auto trade was more than $50 billion during the 1970s. American (and European) losses constituted Japan's gains, as Japan's auto exports were worth over $84 billion during the 5 year period ending in 1980.[113]

The damage to the American industry (and to treasury accounts) could have been much worse. By many accounts, the Japanese have been able to produce cars that were approximately $1500 cheaper than were comparable cars made in America. Consequently, the consensus among Congressional witnesses (reflected in government reports) was that Chrysler (and possibly Ford) could not survive with unrestricted Japanese competition and without some form of federal aid. More troubling for those concerned with the health of the U.S. auto industry was that even GM operates at a disadvantage in terms of productivity to the Japanese. As table 4.9 shows, a new Japanese plant (Toyo Kogyo), with the same number of robots as a GM plant, is two or three times as productive, and less costly to build. The

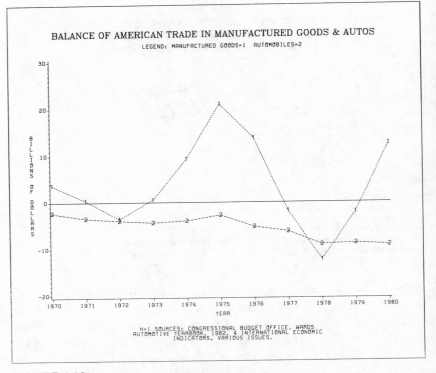

FIGURE 4.12

implication—given higher American labor costs—is that the Japanese industry will continue to be more productive. Hence, without American restrictions of Japanese autos, Japan's surplus productive capacity could have been used to substantially replace much of the already reduced American production. For the Treasury, the costs of the 1980 and 1981 period would have tripled with unrestricted Japanese competition.

Costs to the British Exchequer

1974 was the peak year for the British auto industry. The motor sector was the largest industrial private sector employer with 300,000 direct

TABLE 4.9
Productivity Comparison, GM v. Toyo Kogyo
(Assembly Operations at new plants)

	GM Hamtramck (Detroit)	TK Hofu City (Hiroshima)
size	3.2 million sq. ft.	1.5 million sq. ft.
investment	$600 million	$150–180 million (35,000 million ¥)
employment (direct & indirect)	6,000	1,800[a]
capacity	1120 cars/day	1000 cars/day
robots	155 (approx.)	155 (approx.)
productivity[b]	42.8 hours/car[c]	14.4 hours/car

[a]Includes stamping plant employees located on site. GM's nearest stamping plant is 200 miles from Hamtramck.

[b]Productivity, or man-hours of labor per car, is determined by multiplying total employment by 8 hours to get total man-hours per day. This figure is then divided by total production per day.

[c](40 hours/car assuming 5% absenteeism)

Source: Chilton's Automotive Industries, January 1983. pages 18–19.

and 1 million indirect workers, approximately 5 percent of the total British workforce. The industry was also the biggest single export exchange earner with earnings of £1.3 billion.[114] The industry was believed to directly or indirectly account for over 10 percent of the total of British industrial production.

By 1982, production and employment nearly halved, though the layoffs were not evenly distributed among employers as Ford, UK remained highly profitable. (See Ford & BL profitability and employment comparisons. Figure 4.10 and table 4.5.) These redundancies took place despite a government-imposed incentive designed to keep employees on the payroll. That is, employees made redundant must be given substantial severance pay.[115] Furthermore, these layoffs occurred at a time when British industrial unemployment had increased dramatically, and total unemployment rose to more than 12 percent of the workforce. The costs of transfer payments, lost revenues, and so on of Britain's record levels of unemployment (over

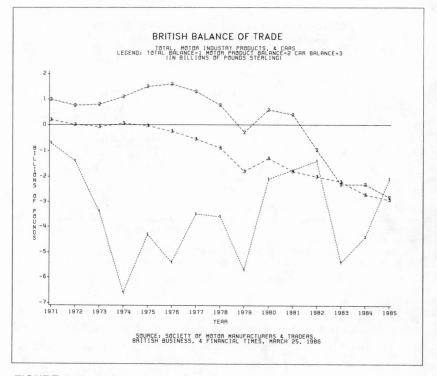

FIGURE 4.13

12 percent) approached £15 billion in 1981–82, of which perhaps
10 percent can be attributed to the auto sector.[116]

The impact of this industrial downturn on the British balance of
trade was also substantial (see fig. 4.13). Though Britain's current
accounts balance remained in surplus, thanks to the discovery of
North Sea oil and a profitable banking and service sector, Britain's
trade balance (i.e. goods/products) was in a staggering deficit of between 2 and 4 percent of GDP in the second half of the 1970s. By
the end of the 1970s, Britain's deficit in the auto trade was between
£1 & £2 billion, or 30 to 50 percent of recent trade deficits.

In a sense, the nine-year collapse of the British industry exceeded

TABLE 4.10
British Car Industry—Possible Outcomes (1985)
Trade, Balance of Payments & Employment Consequences

	1974	High Volume	Consolidated	Reduced	Severely Reduced
Units produced[a]	1.5	(1.9)	(1.5–1.7)	(1.0)	(.7)
imports (000s)	375	575	550–700	1,100	1,300
exports (000s)	565	615	375–500	240	180
balance of trade in cars (in millions of pounds sterling at 1975 prices)					
	65	−90	−150 to −400	−800	−1,000
changes in employment:					
direct	—	−35,000	−50 to −70,000	−105,000	−140,000
indirect	—	−20,000	−40 to −65,000	−110,000	−135,000
total	—	−55,000	−90 to −135,000	−215,000	−275,000

Actual changes (1980)	imports 858,000	production 924,000	payments −1.28 Billion[b]	employment −300,000(est.)

[a]in millions
[b](in 1980 pounds sterling)

Sources: Central Policy Review Staff, *The Future of the British Car Industry*. London: HMSO, 1975. page 111; The Society of Motor Manufacturers & Traders; & the Trade Union Congress, UK.

the "worst case" expectations of UK government analysts. Six years into a ten-year program outlined in a British policy document in 1975, the car industry lies somewhere between "reduced" and "severely reduced" on a chart of possible outcomes (table 4.10).

An examination of table 4.10 indicates that some reduction in industry size was viewed as inevitable, especially with regard to employment and the terms of trade. The degree of employment and trade losses was less certain, and the document reveals that in 1974 the British government still had hopes for a "High Volume" industry—hopes that have been badly confounded.

These massive financial, employment, and trade losses are not necessarily "the bottom of the well" for the British industry. The potential for nearly complete industry bankruptcy (save Ford) was and is present. "Voluntary" quotas and other trade restrictions

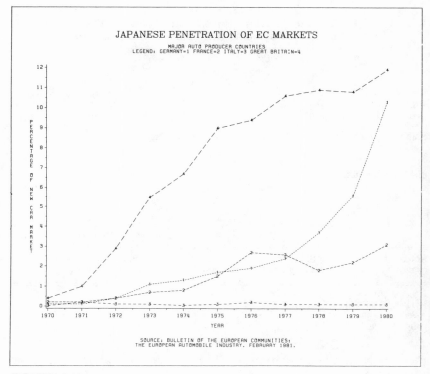

FIGURE 4.14

placed on Japanese imports by Britain and the other three major auto producing European nations have kept Japanese imports to 12 percent or less of their new car sales (See figure 4.14). In sharp contrast, the smaller EC nations have permitted Japanese imports to rise to their "natural" level of between 25 and 45% of the market. (See fig. 4.15, small country markets.) Government policies to protect their markets have required these large countries (with some firm collusion) to attempt to prevent individuals from circumventing quotas by purchasing cars in other parts of the European Common Market. Buyers in Britain had strong incentives to purchase cars in other

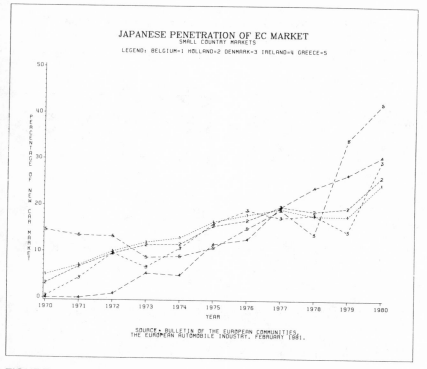

FIGURE 4.15

countries (if possible) as British prices on identical cars were 10 to 30 percent higher than are Belgian prices, as table 4.11 indicates.[117]

The British economy does suffer some losses in consequence of the restrictions on imports. The price differentials are substantial enough so that a recent study suggested that if the British had paid Belgian prices for new cars in 1981, Britain would have saved 0.6 percent of GDP, or £1.3 billion, though the study did not suggest what costs to the GDP would have ensued from the resulting bankruptcy of BL.[118]

TABLE 4.11
Pre-tax Car Prices in Great Britain and Belgium—1983
(net price, in Pounds Sterling)

car by maker	UK £	Belgium £	Difference £	Difference (as % of UK price)
Austin Metro 1000 (BL)	3,451	2,609	842	24
BMW 320	6,899	5,370	1,528	22
Fiat 27	3,411	2,656	755	22
Fiat 131	4,120	3,675	445	10
Ford Escort	3,836	3,069	788	20
Ford Granada	7,470	5,170	2,300	30
Jaguar XJ6	13,106	10,901	2,204	17
Lada 1200 (U.S.S.R.)	2,243	1,706	536	24
Mazda 323	4,334	3,167	1,167	27
Mercedes 230E	8,015	7,256	758	9
Peugeot 505	5,494	4,213	1,280	23
Porsche 924L	8,663	7,687	975	11
Renault 5	3,438	2,625	782	23
Renault 20	6,297	4,806	1,490	23
Rover Vanden Plas (BL)	11,157	7,580	3,576	32

Source: Financial Times, March 7, 1983. p. 7.

Other types of costs

This price difference highlights a second dilemma for government policymakers. Though the short-term opportunity costs of not intervening to the Treasury and national accounts are high, quotas, state subsidies, tax relief, and other interventions in the price structure of markets also generate costs. Generally, these costs of intervention are more long-run, diffuse, and harder to measure—in part because some of the costs accrue to the public welfare. But these costs are nonetheless substantial, and they provide the basic rationale for a key aspect of policy similarity, government insistence on the long-term commercial viability of the auto industry.

One type of direct cost of intervention comes from industrial strategies that drain funds from the treasuries, either through grants or loans, or through changes in tax laws which reduce government income. The British, under authority of Sections 7 and 8 of the Industry Act of 1972 (and the revised Industry Acts of 1975 and 1980) as well as other enabling legislation, have tended to favor direct grants and subsidies. The Americans, with such major exceptions as the "bailouts" of Lockheed, New York City, the Hunt brothers, and Chrysler, have tended to favor the latter method.

British government grants can be divided into two categories; grants to the nationalized industries and private sector grants. Grants to private firms totaled slightly less than £2 billion during the 1981–82 tax year, and had as their public policy purpose one of four areas; regional development, employment subsidies (usually in underdeveloped areas like Northern Ireland), small-business incentives, and aid for new technology.[119] Grants and loans to public corporations, including such institutions of the commanding heights of the economy as British Steel, British Shipbuilding, the National Coal Board and BL, exceeded £3.5 billion in 1981–83, and their total deficit (including loan writeoffs) over the years 1978–1986 is in excess of £10 billion. The total amount of industrial grants has not diminished under Thatcher, as figure 4.16 demonstrates.[120]

Though the private company grants may be justifiable on commercial grounds, few people make such a justification for the public corporations. As we can see from Figure 4.17, the trading losses of the nationalized firms have been substantial since 1971; losses have been made good by the Treasury. These losses have been less per year than the costs of firm bankruptcy to the government. Nonetheless, government subsidies per worker employed at British Shipbuilders in 1981 came to £3500 per worker, a figure smaller than the £4500 per year per unemployed worker cost to state accounts, but still large.[121]

The direct Treasury costs in the United States are largely the result of lost corporate tax revenues. The budget for direct-granting agencies in the U.S. is smaller than in Britain: the Economic Development Administration and the Small Business Administration allocated only $800 million for fiscal year 1984, and the Community Development Block Grants totaled $1.2 billion for the same period.[122] Fur-

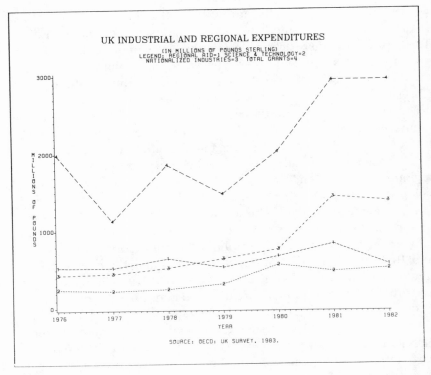

FIGURE 4.16

ther, other subsidy programs (e.g. CETA) have been eliminated. Though the schedule of capital depreciation allowances (the rate at which new machinery can be "written off" as an expense on income tax returns) has been shortened, the main subsidy has arisen from the decrease in corporate taxation as a percentage of total government income. As we can see from Figure 4.18, corporate taxation rose more slowly than personal income taxation until 1981, when the impact of legislation like the "Safe Harbors" bill took effect; corporate taxation then fell dramatically.[123] The other remaining direct costs (e.g. loss of tariff revenue, increase in oil imports due to the restric-

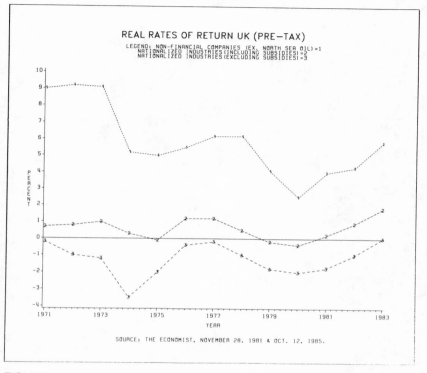

REAL RATES OF RETURN UK (PRE-TAX)

LEGEND: NON-FINANCIAL COMPANIES (EX. NORTH SEA OIL) =1
NATIONALIZED INDUSTRIES (INCLUDING SUBSIDIES) =2
NATIONALIZED INDUSTRIES (EXCLUDING SUBSIDIES) =3

SOURCE: THE ECONOMIST, NOVEMBER 28, 1981 & OCT. 12, 1985.

FIGURE 4.17

tions on the more fuel-efficient Japanese cars) are insubstantial in comparison.

The second type of cost is less measurable, but according to traditional microeconomic theory even more important in the long-run are the distorting effects on the economy by government's intervening in the price structure of markets.[124] In this sort of analysis, prices and profits are signals as to the underlying efficiency of firms and sectors. If a failing firm is saved from bankruptcy by state action, that firm decreases public welfare as it bids factors of production away from more efficient firms and sectors. Prices are higher in consequence. For example, in the context of the auto industry, BL's

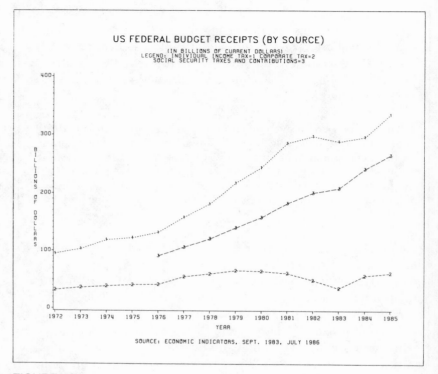

FIGURE 4.18

survival thanks to government subsidies meant that its British component suppliers were able to avoid the price reductions that would
have followed from the elimination of BL's demand. Competitor
firms are harmed, because BL's sales were approximately 19 percent
of the 1983 car market; in the event of its bankruptcy, some of that
market would be gained by the other British producers. Consumers
too are harmed, because the sales price of inefficient producers frequently sets the "floor" price of a product; more efficient firms set
the price of their products to that "floor" price and reap the subsequent profits. Much of the high profitability of Ford, UK can be
attributed to this phenomenon of floor pricing.[125]

Generally, American concerns about the costs of intervention were focused less on budgetary losses and more on the potential harm to the public welfare. The Congressional Budget Office, in reviewing the possible government options for aid to the auto industry, took no overt stand on which options were preferable. Nonetheless, the report concluded:

> There are two broad avenues of approach to these problems [of the auto industry]—one as dealing with them in the context of a national policy to encourage more productive investment, and the other aimed specifically at the problems of the auto industry. The latter would normally be regarded as the less desirable of the two approaches because of its potential for distorting the nation's capital and labor markets.[126]

Though no good estimate of the costs of state intervention is available, they are widely believed to be substantial.

The dilemma we are discussing, the long-term opportunity costs of state intervention versus the short-term efficiency costs of nonintervention, is the dilemma explored in 1942 by Joseph A. Schumpeter in *Capitalism, Socialism, and Democracy*. Schumpeter's thesis begins with a note that capitalism, over the course of decades and centuries, produced a high rate of increase of total output, though it did so unevenly and tumultuously. Capitalism is characterized, not by the static equilibrium found in microeconomics textbooks, but by dynamic disequilibrium. Entrepreneurial opportunities are created by the process of creative destruction that results from disequilibrium.

By the standards of a full employment economy, Schumpeter's capitalism is often woefully inefficient. Many are unemployed as firms go bankrupt, and capital assets and labor are underutilized. For Schumpeter, this short-term inefficiency is not evidence of capitalism's lack of productive potential. On the contrary,

> since we are dealing with a process [capitalism] whose every element takes considerable time in revealing its true features and ultimate

effects, there is no point in appraising the performance of that process
ex visu [visible] of a given point of time; we must judge its performance
over time, as it unfolds through decades or centuries. A system—any
system, economic or other—that at *every* given point of time fully
utilizes its possibilities to the best advantage may yet in the long run
be inferior to a system that does so at *no* given point of time, because
the latter's failure to do so may be a condition for the level or speed
of long-run performance. (p. 83).

For Schumpeter, the trend line of economic growth of "unfettered
capitalism" will have a steeper positive slope than will an economy
with extensive government intervention *precisely because* of the
swings of the business cycle and other destructive elements of
capitalism.

Schumpeter understood that creative destruction was associated
with unemployment and the consequent "suffering and degradation
[and] the destruction of human values."

"Nevertheless, I hold that the real tragedy is not unemployment
per se, but unemployment plus the impossibility of providing adequately for the unemployed *without impairing the conditions of
further economic development.*" (p. 70. emphasis in the original).

Schumpeter also understood that capitalism, the process of creative destruction, was unlikely to survive in the form he described.
Western societies are democratic in that elites compete for votes,
and the voters dislike the trauma and uncertainty associated with
creative destruction. Voters would demand and receive forms of state
intervention that would alleviate the consequences of creative destruction. Furthermore, the rationalist civilization spawned by capitalism employs standards of efficiency to which capitalism does not
measure up, at least in the short-term. State institutions would eventually assume (or direct) the investment functions now undertaken
by entrepreneurs and firms. Socialism, defined as public "control
over means of production and over production itself," is the likely
outcome.

Was Schumpeter right? About socialism, not immediately, though his time line stretches for decades and centuries. About the tradeoff between long-term economic growth and short-term public intervention in the economy? Perhaps so, though the evidence on this point is far from clear.[127] About the unwillingness of the electorate to tolerate the hardships of creative destruction? Certainly. Voters and governments, however, have made compromises unforeseen by Schumpeter in an effort to reconcile the dilemma of long-run growth in the context of the welfare state. Some of these compromises are at the heart of policy similarity.

Summary

The roots of the difficulties facing American and British firms and workers in the late 1970s and early 1980s have been located in an end to American and British market isolation, more efficient foreign producers (and a relatively liberal trading regime), the absence in America or Britain of sources of nongovernmental financing for the weaker firms; and the costs to the states when a sector declines. I believe these features to be collectively responsible for policy similarity regarding the auto industries, though the last, costs to states, was the crucial factor in motivating public policy responses. The strategies adopted by governments to address these problems is the focus of the next section.

THE COMPONENTS OF SIMILARITY

By now, the reader must be wondering what this policy similarity consists of. With regard to the auto industry, it was composed of three elements: (1). the partial reduction by the American and British states of the access to their home markets of Japanese firms; (2). the distribution of the costs of restructuring the industry; and (3). the insistence on both the "commercial viability" and the autonomy of firms, even if at the expense of such policy goals high employment. More broadly: (4). the provision, through the tax code, of incentives to firms to increase capital investment even if at the expense of higher levels of employment or of government revenue. This similarity, I will argue, occurred during a period of economic downturn, and will likely evaporate with the return of better economic times.

I will remind the reader here of my earlier disclaimer about the limits to policy similarity. Britain and the United States have had different public policies toward their private sectors for many decades—socialist alternatives, an elite and (in theory anyway) neutral civil service, nationalizations, and a more-than-half unionized work force[128] are part of Britain's industrial inheritance, but not America's. Part of the point to my discussion in chapter 3 was to convince the reader of these differences. Public policy traditions inspired from these differences in institutions, practices and interests cannot fade quickly; public policy differences will, of course, persist. It is the emergence of similarity, not the persistence of difference, that needs to be explained. I seek to "pick out" the "signal" of policy similarity from the "noise" of divergent traditions and interests.

Access to Markets

Limiting the access of a competitor nation (or a multinational producer) to domestic markets is one of the most effective sources of power a nation has in trade negotiations, especially if the nation has a market with a large effective demand for a given product. This power is not unlimited or unilateral: both the U.S. and Great Britain are bound in part to an international free trade regime by treaties, ideology, and domestic interests (both are major exporters of manufactured products). Yet the threat of blocking access to markets, or being forced to do so by domestic interests (as a result of political pressure or corporatist arrangements), is often sufficient to extract trade concessions from foreign nations or to induce their companies to produce in the domestic markets.

Nonetheless, the ability of nations to restrict access to their markets has diminished. Despite "backsliding" by many nations, the General Agreement on Trade and Tariffs (GATT) process has been successful

TABLE 4.12
Tokyo Round Reduction in Tariffs, average and weighted
average, by sector for ten national markets[a]
(in per cent)

	Calculated on Weighted Average	Calculated on Simple Averge
Industry (ex. oil)	33	38
Raw materials	52	36
Semi-finished	30	36
Finished	33	39
Industrial Sectors		
Wood products	40	
Textiles	20	
Leather & rubber	16	
Metals	30	
Fuels[b]	67	
Chemicals[c]	39	
Transport equip.	37	
Machinery		
Electrical	30	
Non-electrical	43	
Minerals	36	
Other manufacturers	42	

[a]Austria, Canada, EEC, Finland, Japan, New Zealand, Norway, Sweden, Switzerland, and the United States.
[b]excluding petroleum
[c]includes photographic supplies
Source: Fred Lazar, The New Protectionism. Ottawa: CIEP, 1981. page 9.

in promoting an increase in multilateralism in international trade. The so-called "Tokyo round" of the GATT talks (1973–79) produced some substantial tariff reductions (see table 4.12). By 1987, the average tariffs on most products is to be 3 to 4 percent.[129]

In addition to the general GATT tariff reductions, some nations have further reduced trade barriers by forming regional free trade blocks, the European Community being the most prominent among them. The general principle of the EC is that each of its 12 members should have as free access to the markets of the other member countries as it does to its own market. In practice, the industrial and trade policies pursued by the European Governments have produced only "quasi-free" trade as each EC nation has found it expedient to develop its own industrial strategy.[130] Despite the disparate policies, and despite the continuing impediments to free movement of goods, services, and people within the Community, intra-European trade has grown substantially. To take one illustration, Britain's exports to the EC have risen from 23.6 percent of its total exports in 1966–67 to 36.3 percent of the total in 1979–80.[131]

From the perspective of some governments and policymakers, EC membership has had its costs, as the ability of governments to pursue some types of strategies based on restricting access to markets has been greatly diminished. For instance, much of the program of industrial development advanced in various forms in Britain by the Labour Party, the Trades Union Congress (TUC), and the Cambridge Economic Policy Group all require "managed" trade and investment, policies largely precluded by the EC. Not surprisingly, these groups believe that Britain ought to withdraw from the EC.[132]

As tariffs have diminished in importance as trade barriers, new forms have emerged. The explanation for their persistence is straightforward. Assuming that free trade does advance the public good, the manifestations of this public welfare gain is diffuse in the sense that many consumers and producers will gain some small "good" from greater efficiency, although this gain is distant in that it is in the future.[133] The losses from trade, however, tend to be concentrated and immediate. When a steel plant closes, the workers and their community suffer, beginning with the first missed paycheck. In situations where a great asymmetry exists between public good and private gain such that the public good is diffuse and in the future, and private gain (to which the public good is in a negative relationship) is concentrated and immediate, Western democracies have an inherent tendency to aid these private interests.[134] Hence, when one form of trade barrier is restricted, we would expect new forms of to emerge.

The new forms of trade barriers in use within OECD countries are many, but they can generally be categorized as subsidies, regulation, or marketing agreements.[135] For instance, most governments provide research and development funds (directly and indirectly) for some industries, grant export subsidies or tax breaks on exports, employ government purchasing preference schemes, provide regional and manpower grants, and occasionally mandate product regulations that promote domestic products.[136]

The impact of these nontariff barriers on the economies of competitor countries is hard to measure, but even governments not inclined to use the barriers believe themselves bound to at least match the subsidies and policies of their chief trading rivals, or or impose some form of countervailing duties. The alternative is to lose market shares, if not in their home markets, then in other national markets.[137]

Apart from developing matching trade barriers and export subsidies, governments can establish a framework of contingent defenses. That is, when another nation's trading or industrial policies are found to hurt the domestic market of home producers, countervailing duties can be applied. The United States is the nation which has gone farthest in establishing a framework designed to counteract foreign government trade barriers and subsidies. Table 4.13 summarizes the main U.S. contingent trade defense policies.

Several points are worth highlighting with regard to these defenses and American trade policy. The first is that, as the U.S. has the world's largest national market, standards and policies designed by the Americans will tend to govern much of the terms of production and trade, even in non-American markets.[138]

As a result, American antisubsidy action acts, in theory, as a deterrent to overt government subsidization of production.[139]

A second key point is that the 1974 act allows such private interests as domestic firms and unions to bring actions against foreign products, and to appeal International Trade Commission (ITC) decisions adverse to them through the U.S. courts. This decision by Congress is consistent with the classic American regulatory approach: to grant private interests a voice in public affairs by expanding access to the courts to affected parties. The incentives here are obvious. American firms can act to obstruct the sale of a foreign competitor's product by filing charges of "unfair" competition and so on.[140] Ironically

TABLE 4.13
Framework of U.S. Contingent Trade Defenses

Bill/Treaty	Substantive Provisions
1921 Anti-Dumping Act	forbids selling imported goods at "less than fair value" if injury to domestic producers results
1930 Tariff Act	provides for countervailing duties on the importation of subsidized goods; allows for the exclusion of imported goods due to "unfair methods of competition" or "unfair import trade"
1947 GATT	Article 19 permits "safeguard," temporary actions (quotas, tariffs) to protect industries threatened by a sudden rise in imports
1962 Trade Expansion Act	provides for trade adjustment assistance relief where an industry has been harmed by a sudden increase in imports due to a trade agreement
1974 Trade Act	forbids unfair trade practices which are a "substantial cause of serious injury" to a domestic industry; allows private parties to file complaints concerning unfair trade practices in U.S. and non-U.S. markets, and to appeal ITC decisions through the U.S. courts
1979 Trade Agreement	defines injury (1974 Act) as being "not inconsequential, immaterial, or unimportant;" permits countervailing duties on goods subsidized by foreign governments in any of the following ways: provision of capital on noncommercial terms; the provision of goods at preferential rates; granting funds to subsidize loss-making industries; and, assumption of some or all of marketing or manufacturing costs.

Sources: This table is drawn from Fred Lazar, *The New Protectionism*, pp. 27–45; and Congress (U.S.), Joint Economic Committee, U.S. International Policy in the 1980s, pp. 45–6.

enough, given American complaints about European and Japanese trade practices, this causes a particularly discouraging form of trade barrier as the various American standards can be construed as forbidding a normal practice used by firms entering a new market, the selling of a product substantially below cost in order to capture market share (dumping). Further, in addition to the other expenses and technical difficulties of entering the American market, new firms need to factor in lawyer fees and legal obstacles. As it is, from 1975 to 1979, "less than fair value'" petitions were filed against one-sixth of general imports and a quarter of manufacturing imports. As American firms come under increasing foreign competition, the number of petitions is likely to rise.[141]

One particular type of trade restriction used by developed nations is the voluntary quota agreement (VQA) and the orderly marketing agreements (OMA). These devices basically require one nation or a group of nations to "voluntarily" agree to restrict exports to one or more markets on the basis either volume or percentage measures. These agreements were common features of international trade in the nineteenth century, but in the twentieth century, they mostly occurred in the primary products (e.g., agricultural goods) sectors. In the 1970s and early 1980s, however, versions of these market access agreements occurred in textiles (e.g. the Multi-Fiber agreements), shoes, steel, European petrochemicals, some electronic goods, and several other industries characterized by surplus productive capacity.[142]

Quotas and marketing agreements have proven to be fairly effective methods of limiting other nations' access to markets. For instance, some products have a low price elasticity of demand. That is, a 10 percent rise in the price may have a small or negligible short-term effect on consumer demand. Tariffs on products with small price elasticities (e.g. energy supplies, luxury items) might not produce the certain limits to imports that quotas can do. Further, as long as these quotas are "voluntary," they violate neither the GATT rules nor American antitrust laws.

For the nations that are the targets of these marketing agreements, the VQA and OMA have several advantages (assuming the inevitability of some form of restrictions such as tariffs). Unlike tariffs, the subsequent rise in price due to a short fall in supply is returned wholly to the seller. (A price increase due to a tariff increase goes to the tax chest of the collecting government.) Further, the restriction in supply gives the sellers an incentive to change the product mix toward higher quality, more value-added, and usually more profitable sectors of the market. The quota systems have also usually favored the early entrants among the restricted nations and firms, as quotas have tended to freeze existing market shares. New competitors are therefore badly hurt by this arrangement, but for the firms already in the market, the agreements amount to a form of price fixing through a government sponsored cartel.

With regard to their auto industries, both the American and British Governments have used non-tariff barriers to attempt to limit auto imports. Although the use of such barriers is not a dramatic departure from past policies for Britain, marketing agreements are fairly recent for the United States. The specific form of one part of policy similarity (restricting access to markets) was the negotitation of voluntary quota agreements.

Prior to the establishment of the quota agreements, efforts were made by private interests to restrict the access of Japanese cars to American markets. The United Auto Workers (UAW), later joined by the Ford Motor Company, filed a petition with the ITC under the 1974 Trade Act. The petition asked the Commission to find that the Japanese auto industry was the principal cause of injury to the American industry, and to grant temporary relief to the industry by the imposing trade restraints. The ITC rejected the petitions by a close three to two vote.[143] Further, several proposals, especially the "Domestic Content" Bill, were introduced and passed through one House of Congress. The Domestic Content Bill that ultimately passed the House (H.R. 5133) would have required auto companies that import more than 100,000 cars per year into the U.S. to produce 25 to 90 percent (depending on the total volume) of the value of the cars in the U.S. (The UAW estimated that this bill would have created nearly half a million new jobs in the auto industry.)[144]

The significance of these actions was not in the end result—the petition and the bills ultimately failed. Rather, the threat of future restrictions on Japanese auto imports was indicated.

The Japanese Government responded to these threats by imposing a one year quota of 1.68 million cars from April 1, 1981 to March 30, 1982, with provisions for an adjusted quota for each of the next two years.[145] The Ministry of International Trade and Industry (MITI) divided the quota in rough proporation to existing market shares (in thousands):

Toyota, 517–518
Nissan, 453–456
Honda, 348–350
Toyo Konyo, 159
Mitsubishi, 113–114
Fuji (Subaru), 66–70
Isuzu, 17

Suzuki received no allocation, and captive imports were included in the total. (The quotas were extended for a fourth year, expiring in March of 1985, following a decision by the Reagan Administration not to renew. The Japanese government, however, "voluntarily" extended quotas until March 1987.)[146]

The British also negotiated a quota system with the Japanese, though at an earlier date and with (apparently) a wider target range. From 1975 to 1980, Japanese sales were restricted to between 9 and 12 percent of the British market.[147] Japanese auto sales have remained within this target range since that time.

Despite all the attention paid to the Japan's auto exports, the Japanese have not been the major source of imports into the U.K. The EC in general and the American Multinational Corporations in particular are more responsible for the high levels of import penetration of the British market. Since joining the EC the British state has formally waived its right to block the access of cars produced in EC countries to the British market. This has not prevented the British Government from using regulations to limit imports. From 1978 on, for example, every car imported into Britain had to be granted an "approval certificate" that the car met government standards.[148] These certificates effectively blocked personal auto imports from the Continent (where, as we have seen, identical cars are 20 to 40 percent cheaper). The certificates were obtainable only from the auto manufacturers, the people who benefited most from Britain's higher prices.[149]

The American and British Governments were not alone in restricting the access of competitors through non-tariff barriers. All the major auto producing countries, including West Germany, have restricted auto imports via some form of quota. For the Americans in particular, their use is a substantial break with past policies toward the industry.[150]

Distributing Costs

Unless a nation is going to opt out of international trade in automobiles, excluding or limiting competitors is not in itself necessarily a sufficient strategy to ensure a healthy industry. In the case of the U.S. and Great Britain, the domestic industries were not competitive in either price or product with other nations, especially the Japanese. The industries had to be rationalized at enormous cost. GM, for instance, estimated that it would invest more than $80 billion in the 1980s.[151]

The question, then, is who will pay these costs, especially the costs of the smaller firms?

To a large extent, the central governments have. The states have mainly sought to encourage industrial investment through "accelerated depreciation allowances against taxation." This form of state investment subsidy is vastly more substantial than is assistance to individual firms. For instance, in the United States, the capital consumption allowances (with capital consumption adjustment) came to 11.8 percent of the total GDP of nonfinancial businesses in 1982—more than $200 billion. A modified variant, the "Safe Harbors" provision, cost the American Treasury $20 billion in the 1981–82 tax year.[152] This particular device was designed so that money-losing corporations could "swap" tax losses with profitable corporations, lease assets from them, or both. For instance, Ford was able to sell $315 million in tax benefits during 1981 and 1982 in addition to its investment tax credit (spread out over a number of years) of $542 million. Chrysler sold nearly $50 million in credits for the same period, and had $240 million available in tax credits plus $1.8 billion unused "operating loss carryforwards."[153] Profitable corporations were in some cases able to pay "negative income tax," or were refunded more than they paid. The Citizens for Tax Justice were able to demonstrate that such profitable corporations as General Electric, Boeing, General Dynamics, and Dow Chemical had negative tax rates on profits earned in 1981–83.[154]

In Britain, the general tax relief is also much more substantial an aid to British industry than is the panoply of firm-specific assistance.[155] Ford, U.K., for example, listed in its annual report for 1982 (in small print) over £260 million written off in either depreciation, amortization, or accelerated capital allowances, and only £21 million in regional aid. The total U.K. regional aid for the second and third quarters of 1981–82 came to £283 million, only slightly more than Ford's 1982 tax writeoffs.[156]

These depreciation allowances/investment tax credits are not costless for governments. As noted above, these tax incentives are expensive for treasuries at a time when Western governments are generally running substantial budget deficits. These investment incentives also encourage the replacement of workers with machinery, at least in the short-term—a rather puzzling choice for governments to make during a time of high unemployment.[157]

In addition to general industry-wide aid, each government prevented the bankruptcy of the weakest mass-volume producer by providing access to capital markets through loan guarantees, grants, equity buyouts, or other subsidies which allowed the companies to retool, yet remain independent of the government. British Leyland (now called simply BL) was provided, through the auspices of the National Enterprise Board (NEB), £2.138 million from 1975 to March 1983.[158] Chrysler received aid from both nations, up to £72 million from Britain and $1.5 billion in Federal loan guarantees to be overseen by the Chrysler Loan Guarantee Board. The Federal guarantees were the largest ever made to a private corporation, substantially exceeding the $250 million loan guarantees to Lockheed (1971) or

TABLE 4.14
Employment in the US Auto Industry, Indefinite Layoffs
(numbers employed in the United States)

	Total Hourly Workforce	Indefinite Layoffs (August 1980)	Indefinite Layoffs (December 1981)
General Motors	471,000	137,000 (29%)	112,000 (24%)
Ford	190,000	69,000 (36%)	50,386 (26%)
Chrysler	101,000	41,300 (41%)	43,262 (43%)
American Motors	16,000	2,750 (17%)	4,050 (25%)
Total	778,000	250,500 (32%)	209,698 (27%)

Note: In December 1981, over 50,000 other auto workers were on temporary layoff. The totals do not include laid-off workers who have lost recall rights as a result of the length of unemployment.
Sources: Department of Transportation, The U.S. Automobile Industry, 1980, p. 85; Ward's Automotive Reports, August 11, 1980; and Solidarity, January 1982, p. 6.

Penn Central (up to $500 million). The main condition imposed in return for state aid was increased productivity and efficiency.[159]

The industry's workers in both countries were also obliged to bear much of the costs of the restructuring of the industry as each of the major firms laid off up to 40 percent of their work force. (See tables 4.14, 4.15.)

The auto workers unions were also affected by the restructuring of the industries. In the United States, as a condition of aid to Chrys-

TABLE 4.15
Employment in the UK Auto Industry, Changes 1973–1982
(numbers employed in Great Britain)

	no's Employed		Redundancies[a]	% Change
	1982	1973		
BL	80,600	171,296	−90,696	−52.95
Ford, UK	65,200	70,143	−4,943	−7.0
GM	20,123	34,141	−14,018	−41.1
Talbot[b]	6,300	30,883	−24,583	−79.6
Total	172,223	306,463	−134,240	−43.8

[a]Redundant employees are those laid-off by a company and given severance pay with no expectations of future employment by that company.
[b]former Chrysler subsidiary, now part of Peugeot.
Source: Financial Times, December 9, 1982. p. 19.

ler, the UAW and Chrysler were obliged by the Government to negotiate and agree upon wage cuts, union pension loans to Chrysler
and, as a byproduct, increased management consultations with labor.
But, as the loan guarantees were conditional upon the $462 million
in concessions by the UAW, the union was not in a position to
demand a greater voice in Chrysler's decision-making process.[160]

In Britain, the primary costs to the union organizations (not just
in the automobile sector) have come in the form of the trade union
bills. The Industrial Relations Act (1971) appears to have been an
attempt by the Conservative Government to make collective contract
agreements enforceable through the courts, thereby imposing labor
discipline on Britain's workforce.[161] Even after the repeal of the Act,
a number of government reports advocated linking government aid
to such industries as ship building, steel and autos to improved
workforce "attitudes," a reference to the increased militancy of the
various shop-stewards groups.[162]

In recent years, the Thatcher Government has confronted the
unions with a series of bills (the 1980 and 1984 Employment Acts)
designed to make unions legally responsible for mid-contract strikes,
to limit picketing, to prevent secondary strikes, to compel secret
ballots, and to break the automatic union levy, which goes to the
Labour Party. Given the high levels of unemployment, and the
weaker condition of British unions in the 1980s, the Conservatives
will likely continue their attempt to increase "labor discipline,"
should they remain in power.[163]

The Thatcher Government's trade union legislation is perhaps
more important for what it symbolizes about changes in the role of
the British trade union movement than for the specific arrangements
the legislation imposes on union procedures. In a sense, the British
trade union movement had been broadly incorporated into the postwar decision-making process in Britain; union leaders were consulted and courted even by the Conservatives. The leadership of the
trade union movement was too powerful to ignore. As the 1984–85
Miner's strike demonstrates, this is no longer true, at least under the
Thatcher Government.

Trade unions in both countries were successful in raising the wage levels of their members, and in securing relatively decent working conditions, both through strikes and the threat of strikes and through legislation. These favorable terms of work were premised in part on the ability of firms to pass the costs on the consumers. In a world in which Korean car companies compete with General Motors, this practice is less viable. In both the U.S. and the U.K. firms and unions have been experimenting with alternative forms of work organization and compensation, particularly those that link workers' wages to increases in productivity or to the firm's profitability. American and British firms, hoping to induce higher levels of worker commitment, have proposed the adoption of forms of "corporatism" found in Japanese plants, though few have been willing to offer their workers such benefits of Japanese style corporatism as life-time employment. These experimental changes indicate that the power of the trade union movement diminishes as its near-monopoly on labor erodes.

Even though workforces on both sides of the Atlantic have borne much of the cost of restructuring, a large part of these costs has been absorbed by the Treasuries. Welfare-state legislation in Britain and America pays out benefits to workers harmed by market failures. Unemployment benefits and other aid to workers act as a form of subsidy both to the industry and to the employee.[164]

As I noted before, this form of subsidy can be expensive. In 1980, with 250,000 auto workers, 350,000 supplier workers and 100,000 dealer employees unemployed, the Federal Treasury lost $350 million a week.[165] Even after costs began to drop off as Unemployment Insurance and Trade Adjustment Assistance eligibilities (up to a year) expired, total federal costs exceeded $26 billion in 1980 and 1981.[166]

The costs are no less substantial in Britain. In May 1982, a House of Lords Select Committee estimated that each unemployed person cost the British Treasury £5000 per year in transfer payments and lost tax incomes.[167] The annualized figure of £15 billion (at 3 million unemployed) is nearly three times the British Treasury's financial deficit for the 1981–82 tax year; the auto sector layoffs account for 10 percent of these costs.[168]

The costs to auto producers are harder to measure. Both the American and British Governments imposed costs on Chrysler, and the British Government on British Leyland in return for state support. Reductions of overseas production and some personnel changes resulted from state–firm bargaining. Yet, even in the case of British Leyland—where the government became the primary owner—the autonomy of management and of the firm was retained. Shareholders may have suffered losses for which they were largely unreimbursed, but senior management (even under Labour) retained control.[169] This strategy is eminently reasonable given what I will argue was the ultimate aim of the American and British Governments—to produce a commercially viable industry—for to impose long-term costs on management (either financially or in terms of autonomy) would be to act at cross-purposes with the larger aim.

Commercial Viability and the Firm's Autonomy

That commercial viability should have emerged as the goal of both states may not seem to be much of a surprise. [170] After all, both mainstream economists and Marx himself understand capitalism to be a competitive system of production and distribution where success is measured by profits and failures by bankruptcy, however different the languages used to describe the process.

In the last century, however, many more sectors of public and private life, especially in Europe, have been removed from the domain of market decisions because political elites believed either that governments were more efficient at certain types of tasks (e.g. long-range planning) than were markets, or that markets produced unjust consequences.[171] In addition, in Britain as in most of Western Europe, loss-making public industries and services (e.g., British Rail, London Transport) have been kept in business, often at constant or increased levels, on the grounds that some public good (often the maintaining of high employment) is served by these businesses. Even their defenders do not argue that such industries are run on a commercial basis. "Social Accountancy" (or positive externalities) is the usual justification.[172]

During the 1978–1982 recession, the tenor of public intervention changed. The states have not withdrawn from the economies, but they have shifted their emphases toward producing a profitable private sector—in other language, toward increasing accumulation. At least part of this shift is due to concern over the successful industrialization strategies of nations like Japan, the results of which many governments hope to emulate. To that end, the states have sought to remove legal impediments (i.e. regulation) to profitability, and to aid firms through general assistance - in Offe's language, recommodification. The British Government's interest in commercial viability is often dated from the (post-Benn) publication of An Approach to Industrial Strategy in which the Government said that it "emphasizes the importance of sustaining a private sector of industry which is vigorous, alert, responsible and profitable. It intends that the public sector should exhibit the same qualities."[173]

The American deregulation movement has no such clear date; for some in American society, public regulation was never especially palatable. The political successes of the movement date from the late 1970s.[174] In both countries, achieving a viable (i.e. profitable) industry has been defined as the public aim.

Once a profitable industry is defined as being the goal of the Government (and of the senior management of industry), then, given a standardized product and world competition, lower pay raises (even pay cuts), redundancies and productivity concerns become the paramount issues among management, labor, and the government. If firms choose to manufacture standard, price-competitive products, then reducing wage costs per unit of production, thereby increasing productivity, is essential given the high costs of American labor and the low productivity of British labor relative to other competitors. There are, of course, several other options in reducing labor costs within an industry; these include wage indexing and union busting. Indexing wages to productivity increases is an effective strategy only if an industry is already competitive. Given the weak position of the industries vis-à-vis the Japanese, the slow process of gradually improving the companies' competitive position is not a solution to the problems of profitability; BL (renamed Rover) now produces 14 cars per man per year (up from six) and still loses money. Neither is eliminating unions, whatever their current weakness, a viable solution to the firm's profitability. Unions are institutions that have strong political allies in both states, in part because unions have resources that can be converted into political pressures. In both countries, a managed form of industrial restructuring with union acquiescence and government subsidies has emerged as the solution to the problems of the industry.

The insistence by governments on the long-term commercial viability (i.e. profitability) of the auto sector can best be understood in terms of the Treasury, balance of payments, and opportunity costs to States. These direct and indirect costs of government interventions provide the motivation for this key aspect of congruence. Only by restoring firms to some level of profitability could governments avoid these otherwise contradictory costs.[175] The dilemma of the Scylla of state account losses and the Charybdis of the costs of intervention was well understood by government policy makers; under the circumstances, aid which produced a commercially viable firm was the "least bad" solution. Without commercial viability, the drain on the state and national accounts begun in order to prevent deeper losses would continue.

An illustration of this dilemma can be seen in Chrysler, UK's bailout in 1976 following Chrysler's threat to close its British production. The British Government, in a Commons Committee report and in the Executive's response, justified aid to Chrysler in terms of the £150 million unemployment costs and the £200 million balance of payments losses for the first year following Chrysler's closure:

the principal considerations which influenced Government in reaching their decision [was] the unemployment and regional implications, the Exchequer [Treasury] cost and the adverse effect on the balance of payments that would have ensued from the closure of Chrysler, UK[176]

Following an investigation, the Commons Expenditure Committee said that they "... have not dissented from the decision."[177]

The Government evaluated a number of aid proposals, including nationalization, merger with BL, and a grant/loan scheme to induce Chrysler to rationalize its production and integrate it into its European network. The first two options were rejected on the grounds that

> the taking of all or part of CUK [Chrysler UK] into public ownership would have provided no effective solution to the problem, since a State-owned CUK, divorced from CC's [Chrysler Corporation] operations, would have no future. Not only would public ownership, as the Secretary of State informed the Committee, have cost the Government at least £170 million, but it was clear to the Government that CUK could not operate as a company in isolation from its much larger parent. The Government were not prepared to adopt a course which would be both expensive and had no prospect of viability. An alternative takeover option rejected by the Government, that of integrating CUK with British Leyland (BL), is described by the Committee as a recipe for disaster; BL and Lord Ryder had made clear to the Committee that there were very few of CUK's assets that could have been of use to BL, and ... that the opportunities for integration (with BL) were certainly very limited.[178]

The remaining alternative to closure was the grant/loan scheme (to a maximum of £72.5 million over three years), but only should CUK have "prospects of commercial viability." The Government concluded that "a strong and profitable Chrysler Corporation is essential for the success (of the rescue)," and the key to this "was to derive advantages for CUK from association with the operations of other Chrysler companies and thus (obtaining) economies of scale and (providing) a balanced total product range."[179] Chrysler's rationalization (and path, ultimately, to profitability) was to be guided by a planning agreement signed by both the Government and Chrysler.[180]

Though much of what the Government sought to prevent occurred following Chrysler, UK's sale to Peugeot, the remainder of CUK, now called Talbot, continues to assemble cars in Britain.[181]

Another illustration that commercial viability was the best way out of the dilemma was put more starkly in a British Government report entitled *The Future of the British Car Industry*. The report argued that

> Although the social and balance of payments costs of a rapid rundown of the car industry in this country would be serious, this cannot justify preserving employment and maintaining capital in an industry that is declining and has no prospect of achieving viability. The industrial structure of all economies is in process of constant change.... the entire industrial structure in the United Kingdom has altered substantially over the 10 years 1961–71 and changes are expected to continue. Maintaining a particular industry in this country cannot rest on the social and balance of payments costs involved in running it down. The only justification for maintaining an industry is that it has a reasonable prospect of being viable in the longer-term. (pp. 113–14)

The authors of the report were particularly concerned about the long-term consequences of subsidies to BL.

> If BL were to be heavily subsidized for a number of years, it would become impossible for any of the other three motor manufacturers to become or remain viable in the long-term. For example, if BL were to attempt to capture market share by offering concessions to its dealers, leading to a permanent trading deficit which was subsidized by the Government, [we] would expect even the strongest multinational company to be forced to cease its manufacturing operations in Britain. It is for these reasons that the Government must declare its commitment not only to a viable car industry, but to an unsubsidized and internationally competitive British Leyland. (p. 131)

Commercial viability was also the stated aim of American Government aid to the auto industry. For instance, Chrysler's loan guarantees were linked to Chrysler's meeting certain goals toward cost reductions and financing; union concessions and additional private funding from Chrysler's banking and insurance creditors were among the mandated preconditions.

That both governments emphasized viability of firms helps to explain several heretofore puzzling features of government involvement in the industry.

One surprising feature of policy similarity was that both the United States and Great Britain (as well as Western Germany and Canada) have negotiated a series of limited quotas with the Japanese, even though "status quo" quotas do nothing to restore lost production, employment, and government revenues. Quotas only limit future damage, and do nothing to reverse state accounts losses stemming from lost employment. What quotas do, however, is "improve the financial position of domestic firms" as domestic "manufacturers... take advantage of reduced competition to raise their prices."[182] And, by keeping quotas temporary, governments maintain some incentive for auto firms to become more efficient as resumed competition looms (in theory) in the near furture. In addition to providing an incentive for productive efficiency, "voluntary" short-term quotas also avoid the risk of a general trade war, a war sure to damage international producers like Ford and GM.

Another, more puzzling, feature of the similarity of government policy is that neither government has interfered with either the "sourcing" (purchase of component parts) or the "captive importing" (sale of company-built foreign cars) policies of the auto firms. Allowing firms to decide on levels of imports is especially puzzling with regard to Britain, as between 40 and 50 percent of the cars sold by Ford, GM, and Talbot in Britain are imported. These imports total more than a third of British car imports, and have contributed substantially to the run-down of the British industry. The British Government has also raised little objection to the high Japanese "content" of the Acclaim, a car jointly produced in Britain by BL and Honda. The American Government has also not interfered with Ford, GM, or Chrysler's policies (though some of the proposed domestic content legislation would, if passed, impose penalties for importing non-American–built cars and parts).[183] This puzzle vanishes with the realization that corporate profitability is seen as the way out of the Government's financial dilemma, and internationalization of production (especially for a small market like Britain's) is essential for economies of scale, and thus for profitability. The paradox is that the solution arrived at by both governments (firm profitability and autonomy) seems to result in American and British auto firms' locating a substantial part of their production outside the home markets.

The emphasis on commercial viability in the context of the costs to the state also helps to explain the government induced rationalizations of the auto companies. One example of induced rationalization was the Corporate Average Fuel Economy (CAFE) standards imposed on American auto manufacturers in order to reduce America's demand for oil following the first oil crisis. Companies whose CAFE exceeded the standards were to have paid fines that were prorated to the degree of deviation from the standards.[184] Company autonomy was preserved as the strategies of how the companies were to achieve the mandated CAFE was left to corporate management, a management bitterly opposed to the CAFE. Ironically, without this two- or three-year "head start" on the technical requirements for increased fuel efficiency mandated by Congress, the auto industry would have been in much more serious trouble after the oil price increase associated with the revolution in Iran. Other illustrations of state induced rationalizations include performance requirements for further government aid to Chrysler (U.S.) and BL, government induced wage reductions, and tax inducements (depreciation allowances and investment tax credits) for the purchase of labor saving machinery. That these rationalizations would ultimately lead to a reduced labor force was understood by government policymakers, but was deemed necessary to achieve productivity levels approximating those of the most efficient producers.[185]

The emphasis on viability also helps to explain why government assistance in the United States and Great Britain permitted firms to maintain market autonomy, and sought, once the problems of market failure had been solved, to end direct government intervention. In the U.S., tax assistance was made available to industry as a whole, in keeping with the CBO's recommendation, and the quotas and loan guarantees were fixed-term. In Britain, state involvement with many loss-making firms was deeper in that the Government owns them. Nonetheless, following Thatcher's 1979 electoral victory, the Conservatives announced a policy of "privatization;" that is, the selling off to private investors of state-owned companies. So far, sales of Government assets have totaled only £1.8 billion from 1979 to 1983. (The bulk of the value of these sold assets have been energy company assets.) An intention to sell off the profitable parts of all state industries, including BL, has been announced, though only the sale of Jaguar has been consummated.[186]

The emphasis on viability is not necessarily now a fixed feature of American and British public policy. We need to remember that this policy similarity has its roots in a conjunction of four elements, two of which were (more or less) specific to the auto industry[187] and two of which are part of the larger political economy.[188] If these elements no longer reinforce each other, similarity might evaporate, and traditional (divergent) policies reappear. For instance, commitment to profitability did not prevent the Conservative Government from blocking BL's sale to Ford or GM's purchase of Leyland and Rover. Neither did costs to the Treasury induce the Conservatives to settle the very expensive miner's strike. The specific problems of the auto industry were both cyclical (a downturn in economic activity) and structural (a relocation of production to other countries). The coincidence of these cyclical and structural factors magnified the costs to governments of industrial decline. As the world economy recovers, part of the economic pressure on governments will be reduced; partial policy divergence is a probable outcome.

Extending the Argument

My purpose here is to test my argument in a new context to see if this argument about public policy similarity is generalizable beyond the automobile industries of the U.S. and Great Britain. That is, having generated some hypotheses through case comparisons, I will now test to see if Western capitalist governments demonstrate common patterns of public policy toward their firms in general, and, if so, when?

If, as the old saying goes, the tax code is the economic constitution of a society, then the corporate tax code should define the relationship between a government and what few would disagree is in aggregate the most powerful economic institution of market society, the private firm. This institution is assumed by those working in both the neo-Pluralist and the neo-Marxist tradition to dominate government actions toward it, and this dominance is held to be the result of the incentives governments face in modern democratic capitalism, both in the United States and abroad. If this assumption is sound, then we should be able to measure the development of common trends among capitalist societies regarding corporate taxation, should there be any. What is of interest here is not just the changes in the taxes firms pay to governments, but the attempt by governments to redirect the behavior of firms to increase investment by embedding various deduction provisions in the corporate tax code. Focusing on the balance between corporate taxation and firm investment is also useful because the many discussions of trade and competition/industrial policies have obscured the role of taxation systems in protecting and promoting domestic firms in a variety of countries, including the United States. I believe that, in so far as we do find similar policies, these will be the policies of subsidy. I will examine the timing of changing in depreciation and tax credits found in the corporate taxation codes among Western governments in an effort to test my argument about policy similarity.

How do governments' tax treatments of firm investment speak to the issue of policy similarity? I have argued that, in the automobile sector, government policies sought to promote profitable firms through the subsidy of some of the firms' costs while preserving autonomy of firms, even at the expense of government employment and fiscal policies. The study of corporate taxation provides a clear test of this hypothesis because the tax code provisions regulate the

TABLE 4.16
Corporate Taxation as a Percentage of GDP

Country	1965	1970	1975	1980	1983
Britain	2.18	3.46	2.22	2.77	4.10
Canada	3.93	3.60	4.50	3.72	2.46
France	2.47	1.87	1.59	2.14	1.91
Germany	2.47	1.87	1.59	2.07	1.92
Japan	4.07	5.18	4.34	5.65	5.44
United States	4.16	3.79	3.20	3.09	1.60

Source: OECD, Revenue Statistics, 1965–1984.

tax treatment of investment through the embedding of incentives in the code. Hence, the tax code will frame the choices firms will make regarding the organization of production.

As with government policies toward the automobile industry, we start with a position of clear-cut policy divergence. The levels of corporate taxation varied substantially among Western governments and, despite what I will argue is a common trend regarding capital allowances, these difference continue. Table 4.16 gives some indication of the divergences among capitalist countries with regard to levels of corporate taxation.

In the following section, I will create a measure of tax policy toward firms, and will employ statistical procedures to analyze the relationship among tax policy, changes in the level of economic activity, and the taxes firms pay. The data I will use in developing this argument are drawn from aggregated corporate tax returns of nonfinancial enterprises from four countries; the United States, Great Britain, West Germany, and Japan. I conclude from the results of the study that we do find similar outcomes regarding changes in taxes paid by private firms to these governments. The central finding is that, since 1978, these countries increase the subsidy of the capital investments of their domestic firms during periods of economic downturn. We find no common pattern during better economic times. Prior to 1978, government taxation of corporations also demonstrated a common pattern, but the pattern was that the "investment deductions minus taxation" ratio I create rose in periods of increasing economic activity, and declined during periods of decreasing economic activity. That implies that the tax code during the 1969–1977 period served the Keynesean function of an automatic stabilizer.

Several Hypotheses

As I noted above, the purpose of this analysis is to test several hypotheses about corporate taxation policies so as to ascertain:

1. if policy similarity among nations regarding incentives in the corporate tax code and firm investment can be demonstrated;
2. if so, under what circumstances; and
3. if changing levels of taxation-investment are the result of discretionary actions by governments.

My hypotheses are that:

1. as economies turn down,[189] democratic capitalist governments will provide increasing financial aid to firms through investment incentives in the corporate taxation system;
2. as the economies turn up, we will see no consistent cross-national pattern regarding the taxation of firms; and
3. changes in levels of taxation will result partly from the previous year's discretionary government action, as well as from automatic effects built into the structure of the tax code.

In short, Western capitalist nations aid the capital investment of their private firms by providing subsidies in economically difficult times. We will not see a common pattern in good economic times as governments return to other (divergent) policy goals put aside during economic downturns.

Background

Why should governments alter their tax codes so as to encourage their domestic firms to increase capital investments?[190] The argument for the benefits to firms of investment incentives can be illustrated simply. Because of the discount value of money, a dollar paid to you today is worth more than a dollar paid to you next year: you might put that dollar to productive use and earn one year's return on it. The traditional method of depreciating the cost of capital investment is the straight line (or historic cost) method in which a company will deduct a fixed percentage of the cost of capital investment on its accounts—10 percent over 10 years, for example.[191] When depreciation allowances are accelerated, the rental cost of capital is reduced because the cost of capital investment is returned to the investor sooner—the investing firm might be able to deduct 30 percent of the total investment during the first year instead of 10 percent. This will in theory lower the "hurdle rate" beyond which firms will undertake new investments. (See the discussion in the previous chapter on financial theory.) By reducing the costs of new investments only, governments will increase the capital stock, both now and in the future. (Hall and Jorgenson, p. 59)

The link between capital investment and changes in depreciation and investment tax credits has been extensively explored. According to Hall and Jorgenson, the results of their research show that:

> tax policy has been highly effective in changing the level and timing of investment expenditures.... The adoption of accelerated methods for depreciation and the reduction in depreciation lifetimes for tax purposes increased investment expenditures substantially.... the investment tax credit [also] has been a potent stimulus to the level of investment... (p. 11)

Hall and Jorgenson found that changes in the levels of corporate taxation per se did not influence rates of investment by firms: "reduction in the [corporate] tax rate had a small but clearly negative impact on the level of investment." (p. 60) Davies notes that more recent work supports the claims made by Hall and Jorgenson.

> If the investment stimulus per dollar of revenue loss [to the Treasury] is the criterion for judging, both [investment tax] credit and deprecia-

tion are superior to tax rate reduction. The former can easily be limited to new investment, but a reduction in the rate would apply to income from all capital, new and old. Ceteris paribus, accelerated depreciation increases the rate of return on investments and tends to favor assets with a long life. The credit also enhances [firm] profitability but tends to discriminate in favor of short-lived capital. (p. 141)

Apart from empirical studies, the field of corporate finance accepts as a maxim the importance of depreciation allowances and investment tax credits in influencing firm investment. In a concise exposition of the neo-classical theory of investment, Przeworski and Wallerstein(1985) demonstrate that, given an existing level of corporate taxation, depreciation and investment tax credits, and not the effective corporate tax rate, will influence the level of firm investment. The following equation illustrates the optimal level of investment (K^*) needed to produce the rate of return on investments (R'), under conditions of equilibrium. (The full derivation of this equation is to be found in Auerbach, (pp. 912–917.)[192]

$$R' \ (K^*) = (r + \delta) \ [(1 - k - \mu z) \div (1 - \mu)]$$

where

r = rate of interest
δ = per unit replacement rate of capital (economic depreciation)
k = per unit rate of investment tax credit
z = discounted value of future depreciation charges (tax depreciation)
μ = nominal tax rate

The right hand side of the equation is the user cost of capital; the tax treatment of a firm's investment is found in the ratio,

$$[(1 - k - \mu z) \div (1 - \mu)].$$

Put another way, in terms of taxes, $(1 - k - \mu z)$ is the marginal cost to the firm of an additional unit of investment, and $(1 - \mu)$ is the

marginal gain to the firm of that same unit. Hence, looking only at
the tax side of investment, absent taxation, or in the presence of any
tax rate such that $k + \mu z = \mu$,

$$\frac{\text{marginal cost}}{\text{marginal gain}} = 1 = \frac{1 - k - \mu z}{1 - \mu}.$$

Mathematically, it follows that increasing the value of $(k + \mu z)$ will
decrease the marginal cost of investment and induce higher investment on the part of firms.[193]

The reader should note that the neoclassical model of investment
makes a distinction between two types of depreciation: as capital
allowances for purposes of taxation (μz), and as economic depreciation (δ) or the per unit economic replacement rate of capital. Economic depreciation measures loss of value of a firm's capital assets
through normal wear and tear, and is used by firms to calculate the
costs of equipment in the final price of products; δ's value is exog-
enous to public policy, and will not be addressed in this book. The
accounting rate of capital replacement (μz) and the economic rate
of capital replacement (δ) are very unlikely to coincide.[194] Stating
the obvious, the values of μz and k are political choices that governments make regarding the composition of the productive forces
of a society. The choice governments make about the value of the
ratio, $[(1 - k - \mu z) \div (1 - \mu)]$, will strongly influence firm behavior.[195] [All the depreciation data reported later in this analysis
are accounting depreciation (μz), not economic depreciation (δ).]

We have, therefore, both theoretical and empirical reasons for believing that governments can increase the total level of capital investment in a society through use of investment policies. The original
question, "why should governments do this?" is not, however, answered by demonstrating that governments can increase firm investment. The argument that governments should encourage capital
investment is built upon an assumption—that an increase in capital
investment will lead to an increase in economic growth and, presumably, a profitable private sector. Taken at face-value, this as-

sumption does not appear to be sound. Most theories of economic growth concur with the neoclassical orthodoxy that "the marginal product of capital . . . is positive for all levels of the capital labor ratio," but that capital investment is subject to diminishing returns. That is, $f'(k) > 0$ for all k, but $f''(k) < 0$ for all k. Therefore, subsidizing capital investment in a highly develped economy like that of the United States might not be an economically efficient policy, given the opportunity costs involved.[196]

Several factors, I think, have induced governments to overcome this objection, and to subsidize capital investment. The first is that capital is seen as being a proxy measure for technological innovation, which is held to be beneficial. Another consideration is that accelerating depreciation allowances is one method by which governments may subsidize firms (thereby, one hopes, increasing their "competitiveness") without violating the rules of GATT. Of greatest importance is the belief that substituting capital for labor increases productivity, a belief founded in "empirical studies [that] support the idea that as relatively larger amounts of investment increase the capital to labor ratio, a nation's real national product and per capita income grow." (Davies, p. 9)[197]

Though other objections have been raised,[198] Western governments, both of the left and of the right, have introduced some form of investment credit/accelerated depreciation allowances so as to induce higher rates of investment.[199] Other forms of government subsidies (and indeed rates of taxation) are generally dwarfed by the depreciation allowances. For instance, industrial assistance to all British firms under sections 7 and 8 of the Industry Acts totals somewhat less than £5 billion pounds from 1972 to 1981; the British firms in the OECD survey (the largest 1500 firms) received depreciation credit of approximately £45 billion pounds during the same period.[200] American firms claimed $228 billion in depreciation allowances in 1984 alone, $54.5 billion of which was estimated to be investment subsidy.[201] The Office of Management and Budget has estimated the cost during fiscal 1985 of the various depreciation and investment credit "tax breaks" to be $61.5 billion.[202]

Some economists may argue that, if governments really wanted to increase capital investment, governments should then do away with the corporate tax entirely—investment will be an economic decision only—R' (K^*) = r + δ.[203] Corporate taxation has long been the *bête noire* of many economists: double taxation, discouragement of investment, inequitable shifting of tax burdens, inequitable treatment of industries and firms are among the criticisms levied against the corporate tax. Nonetheless, in the United States and all other major industrial countries, corporate profits are taxed now and will likely continue to be taxed. One simple reason for the persistence of this tax is "that there is income there that can be taxed."[204] Ending the corporate tax would entail serious loss of revenues to treasuries. Another reason advanced for not eliminating the corporation tax is that the tax reductions would apply to all capital investment, both new and old, thereby reducing a firm's incentive to increase their current levels of investment. The investment tax credits and the accelerated depreciation allowances would selectively induce new firm investment without depriving the treasuries of a major source of revenue.

In summary, the depreciation allowances and investment tax credits are widely believed to promote additional firm investment independent of the existing rates of corporate taxation. The relationship between depreciation allowances and taxation can be seen as a measure of public policy toward private firms.

Measure

How then can we measure similarity so as to test my hypothesis? Ideally, the most satisfactory way would be to create from publicly available data a model of the corporate tax code of each country, and link changes in the code to changes in economic activity and to the way firms actually responded to these changes. Unfortunately, this approach is extremely difficult.[205] Aid to firms is sometimes treated as confidential information; the British government does not release some types of aid data on the grounds of commercial confidentiality. Another more serious problem is that in some nations civil servants and politicians are reputed to have substantial discretion concerning aid to firms, the data firms need to report to public bodies, and the degree to which firms need to comply with guidelines. Yet another problem, in the cases of the United States and Great Britain, is that the corporate tax code is not neutral among firms and their industries, so that taxes paid by equally profitable companies will vary widely; King and Fullerton report the presence of 81 effective company tax rates in Great Britain during the 1970s.[206] If these problems were not enough, the tax returns of corporations are ultimately a matter of interpretation and litigation, a fact that does not sit well with any attempt to model the tax code.[207] Last, but far from least, the problem of the absence of comparable data, which plagues cross-national research generally, are severe here. For instance, data that match the neoclassical model of investment (e.g. per unit pre-tax profit, per unit post-tax profit) are available for the United States (in the *Survey of Current Business*) but not for the other countries under consideration.

A rougher test of my hypothesis is available. The starting point of my analysis is that, whatever measures I adopt, they must be specific to firms.[208] The private economy consists of firms, and such important variables of analysis as competitiveness, return on investment, economies of scale, etc. are primarily firm specific. The aggregate macroeconomic data used in analyzing national economies rarely reflects the importance of firms as units of analysis. This lack of firm specific data can produce distortions in analysis. For example, Japanese economic policy is generally firm or conglomerate (*Keiretsu*) based, with the government and society frequently bearing the cost of negative externalities produced by firms: hence, analysis of aggregate Japanese data tells us little about Japanese firms. Generally, firms are "healthier" than the overall economic indicators suggest, especially as government policies have had an increasingly microeconomic focus since the mid-1970s.[209]

The most nearly standardized cross-national aggregate firm data are to be found in the "Statement of Income and Changes in Net

Worth of Non-Financial Corporations, Table E,2/N" published annually by the Organization for Economic Cooperation and Development under the title *NonFinancial Enterprise Statements*.[210] This volume is the third part of the Financial Statistics of the OECD series.

Non-Financial Enterprise Statements aggregates the annual reports of nonfinancial enterprises in most OECD countries, and does so in a largely standardized form: the United Nation's *System of National Accounts* is used whenever possible. The American data are drawn from a universal sample; the top hundreds of firms are aggregated for the U.K., West Germany, and Japan.[211] Some countries do not report these data. Of the seven major economies, Canada and Italy do not report their firms' financial returns, and the data for France are based on sample surveys, which vary from year to year. The data from smaller economies are not useful in this study as the economies are not large enough to offset the bias in measurement introduced by the financial effects of several large firms. The data begin in 1969 and, as of this writing, are available for each of the major countries at least through 1984.

The data are reported in balance sheet form. "Gross Product at Factor Cost" is the lead entry, and all other items are substracted from it. After deducting "Wages and Social Charges," we are left with Gross Trading Profit. Gross Trading Profit is overwhelming composed of depreciation (μz), taxes actually paid, dividend payments, interest payments, retained income, and statistical discrepancies. Since these first five elements constitute Gross Trading Profit, the value of the ratio, by definition, approximates 1.

$$\frac{\text{dividend} + \text{interest} + \text{depreciation} + \text{retained income} + \text{taxation}}{\text{Gross Trading Profit}} \approx 1$$

This overall ratio, spread over the universe of firms, remains unchanged by definition.

Depreciation allowance and taxation are, in these data, the primary expressions of public policy toward firms. For each country, depreciation means capital allowances, or the cost of investment that

governments allow firms to deduct from the calculation of profitability.[212] Here, I am interested only in the tax treatment of a firm's
investment, not in economic depreciation per se.

I believe that changes in the balance between depreciation allowances and taxation reveals much about the direction of government
investment policy toward firms. Of course, the raw data, reported in
the current value of the currency of the home firms, is of little use:
we need some control for the effects of inflation and of the business
cycle.

To overcome these problems, I have created a ratio measure of the
taxation relationship between governments and firms. The measure
is:

$$\frac{\text{Depreciation allowances } - \text{ taxes actually paid}}{\text{Gross trading profit } - \text{ (net retained income)}} \approx z_t$$

I believe that this ratio measure has a number of virtues in analyzing cross-national trends in government policy toward firms. First,
because the OECD has reported nearly standard data for each country,
the ratio solves many of the problems of equivalence that plague
comparative research—here, comparable data are reported using similar units of analysis.

The measure also controls for the effects of inflation because all
units are reported in current value of the home country's currency.
We will discover the percentage value, not the absolute value, of the
relationship between depreciation and taxation. The measure also
allows for some account to be taken of changes in the business cycle.
As Pechman has noted, net retained income, but not corporate taxation, are accounted as automatic stabilizers in the economy. (During
more profitable years, corporations will retain more income; during
less profitable years, corporations will retain less income.) By subtracting net retained income from gross trading profit, the denominator will remain relatively stable. Because of lags in depreciation
(costing capital over a number of years) and taxation (deferred taxation, tax carry forwards), the numerator also will demonstrate some

stability in the presence of business cycle changes. Hence, all things being equal (that is, no changes in tax policy), the value of this ratio should change little from year to year.

The measure does have some limitations. It is not strictly comparable to the neoclassical model of investment that is summarized by Przeworski and Wallerstein, although the measure does contain the "theoretically relevant" categories. The data are aggregate data, not per unit data. We also have no figure for the investment tax credit (k); "taxes actually paid" includes the effects of the investment tax credit— $\Sigma(\mu - k)$.

Nonetheless, the data I will use in this analysis is roughly equal to $[\mu z - (\mu - k)]$. Hence, change in government investment and tax policy will be reflected in change in the value of this relationship

In summary, the measure

$$\frac{\text{Depreciation allowances} - \text{taxes actually paid}}{\text{Gross trading profit} - \text{(net retained income)}} = z_t$$

is a measure of the income firms are able to shield via their tax forms through the use of investment incentives. In assessing the overall levels of corporate taxation, we need to understand that taxation is determined not only by the tax rates but also by the deductions firms are permitted to take. By granting deductions, governments seek to direct a firm's behavior to activities sought by the government. So, in the case of the depreciation allowance, firms are permitted to "cost" their capital investments at rates chosen by governments. If governments wish to increase firm investments, they can provide incentives for firms to do so by increasing the capital depreciation allowances. The numerator of the relationship is that part of gross trading profit where governments have an impact on private firms. What is of interest here is not taxes paid, but the redirection of profit to investment through the incentives of the tax code.

In essence, I am arguing that changes in this ratio represent changes in the balance between taxation and subsidy. A systematic increase in the value of this relationship is a subsidy. A systematic decrease in the value of this relationship is a tax. No change in its value is a situation of neutrality.

The primary virtue of this ratio measure is that, regardless of the starting point of each country, I can measure systematic *change* in governments' investment policies (that is, depreciation deductions permitted minus takes actually paid) by measuring change in the value of this relationship. My dependent variable, changes in depreciation minus taxation, will be the first difference of the above ratio. That is, I am measuring year to year *changes* in the taxes paid by corporations. Hence,

$$z_t - z_{t-1} = D^1_t = Y$$

is our appropriate measure of changes in corporate taxation. By measuring *changes*, I can examine trends in investment policy, even though the overall levels of corporate taxation are very different.

Assuming firms (on balance) act rationally, $z_t - z_{t-1} = D^1_t = Y$ will be a reflection of changes in the incentives firms find in the tax code. That is, Y is a measure of the response of firms to changes in public policy, and is therefore an endogenous measure of changes in public policy. I am measuring the cross-national similarities of public policies at a distance. This is a necessary (albeit regrettable) consequence of the inability to model the tax codes of these countries directly.

In the study of the automobile industry, I argued that changing economic circumstances determined when it was that democratic capitalist governments would exhibit common patterns of public policy: economic prosperity would be associated with policy divergence and a return to nationally specific styles of regulation; decreasing economic activity will be associated with similar strategies to promote firm prosperity. Given this argument, one of my independent variables needs to measure change in the rate of economic activity. Unlike much of the previous work done on the relationship between government policies and economic activity [e.g., Cameron (1978, 1982); Katz, Mahler, and Franz(1983)], here I am not trying to assess the effects of government policy on economic activity. Rather, I am attempting to account for the timing and direction of government policies with reference to upturns and downturns in the economy.[213]

As a measure of this independent variable, change in the growth rate of economic activity, I have adopted the Second Difference of Gross Domestic Product (in real terms). The first difference is calculated as follows:

$$[(GDP_t - GDP_{t-1}) \div GDP_{t-1}] \times 100 = D_t^{1}{}_t.$$

The second difference is then calculated:

$$D_t^{1} - D_{t-1}{}^{1} = D_t^{2} = X.^{214}$$

The values of X have been dichotomized into dummy variables corresponding to upturns and downturns in the economy.[215]

The second difference of GDP is useful here for several reasons.[216] First, the second difference measures acceleration and deceleration in the economy, something of interest to economists and managers in investment planning, and to politicians and civil servants in budgeting. The second reason for using second difference data is that Japan has had only one year (1974) in the last 30 where the value of its first difference of GDP was negative. In order to measure the response of the Japanese government to changing economic conditions, I needed a measure of relative economic growth, and the second difference of GDP accomplishes this purpose.

One important point of note is the influence of X on Y, all other things being equal. Changes in economic activity will tend to affect this ratio, but the effects will not be systematic. Hence, absent a common cross-national pattern of public policies regarding taxation and depreciation, regressing X on Y should produce insignificant coefficients. Dividend payments and interest payment are noncyclical, tending to remain at previous levels even when Gross Trading

Profit falls because of changes in the business cycle, and vice versa. Both depreciation allowance claims and taxation exhibit some cyclicality in real terms (though not necessarily in relationship to Gross Trading Profit after net retained income has been subtracted from it), tending to fall during economic downturns. The *difference*, however, between the percentages of trading profit (once net retained income has been subtracted) accounted for by depreciation and accounted for by taxation should not change systematically. *Ceteris paribus,* my expectation is that the value of Y will remain relatively stable in the absence of tax changes.[217]

The result from the United States in 1982 is the case that tests the rule. The 1981 Economic Recovery Act contained, among other things, some provisions that enabled unprofitable corporations to sell unusable tax deductions to profitable corporations.[218] The rate of rate of change for the American Gross Domestic Product was − 5.3%, the fourth lowest value of X in the data set. The Y value for 1982 was .115 (or roughly $46 billion more aid to firms in 1982 than in 1981); this was the fourth largest Y value in the data set. But, only the introduction by the Reagan administration of the sale of tax credits, a highly controversial (and subsequently repealed) action, and other "tax breaks," produced this result.

I have created a second independent variable, changes in public policy. The direct measure of public policy changes (Z) was created from a number of public and private accounting sources. I scored a change in tax or depreciation rules as a 1 if the change was intended to reduce taxation, and as a − 1 if the change was intended to increase taxation. Years of no or little change were scored with a 0. The data were lagged one year. For instance, the changes in corporate taxation introduced by the 1981 Economic Recovery Act were assigned a value of 1 in 1982. The revisions to these 1981 changes were enacted in 1982, were intended to "tighten" the depreciation rules, and were assigned a value of − 1 for 1983.[219]

Z measures government policy changes, but only from the previous year. In a sense, Z is a control variable. X captures the effect of previous government policies - the so-called "automatic" effects of tax codes. Therefore, I hypothesize that both Z and X will have effects on changes in corporate taxation.[220]

Reviewing the argument to this point, I have hypothesized that, in so far as governments have developed policy similarity with regard to aiding their firms, this similarity has been to subsidize firm investment, but only during periods of economic downturn. Using OECD data, I have created a measure of similarity of government investment policy: it is the change in a ratio of depreciation allowances minus taxation divided by gross trading profits (minus net retained income). The first difference of this measure is my dependent variable. One independent variable is change in the rate of economic growth, or the second difference of gross domestic product. A second independent variable is change in tax policy (Z). The effect of these variables will be measured through the use of regression equations: $Y = \beta_1 \text{Downturn} + \beta_2 \text{Upturn} + \beta_3 Z$.[221] I hypothesize $\beta_1 > 0$; $\beta_2 = 0$; $\beta_3 > 0$.

The assumptions that I have made include: (1) depreciation allowances and levels of corporate taxation are useful measures of the subsidy and taxation; (2) firms on balance act in an economically rational manner; (3) changes in Y due to changes in X are the result of changes in the incentives firms find in the corporate tax codes; and (4) Y has stable properties and no systematic bias.

The method I will use to conduct this investigation will employ regression analyses. The logic of the argument is that, in using pooled cross-sectional and time-series data, a statistically significant result indicates the presence of a cross-national pattern. No significant results mean no common pattern.[222] The data will be split into samples from the 1969–1977 period and from the 1978–1984 period. This will allow me to examine the stability of the relationship over time.

When using pooled cross-sectional, time-series data, some analysts argue that the use of GLS (generalized least squares) procedures rather than the more usual OLS (ordinary least squares) procedures is necessary, given the nature of time series–cross-sectional data and the assumptions made in OLS procedures.[223] The GLS estimate techniques followed here are described in White and Horsman (1985), and these follow Kmenta (pp. 512–514) and Judge, et al. (p. 518).[224] This model corrects for heteroskedasticity and autocorrelation. More efficient estimates are obtained by accounting for contemporaneously correlated residuals.

Tests

I will begin the analysis by examining the relationship between X and Y. Consider four types of associations between X and Y from a test of $Y = \beta_1$ (downturn) $+ \beta_2$ (upturn), where upturn and downturn are dummy values of change in economic activity - X. These are as follows:

1. No Association. X has no statistically significant effect on Y, which is the joint null hypothesis $- \beta_1 = 0$ and $\beta_2 = 0$ for upturn and downturns in the economy. Theoretically, this would imply no cross-national pattern whatsoever;

2. Direct Association. Y varies directly with X; a decrease in business activity produces a decrease in business investment and in tax collections, but the decrease in investment will be proportionally larger than the decrease in taxes collected. An increase in economic activity will produce a larger investment effect. We would find statistical significance in X's effect on Y; upturn's β will have a positive sign and downturn's β will have a negative sign.[225] Theoretically, this would imply that the corporate tax codes of Western nations do not function as stabilizers in the economy;

3. Inverse Association. Y varies inversely with X; upturn and downturn dummies would be statistically significantly related for all values of X, and the signs of the values of X and Y would be opposite—upturn's coefficient would be negative and downturn's coefficient would be positive. Theoretically, this result would imply that we do find a cross-national pattern in which the similar policies are aimed at stabilizing the economy; and

4. Partial Association. Y varies inversely with X, but only when X is negative—the downturn dummy is the only statistically significant effect $- \beta_1 > 0$. Theoretically, this would imply that policy similarity

occurs only during periods of economic downturn: my original hypothesis.

The equations have been constructed on the presumption that X and Y have some association. I have dichotomized the values of X into positive and negative values: dummy variables. To these dummy variables, I have added a variable, Z, a measure of the previous year's changes in taxation policy. Stating my hypotheses for Z:

ZH_0 = no effect on Y from changes in the tax code;
ZH_1 = effect on Y from changes in the tax code. A positive sign means that the policy achieved its intended effect, a negative sign means that the policy produced unintended consequences;

Z measures changes in tax policies, and the influence of Z on Y is only for the *following* year's tax results. In the second and all subsequent years, the effects of tax policies are captured in the X variable. In other words, Z represents the marginal change in the tax code; the full effects of a nation's tax regime is estimated through Y = β_1 (downturn) + β_1 (upturn).

The main regression equation is reprinted below. For all equations, p. $<.1$ is denoted by $*$; p. $<.05$ is denoted by $**$; p. $<.01$ is denoted by $***$. As noted above, because the dummy variables sum to one, the coefficient has been suppressed.

Equation #1—1969–1984

$$Y = \beta_1 X_1 + \beta_2 X_2 + \beta_3 Z$$

where

X_1 = downturn in economy (dummy)
X_2 = upturn in economy (dummy)
Z = change in tax policy

	Estimated Coefficient	Standard Error	Standardized Coefficient	T-Statistic for H_0
X_1	0.0138	0.0059	.138	2.33**
X_2	0.0125	0.0069	−.125	−2.04*
Z	0.0250	0.0073	.312	3.40***

$$R^2 \text{ (adj.)} = .34$$
$$DW = 1.84$$
$$\rho = 0.06$$
$$N = 64.0$$

The first equation's results provide mild support for hypothesis three—inverse association. The downtown dummy and the Z variable have significant coefficients (at the .05 and the .01 levels, respectively) with appropriate signs. Because these coefficients are each statistically significant, we know that that $X => Z => Y$ is not the "driving factor" in this equation; each has an independent effect.[226] The rate of corporate taxation does fall during periods of economic decline, and discretionary public policy changes by governments have a strong positive effect on taxation. We can reject the null hypothesis of no increase in corporate taxation during better economic times as the T-value of the coefficient is significant at the .05 level, and the coefficient's sign is in the expected direction. From these results, I conclude that: democratic capitalist countries do show a common pattern of subsidizing corporate investment when the economy is in decline—$\beta_1 > 0$; that discretionary government policy is effective in bringing about these changes—$\beta_3 > 0$; and that overall level of taxation rises during periods of economic upturn—$\beta_2 < 0$, though the values of the coefficients indicate that the upturn effect is substantially weaker than are those of the other two variables.

The next test is to see if the patterns in depreciation/taxation rates have changed over time. The data sample has been split: 1969–1977 and 1978–1984. 1978 was chosen as the midpoint because half the cases where $X < 0$ occurs are above and below this point. Two equations, similar to the first equation, were run for each period.

POLICY SIMILARITY

Equation #2—1969–1977

$$Y = \beta_1 X_1 + \beta_2 X_2 + \beta_3 Z$$

where

X_1 = downturn in economy (dummy)
X_2 = upturn in economy (dummy)
Z = change in tax policy

	Estimated Coefficient	Standard Error	Standardized Coefficient	T-Statistic for H_0
X_1	0.0149	0.0045	.145	3.31***
X_2	−0.0238	0.0054	−.234	−4.41***
Z	0.0488	0.0078	.597	6.23***

R^2 (adj.) = .76
DW = 1.84
ρ = 0.07
N = 36

Equation #3—1978–1984

$$Y = \beta_1 X_1 + \beta_2 X_2 + \beta_3 Z$$

where

X_1 = downturn in economy (dummy)
X_2 = upturn in economy (dummy)
Z = change in tax policy

	Estimated Coefficient	Standard Error	Standardized Coefficient	T-Statistic for H.
X_1	0.0397	0.0075	.436	5.30***
X_2	0.0052	0.0054	−.057	−0.96
Z	0.0046	0.0084	−.062	−0.54

R^2 (adj.) = .74
DW = 1.70
ρ = 0.13
N = 28

Are these different equations? I followed Pindyck and Rubinfeld procedures in testing regression coefficients. (1981, pp. 117–118). That is,

$$\frac{(ESS_r - ESS_{ur})/Q}{ESS_{ur}/(N - k)}$$

The test on the coefficients indicate that equations 2 and 3 are different equations.[227] Hence, we need to analyze these as separate periods.

The results of the two equations suggest that my hypothesis of no increase in corporate taxation during better economic times has been refuted for the 1969–1977 period, though not for the 1978–1984 period. For the former period, all the coefficients are highly significant (p. <.01) and have signs in the expected direction. No autocorrelation is present; the DW number is above the d_u threshold. We can conclude for the 1969–1977 period in these four countries that corporate taxes rose during economic upturns; corporate taxes decreased during economic downturns, though this effect is much weaker than that of the other two variables; and discretionary government action strongly and positively influenced changes in the levels of corporate taxes paid. In short, we do find policy similarity, but not of the sort that I had hypothesized.

These results are probably not surprising to those readers who were schooled in Keynesean economics and who think of corporate taxation as one element in government's macroeconomic toolchest of instruments for stabilizing and controlling the economy.[228] We do find policy similarity regarding corporate taxation, but this similarity seems to have been a Keynesean one with taxes going up as well as going down. Specific changes in depreciation rules and corporate tax rates, not only "built-in" stabilizers, strongly influenced changes in the levels of taxation: political bargaining, not bureaucratic self-regulation. Note, too, that the value of the standardized coefficient for the downturn variable is substantially smaller than that of the upturn variable, implying a secular decline in the investment/taxation ratio.

We cannot advance this argument for Keynesean similarity for the 1978–1984 period. The results from the equation 3 indicate that we cannot demonstrate that corporate taxes rise when the level of economic activity also rises—the coefficient of X_2 is not significant. Corporate taxes still fall when the economy slows - X_1's coefficient is significant (at the 99% level.) The implicit Keynesean link seems to have been broken. We also can no longer reject the hypothesis that these changes in Y are the only result of "automatic" features of the tax code—Z's coefficient is not significant. Such policy similarity we find regarding corporate taxation now occurs only during economic downturns. About corporate taxation in better economic circumstances, we find no pattern.

My interpretation of these results is that these reflect an increasing concern by governments for the "supply-side" of the economy. In essence, investment is subsidized and taxes do not automatically go up as economic activity increases. This outcome coincides with the policy recommendations of advocates of a "supply-side" economic policy, though this apparent association between policy effect and economic theory may be a coincidence.

Another aspect of the equation suggests that corporate taxation has recently come to be used as a microeconomic tool of industrial policy.[229] Paradoxically, the absence of a statistically significant effect from Z (changes in taxation policy) has persuaded me of this. As I reviewed the data from the late 1960s and early 1970s, I had no difficulty in "scoring" Z. Changes in the tax code/depreciation rules were generally "all encompassing" and fairly simple. For the data from the 1980s, assigning a value to Z became quite difficult. Changes in the tax codes were often industry, regionally, and sometimes firm specific. The American corporate tax code, for instance, had become highly discriminatory among industries.[230] I believe it is this difficulty in measuring those changes in public policy introduced by the microeconomic focus of recent corporate tax changes, and neither an absence of public policy nor its ineffectualness, that accounts for the insignificant value of Z in this period.

These results parallel some of the findings regarding the automobile industries. Prior to 1976, the British government used policies toward the automobile industry as an adjunct to its overall demand-management of the British economy, though the American government did not. Both governments adopted policies in the late 1970s and early 1980s to reinforce the financial position of firms through accelerated depreciation allowances, tax forgivenesses, export subsidies, and the like. A return to relative prosperity did not deprive these companies of these tax breaks.

This evidence suggests that one assumption of neo-Marxist and neo-Pluralist analysis—that market societies show a strong degree of policy similarity toward private firms—is partly sound in the case of corporate taxation and investment subsidies. The thesis of common patterns of public policy apparently needs to be qualified, however, to periods of economic downturn. The appropriate question seems to be when—not if—market societies demonstrate common patterns of policy.

In summary, the 1978–1984 equation suggests that policy similarity regarding corporate taxation occurs during periods of economic downturn and that this common policy is to subsidize firm investment. Taxes do not automatically rise when economic activity increases, though taxes did so rise in the 1969–1977 period, a time when changes in taxation are positively affected by discretionary public policy. In the 1978–1983 period, major changes in tax codes did not produce a measurable change in taxation.

Summary

My original question was, to what extent do we find that, cross-nationally, government aid to firms is influenced by changes in economic conditions?[231] My conclusions are straightforward. We do find some similarity among the United States, Great Britain, West Germany and Japan. The 1969–1977 and 1978–1984 periods, though, demonstrate different patterns of similarity. The early period shows that taxation increased as the level of economic activity increased, and decreased during downturns. This similarity is partly the result of discretionary changes in tax policy. We can demonstrate only the tax reduction during the 1978–1984 period. In both periods, similarity during downturns consists in the reduction by governments of the amount of capital withdrawn from private corporations.

I draw several inferences from these results. The first regards industrial policy. These four governments do have a common denominator in terms of industrial policy, and it is to subsidize the investment by firms in capital equipment. Governments have in recent years sought to promote economic growth by stimulating firm investment, thereby, one hopes, increasing the productivity of firms, lowering per-unit labor costs, and increasing overall national economic prosperity.[232] Those analysts who presume that what the United States has now is no industrial policy are much mistaken.

Second, these results seem to capture some of the shift from a concern by policymakers with macroeconomic adjustments of the economy to a concern with 'supply-side,' private-sector investment. We also find some indication that the corporate tax codes have an increasingly microeconomic focus.

Returning to the issue raised in the introduction to the book, the first-order question—does capitalism generate common structural imperatives among market societies?—seems to me to be best replaced with the second-order question—when, and under what circumstances, does capitalism do this?

Conclusion

Schumpeter could find no solution to the dilemma of capitalism—when we intervene in markets to promote short-term efficiency, we impair the long-term growth of the economy. Creeping socialism, brought about by democratic processes, resolves this contradiction, though not without producing a less innovative and less prosperous society.

For the problem of dynamic disequilibrium, modern states have evolved strategies other than the socialism defined by Schumpeter. The position of firms as the agent of society's investment has not eroded. In fact, through the tax code, the states provide investment incentives that seek to induce corporate investment while preserving firm autonomy—public control of investment has not emerged as a common pattern among capitalist countries. The tax code has vested corporations with the public function of resolving the dilemma of short-term efficiency and long-term growth. This vesting is conditional, however; we now find evidence for its presence the countries surveyed only during periods of economic downturn.

When public functions are assumed by private actors, two problems of democracy are raised—the problem of voter choices and the problem of agency.

For Schumpeter, democracy was a process whereby competing elites offered differing agendas and programs to voters, voters would choose among these elites, and the elites would then implement the agendas. Have voters in capitalist countries chosen among competing agendas and, in each country, decided during periods of economic downturn to give investment and employment functions to private firms? Or, are voters constrained in their choices in ways not foreseen by Schumpeter? Put another way, either (1) governments and voters of market societies have congruent interests with their domestic firms such that government policies give investment and employment functions to firms, or (2) (à la Lindblom) democratic capitalist governments have few other options in periods of economic downturn than to provide incentives in order to induce their firms to invest.

The problem of agency concerns the issue of how to arrange the regulation of corporate behavior so as to achieve the ends desired by the voters, assuming that voters have chosen to surrender public functions to private firms. We have no basis for assuming that the interests of corporations and the interests of society will necessarily coincide—common problems, negative externalities, nonproductive rent-seeking activity are normal occurrences. In theory, society constrains firms and individuals from engaging in harmful activities through laws—corporations are entities created by government, after all. But, what if the ability of government to regulate corporations is constrained at times?

These questions and issues will be addressed in the next two chapters.

5.
EXPLANATIONS FOR SIMILARITY

The Argument in Review

THE ARGUMENT MADE to this point in the book is that, starting from different points in the early 1970s, the American and British policies toward their industries have developed a similarity that had its origins in a crisis of market competition and took the form of similar solutions to this problem.

The common problem is as follows: Each nation's auto producers developed in a sheltered market. For different reasons, the demand profile (types of cars sold) of the markets shifted toward those prevailing in the rest of the world, and the barriers to auto imports were thereby reduced. It was as though the barriers of an ecologically unique environment had been breached, and the indigenous forms were maladapted to their now changed environment. The result was that American and British auto makers were at a competitive disadvantage within their own markets to Japanese and German automakers. To regain market shares lost to foreign competition required extraordinary capital expenditures at a time when relatively little long-term or equity financing was available. This problem was especially acute for smaller producers—Chrysler and British Leyland. This is so because, although the costs of rationalization and new product developments are similar for the large and small companies, the internal resources and the credit worthiness of the small companies (measured by the "gearing" or debt/equity ratio) are not. Thus, with the financial markets and banks geared at the time for short-term lending, Chrysler and BL had difficulty raising capital, especially as the prevailing rates of return in 1981 from London Eurodollars funds was 16.5% and from the U.S. Federal Funds 16.38%. In the changing oligopolistic market of autos, smaller firms were squeezed out of the capital markets.[1]

The governments had a limited set of policy options with which to respond to the likelihood of the bankruptcy of one or several auto firms. Both nations restricted the access of Japanese competitors to their markets via a quota system. Both nations sought to redress the underlying problems of the auto industry by attempting to direct the rationalization of the production process and encouraging the development of competitive products, while preserving the the market autonomy of the firms. The states did this in the course of bargaining over the allocation of resources and distribution of the costs of rationalization with management and labor. In both cases, the states absorbed part of the cost of the adjustment process, and in part the state forced the others (principally labor) to absorb the rest. The final aim of the governments was to encourage a commercially viable industry.

The states also rejected several options. First, they avoided the demand stimulation of the economy, even though increased consumer demand might have alleviated the auto slumps of 1974–76 and 1979–82. They did this for several reasons. As the British discovered in the 1960s, an increase in demand frequently sucks in imports, precipitating balance of payments problems. Of greater significance was the shift away from Keynesean economics by governments, and the development of an "expectations trap." The premise of the problem is the by now widely accepted monetarist position that an increase in demand sparked by the government (via a growth in the money supply, or an increase in government expenditures without tax increases, or a cut in taxes without cuts in expenditures) is inherently inflationary. This then discourages business investment and, to avoid this, government demand stimuli should be avoided. Hence, the state policies in most OECD countries of "tight money," higher interest rates, and reduced government demand during the early 1980s were aimed at encouraging business confidence. Unfortunately, long-term investment policies (made in the expectations of future profits, growth, and productivity) were limited by low consumer demand and high real interest rates, which made it all the more difficult for heavily indebted companies like Chrysler to raise capital, thus pushing such firms toward bankruptcy.[2]

The American and British governments also chose not to engage in state planning for the auto sector, preferring instead to leave firms autonomous from the state while offering incentives for change. None of the models of state planning (socialist, cooperative, or directed) is possible at the moment given the political climate in these countries.

The socialist model—at least that articulated by the Labour Party in the 1974–75 period—would require, above all, a restriction of the ability of investors, bankers, and others to shift capital from one investment to another. State planning becomes impossible without such a restriction. Even if this were politically possible, the economic consequences would be severe. Both the U.S. and Britain have historically permitted free movements of capital, and numerous investments have been made and institutions (e.g. Lloyd's, banking services) developed on that presumption. A shift in that premise would threaten these services, produce a run on currency as divestments occurred, and threaten a loss of—at a minimum—international credit investments.[3] Britain's net earnings from the services trade alone equaled 1.7 percent of the 1982 Gross Domestic Product. For the U.K., international credit funds supplied approximately 18 percent of all British credit in 1979. The American figure was nearly 8 percent for 1978. By way of comparison, the Japanese figure in 1979 was 0.2 percent. Simply, the evolution of institutions of international capitalism in the United States and Great Britain make a socialist solution to these problems unfeasible.[4]

Several alternative forms of selective planning do exist. John Zysman describes these as (1) the state-led credit based (directed), and (2) the negotiated, bank-led (cooperative) systems of industrial adjustments. The first system (Japan, France) depends on credit controls (and loan prices) being administered (individually and discreetly) by the state. The second (West Germany) requires close linkages among government, industry, and the handful of dominant banks. Neither in the United States nor in Great Britain do the institutions for these forms of planning currently exist.[5]

Thus, the options chosen by the two countries were constrained by the institutional capacities of their political economies (and by the prevailing economic ideologies) to attempting to change both market access and distribution of costs while creating ad hoc institutions (the Chrysler Loan Guarantee Board, the National Enterprise Board) that provided aid, and granting general business assistance through the tax laws.

This last pattern, subsidizing the investment of private firms, is sometimes true of the Federal Republic of Germany and Japan as well. The congruence of tax policies among these four countries is limited, however, since 1978 to situations of economic downturn.

Explanations for State Intervention

This book has focused on a description of the development of a similarity in the United States and Great Britain with regard to automobile policies. The argument has focused on the problems to which the states responded and the policy tools they used. Little attention has yet been paid to the issue of why the states intervened, nor to which explanations of state intervention are useful for an understanding these events.

In the course of evaluating various explanations for the policy similarity, there are several I will not examine despite their great importance. These are explanations that have as their units of analysis domestic actors, institutions, bargaining processes, cultural factors, or other variables specific to a nation. As I am assuming that policy similarity is due not to chance but to some common variable or process, I will review only those explanations which do not depend on peculiar national factors but instead focus on theories which can be applied cross-nationally.

The justification for this method of analysis is appealingly simple. Imagine four different political economies (A, B, C, & D) in which we find a common policy outcome, θ. If we discover a common set of elements, α in A through D, we would attribute explanatory power to the $\alpha \rightarrow \theta$ relationship if (a) α precedes θ, and (b) no other common element or set of elements is present that has "theoretical relevance." This method allows us to escape from the "historical cure," and to look for common structural features. We otherwise remain in the domain of the ungeneralizable case study.

Obviously, a focus on domestic actors, institutions, political bargains, and other historically specific factors is crucial for most analysis in political science. Indeed, explaining policy divergence among capitalist countries requires a historical framework that examines domestic actors and interests. But as a common policy is the outcome to be explained, cross-national explanations are in order.

The standard I use in evaluating the utility of theories is whether a given theory of the state is able to accommodate the substance and direction of similarity while remaining falsifiable. I am looking for the "best fit" in terms of the expectations drawn from the theories matched to actual outcomes.

Generic, cross-national explanations for state intervention in the troubled industries of Western democracies include (a) societal pressures, (b) ideology, (c) underlying processes or problems specific to a stage of capitalism, and finally, (d) the state's own interest.

Societal Pressures

Political pressure—the economically rational voter

In the academic debates on the relationship between state and society, most writers seem to view the state's actions as either constrained or driven by some significant actors, such as the voting public or members of a class, an interest group, or a specific producer group.[6] The central point is that the politicians who govern the state act in response to some significant group in order to either gain political/electoral benefits or to avoid similar types of costs.

The "logic of political costs" argument has a number of mechanisms through which society might direct or influence state interventions. The first mechanism is through the voting process such that individual voters respond in a Downsean fashion to changes in their personal economic conditions.[7] Donald Kinder has referred to this as the "pocket-book" citizen view of democracy.[8] The argument would be that the state intervened to protect individuals from the direct consequences of in industry's decline so that the politicians who run the state would then maximize favorable electoral results. Employment and changes in real personal income are the "public goods" that the interventionist state would seek to deliver.

The second mechanism is that the voters respond positively to perceived changes in the general economic conditions (the "sociotropic citizen" in Kinder's words), not just to their personal economic positions.[9] Hence, any sectoral decline would have political ramifications for political leaders beyond those resulting from the anger of those who were personally affected. This social analogue to the Keynesean multiplier effect would take effect through the way in which the media influence the voters' perception of economic changes. The interventions by the states in the auto industry would then be seen as attempts at image-making as well as the avoidance of short-term changes in the general economic conditions.

In either case, policy similarity would be the result of democratic politics in the welfare age as politicians compete for the allegiance of voters and for political power. We would expect policy similarity not just in the United States and Great Britain, but in any democratic, industrial nation where politicians are held electorally responsible for market failures. We would also expect the propensity of states to intervene to vary in proportion to the size of the market failure.[10]

In general, the "economically rational voter" argument, especially in its "socio-tropic" version, seems to be a useful one in explaining some forms of state actions in Western democracies. But, this argument is not of much help here. One reason is that the type of state aid offered to the auto industries in both countries, and to private firms in general, was "supply-side" directed. That is, the industries gained access to capital (or to capital markets) for the purposes of making long-term investments. The time horizon of the auto industry, from investment to final product, is in years if not in decades. The time horizons for politicians are notoriously short, especially in the United States. Thus, even if there is a "political business cycle," neither long-term aid to the auto industry nor general investment subsidies fits this pattern.

Indeed, government aid induced substantial layoffs, wage reductions, and other production cost reductions, all aimed at firm profitability, not at high levels of employment. More generally, the American and British Governments seem to be subsidizing the substitution of "capital" for "labor" in the production process. Using the depreciation allowance data reported by the OECD in the *Non-Financial Enterprise* data as a proxy measure for capital, and the wages paid to employees as a proxy measure for labor, we find that, when we divide wage costs into depreciation the ratio has increased in value since the late 1960s. In the U.S., the ratio changed from .129 in 1969 to .172 in 1982, in Britain, from .167 to .257[11] I therefore conclude that the main form of state intervention did not have the broad (short-term positive) impact on the voters that we would have expected from state policies if the state were responding to this form of societal pressure. We would have expected either demand stimulation policies or high-tariff policies—policies that would protect employment.

Another problem with the voter version of the political costs explanation is that, at least in Great Britain, the voters seem to be holding governments less accountable for economic problems than they did in the past. The voters seem to sense that politicians and governments are faced with economic problems beyond their control. Thatcher's reelection in 1983, despite Britain's massive economic decline during her first Government, seems to confirm James Alt's argument that the linkage has been weakened between the economic performance of the government and the electoral responses ("declining expectations"). Certainly Thatcher and Reagan have been willing to cut state services despite potential voter anger. But, though politicians from areas most affected by the bankruptcy of auto firms (e.g., Michigan, Midlands) clearly are the target of voter pressure, the linkage on the national level is not clear.[12]

Political Pressure—Interest Groups

The argument that policy outcomes in Western democracies are the result of either the competition of general interest groups, usually aggregated into political parties (Pluralism), or the influence of a narrow range of resource-rich producer groups (Neopluralism) has informed much political theory and research in America since the Second World War. The utility of these research frameworks in explaining some types of policy outcomes is generally accepted, even by those who work within a Marxist framework.[13]

The mechanism by which interest groups exert their pressure is often said to have two aspects or faces.[14] The more visible aspect comes from the drive by interest groups to gain resources from the state or to place issues of concern to them on the state's agenda. The mechanisms through which this process occurs in (generally) noncorporatist societies like the United States and Great Britain is the mobilization of resources which are transferable into political power. Traditional pluralist analysis focuses on the mobilization of interest group members into supporters and voters of candidates who favor their cause.[15] A politician's "payoff" comes from the added support of those personally affected by his actions, a situation the outcome of which would be similar to that of the "pocket-book citizen" view of the political process.

For Neopluralist analysis, the focus is broader, and encompasses the second aspect of influence—the power to prevent issues from arising on the state's agenda. Groups can have an impact beyond their membership if they either control resources which can be translated into wider support (through campaign contributions or media advertisements) or control a critical, not easily coercible or replaceable resource central to economic growth (i.e. capital).[16] In the first instance, the mechanism of influence is mostly financial, a resource with which politicians generate support. In the second case, power is more "structural." That is, those who control or own investment resources (capital) have, in aggregate, a determining role in the level of economic activity in Western capitalist societies. If we accept the proposition that voters hold politicians responsible for the performance of the economy, then this gives capitalists and corporate managers power over political leaders. As capital (or investment funds) is a liquid and easily transferable resource, those who control capital need to be induced by policies aimed at "business confidence" into making (or maintaining) investments that lead to economic growth and, of particular importance, employment.[17] The importance of business confidence has percolated down to the electorate such that one of the measures Kinder used to assess popular satisfaction with the President is the voter's assessment of business conditions.[18]

What unites all these variants of interest group analysis is that, in the long run, political leaders find that the wishes of interest groups (including business) are translated into electoral support (or the lack of it) and political power (or its deprivation). As a result, even though the Pluralist and Neopluralist frameworks are of great use in understanding much of democratic political life, these frameworks are not of much help in understanding the development of this policy similarity. This is true since, as I have already mentioned, the type of state aid was sufficiently long-term to have little immediate (3–5 years) impact on the electorate.

Another aspect of state intervention in the auto industry (and private firms more generally) that does not fit with pluralist expectations is the extent to which labor groups in the auto industry were obliged to absorb massive layoffs and economic dislocations. The willingness of the state to refuse to shelter employees from the market consequences of industrial decline is surprising given that groups tied to labor unions, the Labour and Democratic parties, were in executive power for much of the late 1970s. This is particularly surprising given that both parties believed (and some evidence suggests) that economic growth is tied to "demand-side" policies. Even for groups that represent business interests, there does not seem to be any instrumental linkage between groups like the Confederation of British Industry and state outcomes. Finally, other interest groups have been unsuccessful in pushing the states when what is at stake is not the allocation of resources within existing institutions or political agendas, but the creation of new institutions of administration.[19]

Both the "economically rational voter" explanation and "interest group influence" depend on electoral pressure, at some level, for the mechanism of societal influence. I have argued that these perspectives are not useful here because the way in which similarity occurred does not "fit" with the expectations concerning the timing, forms, and substance of state intervention derived from either of these perspectives.

Institutional Pressures—Corporatist Institutions

Though direct or indirect electoral pressure might not have produced policy similarity, the possibility exists that previous political struggles have shaped state institutions such that the state responds to the wishes of societal actors through a process internal to the states' policy making. The agendas of the states could be so shaped by previous political struggles that issues of concern to central political actors (i.e. labor and capital) are automatically issues of concern for the state—I have already noted that welfare and other market failure costs are so embedded in state structures. As we know from Stephen Krasner's work, the capacities of governments vis-à-vis their societies vary, so it should not surprise us that the agendas of the relatively "weak" states like the U.S. should reflect societal concerns.[20]

There seems to be at least one mechanism through which this reflection might occur without reference to electoral pressure. The mechanism is corporatist institutions embedded in the state structure.

The literature on social corporatism has been described as something of a growth industry.[21] The most widely quoted definition of corporatism is that of Philippe Schmitter.

Corporatism can be defined as a system of interest representation in which the constituent units are organized into a limited number of singular, compulsory, non-competitive, hierarchically ordered and functionally differentiated categories, recognized or licensed (if not created) by the state and granted a deliberate representational monopoly within their respective categories in exchange for observing certain controls on their selection of leaders and articulation of demands and supports.[22]

In some sense, corporatist institutions are a continuation of the process of the incorporation of the members of producer groups into the political life of Western democracies begun in the nineteenth century.[23] As the sphere of the public domain has broadened to include once private matters like wage and price contracts, producer groups have found their interests "articulated" by these associations.[24] As Katzenstein shows in Small States in World Markets this process seems especially well advanced in small societies with open economic markets or in societies where wage guidelines (and hence control of wage costs) are a central concern of the state. Corporatism is then both a policy in itself and a policy-generating institutional arrangement. The oft-cited advantage of corporatist institutions is that they channel political participation, and avoid pluralist stagnation.

This explanation is of little help to us since corporatist institutions did not emerge as part of the solution to the auto industry crisis in either country. In fact, part of the similarity occurred through the reduction of labor's voice in the restructuring of the industry. This is not surprising as the conditions for corporatist institutions are present weakly, if at all, in the United States and Great Britain. For instance, despite a long history of (voluntary) tripartism in Great Britain, labor organizations (with scores of competing unions) and business organizations remain neither ordered nor compulsory.[25] Interestingly, in the case of Chrysler's near bankruptcy, when the American state intervened, it forced upon management and labor wage restraints/cutbacks and management consulting agreements more reminiscent of European corporatist patterns. These arrangements have not been accepted by Ford or by GM, and Chrysler showed some reluctance in allowing the UAW's new leader, Owen Bieber, onto its corporate board.

The Functional Needs of Capitalism

Those who work within the Marxist framework have a number of potential society-centered explanations for policy congruence among Western democracies. One of the dominant variants of recent neo-Marxist analysis understands state policy action within Western democracies as a product of the functional requirement that the state maintain the conditions for legitimation of the existing political and economic order (the widespread acceptance of a regime as just) at the same time the state maintains the conditions necessary for capital accumulation (high rates of profits and investments). In short, policy actions by a state are caused by the anticipated outcomes.[26]

In the case of capitalist states, the requisite outcomes are the maximizing of both popular support and a profitable and growing capitalist sector. Over time, the aggregation of state policies aimed at legitimation and accumulation becomes a capitalist regime or structure.[27] Within this structure, policies frequently have irreconcilable or contradictory goals and methods. For instance, in times of economic crisis, maintaining profits for industry (accumulation) may be possible only by squeezing wages and transfer payments, producing varying levels of dissatisfaction with the state among those who have been squeezed. In order for the state to reconcile these potentially contradictory aims, most neo-Marxists agree that the democratic state requires a degree of autonomy from individual interests or particular capitals.[28] That is, the state achieves this modern day "General Will" (capitalism's general interests) by ignoring the "Will of All" (the specific interests of the capitalist class). Most neo-Marxists also agree that, should these requisites of the capitalist state prove to be incompatible, the accumulation function will take precedence, and the "facade of bourgeois democracy" will yield.[29]

The logic of this argument then is that state policies are a product of the dynamic between the functions of legitimation and accumulation, and that state policies will change in order to maximize these as the political and economic parameters of the state change. Thus, as the needs of the capitalist state change, so too will the policies. Generally, these policies will have accumulation as the central focus since, under capitalism, the state has an "institutional self-interest" in the accumulation process.[30] As we have seen under our previous discussion of "business confidence" and the power of the business classes, without steady accumulation (investments), economic growth and popular support for the capitalist state soon diminish. Since policy similarity would be understandable as resulting from this dialectic of these state functions, we would expect similarities in state outcomes any time capitalist states were confronted by common problems. Similarity, following from this argument, may then be generated from state functions. As capitalist states have common functions, when the world economy undergoes an economic downturn, we would expect the various capitalist states to seek to restore the accumulation process.

All the policy actions that the American and British states took to restructure their auto industries are describable in terms of accumulation and legitimation. The long-term nature of state aid can be understood as being aimed at guaranteeing the profitability and survival of a key sector of the economy. The heavy costs of the restructuring which accrued to labor can be seen as part of the effort at guaranteeing accumulation by reducing wage costs and improving efficiency, even though the social costs to the state increased and auto labor unions increased their political pressure. The opposition to state intervention by segments of the business community can be explained away as a manifestation of the particular interests of some fraction of capital. In fact, the "functional needs of capitalism" explanation has provided the best "fit" for describing this congruence process yet. I will argue in the final section that the tradeoff between legitimation and accumulation is an important issue in any normative discussion of politics—what ought the democratic capitalist state do?

Nonetheless, this explanation is unsatisfactory for an understanding of the form and direction of similarity. The main problem is that functional explanations are incommensurable with the kinds of evidence and issues we discuss here. The neo-Marxist framework provides us with categories of understanding about which institutions, processes, and causal structures are important. It provides us with a language of description, not a series of falsifiable hypotheses.[31] If the policy similarity had been in the direction of the creation of institutions of labor incorporation, the building of total tariff barriers to imports, and the use of policies of demand stimulation, we would not then reject the neo-Marxist framework, as we would the argument that I will later advance; we would instead be able to talk about state actions in terms of the legitimation function of the state as well as the need to protect domestic capital. As a result, this framework gives us no basis for explaining why the state intervenes in one case and not in another. We cannot explain a similar type of policy intervention in the auto industries of the 1970s.

In part, the problem in applying the neo-Marxist framework to the issue of congruence is rooted in the the nature of functional explanations, under which category most neo-Marxists explanations fall.[32] First, functional explanations are generally teleological. As Percy Cohen has written,

> A doctrine or theory is said to be teleological if it explains the existence of some phenomenon by asserting that it is necessary in order to bring about some consequence: more specifically, teleological theories are said to explain one thing by showing that is has beneficial consequences for another. The principal objection to this is that the explanation treats an effect as a cause.[33]

This is no problem if action is intended or purposive. But, as we have seen in our discussion of interest groups, no instrumental linkkage can be traced between interest associations (capital) and the state.[34] This leaves the claim that the capitalist state acts for capital even without links to the capitalists, a claim which is necessarily unverifiable. This claim is a little like Marx's claim that "No social order ever perishes before all the productive forces for which there is room in it have developed; and new, higher relations of production never appear before the material conditions of their existence have matured in the womb of the old society itself."[35] It quite possibly might be true, but we can only know so well after the fact, if at all.

In this section, we have briefly reviewed several explanations which posit that state policy outcomes are generated from societal pressure, be the mechanism political pressure, institutional pressure or the functional requirements of a system. Although each variant of the societal pressures explanation has been found by other researchers to have descriptive (and sometimes) predictive utility in the understanding of state outcomes. I have argued that the expectations we draw from the use of these explanations either do not fit the evidence of this case, or, in the case of neo-Marxist analyses, are incommensurable with the specific problem of congruence.

Ideology

Another potential explanation for policy similarity might be the evolution of an ideology shared among the political elite of the United States and Great Britain: ideology here meaning the organizing metaphors about state, economy, and society (e.g. Conservatism). The argument does have some initial plausibility as both President Reagan and Prime Minister Thatcher (and many members of their parties) see themselves as Conservatives, are adherents of a "free market" political economy as a solution to economic problems, and are admirers of the work of Professor Milton Friedman of the University of Chicago. (Friedman himself has doubts about the rigor of the commitments of Reagan and Thatcher to monetarism.) On a more general level, the "Keynesean consensus" of demand-side management seems to have broken down and has been replaced by a

concern for supply-side government economic policies and a reduced tax burden for the wealthy; policy congruence may thus be
generate from the acceptance of supply-side–monetarist economics
on both sides of the Atlantic.[36]

But, ideology in this sense cannot be used as an explanation for
the congruence of state interventions as state intervention in both
countries was designed to prevent the full operation of market forces.
It is true that both states have become more concerned about long-
term investment, and have changed tax policies to reflect this concern, but the quota systems (voluntary or otherwise), subsidies, and
special tax breaks for the auto industry are hardly consistent with a
free market system. As Chrysler and BL were the victims of market
operations, they presumably deserved their fate of bankruptcy. Both
Reagan and Thatcher largely continued the policies of their predecessors with regard to the auto industry, a result that we would not
expect if policy similarity resulted from ideological conviction.[37]

Common Underlying Problem

Another set of explanations is available that relies neither on societal pressures nor on ideology for an understanding of the process
of congruence. The writers who share this assumption would see
similarity as emerging from a common problem of capitalist or political development. In each case, either the capitalist economy or
the political institutions (and in some cases, both) of the United
States and Great Britain are suffering from a common crisis, a crisis
which threatens the legitimacy of the political system.

The Crisis of Capitalism

Many of the scholars in Economics and Political Science who work
within the Marxist framework accept as both a premise and a fact
that the capitalist systems of early industrializing countries like the
United States and Great Britain are in a crisis, and that this crisis is
an irreversible, and ultimately fatal, consequence of the logic of capitalism. The evidence of this crisis is manifested through a slowing

down of the accumulation process, or (analytically the same thing) of the tendency of the rate of profit to fall.[38]

Marx believed that the tendency of the rate of profit to fall was central to the process of the transformation to socialism. He wrote in *Grundrisse*:

> This is in every respect the most important law of modern political economy, and the most essential for understanding the most difficult relations. It is the most important law from the historical standpoint. It is a law, which despite its simplicity, has never before grasped and, even less, consciously articulated. [P.748]

This "tendency" may be central, but it is by no means simple. The starting point of his argument was the "organic composition of capital." By this, he meant that:

> The composition of capital is to be understood in a two-fold sense. On the side of value, it is determined by the proportion in which it is divided into constant capital or value of labor-power. This latter composition is determined by the relation between the mass of the means of production employed, on the one hand, and the mass of labor necessary for their employment on the other. I call the former the Value-composition, and the latter the technical composition of capital.

By the "accumulation of constant capital." Marx meant "the accumulation of labor time performed in the past (often called "dead labor") and embodied in the means of production."[39] Since by definition profit can be derived only from variable capital (i.e. labor and not technology), Marx assumed no technological monopolies and limited barriers to market entry; and since constant capital ("dead labor") increases, the net consequences were to be decreasing profits, a growing reserve army of labor, monopolization, underconsumption, and a general secular economic crisis.[40] As profits (and accumulation) fall, the capacity of capitalism to renew itself as a social relationship (between owners and workers) falters, the legitimacy of the state is weakened, and ultimately capitalism fails.[41]

In recent years, the pre-tax profit rates in the United States and, especially, the United Kingdom have decreased at the same time Western societies have seen an end to high growth and the development of stagflation. Along with this development has come a renewed interest in Marx's argument about the falling rate of profit and the inevitable crisis of capitalism.[42] Though most authors agree on the general principle, they disagree as to the mechanism through which profit falls (though some concede possible multicausality).

The first mechanism is the "rising organic composition of capital," or the notion that "surplus labor" required in production decreases as production becomes more automated unless the "rate of exploitation" is increased to offset this development.[43] The second argument is the underconsumption hypothesis, a variant of which was made famous by Baran and Sweezy.[44] Following Weisskopf, this theory hypothesizes, first, that the process of capitalist development involves a shift in favor of profits (or the profits of large oligopolist corporations) and against wages (and the profits of small competitive firms). Assuming secondly that the propensity to consume out of wage income is significantly higher than is the propensity to consume out of profits (especially oligopoly profits), "this distributional shift implies that consumption demand (C) will not keep pace with the growth in income (Y) so that C/Y will fall ... and will result in a decline ... in aggregate demand (D)."[45] The third mechanism is the "profit squeeze" or "rising wages" variant. Wright says that:

> The essential argument of the profit squeeze is very simple: the relative share of the national income going to workers and to capitalists is almost entirely a consequence of their relative strengths in the class struggle. To the extent that the working class develops a strong enough labor movement to win wage increases in excess of productivity increases, there will be a tendency for the rate of exploitation to decline and thus for the rate of profits to fall (to be squeezed by rising wage bills). Such a decline in profits results in a corresponding decline in investments and thus even slower increases in productivity. The end result is economic crisis. Conditions for profitable accumulation are restored when, as a result of the economic crisis, the reserve army of the unemployed increases to the point where the bargaining power of the working class is weakened. This enables the capitalist class to

increase its share of the national income and thus escape the squeeze on profits, at least temporarily.

As Wright has noted, these analyses are at least in part incompatible.[46] The "rising wages" hypothesis assumes the successful resistance of the working class to an increase in the rate of exploitation. The underconsumption hypothesis assumes a rise in the rate of exploitation, as does the "rising organic composition of capitalism" thesis. Fortunately, we need not choose among them for the moment, but instead, concentrate on the implications that the "tendency of the rate of profit to fall" has for our problem of congruence.

If this argument is correct, then the problems of the auto sector are part of a larger problem confronting the capitalist states in the late monopoly stage of capitalism. We would not be surprised that states would develop a policy congruence to solve similar problems. In terms of this variant of neo-Marxism, we would be surprised if capitalist societies in similar stages of the transition to socialism did not develop policy similarities with regard to central industries. In fact, in both the United States and Great Britain, the governing parties have expressed "concern" about corporate profitability in light of the recent depression, made some changes in the depreciation and investment allowances aimed at corporate profitability and investment, and provided long-term aid to the auto industries which had as its final aim the profitability of the producing companies.

Some recent empirical work, however, challenges two aspects of this central thesis of a secular decline in the profit rate. Joseph Pechman and Richard Jankowski have each demonstrated that, although pre-tax profits have fallen, post-tax profit rates have not.[47] They further argue that this is not the result of a conscious decision by the state to to bolster corporate income, but rather is the consequence of a gradual rise in debt financing (as opposed to equity financing). If Jankowski, in particular, is correct, then the central premise of this form of the neo-Marxist argument is unsound.

Jankowski computes the corporate nonfinancial post-tax profit rates by subtracting from the sum of corporate profits and interest

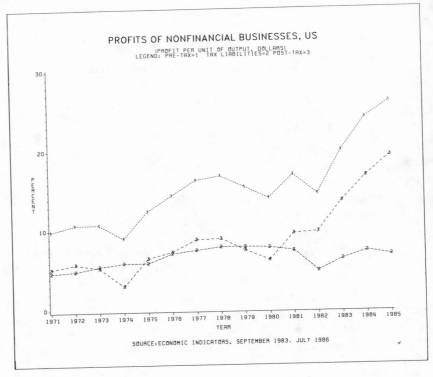

FIGURE 5.1

receipts the corporate tax liabilities, and divides the total by capital stock and inventories. After controlling for fluctuations of the business cycle (by adding a variable for capacity utilizations), he found "no evidence of decline during the 1970's in the [American] post-tax profit rates."[48]

Jankowski next asked whether or not this divergence between the pre and post-tax rates is the result of the American state intervention in propping up declining profits. He notes that "the effective tax rate on corporate profits has declined."[49] He follows Pechman's analysis of this decline when he notes that the overall tax rate for the upper bracket of corporate profits has decreased only marginally (52% to

48%), and that most of the changes in effective tax rates between 1947 and (presumably) 1981 were due to changes in the depreciation allowances and investment tax credits, as well as to the shift to debt financing of corporate debt. Jankowski reasoned that "if tax legislation [had been] enacted with the effect of increasing the post-tax profit rate, the ratio [of the pre-tax to the post-tax rate] would be expected to increase at the time of its effective implementation."[50] He found no such results, and argued that "none of the tax changes tested had a significant effect on the ratio of profit rates."[51] He instead argued that the shift from equity to debt financing by corporations is to take advantage of a long-standing feature of OECD taxation policies, that interest payments on bonds and loans are not taxed, but dividend payments to equity holders are. This, he says, is largely responsible for the changes.[52] He concludes:

> Therefore, arguments for the state's essential role in capital accumulation (cf. O'Conner, Habermas, Poulantzas, and many, many others) find no support in this crucial case of the pre-tax profit squeeze. If the state's intervention is not required in this area of paramount importance to the reproduction of capitalism, either its interventionist character is brought into question, or its intervention is restricted or necessary only in much more political matters.

Without necessarily accepting Jankowski's last conclusion, I believe that his argument (that the post-tax rate of profit has not fallen) to be essentially correct. Corporations in the United States and Britain have shifted towards debt financing, which—since dividend payments are included in the profit category but interest payments are not—means that both the pre-tax and the post-tax profit rates will almost by definition fall.[53] In the United States, the cumulative nonfinancial corporate debt to equity ratio was 39.1 percent in the 1968–73 period. By 1976–79 period, this figure rose to 74.3 percent.[54] For both the United States and Great Britain, the thesis of the declining rate of profit does not seem to hold, and thus can not be used to explain policy congruence.

TABLE 5.1
Real Labor Costs and Productivity
(% change per year)

	Real Labor Costs (manufacturing)		Productivity (industry)	
	1960–73	1974–80	1960–73	1974–80
U.S.	5.1	1.9	2.8	0.5
Japan	14.4	7.6	9.0	4.7
Germany	6.4	2.5	4.7	2.9
France	8.2	2.1	5.7	3.2
Britain	3.6	−0.9	3.6	1.7
Italy	9.2	2.5	5.7	2.1
Canada	6.5	1.0	4.2	−0.2

Source: OECD, Economic Outlook, December 1982, p. 39.

Crisis in the production process

The Marxist crisis explanation is not the only variant which sees political problems (and their solutions) as being rooted in the process of production. In recent years, economists have noted the higher productivity of Japan, Germany, and France over that of the United States and Great Britain, and have linked this fact to the higher growth rates in the former countries (see table 5.1).

This relationship, spurious or not, has sparked a genre of "industrial crisis" literature in Great Britain, and more recently, the United States.[55] Most of these analyses are country specific: Britain's decline is often linked to imperial commitments, imperial trade patterns, dominance of financial interests over manufacturing interests, remnants of feudal values, or an ideological consensus among political elites in Britain for an overvalued currency. These factors are only recently, if at all, related to America's industrial problems.

One sort of analysis that does possibly apply to both countries is one which locates industrial decline in an aging industrial process, a process which emerged in both countries in the nineteenth century. This process for the manufacture of goods evolved into large scale, machine intensive, production characterized by sharp, hostile, divisions between management and labor, and by the emergence of oligarchies in sectors of the economy.[56]

As Robert Reich, among others, has argued, the oligopolistic markets and bureaucratic managerial structure of American and British industries are not adaptive to rapid change.[57] Reich wrote that

> The central problem of America's economic future is that the nation is not moving quickly enough out of high-volume, standardized production. The extraordinary success of the half-century of the management era has left the United States a legacy of economic inflexibility. Thus our institutional heritage now imperils our future.[58]

As multinational firms (and industrializing nations) begin production in lower labor cost countries (using comparable technology), American and British firms are increasingly unable to produce at home and still compete with these new producers. Reich sees no direct solution for the United States or Great Britain except for government, business, and labor cooperation aimed at creating a more "flexible" and factor-intensive production system. The implication is that the model to be followed is the "sun-rise, sun-set" industrial policy of Japan.[59]

Reich's analysis emphasizes organizational rigidities in both the production process and the political system as the key to the understanding of industrial decline. Reich's argument has some illuminating aspects in this regard, especially in his discussion of the origins and the effects of "paper entrepreneurialism."[60] Reich's analysis, however, is not helpful for us as his "cooperative solutions" focus obscures a central dilemma facing governments—that part of the decline of the American and British industries is due to firm strategy in relocating production (e.g. Ford to West Germany) or buying equity in or concluding agreements with foreign producers for the purpose of importing cars into the domestic markets (e.g. GM with Isuzu, Chrysler with Mitsubishi). To suggest greater cooperation between government and labor, on the one hand, and industry on the other is to ignore the differences in interests among the parties.

A second problem that limits the utility of Reich's analysis for us is that automobile production requires machine-intensive, mass production in order to achieve economies of scale in the popular automotive market. His proposals for a shift to the production of "precision-manufactured," high value goods would, if applied to the United States and Great Britain, take both out of the mass production automobile market.

Another explanation which examines both product and production process as a clue to economic changes is the "product cycle" theory first advanced by Raymond Vernon.[61] Product cycle theory treats production and trade historically and relationally. That is, the analysis begins with the innovation of a product and its subsequent production within a large market. The surplus production is exported to other advanced countries, thereby creating a demand for that product in the importing countries. Once the demand in the other advanced countries is great enough to exploit scale economies, production begins in the other markets, and "the product becomes sufficiently standardized that price competition becomes important."[62] If wage costs are significant for production costs, and the product is standardized, this product cycle may recur in other low-wage countries either as a result of multinational firm strategy or the industrializing policies of low wage countries or both. Ultimately, production in the original innovating country declines as its production costs squeeze exports and make imports competitive.

The developments in the world auto industry do approximate the first two stages of Vernon's description, though not as of yet the third.[63] Both the U.S. and Britain can be seen as innovating countries (along with Germany) in aspects of automobile production. Further, as the product became standardized (i.e., the world cars of the 1970s), both nations suffered import penetration, though not necessarily because of high wage costs. Vernon's thesis is nevertheless only of limited value for us in understanding policy similarity.

The strengths of this thesis for our problem include its units of analysis. By focusing on firm investment choice as being a function of expected product costs, Vernon's analysis gives us some basis for understanding how national industrial production can decline although firms continue to prosper. Further, by focusing on the relative costs of national labor (per unit of production), as well as the relative size of domestic markets, Vernon provides us with some criteria for predicting where firms will choose to invest and produce. Additionally, we can anticipate from his analysis that government policy actions with regard to mature industries (those with standardized products) will aim at changing the price structures of domestic markets by raising barriers to entry, reducing labor costs, and attempting to induce firm investments. All this has occurred.

Nonetheless, aspects of Vernon's thesis are not helpful here. The rapid changes in both product and process in the auto industry may mean that the product cycle is restarting, implying a limit to divestments in the older industrialized countries. This is in part because economies of scale, more than wage costs, seem to be of central importance in achieving a low-cost product. As we have seen in our previous discussions, the requirements of achieving these economies of scale in autos usually can be met only by an advanced industrial nation with access to a large market. A final problem limiting the utility of product cycle theory for us is that, though we can extrapolate about government action from Vernon's theory, he has no place for the state in his theory. He treats it as an exgoenous variable, rather than as the critical determinant of firm choice.[64]

Political and economic sclerosis

One "crisis" thesis that has received much attention since its publication in 1982 attributes declining growth rates and industrial stagnation, not to a crisis, but to the lack of any *destructive crisis*. Mancur Olson's much praised, much damned *The Rise and Decline of Nations: Economic Growth, Stagflation and Social Rigidities* (New Haven: Yale, 1982) lays claim to be able to explain much of political, social, and economic behavior through the application of concepts derived from public choice economics.[65] Olson concludes his book by saying

The theory offered here is certainly a simple one. . . . [it] is consistent with the rapid postwar growth of West Germany and Japan, with the slow growth and ungovernability of Britain in recent times, and at the same time with Britain's record as the most rapidly growing country in an earlier time. It is consistent with the slower growth of the northeastern and older midwestern regions of the United States and with the faster growth of the South and the West—and offers a statistically significant explanation of the growth of the forty-eight [Sic] states as a whole.

The theory also is consistent with the rapid growth of the six nations that founded the Common Market, the rapid growth of the United States throughout the nineteenth century, and the rapid growth of Germany and Japan in the later part of the nineteenth and early twentieth centuries. The theory fits the growth of Britain and Holland and (less clearly) of France in the early modern period and their roles in the rise of the once-backward civilization of Western Christendom. It explains the decline of old cities in the midst of these expanding countries and the scattered, transactions-intensive putting-out system. The theory, is consistent with the phenomenal postwar growth of Korea, Taiwan, Hong Kong, and Singapore and with the guild-ridden stagnation of the China that was first exposed to European pressure, not to mention the similar stagnation in India. Finally, the theory fits the pattern of inequalities and the trade policies of many of the unstable developing countries, and a number of other facts as well.[66]

I cannot here evaluate the soundness of Olson's assumptions and premises, nor the validity of his arguments. Others have attempted this. Our purpose will be to see if his argument is of use in explaining policy congruence.

The core of Olson's argument can be understood through the metaphor of sclerosis. He assumes that economic growth is a function of a lack of restraint on factors of production, and that "collusions" and "distributional coalitions" are key restraints either directly (e.g. unions) or indirectly through pluralist pressure on the state. He argues that "Stable societies with unchanged boundaries tend to accumulate more collusions and organizations for collective action over time" (p. 74). In consequence, "distributional coalitions slow down a society's capacity to adopt new technologies and to reallocate resources in response to changing conditions, and thereby reduce the rate of economic growth" (p. 74; chapters 2 and 3 set out "the logic" and "the implications" of the argument). He then analyzes country histories to see if his argument has any explanatory power. Olson focuses much attention on Britain.

> The logic of the argument implies that countries that have had democratic freedom of organization without upheaval or invasion the longest will suffer the most from growth-repressing organizations and combinations. This helps explain why Great Britain, the major nation with the longest immunity from dictatorship, invasion, and revolution, has had in this century a lower rate of growth than other large, developed democracies. Britain has precisely the powerful network of special-interest organizations that the argument developed here would lead us to expect in a country with its record of military security and democratic stability. The number and power of its trade unions need no description.... In short, with age British society has acquired so many strong organizations and collusions that it suffers from an institutional sclerosis that slows its adaptation to changing circumstances and technologies. (pp. 77–78)

He examines the U.S. in regional terms, and finds in the industrial Northeast a variant of sclerosis.

> When we look at cities and metropolitan areas we see the same tendency for relative decline in the places that have had the longest time to accumulate special-interest groups. The best-known manifestation of this and of the ungovernability brought about by dense networks of such coalitions is the bankruptcy that New York City would have suffered in the absence of special loan guarantees from the federal government.... But New York is only a prototypical case.... all the great cities to the north and east of a crescent extending from just south of Baltimore to just west of St. Louis and Milwaukee are in difficulty. In general, the newer cities of the South and West are in incomparably better shape. (pp. 114–16)

He directly compares the U.S. and the U.K. with regard to older industries, and says that what evidence he has

> is surely consistent with the hypothesis that the United States as well as Britain does relatively badly in older industries and heavy industries that are especially susceptible to oligopolistic collusion and unioni-

zation. No doubt other factors are also relevant, but the fact that wage rates in the troubled U.S. automobile and steel industries have been very much higher than the average wages in American manufacturing tends to confirm . . . [the] hypothesis that the present theory is part of the explanation. I would also not be surprised if in these troubled industries there have been excessive numbers of vice-presidents and other corporate bureaucrats with handsome perquisites. (p. 116)

In opposition to American and British stability (and declining growth rates) are the experiences of Japan and West Germany. What characterized their experiences was "revolution and occupation, Napoleonism and totalitarianism" which "have utterly demolished most feudal structures on the Continent [and Japan I might add] and many of the cultural attitudes they sustained" (p. 83). He reviews the evolution of fascism in both countries and the subsequent Allied occupations, and claims that the "distributional coalitions" in each country "have been emasculated or abolished by totalitarian governments or foreign occupations" (pp. 75–77). Japan and West Germany will not likely sustain high growth rates since, "The theory here predicts that with continued stability the Germans and the Japanese will accumulate more distributional coalitions which will have an adverse influence on their growth rates" (p. 76).

Olson's most important policy conclusion is that "There is no substitute for a more open and competitive environment. If combinations dominate markets throughout the economy and the government is always intervening on behalf on special interests, there is no macroeconomic policy that can put things right" (p. 233). Actions that he recommends include policies to provide incentives to businesses to reduce wage increases, to moderate price increases, and to hire additional workers in order to combat high rates of "natural" unemployment (pp. 232–34).[67] Though Olson refrains from directly calling for state intervention to break the power of labor unions, a group that he blames for "preventing the mutually profitable transactions between the involuntarily unemployed and employers," he clearly believes unions to be a serious obstacle to economic growth (pp. 201–5, 232–37). This is especially so since unions are an obstacle to the adoption of new technologies and to the shifting of resources (and jobs) from less profitable to more profitable sectors.

Olson's logic, when applied to our problem of policy similarity, is of limited analytic help even if his overall argument is valid. This is, in part, because he has a pluralist understanding of how governments operate, a form of analysis that we have found to be of use in only a few aspects of our problem. But the larger difficulty is that his theory does not fit the evidence. As we have already seen (in chapter 3), one central feature common to the U.S. and Britain is that each country has a mobile and largely unrestricted investment capital market, a situation which under Olson's argument ought to be a significant contributor to economic efficiency. Japan, France, and to a much lesser extent, West Germany, by way of contrast, have capital markets in which prices and investment levels are set through bargaining or other forms of political "collusions." The results are that the levels of per capita industrial investment—a key precondition for economic growth—have been substantially lower in Great Britain and the United States than in Japan, France, and West Germany for several decades. American and British investors and firms have exploited higher rates of return available in foreign countries. This is of special significance in the auto industry as American auto manufacturers have chosen to establish foreign subsidiaries rather than to invest in the United States for the purposes of exporting to other markets. Although this is a rational policy for the firm given the world investment incentive structure in autos, the consequences have included a decline in American and British production. The one major capitalist country where these firms were politically excluded from investing was Japan, and it is Japan's auto companies that have grown most during the past 20 years. In fact, the scale of impediments to the free operation of world market forces in Japan is legendary.

These "collusions" occur in sectors other than in Japan's auto industry. As Chalmers Johnson demonstrates, Japanese "collusions" are credited with much of Japan's economic growth.[68] Further, several features of Japanese society which have also contributed to Japan's growth are residues of Japan's recent feudal past. Among the residues, which survived fascism, war, and occupation, are the *zaibatsu*, a clan type of social organization which became the basis of many corporations, including such famous names as Mitsubishi, Nissan, and Toyota.[69] Of all the major auto producers, only Honda, the fifth largest auto producer in Japan, is a postwar company. The strong sense of reciprocal loyalty between the company and the work force, and the commitment to productivity which apparently characterizes Japanese workers, have been traced as well to the persistence of feudal values which are "adaptive" for industrial production. Another apparent residue is Japan's tradition of consensual bargaining. Japan's success may, in fact, lie in its not having a "more open environment." Olson's argument, for all its rigor, simplicity, and explanatory power, is too sharply at odds with the facts of the auto industry to be of any help here.

State Interests

For many social scientists working within one of the pluralist, neopluralist, or Marxist frameworks, the notion that the state may have its own interests is an oddity. The core assumptions of these frameworks is that political institutions are directed by, or act for, important societal actors. To talk about state interests is to reify politics by abstracting the political bargaining process through the use of rational actor models—models that overlook the "pluralist roar" of politics.[70]

Several traditions in the social sciences exist for which "state interest" is an important concept. For instance, in international relations, we find political scientists talking about the "national interest" as being the maximization of state power in the context of the international arena.[71] Though the definitions of power vary (military power, hegemonic interests), as do the understandings of how the process of state interests are defined (ideology or perceptions of elites, bureaucratic rationality), the underlying assumption is that the state interest is separable from, and superior to, the interests of social actors. Even in cases where the state seems to be acting in a way consistent with the interests of important social actors, some analysts have argued that this was so because the "managers of the national interest" had defined the national interest such that it coincides with these other interests.[72]

Another tradition that employs a "state interest" explanation for political outcomes sees states as aggregations of roles, norms, belief structures, and expectations into which individual actors are slotted and socialized. The doing of one's job becomes an end in and of itself; utility is defined in terms of one's job. Even those who do not work within the Weberian framework of bureaucratic rationality borrow insights from this framework.[73] For instance, Stephen Krasner, who seems to be more indebted to Pareto than to Weber, nonetheless describes his main assumption as being that "it is useful to conceive of a state as a set of roles and institutions having peculiar drives, compulsions, and aims of their own that are separate and distinct from the interests of any particular societal group" (page 10).[74] Many other authors who have dealt with national policymaking, economic policymaking in particular, focus on either the identity formation or the ideological beliefs of actors in governmental roles as keys to the understanding of state outcomes.[75]

What links the realist and the bureaucratic rationality traditions is the common assumption that individuals in governmental roles can act for the state's interest and that state officials are not necessarily captives of pressure groups or followers of personal whim. I share this assumption, an assumption that makes a state's interest explanation of politics possible.

I am advancing a form of "state interest" explanation for policy similarity. Unlike other variants of state interest argument, interest is here defined only by the optimization of (a) government and national revenue, and (b) the public welfare by the state. That is, the state seeks to resolve Schumpeter's dilemma of long-term growth and short-term efficiency. This definition of the state's interests is not normative; I in fact do not think state interests ought to be defined in such a pecuniary manner. Nor is this a rational actor model; in many ways, a broader definition of interests would be more "rational" or "effective" for states. I am simply arguing that the similarity of governmental policies toward the auto industry in particular, and firm investment in general, best fits a thesis which explains outcomes in terms of states seeking to avoid long-term hemorrhaging of state and national accounts: a narrow reflection of bureaucratic and agency interests. This is also not to argue that other explanations have no analytic value; the behavior of politicians of Michigan and the Midlands conforms closely to pluralist expectations, and the structural Marxist explanation also accommodates these changes in policy. But only a state's interest description can explain the long-term nature of aid, the massive layoffs of labor in both countries, and the insistence by the states that the firms achieve commercial viability.

What is the essential element of this conception of the state that gives it analytic utility here? It is the "structure of incentives" facing political elites imposed by the bureaucratic order of the welfare state—welfare in the broadest sense of the word. I contend that, owing to aspects of the welfare state, policy similarity has recently developed among advanced capitalist countries in economically difficult times because of the economic consequences to public welfare of large-firm failures *and* the economic consequences to public welfare of state subsidies to failing firms. Promoting firm profitability and firm investment is a strategy that potentially reconciles this dilemma.

From where did the welfare state come? Physical devastation, economic deprivation, political debilitation, and human degradation were the consequences of the slow (1914–1945) collapse of the liberal "laissez-faire" order. Liberal states were all too vulnerable to the ideological incitements of anti-market social movements, especially when markets themselves suffered catastrophic collapse. Modern Welfare Capitalism is not as vulnerable as the liberal regime, but its legitimacy rests fundamentally on its ability to "deliver the goods," an ability predicated upon regulating fluctuations in the business cycle, and upon mitigating the consequences of market failures.[76]

Two models of welfare capitalism emerged. The first, the postwar Keynesean consensus, presumed that both social peace (legitimacy) and prosperity (efficient allocation of available resources) were to be had by creating bureaucratic institutions through which the inefficiencies of the market would be more or less automatically corrected. Schumpeter's warning—that these arrangements eroded the preconditions he foresaw as being necessary for long-term growth—went unheeded. As a consequence of this Keynesean consensus, market failures were institutionalized as part of the domain of bureaucratic politics; economic efficiency became the central item on the agenda of the state. The key proposition was that economic management of the economy was to be as *nondiscretionary* (for politicians) as was possible.[77] Automatic stabilizers—unemployment insurance and other transfer payments—promoted both equity and efficiency, and did so without the "visible hand" of politicians. We had, instead, the "hidden hand" of the countercyclical state.[78] We should note, however, that the form of intervention was primarily macroeconomic. Markets are essentially preserved in this model. When added to the general growth in the 1950s and 1960s of the welfare state among Western countries, the "automatic" expenditures provided a framework of "entitlements" not easily changed by political elites.[79]

The second model was the French, Japanese and, (recent) German versions of indicative planning.[80] This model, as Shonfield convincingly argued in his *Modern Capitalism*, was not adopted by the United States or Great Britain. The essence of this model is the exchange of information among industry and government officials, sometimes codified in production and other planning targets, and sometimes enforced by government officials through financial and other incentives and disincentives. This microeconomic and firm-specific industrial strategy was held responsible by analysts like Shonfield for the high rates of growth for France and Japan in the 1950s and 1960s. By the end of the 1970s, American analysts involved in the industrial policy debate were frequently championing this model of selective intervention as one the United States should adopt in some form.

We do find a common denominator among these countries in some social expenditures. If, after all, the welfare state promotes the economic good, we should not be surprised to discover that Western governments have generally adopted it. Although we do find national variations, welfare states have some common features. Most governments have countercyclical budgetary and expenditure rules, most states spend over half of government expenditures on "social" expenses, personal taxation is progressive to a degree, and the unemployed receive some type of social insurance. In fact, the OECD claimed that one feature of the western welfare system is "a tendency towards international convergence."[81]

Both the social expenditures of the welfare state and the model of selective intervention had their critics, even before the dissolution of the "Keynesean consensus." These expenditures undermined personal liberty: or, they promoted indolence among the lower classes: or, they were based on the false premise that fiscal policy mattered— attention to the money supply mattered much more: these were some of the criticisms mounted. These voices were little heard before the economic troubles of the 1970s, troubles that seemed to confound the work of Keynesean and post-Keynesean theorists. High inflation *and* high unemployment *and* slow-to-no growth were unexpected fellow-travelers. With these troubles came the challenge to the prevailing orthodoxy—perhaps the welfare state and the mixed economy did not promote short-term economic efficiency.[82] Commenting on this debate, the OECD wrote:

> The relatively poor performance of the OECD economies since the early 1970s has been accompanied by some reassessment of the consequences of large and growing public sectors. The last ten years have seen a significant change in attitude. Rather than being widely regarded as a major contributor to economic growth and macroeconomic stability, the view that the growth and financing of the public sector has, on balance, stifled growth now attracts widespread support. Although it is recognized that the public sector still has beneficial effects, it is argued that these benefits cannot justify the damage done.[83]

Alternative theories of both the political right and left were revived as intellectual contenders to the mixed economy, though the left critiques have had little practical political influence.

The particulars of indictment against the welfare state and the mixed economy were primarily microeconomic in orientation, and concerned both economic and political activity. Regarding economics, critics charge the state with two types of offenses. On the expenditure side, the state was thought to reduce (a) the incentives of the poor to find work because of its overly generous benefits, (b) the opportunity of the unemployed but willing to find work because of minimum wage rules and other "restrictions on free contracting," (c) the mobility of the working class through housing subsidies, and (d) the efficiency of all other labor markets by generally interfering with the price and wage structures—the "rational expectations" critique. On the taxation side, the state was seen to distort the incentives for saving and investment. Social security reduced the incentive of people to save for old age. High marginal tax rates reduced the incentive of the already-prosperous to continue to work and to invest. Corporate taxation was charged with being a "double tax," and with preventing "efficient" investment. In essence, the charge was that the state transferred funds from economically efficient classes to less economically efficient classes. Reducing the welfare state would then, ceteris paribus, promote economic efficiency by reducing distortions in markets.

The political critique of the welfare-state–mixed economy centered on the "rent-seeking" side of the state.[84] Interest groups and other social groups were competing for state "welfare" or subsidies, and were helping to make nations "ungovernable." Certainly, huge sums are committed by Western governments towards "entitlements," and these are not usually "means-tested." Table 5.2 gives estimated figures for the 1985 American budget. Even firms were hypothesized as inducing regulation as a strategy of seeking rents.[85] Mancur Olson's work in his Logic of Collective Action and The Rise and Decline of Nations fits within, and extends, this tradition. In sum, these analyses

TABLE 5.2
U.S. Federal Spending—1985 estimates

	$Billions	% of Budget
National Defense	273.5	(28.2)
Transfer Payments	460.4	(47.5)
Revenue Sharing	53.6	(5.5)
Other Operations	59.0	(6.1)
Net Interest	121.9	(12.6)
Transfer Payments Means Tested		
Entitlements	49.7	(5.1)
Non-Entitlements	30.7	(3.2)
Not Means Tested		
Entitlements	370.4	(38.2)
Non-Entitlements	9.7	(1.0)

Source: U.S. Congress. House of Representatives. Committee on the Budget. *Non-Means-Tested Entitlement Reform Programs.* Hearing, March 1, 1983.

conclude that the welfare state is too easy to loot, and that Shonfield's hope for a value-neutral civil service above politics is a nonstarter.

Critical evaluation of these contending arguments is difficult. The lack of consensus within the economics profession is a testimonial to this.[86] The OECD has attempted to sort out some of these claims. They concluded:

Whether the shift from optimism to pessimism regarding the economic impact of a growing public sector is justified has been and remains an open question. At the micro-economic level it is difficult to identify adverse effects of taxation and social security on labor supply, labor demand, saving or investment.... At the macro-economic level, preliminary cross-country comparisons undertaken by the [OECD] Secretariat have failed to reveal an inverse relationship between public sector size and economic performance as reflected in GDP growth rates, unemployment levels and inflation rates, or between public sector growth and inflation rates. However, the trend deterioration in economic performance in the OECD area is real enough, and so are large and growing public sectors. It may as yet be difficult to attribute the former to the latter, and *those who do so may be forced to rely on arguments which are difficult to substantiate, but there is a ready willingness to adopt such a view, and in recent years it has been having a growing influence on economic policy.*[87] (my italics)

The transfer payment features of the welfare state, in conjunction with these conflicting views about the welfare and interventionist state, make up the "incentive structure" that faced politicians and civil servants in Western countries in the late 1970s and early 1980s. As we know, many firms failed during the structural and cyclical economic downturns of 1979–1983. Political elites were constrained by the practice and theory of the countercyclical state to (initially) protecting employment and, later—and more crucially—to avoiding the failures of large firms.[88] To have done otherwise would have been at odds with the "good sense" of promoting public welfare, at least as understood by economists of the postwar era. To not prevent large firm bankruptcies would automatically trigger state expenditure and multiplier losses to society as a whole; resources would be under-utilized. To prevent large firm bankruptcies would distort markets, provide a "demonstration" effect for other troubled firms, and help delegitimate the notion of a neutral market; capitalism is a process of creative destruction. Providing capital investment assistance (and limited trade protection) was the optimum choice given these constraints. "Commercial viability" meant in practice the reduction of demands on the state, but done in the interests of reconciling short-term efficiency and long-term growth. The bailing-out of firms, investment tax credits, corporate tax "forgivenesses," deregulation, etc. were therefore all "rational" acts for political and bureaucratic elites, given the above incentives imposed by the welfare state, *and the beliefs about economics* that inform public policy. The "independent variable" driving policy similarity is therefore a search for economic efficiency—in almost Hegelian fashion, a form of reason's progress, only mediated through the welfare state[89]

The implications of economic efficiency defining a "state's interests" will be discussed in the following chapter.

Assessing Theories Of The State

This framework—the incentive structure of state interests posed by welfare capitalism—accommodates the events involving the auto industries very well. Of the falsifiable theories of the state, only a state-interest argument can explain the insistence by governments on "commercial viability" of firms while tolerating extensive overseas outsourcing by auto firms. Only a state-interest argument can explain the state subsidies for the replacement of labor by capital in the auto industry and in other industrial sectors. Only a state interest argument can explain the "long-term" nature of state aid. Only a state interest argument can explain the recurrent cross-national government practice of "bailing out" large firms and banks, but not smaller firms or banks, even though the total value of these "smaller" failures is large.

Other theoretical perspectives are nonetheless useful. For instance, several of the "common crises of capitalism" arguments, particularly those focusing on the relationship between governments, and the structure of financial institutions, and the effect that this has on the prevailing rates of return and overall investment, do help explain differing economic outcomes (e.g. cost of capital to firms) between the United States and United Kingdom on the one hand, and Japan, France and West Germany, on the other.[90] These factors were not the decisive influence shaping public policy in this case, however. In many cases, particularly that of neo-Marxism, writers are simply using different language to describe the same phenomenon. For instance, Claus Offe uses the phrase "accumulation" to describe the process of what is otherwise called capital investing. He describes as "recommodification of labor units" the process of training workers to make them more employable. The neo-Marxist framework, as exemplified by the work of Offe, Epsing-Anderson, Roger Friedland, and Fred Block, is theoretically subtle and historically sensitive. The acceptance or rejection of the neo-Marxist framework is almost an aesthetic judgement, rather than a matter of verification and refutation. Other frameworks for understanding state actions would be

useful given different policy outcomes. For instance, if a public policy similarity that protected levels of employment in some way had
been discovered, I would have taken this as evidence for Lindblom's
version of neo-Pluralism. Only the "orthodox Marxist" and the "public choice" positions are more or less without analytic utility here.
In both cases, the analysts have too limited a view of the state to be
of much use in this study.[91]

It follows then that, despite its utility here, a state interest argument
of this sort, or any other, is not a universal political explanative. A
state interest argument cannot, for example, be readily used to understand the initial emergence of the welfare state, or its expansion.
This argument is useful only in the context of an existing regime of
welfare capitalism, one in which promoting public welfare is already
embedded in the domain of state responsibilities. The state interest
argument is also not of much help in understanding public policy
divergence. I had earlier argued that, as good economic times return,
governments will likely resume their previous (divergent) public
policies toward firms: differing mixes of regulation, *dirigisme*, indicative planning, nationalization, codetermination, and so on. Although I have no reason for believing that a state interest argument
has nothing to say about cross-national divergence, neither can I
demonstrate its utility. About public policy divergence then, silence.
Even in situation in which economies are in decline, government
policymakers do not always optimize state interests, even when the
incentives are strong to do so; Joel Krieger has pointed out that the
facts of the miners' strike do not fit a state-interest argument. "State
interest" is, at best, a useful approach to the study of public policy
part of the time.

Falsifiable political and social theories are like that—useful only
sometimes. A theory whose proponents claim otherwise is either a
language of description, which tells us what categories and problems
are important *a priori*, or else hopelessly parsimonious, and thus
unable to handle the complexity of human interactions.[92] We need,
therefore, constellations of theories of the state rather than a search
for a single unifying theory. We need to ask "second order" questions

about political economy and the state. "How autonomous is the state?" "Are Western nations converging?" "Is planning efficient?" "Are markets beneficial?" should be replaced by "when is the state autonomous?" "under what circumstances do nations demonstrate convergence?" "when is planning efficient?" "when are markets beneficial?" These last are questions of political science, the others are of political theology.

6.

CONCLUSION

I HAVE ARGUED THAT a policy similarity has developed between the United States and Great Britain. The core of similarity has been that, in order to minimize the inevitable short- and long-term financial consequences of industrial decline, both nations have taken steps to restore their auto industries to profitability. The argument makes a specific prediction from this case study. The British and American governments will opt for commercial viability in restructuring operations where an industry is hit by a structural shift in production and a business cycle downturn, even at the cost of employment and other policies. The argument also predicts policy divergence, or a return to previous policy goals, as good economic times return and costs to the treasuries fall.

The argument has been generalized to changes in corporate taxation in the United States, Great Britain, West Germany, and Japan. From 1978 on, we find a common pattern among these capitalist countries, and this pattern is to subsidize the investment of their private corporations during periods of economic downturn.

I also contend that a state-interest explanation provides the best fit for this similarity, even though state interest in this sense is only a narrow reflection of treasury and national accounts. Using the state-interests framework, we can understand the use of quotas instead of tariff barriers, the sudden emergence of general business tax aid and the deemphasis on deregulation and other Government policies, as well as the massive loss of employment,—a loss abetted by the Governments in a number of ways. This analysis also accommodates the paradox that the governments have permitted the auto firms great autonomy, even though they have used this autonomy to transfer a significant part of production out of the U.S. and Britain, and to replace labor with capital.

The state-interest explanation does have specific limitations as well as strengths. It is really useful only for understanding how states respond to economic and social questions that are already "embedded" in the state structure. The welfare consequences of market failures are one such "embedment." But, such an explanation is of little help to us in understanding how such issues become institutionalized in the first instance. "Why the welfare state?" is a question beyond the scope of a state-interest argument, as is the more mundane question of why welfare and other such costs have achieved the status of automatic, rather than discretionary, costs to states. To understand how state agendas change, and how new state institutions are created, we need refer to one of several of the societal-pressure arguments.

The argument about policy similarity and state interests is applicable to other industrial sectors in Western nations. The general issue is that of competitiveness. As I noted in my introduction, work by the French economist Jacques Mistral suggests that both the British and the American economies are in the midst of a long-term deterioration in industrial competitiveness. This implies a steady erosion of the terms of trade in manufacturing as well as a loss of home markets as foreign firms sell into once isolated markets. The auto industry is thus a specific case of a general trend.[1]

This structural problem in the manufacturing industries has been reinforced by government policies, in both the developing and developed world, to construct world competitive industries in a variety of industrial sectors. The major consequence of these government industrialization and competition strategies has been a general world surplus capacity, a capacity subsidized by states. The resulting dynamic disequilibrium in international trade has produced a general strain on the free trade regime among democratic capitalist countries, just as the domestic dynamic disequilibria described by Schumpeter produced a strain on domestic laissez-faire regimes.[2]

These underlying factors affect nations in different ways, as I have already argued. Even so, the postwar growth regime (with its prisoners' dilemma overtones) and the welfare social systems have produced a strong set of structural constraints confronting Western governments. The development of broadly similar industrial policies—that is, similar strategies—will be the general form of industrial strategy given the incentive structure confronting states. Policy similarity is normal politics under extreme conditions.

If my argument about policy similarity, and state interest as its explanation, are correct, several issues follow. If state interest does supersede the role of private interests in producing policy, then more attention needs to be directed at how states define interests, what the likely consequences of similarity based on state interests are for private actors, and what justifications and normative assumptions are associated with public policies.

The first issue—how states define interests—I did not address in this work. I treated the state as a black box, and inferred the substance of my argument from the circumstances and outcomes of policy. This was a choice made on the basis of the evidence available to me given my resources. Nonetheless, studies of bureaucratic and legislative politics are the natural outgrowths of a state-interest argument. The second question, the consequences of state policies for private actors, will be treated in the following section. Afterward, I will analyze the justifications and normative assumptions inherent in the use of economic efficiency as the criterion of the state's interest, and will propose alternative bases for public policy. My purpose there is not to judge the merit of one set of assumptions over another— this issue can only be decided through democratic politics. I wish only to illuminate for discussion the range of alternatives.

Social and Economic Implications—Private Interests

The end of home market isolation and the introduction of general world competition has altered the balance of relations among state, firm, and labor in many countries. The presumption upon which manufacturing sectors in large markets have operated was that the costs of slack management practices, state policies, and high wages (that were not linked to productivity gains) could safely be passed on to consumers. Social institutions (e.g. communities) and economic networks (e.g. supplier arrangements) were also constructed on that premise. The addition of foreign competition with lower per unit labor costs has challenged this presumption, and threatened these economic and social arrangements.

The financing of the industrialization strategies of Third World countries by Western banks and investors has inadvertently also further complicated the relations among firm, state, and labor in the developed countries. The Newly Industrializing Countries (NICs) were lent money, and investments were made, on the presumption that the loans and investments could be repaid through the export of goods back to First World countries. Social and economic relations in the NICs are no less threatened by a change in the world free trade regime than are domestic relationships by the retention of this regime. We know that some countries' workforces, firms, and investors will suffer.

Labor and management confront the initial series of strategic choices, and these choices are restricted, at least in the production for the mass market. Lower per unit costs are achievable in a limited number of ways, and all of them impinge on either the wage benefits or the traditional practices and rights of the working class. Increased automation, wage cuts, overseas investment, and "outsourcing" for component products are all methods of reducing costs that cut the total wage bill. Flexible production processes and new authority structures promise to lower costs in some industries, but require substantial work rule concessions.

Labor institutions can only react to the change precipitated by this new competition. Labor has neither the financial resources nor the organizational capacity to establish productive relations that can act as a viable alternative to firms and market capitalism. The shrinking of its resource base, and the current electoral weakness of its political allies, make it unlikely that governments and labor will ally to halt this new competition and its consequences. Furthermore, the consensus behind some form of market competition extends, in practice at least, now from right to left in Western democracies. Labor can at best retard change.

The most substantial change for labor is that the quality of life for working people will likely diminish. Some evidence exists already in America that the workforce is "bifurcating," with two-income professional families growing more prosperous while the working class drops in income and life opportunities.[3]

More important still, in a human sense, is the diminishing quality of life through a loss of community and family life. "Efficient" economies require a fluid factor market and a migratory labor force. As the mill and mine towns which sprang up in response to the economic relations of the early industrial era dissolve, so too does the "community" built upon now rotting economic foundations. This loss of community is not a particularly new feature of Western life. But, unlike other postwar migrations, the loss is often involuntary and is occurring at the same time as other social and economic expectations are under assault. In a sense, market competition includes the values people hold. "At what point do the wages I can earn elsewhere outweigh family and community ties?" is a question asked by people in times of social and economic change. Thanks to market isolation and general prosperity, it was not a question that was pressed upon unionized America during the postwar era. It is now with us again.

The diminishing power of labor is a concomitant of the increasing power of firms. Because of the incentives governments confront, economic growth and its precipitator—plant and capital goods investment—now have top priority in public policy. Because investment is essentially a voluntary act, firms must be induced, not compelled, to invest. They can choose where to invest, and in what fields—possibly shifting product and service lines—or even choose not to invest at all. Stockholders rarely object to higher dividends in lieu of higher investment. Public policy in Western nations increasingly reflects the fact that firms have many strategic choices, only some of which coincide with governments' policies.

One manifestation of this change in public policy is to be found in income tax policies. Economists widely believe that investment is a function of savings (as well as exchange rates and relative sectoral returns within a country). As the upper class has a greater marginal propensity to save than does the lower class, the level of investment should increase as the overall wage bill is reduced. According to this argument, firms, and the upper class in general, should therefore receive a larger share of national income in order to spur investment. More efficient growth is said to be a likely result of these tax policies. This pre-Keynesean model of growth has reemerged in American and British tax policies in the 1980s, and has always been present, some argue, in France and Japan.[4]

All of this is not to say that the managers of firms are free from constraints. Foreign and domestic competition has its effects. The financial markets in particular impose a certain kind of discipline on firms, a discipline which mandates high returns relative to other firms. While the neoclassical theory of the firm has few real-world embodiments, the theory's cathexis (or, preoccupation) on profitability as management's moral duty has a greater grip on the sensibilities of investors and managers alike in competitive markets. This then can only enhance management's willingness to treat the workforce and the state as means to the end of profitability. Managers, who in years past would have been reluctant to close less profitable plants, cut wages, and reduce the workforce, may find social responsibility a more costly proposition. While this will undoubtedly not mean a return to the "Working Class Manchester" of Friedrich Engels, it will mean a further diminution of labor's value—value in both the material and intrinsic sense.

Issues for the State

A Definition Too Narrow

The various institutions of states and, in theory, the electorate also confront choices that result from economic and social change. Minimally, the social and physical infrastructure needs to reflect population trends. New sewers, old-age homes, and prisons are part of the stuff of social change. To date, most governments have absorbed some of the costs of social change, but they have done so in a selective and ad hoc way. For displaced workers, the state's remedy has been to temporarily replace part of the lost income of individuals. For firms, tax subsidies and market protection have been the remedies. For the general problem of economic decline, government policies aimed at promoting firm investment have been undertaken.

Nevertheless, the state interest here described is really only a narrow reflection of the current agendas of state institutions, and not that of any overarching state purpose. Government agencies generally respond only to policy problems that are already in their domain. Other problems—even those posing a general threat to the effectiveness of other public policies—are usually ignored. Furthermore, governments are rarely so organized that the interrelatedness of public problems is reflected in public policy. Western states have no "Ministry of Social Well-Being and Public Purpose." The longer-term social consequences of current problems in particular receive little attention from state institutions or the electorate.

A broader definition of cost and state interest is available than the notions of cost and interest that underpin the policy similarity. A cost-benefit calculus that incorporated a positive value variable for community—one that reflected the social value of community[5] to society—would likely produce different forms and instances of state intervention. At a minimum, we would be unlikely to provide tax writeoffs for plant closures for those companies relocating production overseas. Production facilities upon which entire communities depend would be more likely to continue producing than they now do. After all, sociologists have long known that communities are repositories of social values, especially those that reinforce the general social order. As such, communities act as social glue, defining both acceptable and deviant behavior. To lose community is to lose a referent network of norms, role expectations, and other ingredients of "meaning." Further, older communities come complete with housing stock, physical infrastructure, and social services, not to mention an existing plant and capital stock. State interventions that reflected the economic and social costs of relocation might benefit societies in the following ways: family structures would more likely remain intact; people would remain employed, thus retaining work habits and self-esteem; state costs for jails, old-age homes, drug and alcohol rehabilitation, and other such "dislocation" costs would be reduced; and finally, the social order itself would be strengthened. The transaction costs (broadly conceived) of economic and social change would be lessened. State interests would be more effectively and efficiently served. Perhaps long-run economic growth would be diminished, as Schumpeter suggested, but is growth in the rate of total output the main purpose of the state?

Efficiency, Ethics, and Public Policy: Upon What Basis Ought We To Make and Choose Policy?

The reader will note that the writer has shifted voice. I have described similarity, explained it in terms of state interests, and suggested what implications all this has for the actors in this process. I am now arguing that governments should have a broader definition of interest, one that defines community as a social good. I could (and do) argue that, in the long run, such a notion of interest would be cheaper in some economic and social calculus than current policies. I could then defend a social outcome I desire by more or less using standards of efficiency (i.e. getting more "good" or "utility" out of a given input) with only minor violence to accepted notions of public welfare.

In a book with a readership of social scientists, to argue that my position is more efficient would be a wiser strategy than for me to argue that my position is more "just." The metaphor of efficiency is a powerful one in political and economic discourse, summoning images of value-neutrality. The image of justice is vague, and we are rightly suspicious of it. In consequence, efficiency is frequently the standard upon which state policies are undertaken and justified; it is now one (if not the only) accepted norm for public policy. Nevertheless, efficiency is also a mask under which the analyst's values are hidden. For instance, my belief in the virtue of this broader definition of interest is grounded not in a belief in efficiency as the just end of public policy, but rather in a different set of values. If Schumpeter could demonstrate that it really would promote growth in decades and centuries to come if the state were to let towns and regions wither, and to impoverish the working class, I would not then change my mind. Efficiency in state accounts is a subsidiary, not core, value for me.

My aim in this section is to discuss some of the values and assumptions inherent in the use of economic efficiency as a standard for public policy. My ultimate purpose is to match these assumptions and values to those of other standards that might serve to guide public policy. I do not come to judgment about the moral merit of any of these—this choice is that of the electorate. I wish mainly to show that we do have choices.

Efficiency, most everyone would agree, provides in general a useful framework for evaluating things. Efficiency, in its engineering, business, and social senses, has been the standard measure of good performance for most of the past century—part of the development of "rationalist" civilization.[6] The promise of efficiency is that of a value neutral, rational method of arranging human affairs so that the ratio of benefit to harm is increased.

The promise, however, is as ambiguous as is the word. In the 1931 Edition of the *Encyclopaedia of the Social Sciences*, the text under the heading "Efficiency" read in part

> The tremendous emphasis on efficiency and the widespread use of the term in the sense of the business or pecuniary efficiency have obscured the real nature of the term and created the popular belief that efficiency is desirable per se. Hence it has been accepted as an indictment of trade unions to say that they are opposed to efficiency or of public operation of industries to say that it is inefficient. Strictly speaking, efficiency is a purely abstract and colorless term. It relates simply to the ratio of results achieved to the means used. It follows that there

is no such thing as efficiency in general or efficiency as such—there are simply a multitude of particular kinds of efficiency. Actions and procedures which are efficient when measured with one measuring stick may be inefficient when measured with a different measuring stick.[7]

Thus, the measurement of efficiency, as with the statistical measures of other abstractions, depends crucially on the grounding assumptions of the investigator. And these assumptions are inevitably a reflection of the investigator's values. For instance, an investigator who judges a government's effectiveness by its efficiency in promoting liberty or individual choice will have a different measure of efficiency from someone whose first principle is social equality.

This understanding that efficiency has meaning only in light of the investigator's beginning assumptions has been overlooked in the general acceptance of economic efficiency as the general standard in public policy. I will argue that the acceptance of efficiency as a legitimate norm for public policy produces serious problems. I will also argue that alternative criteria for evaluating the contribution of policies to public welfare (and different definitions of public welfare) are available, though I do not suggest one or another as being preferable. That choice is the electorate's.

Efficiency's Ethos

The "popular belief that efficiency is desirable per se" is a unique characteristic of late-nineteenth and twentieth-century thought, but the social origins of the "virtue of efficiency" predate this period. In the most important sense, the idea of efficiency is yet another example of what Weber called the "progressive rationalization of modern life." Weber's thesis, that the origins of capitalism are to be found not only in material conditions but also in "the ability and disposition of men to adopt certain types of practical rational conduct," is important here because he argued that this "disposition" toward "rational conduct" is generalized to all other aspects of life.[8] Weber seems to have two important mechanisms of generalization. The first is that of economic competition or "what everywhere and always is the result of such a process of rationalization: those who would not follow suit had to go out of business."[9] The second mechanism is the process of political and social bureaucratization of domination.

> [The]...rational bureaucratic structure of domination...[has] develop[ed]...far reaching and general cultural effects...quite independently of the areas in which it takes hold....bureaucracy promotes a "rationalist" way of life...[and] furthers the development of "rational matter-of-factness" and the personality type of the professional expert. This has far-reaching ramifications....Since bureaucracy has a "rational" character, with rules, means-ends calculus, and matter-of-factness predominating, its rise and expansion has everywhere had "revolutionary" results...as had the advance of "rationalism" in general.[10]

Efficiency, then, is one measure of the rationalism of bureaucratic organization. As bureaucratic procedures have gained acceptance as the legitimate form of economic, social, and political organization, so too has efficiency gained legitimacy as its appropriate measure.

The act of measuring efficiency and applying these standards to organizations, however, has transformed the meaning of the concepts of which it is the measure. The Utilitarians, whether act or rule utilitarians, shared the assumption that "social good" or "utility" ought to be the proper aim of states. In the broadest sense, the good society was one so constructed that the summation of the pains and pleasures of individuals produced the largest possible margin in favor of pleasure. Much was lost in the translation of this "calculus of hedonism" from philosophy to economics.

The central loss was in the meaning of "good" and "utility." The philosophical meaning included intrinsic value, a value not necessarily quantifiable by objective criteria. As used by economists like Jevons and Marshall, utility has come to mean "value in use." We know something's "value in use" by what people are willing to exchange for it. The "price" of a good—its value in use—we can understand only in terms of the marginal utility of the last unit of it for an individual against the marginal utility of other goods—indifference analysis. This transformation of meaning is crucial for the mathematization of economics, and it has allowed economists to understand some heretofore puzzling phenomena.[11]

But we should not lose sight of the biases it introduces into the examination of utility and efficiency.[12] First, only individual preferences for commodities (and time) can be easily measured. Those "social commodities" and basic "rights" of citizenship (and human existence) that were part of the philosophical utilitarian conception of the "good" are not accommodated in the economic conception. Secondly, the emphasis on the maximization of "good" or "pleasure" has been changed to the maximization of individual choice—choice among commodities. Thirdly, the usual measure of economic efficiency is the net benefit criterion—average or paretean. This is usually understood in terms of increases in real income, a measure which—barring metaphysical contortions of the concept of negative externality—excludes crucial public "quality of life" concerns. I have previously discussed the problem of the internal validity of these measures of efficiency. We need add to this the threat to the external validity of these measures posed by the fact that only a narrow range of important data about the "good" is quantifiable. The apparent value neutrality of economic analysis obscures the biases inherent in a view of the "good" as individual consumption.

Efficiency and its Application to Political Life

This discussion of efficiency and utility is important in a study of public policy toward declining industries because it raises what many take to be the central problem facing states—that of distributive justice. Inevitably, the question of political intervention in the economy raises the issue of equity in the distribution of resources. Using economic efficiency as the standard for justifying when to intervene may appear to be value-neutral, but we know this standard to measure only a narrow range of the "good." In consequence, this standard biases the issue so that intervention is usually directed at achieving "efficiency" in terms of price. This standard does not always produce results that favor the "efficient," or capitalist, class, but it does have a bias against nonmarket factors like community or "rights." The perceived justice of this distribution, and its political consequences, are also among the factors ignored.[13]

The distribution of goods is a problem which lies in the domain of governments. Even those who favor limited government, and argue that distribution is, and ought to be, only a function of markets, understand that the enforcement of the distribution of goods is the major function of government. Adam Smith, no friend of encroaching government, wrote

> Men may live together in society with some tolerable degree of security, though there is no civil magistrate to protect them from the injustice of ... passions. But avarice and ambition in the rich, in the poor the hatred of labour and the love of present ease and enjoyment, are the passions which prompt to invade property.... Wherever there is great property, there is great inequality. For one very rich man, there must be at least five hundred poor, and the affluence of the few supposes the indigence of the many. The affluence of the rich excites the indignation of the poor, who are often both driven by want, and prompted by envy, to invade his possessions. It is only under the shelter of the civil magistrate that the owner ... can sleep a single night in security. ... The acquisition of valuable and extensive property, therefore, necessarily requires the establishment of civil government. [231–32]
> Civil government, so far as it is instituted for the security of property, is in reality instituted for the defense of the rich against the poor, or of those who have some property against those who have none at all. [236][14]

Smith's pessimism concerning the fate of ordinary people was mild in contrast to the classical economists who followed him. Regardless of the justice they saw in the then current distribution of goods, economists from Marx to Malthus agreed that the majority of humanity was bound to suffer pauperization under capitalism. Richard Hofstadter pointed out that long before the advent of Social Darwinism and the philosophy of survival of the fittest, economists had evolved an understanding of human behavior in terms of scarcity, struggle, and competition.

> ...classical economics already had its doctrine of social selection. Since it had been one of the great figures of the classical economic tradition [Malthus] who had led Spencer, Darwin, and Wallace toward the evolutionary theories, the economists might have had some justification for proclaiming that biology had merely universalized a truth that had been in [economists'] possession for a long time.[15]

The truths of the "iron law of wages," pauperization, and natural selection presented liberal governments with the tradeoff between economic and political freedoms. Distributive justice was an irresolvable issue in class war. After all, given universal suffrage, would not the majority end capitalism, and seize and redistribute property? In every capitalist country, the enforcement of the distribution of goods produced by capitalism took precedence over majority rule. Given the assumptions of classical economics, such that efficiency was a desirable attribute of government, it was applied to maintaining police order and to fiscal prudence: not to promoting growth or equality.

The cataclysms of war and depression redefined the roles of government with regard to distribution. The desperate poverty of unemployed, marginalized workers, and the threat to political stability that this was thought to pose, produced many of the institutions of welfare capitalism, liberal (i.e. laissez-faire) principles of political economy notwithstanding. The efficiency of authoritarian regimes in promoting economic growth was an important prod to expanding state involvement in Western democracies. In addition, we should remember that, even before Keynesean policies, many non-Marxist economists (e.g. Thorstein Veblen, Joseph Schumpeter) saw some form of state planning as inherently more efficient (at least in the short-term) than traditional capitalism. This conjunction of massive market failure, prospering enemy authoritarian regimes, and alternative theories of public economy resulted in the promotion of economic growth and the presence of a welfare system being defined as possibly the central legitimate task of the state. Political discourse was henceforth to focus, not on the value of these new goals, but on the most efficient strategy (and party) to their achievement. A few "free-marketers" objected, but real-world failure was no respecter of the intellectual rigor of libertarian liberalism.

The possibility that this new compromise over distribution (i.e. both growth and welfare) involved two potentially contradictory goals occurred to very few before the 1970s; Schumpeter was the major exception.[16] In the first place, the political problems of distributive justice were eased in the Western democracies by the postwar growth. In part, economic growth "floats all boats" and lessens the political demand for, and the economic consequences of, the redistributive policies of the welfare system. Growth made possible the "Great Society" programs, "social engineering," and the institutionalization of welfare expenses.

The second factor in easing the political problems was the perception that "technocratic" politics had provided a method for solving distributional problems. To repeat myself—the promise of efficiency (here, technocratic politics) was of a value-neutral, rational method of resolving distributional problems. The difference now between this politics of efficiency and those of the late-nineteenth and early-twentieth century was that economists no longer believed in the inevitability of widespread poverty and rigid income distributions. Keynes taught that a well-managed economy could both achieve growth and eradicate poverty.

The particular benefit to states of technocratic politics consisted in limiting the domain and the intensity of political struggle. The endless political battling over the allocation of government resources could be circumvented by delegating decisions to bureaucrats, thus making the process appear in the political arena as categorical and nondiscretionary. It is bureaucrats matching people to categories, not interminable political bargaining over who gets what, that characterizes modern welfare capitalism. The allure of technocratic politics was widespread enough so that professional schools were set up by many of the nation's most prestigious universities to teach the science of politics and public management.[17]

These twin phenomena of economic growth and technocratic politics produced in most Western countries a period of relative political consensus during the 1950s and 1960s. The ideological politics of the early part of the twentieth century were little in evidence. "The End of Ideology" was Daniel Bell's summation of this period.[18]

The relative consensus dissolved as the economies of the Western nations slowed in the 1970s. Both the standards of technocratic politics and the definition of growth/welfare as equally important state functions have come to be threatened. Older issues of distributional politics have reemerged. Forgetting for a moment that political turmoil over distribution is the usual, not the deviant, case in politics, various academics advanced "overload" or "crisis of democracy" theses. These saw "excess participation" by interest groups as imperiling the political stability of Western societies, a true but historically obvious proposition.[19] Institutional change that limited or structured political demands was seen as the best solution to this problem.

These proposals, however, missed the point. Simply put, many economists now believe that a resumption of economic growth requires (at least in the sort-term) redistribution of income away from the consuming class (the majority of us) toward the saving class. In low-growth situations, the compromise of growth and welfare is now seen as being really a tradeoff. Democratic states must—there the argument goes again—shift income from the majority. No wonder that taxes and distribution are again the subject of intense ideological debate. The crises theorists are right in saying that states now confront problems that political institutions cannot now adequately handle. But, can any institution adequately handle the dilemma in which democratic capitalist states ask the majority to surrender income to the already rich?

The problem is located in the very nature of the tasks that the state was being asked to perform, and in the methods available to states to perform them. The method of adjusting income distribution has been through bureaucratic politics. But, technocratic politics cannot handle this issue. The very claims about what is "necessary" or "efficient" do not hide the interests involved, and what are most claims about distributive justice but self-interest mediated through self-serving values and self-serving rhetoric?[20]

The larger problem is that governments confront potentially irreconcilable incentives and obligations; these "irreconcilables" are often called contradictions. A contradiction "is the tendency inherent within a specific mode of production [e.g. capitalism] to destroy those very preconditions on which its survival depends....the necessary becomes the impossible, and the impossible becomes the necessary."[21]

The originator of the meaning of this sense of contradiction is Marx. For him, contradictions were economic in origin, with devastating political and social consequences for existing institutions; I have already discussed at length the "tendency of the rate of profit to fall," one major contradiction for Marx. However, my discussion of the relevant potential contradictions has its roots more in the work of Max Weber on legitimation and with Joseph Schumpeter on creative destruction.

The first major contradiction is between government legitimacy and the efficient accumulation of investment funds by firms. The primary insights into this problem are to be found in the work of Claus Offe and Jürgen Habermas. Although I have previously rejected Offe's work as not being adequate for an understanding of the forms and substance of policy congruence, his work (and that of Habermas) gives us a language of description with which to explore the dimensions of the problem of public policy and economic efficiency.

The argument is as follows. Legitimacy—the extent to which people believe the existing rules and institutions to be just—is a political concern. Governments seek to gain and maintain legitimacy. Some aspects of maintaining government legitimacy interfere with the efficient accumulation of investment resources in the private sector and vice versa. Each, however, is a necessary compliment to the other; both are necessary conditions for stability. We have seen one illustration of this contradiction in our discussion of the dilemma confronting democratic governments as they redistribute income from the consuming class to the already wealthy while attempting to persuade people of the necessity and efficiency of this policy. Offe sees three specific tradeoffs between legitimacy and efficiency. These are:

> 1). the prohibitive political and economic costs in advanced capitalist economies of maintaining full employment of both capital and labor (owing to the decreasing marginal returns);
>
> 2). the increasing demand on governments to provide costly programs and incentives to make workers employable by the private sector (with education, manpower, regional, and other policies); and
>
> 3). the changes induced by the non-market state services sector (e.g., education, welfare) in the perceptions of those who are involved with it about what is legitimate and appropriate (so that, for instance, welfare is seen as a legal and moral right by its recipients, and not as an act of charity.)[22]

All three "empirical phenomena" undermine the equilibrium between the state's need for legitimacy and the state's need for efficient accumulation, an equilibrium that Offe apparently believes (as do I) existed in the 1950s and 1960s. These phenomena are clearly now at work in Western societies, and help explain the return to ideological politics and the general inadequacy of technocratic politics.[23]

A second level of contradiction operates at the cultural level, though it has an impact on the state. Weber argued that Protestant asceticism was an essential precondition for capitalism, but that, once asceticism became a component of capitalist culture, the religious and moral underpinnings of capitalist society were dispensable, and vanished.

> Since asceticism undertook to remodel the world and to work out its ideals in the world, material goods have gained an increasing and finally an inexorable power over the lives of men as at no previous period in history. Today the spirit of religious asceticism—whether

finally, who knows?—has escaped from the cage. But victorious capitalism, since it rests on mechanical foundations, needs its support no
longer.[24]

Weber was concerned with the necessity of a moral ethic to the
workings of capitalism—capitalism and the moral virtue of the individual. Daniel Bell and Irving Kristol have shifted the argument
to one of capitalism and moral legitimacy—that the political legitimacy of capitalism requires a general belief among ordinary people
that capitalism somehow produces (on balance) morally just outcomes—that virtue will usually be rewarded.[25] Bell notes that several
features of capitalist society undermine the traditional link between
capitalism and moral virtue. These features are the consumer culture
(as promoted through advertising) and (less clearly in Bell's argument) the systematic promotion of acquisitive individualism
("what's in it for me?") as capitalism's central virtue. Capitalism
promotes free markets in all spheres, including those of moral values,
thus leaving itself vulnerable to political counterattack and
delegitimation.

The argument may be overstated, but the central notion of moral
legitimacy as being crucial for capitalism's survival is sound. "Moral
Sentiment" seems to be one of the irreducible prisms through which
people understand their world. "Moral Sentiment" seems to attach,
through long years of exposure, in particular to the outcomes produced by existing political and social relations—the wellspring of
legitimacy in one sense. Even the market economy seems to have
had some of its features so legitimated—despite its apparent ran-
domlessness—because it has brought prosperity to many people.[26]
Political, social, and economic events are therefore all subject to
moral judgement. States, as they intervene in the economy, need to
meet not only its own general standards of efficiency, but those of
"moral sentiment" as well. This is a difficult task, as people show
no inclination to accept unfavorable outcomes simply because the
"market" so ordains.[27]

In sum, economic efficiency (and its liberal utilitarian foundation) has its difficulties in acting as the origin of public policy or as the justification for public policy. It is not value-neutral, it is subject to a variety of "irreconcilables" or contradictions, it is not always (or even intended to be) just, and it does not specify unique solutions. Very well—but if not efficiency, then upon what other ethic can we base public policy? Which other normative theories available to us are useful in deciding when, and how, we should intervene in non-competitive industries?

Alternative Bases for Public Policy

I take economics and standards of economic efficiency to be "consequentialist" in world view. That is, what works is good, what works better is better. These other possible bases for public policy are primarily nonconsequentialist. That is, rights are vested in individuals or in groups, and competition and social allocation of resources are then constrained by rights. Three alternative non-consequentialist types of theories are discussed here, though each of these also seems to also have practical problems. These are libertarianism, communitarianism, and the work of John Rawls.

The libertarian position rejects the right of the state to intervene in the economy except to enforce the most basic "free market" rules of the game.[28] Libertarians reject both social justice and efficiency as claims for state intervention. Friedrich Hayek has gone so far as to say of the notion of "social justice" that

> it is a sign of the immaturity of our minds that we have not yet outgrown these primitive concepts [social justice] and still demand from an impersonal process [markets] which brings about a greater satisfaction of human desires than any deliberate human organization could achieve, that it conform to the moral precepts men have evolved for the guidance of their individual actions.[29]

The root of this argument is that liberty is the ultimate value, and all other values are, or ought to be, derivative.

In the context of asking about the direction of modern state intervention, this argument is in practice something of a *non sequitur*. In the first place, markets are already hopelessly structured by state interventions in many subtle and not so subtle ways. To ask on what basis we should choose policies and to be told not to choose is to ignore reality. More to the point, many of the state interventions are the consequence of market failures, the largest of which—the Great Depression—caused the overthrow of a number of market systems, including that of Professor Hayek's homeland. Legitimacy and social justice, no matter how immature the impulse, are ignored by states only at their peril.

John Rawls' *A Theory of Justice* (henceforth, TJ) provides another standard for judging and justifying public practices.[30] TJ has had enormous impact, not in the least because it provides something of an intellectual justification for the liberal welfare state. Without providing the detail of the argument, the relevant features seem to be that institutions and practices of states should be so structured such that public actions would not be undertaken unless the least well-off were to benefit—the difference principle. In Rawls's thought experiment at least, we would agree to these institutions and practices because, acting from self-interest, we all would come to consensus about institutions and practices from behind a "veil of ignorance;" we would therefore not know our future economic and social position. In this position of ignorance, Rawls argues that reasonable people would produce the following principles:

> First, each person participating in a practice, or affected by it, has an equal right to the most extensive liberty compatible with a like liberty for all; and second, inequalities are arbitrary unless it is reasonable to expect that they will work out [to the benefit of the least well-off], and provided the positions and offices to which they attach, or from which they may be gained, are open to all.[31]

Some of the problems of personal interest, incomplete information, greed, and so on are partially eliminated as the individuals and officials participating in those practices are freed from the burden of calculating how their individual decisions affect the worst-off as the schema at large is structured to protect these people.

Rawls has given us a standard for assessing the justice of practices. This standard, justice as fairness, has several immediate applications for us. The first issue is whether or not the state should be able to aid auto workers and their firms; the second is whether or not the income distribution alleged to be necessary for efficient growth is just. Hence, should the investment of private firms be subsidized given these two principles?

Initially, permitting the state to aid the auto sector seems to be in violation of the injunction to avoid inequalities unless they work to the benefit of the least well-off. The shareholders and managers are in no sense the least well-off. Neither are the auto workers the worst-off in the society, and perhaps not even in context of the practices of the auto industry; they constitute something of a labor aristocracy, and their high wages have induced companies to follow capital intensive, rather than labor intensive, methods of production. To aid them, and the unionized industrial workers in general, is to perpetuate an existing inequality. Reading Rawls in this way would lead us to provide less support for the auto industry than would a utilitarian calculus.

This objection can be met in two ways. First, as a result of the multiplier effect, maintaining the income levels of auto workers would, at least in theory, avoid a net loss to everyone in the local economy. Secondly, the unemployed industrial workers join, after their benefits expire, the least well off group in society, both in terms of income and life opportunities. Certainly, the loss of work and community would impair the life-chances of the children of the workers. To aid them is to prevent them from becoming the least well-off.

The second issue is the more important one; it goes to the heart of the justification of firm autonomy over investment and inequitable income distribution. The claim is made that, in order for economies to grow efficiently, the least well-off need to be made even less well-off, and the well-off need to be made even more well-off—the indifference principle if you will. Rawls addressed this issue of just savings in the context of justice between generations. He said:

> Some may go further and maintain that inequalities in wealth and authority violating the second principle of justice may be justified if the subsequent economic and social benefits are large enough. To support their view they may point to instances in which we seem to accept such inequalities and rates of accumulation for the sake of the welfare of later generations....It was precisely the inequality of the distribution of wealth which made possible the rapid build-up of capital and the more or less steady improvement in the general standard of living for everyone. [TJ, pp. 298–99]

The argument, then, can be made to turn solely on improving the situation of the standards of living of future generations of the working class.

> ...Whenever the constraints of justice in a matter of savings are infringed, it must be shown that circumstances are such that not to trespass upon them would lead to an even greater injury to those on whom the injustice falls. [TJ, p. 299]

The question would then seem to hinge on one of two empirical issue: "does "trickle-down" economics lead to greater economic growth?" or "does creative destruction require little alleviation of the consequences of economic failure?" Practices should be adjusted to reflect the answers. Should the answers be yes, we would face a paradox. The logic of the argument would lead us to the following conclusion: those things that promote growth, as long as the least well-off benefit more than they otherwise would, are just.[32] Though with different beginning assumptions, this position is indistinguishable in practice and in end result from some versions of the economic efficiency argument. Perhaps the Almighty really does manifest Himself through all things, vulgar and sublime.

But this would be a misreading of Rawls' intention. In a subsequent article, he indicates that he was referring only to a savings rate consistent with "a material base for making equal liberties effective."[33]

Beyond this point justice requires no further accumulation of wealth and net savings may drop to zero" [FG, p. 544–45]. Rawls is in fact willing in some circumstances to surrender economic growth if it would require too much inequality. Justice "does not enjoin a continual increase in the general level of wealth, but only that the existing (and possibly constant) social product be distributed in a certain way " [FG, p. 545.]. As the issue for us in discussing economics and redistribution is not "shall we grow?" but rather "how may we most efficiently grow?", the argument in favor of the current redistributionary policies cannot be held to be just.

Rawls' argument is an internally consistent alternative standard for evaluating political action—one at odds with prevailing practices, and radical in its implications. Few Western politicians would call for an end to the growth regime on grounds of justice. But, it is a persuasive alternative normative standard to economic efficiency.

The final basis for action is one which treats community as a necessary and irreplaceable means for the attainment of some human good. Many different theorists are communitarians in this sense; corporatism, feudal collectivism, communism, and syndicalism, all share this view of community. The view as to what constitutes the good, of course, differs. For Marx, the good was an end to alienation and exploitation, and a reintegration of our social selves. For Aristotle, the goodness of a community was in its ability to bring out the goodness of individual. But, the individual reaches his/her potential only though community.

This is a puzzling notion for liberal theory; the community is generally thought to have no end but those of its individual members. Community as prior to the individual is in fact the antithesis of liberal thought, a challenge to the assumptions of individualism. Aristotle, in many ways the first of the political communitarians, made this explicit.

> ... it is evident that the *polis* [city-state] belongs to the class of things that exist by nature, and that man is by nature an animal intended to live in a *polis*. He who is without a *polis*, by reason of his own nature

and not of some accident is either a poor sort of being, or a being
higher than man... [Politics, 1253 a 9]
...the *polis* is prior in the order of nature to the family and the individual. [Politics 1253 a 12.]

Aristotle's assumption about the priority of community is shared by
social corporatist theories of society, be they Christian corporatism
or Marxist. Some higher end is to be found only through the collec-
tivity. Again, Aristotle: "...the end of the state is not mere life; it
is rather a good quality of life" [1280 a 6]. Economic prosperity is
not what Aristotle means, however: "it is not the end of the state to
provide an alliance for mutual defense against all injury, or to ease
exchange and promote economic intercourse." Rather, "any *polis*
which is truly so called... must devote itself to the end of encouraging goodness [of its citizens]" [1280 b 8]. In essence, community
constitutes moral association, to which economic exchange is clearly
an inferior act. If we accept the premise as true, preserving community—even if not exactly Aristotle's *polis*—ought to be the end
of policy, as community is the highest of associations.
    This argument does have its strengths as it provides us with a
standards for state intervention. Utilitarianism cannot tell us how
we should evaluate a situation in which either many will suffer a
small financial loss or a few will suffer serious financial and community losses. Communitarians value community: they would judge
that the many should suffer a little. For some communitarians, gains
and losses of the community are not even understandable in terms
of the gains or losses to individuals. And what if, over the course of
time, these small losses produce a less efficient and less prosperous
society than that of others? The communitarians answer that economic growth is no measure of the quality of life; perhaps too much
economic growth undermines this quality.[34]
    In contrast to the United States, the communitarian ethic and the
recognition of the importance of the "quality of life" seems to be
deeper in Britain.[35] Britain has grown more slowly than other major
countries, in large measure because her politicians undertook non-

market solutions to social problems. But, her streets are clean and infinitely safer than those of America, and her lower class receives medicine and housing as a right. London is not filled, as is New York, with tens of thousands of homeless and destitute people; missing teeth, rotting feet, and pints of Mad Dog 20/20. The communitarian ethos is in bad repute among Britain's current liberal leadership. But, they should be forewarned that too much policy similarity with the United States will have its costs.[36]

Despite its humanitarian overtones, community as the inspiration and the end of public policy has practical problems. The argument, when taken to its extreme, could be used to block any social and economic change. Economists cite buggy-whip manufacturers and carriage makers, but the point is well taken that some social and economic change is inevitable in a world where innovation occurs.

Perhaps a more crucial problem is that the community argument assumes a homogeneous population. Unless values and norms are well defined and widely shared, the formulation of public policy is bound to produce intense political conflict as groups with different values and interests each seek to have its values codified into law. The danger is particularly acute where religious differences are pronounced, as the current debate in America over abortion reminds us. In heterogeneous situations, the communitarian ethic will likely split communities.

Should value consensus be achieved (at least in the United States) the least common denominator will inevitably be Christian tradition. Several social movements have attempted to transform the U.S. into a Christian commonwealth (e.g. Women's Christian Temperance Union, the Moral Majority). Mercifully, they have failed. We should understand that the "deep structure" of American society may be communitarian, but it need not be and probably is not tolerant and humane.

Thus, we have a dilemma. Current policy is based only upon a reflection of a narrow and not very "rational" definition of state interest, but all of our other alternative bases for political choices are also compromised in their practical applications. Each is partly flawed in its vision and consequences. We also have no "objective" standard for choosing among them. Our choices can really be based only on our antecedent values. Do we prefer growth to equality, to community, to liberty?

The reader may by now be convinced that the "science" of this political analysis is gone. In truth, political science can take us no further. Political art and moral vision are the only guideposts left to us in choosing the "ought" of politics. But, the purpose of this discussion is to remind us of the consequences of our choices, and that we even have alternative choices. The electorate may still prefer economic efficiency as the standard of public policy. But, they should be offered other paths.

Appendix

MAJOR CHANGES IN EFFECTIVE TAX RATES— EXPLANATIONS FOR SCORING OF "Z"

Japan

1972　Capital Gains for land sales taxed at 15%, up from 10%. (-1)

1973　Top corporate tax rate raised to 40% from 36.75%. (-1)

1974　Capital gains from land sales taxed at 20%, up from 15%. 10% surplus profits surcharge applied to corporate profits. (-1)

1975　Tax rates reduced for small and medium-sized corporations to 6% and 9% respectively. (1)

1979–1980　Addition depreciation for Plant and Equipment valued over ¥100 million decreased from 33% to 27%. (-1)

1980–1981　Top corporate tax rate increased to 42% from 40%. (-1)

1982　Minimum salvage value of fixed assets increased from 5% to 10% of acquisition cost. (1)

West Germany

1977　Top corporate tax rate raised to 56% from 52.53%. (-1)

1980–1981　Depreciation on equipment accelerated; first year allowance raised from 22.7% to 27.3%. (1)

1981–　Maximum first-year accelerated depreciation allow-
1982　　ance raised to 30%. *(1)*

United Kingdom

1970–　Top corporate tax rate cut from 43.13 to 40%. *(1)*
1971

1973　Top corporate tax rate raised from 40% to 49%. *(-1)*

1974　Acquisition of new and used plant and machinery eligible
　　　for 100% 1st-year depreciation. *(1)*

1974–　"stock-relief" passed, effectively eliminating cor-
1975　　porate taxation. *(1)*

1981　First-year depreciation allowance for industrial building in-
　　　creased from 50% to 75%. *(1)*

United States

1969　Investment tax credit removed, effective 1970. *(-1)*

1971–　Reinstatement of investment tax credit; liberalization
1972　　of depreciation lifetimes to + or − 20% of former guide-
　　　lines. *(1)*

1975　Increase in investment tax credit. *(1)*

1978　Top corporate tax rate cut to 46% from 48%; increase in
　　　capital gains holding period from 6 months to 1 year. *(1)*

1980　Maximum corporate capital gains tax decreased from 30%
　　　to 28%. *(1)*

1982　Economic Recovery Tax Act of 1981 initiates accelerated
　　　depreciation system, tax swaps, and "safe-harbors." *(1)*

1983　1981 ERTA amended: "safe-harbors" restricted, depreciation
　　　rules "tightened." *(-1)*

Sources:

Business International Corporation. *Investing, Licensing, and Trading Conditions Abroad.* Various issues, 1970–1985.

Horst, Thomas. *Income Taxation and Competitiveness.* Washington: National Planning Association, 1977.

Ministry of Finance (Japan). Tax Bureau. *An Outline of Japanese
Taxes.* Tokyo: various years.

Kay, J. A. and Mervyn A. King. *The British Tax System.* Oxford: Oxford University Press, 1978.

King, Mervyn A. and Don Fullerton. *The Taxation of Income from Capital.* Chicago: University of Chicago Press, 1984.

Price Waterhouse. *Corporate Taxes: A Worldwide Summary.* Various issues.

U.S. Congress. Joint Economic Committee. *The Corporate Tax Code as an Industrial Policy.* Washington: GPO, 1984.

NOTES

1. Overview

1. Robert R. Alford and Roger Friedland, *Powers of Theory*, p. 1.

2. Most social scientists are aware of the problem of inductionism posed in David Hume's *Enquiry Concerning Human Understanding*. "Nature will always maintain her rights, and prevail in the end over any abstract reasoning whatsoever.... All inferences from experience are effects of custom, not of reasoning.... All belief of matter of fact or real existence is derived merely from some object, present to the memory or sense, and a customary conjunction between that and some other object.... experimental reasoning [therefore] is nothing but a species of instinct" (Hackett edition).

"Deduction leading to falsification" as a research method, which Imre Lakatos terms "naïve falsificationism," also has not been accepted in the social sciences as the exclusive method of research. (See Lakatos, *The Methodology of Scientific Research Programmes: Philosophical Papers*, 1:20–93; Donald N. McCloskey, *The Rhetoric of Economics*, pp. 13–19.) In practice, a more limited form of "deduction-falsification," with a "whiff of inductivism" (Lakatos's phrase) is the more usually accepted methodology. See Mark Blaug, *The Methodology of Economics*, Ch. 15. In essence, the question of methodology in the social sciences distills to "what problems, procedures and practices do I, as member of field X, need to follow to be persuasive within my research community."

"Sophisticated methodological falsificationism"—again, Lakatos's phrase—probably is the most widely accepted method in the social sciences. But, as those of us in the social sciences (especially in interdisciplinary fields of research) know, research cultures differ substantially among disciplines and within subfields of disciplines.

3. One very interesting theoretical treatment of public policy is found in Robert E. Goodin, *Political Theory and Public Policy*.

4. Katzenstein, *Small States in World Markets*, p. 21.

5. John Freeman of the University of Minnesota once suggested that two research cultures are to be found in the study of political economy. One, he termed the Social Science Research Council (SSRC) model, and this he characterized as involving careful historical and comparative analysis, usually done through interviews and archival research. The other, the National Science Foundation (NSF) model, employs data collection and quantitative analysis.

6. Regarding the rules of deduction, see John Neville Keynes, who in *The Scope and Method of Political Economy* (part of which is reprinted in Daniel Hausman, ed., *The Philosophy of Economics*) advanced what he took to be the proper rules of deduction in his chapter 7 (pages 85–93 in the Hausman volume). Keynes's approach to method is far from dogmatic, and reads, three quarter's of a century later, closely to Lakatos's prescriptions for deduction mixed with inductive leaps. Neville Keynes praises "Adam Smith's freedom from excess on the side either of à priori or of à posteriori reasoning. He rejected no method of inquiry that could in any way assist him in investigating the phenomena of wealth" (pp. 74–75).

Those who work within the interpretive tradition in the social sciences frequently quote Weber on the impossibility of separating human action from its meaning context. Weber wrote, in *The Methodology of the Social Sciences*: "The fantastic claim has occasionally been made for economic theories—e.g., the abstract theories of price, interest, rent, etc.,—that they can, by ostensibly following the analogy of physical science propositions, be validly applied to the derivation of quantitatively stated conclusions from given real premises, since given the ends, economic behavior with respect to means in unambiguously 'determined.' This claim fails to observe that in order to be able to reach this result even in the simplest case, the totality of the existing historical reality including every one of its causal relationships must be assumed as given and presupposed as known. But if this type of knowledge were accessible to the finite mind of man, abstract theory would have no cognitive value whatsoever (p. 88)."

Regarding economists' acceptance of the formal testing of hypotheses, see Lord Lionel Robbins, "The Nature of Economic Generalizations," in *The Nature and Significance of Economic Science*, (reprinted in Hausman); and Milton Friedman, "The Methodology of Positive Economics," also reprinted in Hausman's useful volume. By no means am I unaware of or, more importantly, unsympathetic to the criticism launched against the formalization of historically determined phenomena in the search for law-like precepts.

7. See Claus Offe *Contradictions of the Welfare State*.

8. Katzenstein describes these as the liberal and the statist traditions. He adds a third model, democratic corporatism, which he argues characterizes the smaller European countries. *Small States...*

9. This is the assumption implicit in Mancur Olson's *The Rise and Decline of Nations*, for instance. Many textbooks in economics and finance make this assumption explicitly.

10. Keynes, of course, wrote "the decadent international but individualistic capitalism" where I substituted "public interventionism"—poetic license. John Maynard Keynes, "National Self-Sufficiency," *The Yale Review* (Summer 1933), vol. 22.

11. The conquering of the business cycle was held to be the singular triumph of Keynesean economics, though a further smoothing of the business cycle, Andrew Shonfield argued, was to be had from the adoption of indicative (or coordinated) planning. See his *Modern Capitalism.* He maintained that position, even in the face of the economic instability of the 1970s, and the increasing international composition of trade in his *In Defense of the Mixed Economy*, chs. 3, 12. Schumpeter notes, in *Capitalism, Socialism, and Democracy*, that leveling the business cycle may have long-term detrimental effects on economic growth—short-term organization of society's resources does not necessarily produce long-term optimization. Keynes's reputed reply—in the long-run, we're all dead.

The recent cutbacks in employment at Renault and throughout the steel industry seem to indicate the protecting employment will no longer be a central goal of the Mitterrand government.

12. See the essays by Krasner, Ruggie, and Strange in Stephen Krasner, ed. *International Regimes.*

13. The substantial intervention in the domestic markets by the Japanese and French states in the postwar era is well documented; a review of the literature can be found in Dennis P. Quinn and Robert Jacobson, "Industrial Policy Through the Restriction of Capital Flows," in which the consequences of industrial policy in recent years are assessed. Gary Saxonhouse has argued that Japan's institutions acted as substitutes for market mechanism, but that these institutions were neither superior to market mechanisms as methods of resource allocation nor copyable by other countries. Saxonhouse, "The Micro- and Macroeconomics of Foreign Sales to Japan."

Comparative economic growth rate data is open to various questions and varying interpretations—are we really measuring alike phenomena? what does this say about quality of life? and so on. The "yearly change in real gross domestic product" from 1960 to 1982 for Japan was 7.3% and 4.3% for France, the highest and second highest figures for the major OECD countries during that period. (Organization for Economic Cooperation and Development, *Historical Statistics, 1960–1982*, p. 44.) The American and British figures were 3.1% and 2.1%, respectively.

14. Paul Krugman, "New Theories of Trade Among Industrial Countries," *American Economic Review*, pp. 343–47. See also P. K. M. Tharakan, ed. *Intra-Industry Trade*.

One point of note is that even those who have advanced these models do not necessarily conclude that the U.S. should adopt trade restraints. Although it might be rational for any one country to adopt protectionist industrial strategies, the collective consequences to global welfare (especially for the Third World) of all countries adopting restraints are not good. In a sense, these models propose that protectionism–free trade decisions are a sort of prisoner's dilemma.

15. Dennis C. Mueller, in *Public Choice* provides a summary of the work of Buchanan, Tullock, Olson and others who work from the public choice perspective.

16. Milton Friedman, in several published reports, has explained Britain's continued economic decline under Thatcher's government as resulting from the Conservatives' failure to stay the course. He is quite right that the British state maintained its extensive interventions in various markets throughout the Conservatives' reign.

17. Elasticity is a concept that allows us to measure the changes in demand for a product relative to changes in its price (dY/dX). When a country's demand for imports is more elastic than is other countries' demand elasticity for its exports, the country will, among other problems, suffer balance of trade problems in early stages of business cycle recovery.

18. See Jacques Mistral, "Competitiveness of the Productive System and International Specialization," and his "Economic Growth of Nations and International Competitiveness," originally a talk presented at Columbia University, September 13, 1984. See also Attiat F. Ott, "An Industrial Policy for the United States."

19. Quoted from Organization for Economic Cooperation and Development, *Competition and Trade Policies: Their Interaction.*

2. The World Auto Industry

1. Organization for Economic Cooperation and Development, *Long-Term Outlook for the World Automobile Industry* (1983), p. 7.

2. James Laux, "The Genesis of the Automobile Revolution," p. 47.

3. The authors of the MIT study of the automobile industry regard this development in Europe as being a production innovation on a par with that

engineered by Henry Ford, and as an important precursor of the Japanese form of "Flexible" production. Alan Altschuler et al., *The Future of the Automobile*, ch. 1.

4. Alfred D. Chandler, Jr., ed., *Giant Enterprise*, p. 5.

5. For a discussion of the Sloan method of management, see Chandler, "GM's Innovations in Management . . . and Marketing," pp. 111–75.

6. Laux, "Genesis," pp. 79–90, 112.

7. George Maxcy, in his *Multinational Motor Industry* has argued that "almost all foreign investment decisions have been prompted by tariff barriers to exports. . . . foreign direct investment in the automotive industry has almost always been defensive investment" (p. 270). See also pp. 84–86.

Ford and General Motors were not entirely welcomed in Continental Europe, even after they had substantial investments in those markets. Ford was effectively squeezed out of Italy in the 1930s, GM was prevented from purchasing Citroen in France in the 1930s, and the Nazi Government (no surprise here) showed strong preference for indigenous producers (e.g. VW's ancestor, Auto-Union) over GM's Opel and Fordwerke.

8. U.S., Congressional Budget Office, *Current Problems of the U.S. Industry and Policies to Address Them*, p. 38.

9. Though almost all observers of the world industry credit the Japanese government as being the crucial element in the development of Japan's "infant industry," some controversy remains as to the importance of government policies from the 1960s on in the success of Japanese firms. See for instance Robert E. Cole and Taizo Yajusiji, eds., *The American and Japanese Auto Industries in Transition*, in which little credit is given to the Japanese state for the industry's success.

10. Marina v. N. Whitman, *International Trade and Investment*, pp. 11, 13.

11. Sanjaya Lall, "Prospects for Automotive Transnationals in the Third World," pp. 13–30.

For an innovative discussion of the development of the auto industry in a developing context, see Douglas C. Bennett and Kenneth E. Sharpe, *Transnational Corporations Versus the State: the Political Economy of the Mexican Auto Industry*.

12. The material in this section is drawn from C. S. Chang, *The Japanese Auto Industry and the U.S. Market*. Chalmers Johnson, *MITI and the Japanese Miracle*, and William C. Duncan, *U.S.–Japan Automobile Diplomacy*. The most recent (and most complete) study available in English is Michael A. Cusumano, *The Japanese Automobile Industry: Technology and Management at Nissan and Toyota*.

13. Quoted in Duncan, p. 74 and Chang, p. 49.

14. See Johnson, *MITI*, pp. 286–89 for a discussion of Mitsubishi's break with MITI.

15. Hyundai entered the American market in February 1986. By the end of August, Hyundai's Excel had become the leading foreign import in the American market, with monthly sales of 20,000. Hyundai's Pony had comparable success in Canada. *New York Times*, October 3, 1986.

16. Organization for Economic Cooperation and Development (hereafter OECD), *Economic Surveys: Canada*, p. 63.

17. Canada instead chose to negotiate the Auto-Pact treaty with the U.S., a treaty that joined the two nations into one basic market, while using incentives and grants to induce the American companies to produce in Canada. See Ross Perry, *The Future of Canada's Auto Industry.*

This policy has resulted in Canada's becoming an auto exporting nation (to the United States). One third of Canada's 1983–1984 trade surplus originated in automobile sales. Not all of Canada's success can be attributed to Canadian government policy, however. Canada's plants produced a disproportionately large share of full-sized cars and vans, and therefore benefited from the decreasing price of oil and the consequent rise in sales of full-sized cars and vans. Ironically, Canadian critics of the American automotive manufacturers in 1979 and 1980 cited the Canadian industry's reliance on large cars as evidence that the American industry was unconcerned about the fate of the Canadian plants. See "Canada's Lucky Car Industry," *The New York Times*, October 17, 1984.

The Korean automobile industry has developed rapidly, producing 236,000 automobiles in 1985, an increase of nearly 350% since 1981. The industry will have the capacity to produce 750,000 cars by 1987. Since the Korean market is quite small (107,000 cars sold in 1984), most of these cars are intended for the export market. While the industry has successfully exported cars to Canada (owing to an exemption from tariff duties), restrictions on Korean cars are in place throughout much of Europe. The Korean automotive firms may avoid trade restrictions in the American market because of the links between Korean firms and American firms (e.g. Daewoo Motors and General Motors). Should trade restraints be placed on Korean entry into the American market, Korean manufacturers will have only a small domestic market to sustain them.

A third method of creating an auto industry is for a nation to induce an MNC to sign a "turn-key" or technology agreement whereby, for a fee, the MNC issues licenses for technology or builds an assembly plant or does both, and then "turns over the key." FIAT signed a number of such agreements in Eastern Europe, principally with the Soviet Union and Poland. FIAT may now regret such deals. The new Yugo car, selling in the United

States in 1986 for $3990, is a FIAT 128 with minor modifications. The LADA, sold in Canada, is also a FIAT "knockoff." Not coincidentally, FIAT has abandoned the North American market. FIAT, however, remains one of the few profitable "mass" car producers.

18. Peter F. Cowhey and Edward Long, "Testing Theories of Regime Change," pp. 175–76.

19. See *Financial Times*, September 5, 1985; and OECD, *Long Term*, pp. 21–51. The *Economist* reported that GM operated at 98% of capacity in 1985, Ford at 87%, and Chrysler at 95%. Western European producers, on the other hand, had a spare capacity of 2.5 million cars in 1985. October 25, 1986, p. 83.

20. Daniel T. Jones, "Technology and the U.K. Automotive Industry," pp. 14–27.

21. Krish Bhaskar, *The Future of the World Motor Industry* (London: Kogan Page, 1980), pp. 350–54. Cowhey and Long, "Testing Theories," give a figure 6 million units higher than does Bhaskar.

22. Cowhey and Long, p. 174.

23. This means that motor vehicles are useful in helping to produce other goods (e.g. bringing things to markets) and that a country's work force will work harder if autos are within the price range of the middle to lower middle class.

24. In the business policy literature, a distinction is often made between products that are "price competitive" and those that are "quality competitive." Products that compete on the basis of price tend to be standardized, which means that the product is fairly uniform and the technology needed to produce it is widely available. Hence, firms will have comparable "capital endowments" as they produce the product, and lower per unit wage costs will usually be decisive for sales. These produces are often aimed at the "mass" market. Products that compete on the basis of quality tend to be specialized products, aimed at a specific market, one in which consumers tend to be less sensitive to changes in price and more sensitive to changes in product quality. Specialized machinery and skilled labor is often required to produce these products. Unlike "standardized" products, these goods are less vulnerable to wage-based price competition. Historically, countries like the U.S., with more equitable distributions of income, had developed "mass" markets; those with less equitable distribution of income (e.g., Western Europe) have tended to develop specialized markets. Markets develop traditions so that, even should income become more equitably distributed, the preferences of the consumers may remain that for "elite" goods, and vice versa.

The automobile is characterized by both types of goods—the Chevy Chevette and the BMW 528i. In the "mass" market, wage and labor organization costs matter to the ability of the firms to capture market share as consumers tend to be price sensitive. Since firms have comparable capital endowments, East Asian countries—with lower wages and higher productivity—successfully captured much of the mass market. Newly industrializing countries, or countries without a large domestic market, tend to enter this market—Yugoslavia and Korea are the most recent entrants. GM and Chrysler hope to capitalize on the competitive advantage of East Asia by developing joint production networks with Korean, as well as Japanese, firms. In the specialist market, prices matter less. Quality and brand-name appeal sell cars, and here wage costs are secondary as a basis of competition. Smaller production runs are possible, and scale economies are achieved in part through skilled labor, and not through capital intensive production. Specialist producers are less vulnerable to import competition. Being a specialist auto producer does not guarantee success, however. Germany's specialist producers—BMW, Porsche, Daimler-Benz, Audi—have fared well; Britain's—Triumph, Rover, MG—often did not. In practice, most large firms attempt to service both markets.

25. The classic discussion of economies of scale is to be found in F. M. Scherer, *Industrial Market Structure and Economic Performance*, especially chapter 4. The first extended discussion of specialization and the division of labor is to be found in Adam Smith's *The Wealth of Nations*. Smith argued that the extent of specialization is limited by the extent of the available market. Hence, we would expect, following Smith, that economies of scale should increase as barriers to trade diminish, and vice versa. Some analysts have argued that economy of scale is somewhat of a misleading concept, and that firms can achieve scale economies under widely varying circumstances. We do know that several of the smaller Japanese firms are profitable despite limited production runs.

For an discussion of recent and possible future changes in the structure of production, particularly with regard to production by "specialist" firms, see Charles F. Sabel, *Work and Politics*, especially chapter 5. See also the discussion of robots and reprogrammable machines as applied to assembly lines in Alan Altschuler et al, *The Future of the Automobile*.

David Friedman has argued that those automotive producers that develop a "small and flexible" production system do not necessarily suffer serious cost disadvantages in comparison to the scale economy producers, and that the "flexible" producers benefit from a wider range of products (presumably corresponding to markets "niches") than do standardized producers. Friedman prints a table showing that Japanese producers have many more different auto bodies and engines than do American producers. He warns that firm strategies that rely on standardization may have serious public policy consequences, and recommends that the U.S. government develop policies to redirect corporate strategy (David Friedman, "Beyond the Age of Ford"). I have some reservations about this analysis. The Japanese auto firms do have a "flexible" form of production with a diverse product line. We cannot assume, however, that firms in other countries are capable of replicating their success. A wide range of products cannot account for Japanese profitability. For instance, if we were to list the various range of cars available from British car companies in the 1950s and 1960s, we would see that Britain's specialist auto industry was flexible before flexible was fashionable. Unfortunately, they were not profitable. Nor can robotization account for the success of Japanese firms. Honda's Marysville, Ohio plant is both profitable and one of the least automated plants in the States. A favorable yen/dollar exchange rate, cheap prices on supplier parts, a well-developed reputation for quality, and a highly productive work force would have produced a profitable Japanese auto industry, independent of a diverse product range and flexible production systems (see the Cusumano's conclusion in his *The Japanese Automobile Industry*). I suspect, therefore, that the key adjective in "Japanese flexible production" is Japanese and not flexible. Hence, I am doubtful that the U.S. government is capable of successfully redirecting corporate strategy toward a "market niche" approach.

26. Maxcy, *Multinational Motor Industry*, pp. 199–202; D. G. Rhys, "Economies of Scale in the Motor Industry"; Peter J. S. Dunnett, *The Decline of the British Motor Industry.*

27. Dunnett, pp. 22–25; Bhaskar, *Future of World Motor Industry*, p. 358; and United Nations Center on Transnational Corporations, *Transnational Corporations in the International Auto Industry.* New York: United Nations, 1983, p. 21.

28. Ford Motor Company, *Annual Report*, various years; Ford, UK, *Annual Report, 1982*; and General Motors, *Annual Report*, various years.

29. *Financial Times*, February 11, 1986.

30. See Altschuler *The Future of the Automobile*, ch. 9, and Harry C. Katz, "Collective Bargaining in the U.S. Auto Industry."

31. On routinized work, see Abernathy, *The Productivity Dilemma*; Paul Willman and Graham Winch, *Innovation and Management Control*, pp. 172–191. On Fordist practices, cf. Abernathy and Charles Sabel, *Work and Politics*. On the Taylorist model, see Michael Burawoy, *The Politics of Production*. He describes the Anglo-American model as the of "market individualism," though he does note the important differences among the

American and British factory "regimes." Martin Weitzman *The Share Economy*; and James Meade, *Alternative Systems of Business Organization and Worker's Renumeration* offer proposals for reform.

32. This situation, of course, describes the circumstances of early capitalism.

33. OECD, *Long Term* ..., p. 64.

34. Whitman, *International Trade*, p. 12; United Nations, pp. 148–50.

35. For instance, British hourly wage rates are much lower than are those of Germany, and BL (now Rover, Plc.) boasts that its per worker productivity "at 14 cars per man year is already up to the best in Europe." Nonetheless, BL lost £138 million in 1985, GM (Vauxhall) lost £47.4 million, and Talbot (Peugeot, née Chrysler) lost £12.8 million in 1985. BL, Plc., *Annual Report & Accounts, 1985; Financial Times*, February 11, 1986; *Financial Times*, "Vauxhall Pays the Price of Success," March 20, 1986; Peugeot Talbot Motor Company Limited, *Annual Report, 1985*.

36. Toyota, Mazda, Honda and Nissan have subsequently established foreign production subsidiaries in the U.S. and elsewhere.

37. *Chilton's Automotive Industries*, January 1983, pp. 189–191.

38. Cusumano, *Japanese Auto Industry*, pp. 192–93, 383.

39. The sources of this cost advantage will be discussed in a later chapter. The American figure is a composite drawn from the 1980 and 1981 studies of the American auto industry by the Department of Transportation, *The U.S. Automotive Industry 1980*, p. 40; 1981, p. 15. The European data come from the Commission of the European Communities, The European Automobile Industry, p. 18.

40. *U.S. Automotive Industry, 1980*, pp. 51–52.

41. Congressional Budget Office, p. 38.

42. Maxcy and Bhaskar seem to agree on this point, though the authors of the UN study believe that the Japanese will remain slow to invest in other countries (pp. 85–88).

43. See Gilbert R. Winham, *The Automobile Trade Crisis of 1980*, pp. 31–32; U.N., pp. 85–88. The production capacity will be distributed as follows: Honda, 300,000 cars in two plants, one in Ohio and one in Michigan; Nissan, 125,000 in one plant in Tennessee; Toyota/GM (NUMMI), 250,000 in one plant (Fremont, California); Madza, 240,000 in one plant (Flat Rock, Mich.); Mitsubishi, 180,000 in one plant in Illinois; and Toyota, 200,000 in one plant (Georgetown, Kentucky). These plants will increase the automobile production capacity of the U.S. industry by 14% over 1985. *Financial Times*, September 5, 1985.

44. Ford, UK, *Annual Report, 1982*, p. 23. Ford's European operations have not been as profitable in recent years. Ford, Europe accounted for 21.4%

of external sales in 1983, 16% in 1984, and 16.6% in 1985. It accounted for 15% on net income for the Ford overall in 1983, 5% in 1984, and 13% in 1985. Put another way, the % net income to % sales ratio was .7 in 1983, .3 in 1984, and .8 in 1985. The erosion of Ford's European profitability can be explained by the fierce competition for market share among the six leading European producers. Ford Motor Company, *Annual Report*, various years.

45. U.N., pp. 80–83.

46. See Whitman, *International Trade*, discussion of this, pp. 17–20.

47. *Ward's 1982 Automotive Yearbook*, p. 134.

48. Alfred Chandler, in his *The Visible Hand*, argued that vertically integrated companies enjoyed a crucial competitive advantage over less integrated companies during periods of business cycle downturns.

49. The *Wall Street Journal* of October 7, 1986 reported that Ford's internal value-added was now 50% of the total cost of production.

50. This "back-door" method of avoiding quotas has been noted by Western European governments, especially the Italian and the French, but has yet to be obstructed. *Wall Street Journal*, March 11, 1983, p. 30.

51. The "voluntary" quotas were set at 1.6 million cars exported into the American market. After April 1984, 2.3 million Japanese cars were permitted to enter the American market, 314,000 of which are "captive" imports. The three producers that provide most of the captive imports, Mitsubishi, Isuzu, and Suzuki, received the largest percentage increase in export allotments. *The New York Times*, Oct. 27, 1985.

52. One important determinant of the ability of auto firms to carry out corporate strategy—indeed, a determinant of corporate strategy—is the relative financial capacity of the firms to generate investment money. These capacities range from Toyota's, one where the company has no long-term bank debt, to BL's, where the company would not survive without government grants. The issue of finance will be discussed in later sections.

53. Specialist auto makers guard their reputations with a zealotry. As an illustration, BMW executives were quoted, in a recent article in the *New York Times*, as complaining that BMW's were in danger of being seen as the "Scarsdale teenager's" typical high school graduation gift, an image apparently not sufficiently "upmarket" for them.

54. David Teece has used the phrase "economies of scope" to describe situations in which manufacturers are able to profit from the production of related products or variants of the same product. For instance, a four cylinder engine and a six cylinder engine usually will be produced on different assembly lines with different machinery. Though the firm producing the engines will not achieve the same scale economies if it were to manufacture one engine, the firm will achieve some saving. New buildings and new

suppliers will not be needed, and so on. See David J. Teece, "Economies of Scope and the Scope of the Enterprise," pp. 223–47.

55. Toyota Motor Corp., *Annual Report, 1985*. OECD, *Long Term*. . . . See Appendix B, pp. 109–116. The conclusion reached was that only American firms approximate the "world car" model of product development. The report does note that Britain and Italy have developed a competitive component market that is independent of the major automotive producers.

56. *Economist*, July 12, 1986; *Financial Times*, March 18, 1986.

57. See OECD, *Long Term* . . . , ch. 2, and J. C. Tanner. *Saturation Levels in Car Ownership*, pp. 1–8.

58. OECD, pp. 16–20.

59. The 1985 numbers were calculated from various issues of the *Financial Times* and *Ward's Automotive Report*.

60. The European car market is defined as including the European Community and several Scandinavian countries. The six major producers are (ranked by market share in 1985) Volkswagen (12.9%), FIAT (12.2%), Ford (11.9%), Peugeot (11.6%), General Motors (11.4%), and Renault (10.7%). The magnitude of market shares has been relatively stable. The 1980 figures (in order) were 12%, 11.8%, 11%, 14.6%, 8.4%, and 14.7%. Ironically, both the biggest market share "winner," GM, and the biggest losers, Renault and Peugeot, have lost substantial sums of money during the past 6 years, over $2 billion in the case of GM's European operations. The six smaller "major" producers are BL (now Rover), SEAT (now part of VW), Daimler-Benz, BMW, Volvo, and Alfa Romeo. BL, SEAT, and Alfa have been consistently unprofitable. Daimler, BMW, and Volvo are "specialist" auto producers. These companies have been profitable, but, as the exchange-weighted value of the dollar falls, may become less so as their American markets shrink. See *New York Times*, June 2, 1985; *Financial Times*, April 25, 1985; *Financial Times*, February 4, 1986.

61. Ford Motor Company, *Annual Report, 1985*.

62. These figures are calculated from the Annual Reports of each of the major auto firms. These numbers understate tax subsidies. Depreciation allowances, tax deferrals, and tax reductions from (the now discontinued) DISC (Domestic International Sales Corporation) are not included here.

63. Quoted in the *Financial Times*, February 15, 1985. The quotas were said to cost the U.S. consumer $16 billion in the first four years of enactment.

64. *Financial Times*, February 20, 1986; *Ward's Automotive Yearbook*, 1983.

65. *Washington Post, Weekly Edition*, November 25, 1985. The Post reported that, of the 1984 model cars rated by consumers as being of good quality, only one of the top ten (#10 at that) cars was made by a domestic

manufacturer—the Lincoln Continental. Only 21 percent of American car buyers were reported as believing that American made cars were of better quality than were Japanese cars.

66. *New York Times*, August 24, 1986.

67. See the discussion of sectors like steel in the volume edited by Susan Strange and Roger Tooze, *The International Politics of Surplus Capacity*.

68. Martin Anderson, *Financial Restructuring of the World Auto Industry*, p. 4.

69. Richard Philips and Arthur Way. *The West European Automotive Industry*, p. 96.

70. See Charles Lindblom's statement of this problem in his *Politics and Markets*.

71. On exports, see Economist Intelligence Unit. Quarterly Economic Reviews; Japan: Annual Supplement, 1981, p. 17. On imports, *Financial Times*, February 14, 1986.

72. Commission of the European Communities. The European Automobile Industry, p. 25.

73. See David J. Ott and Attiat F. Ott, in *Federal Budget Policy*, pp. 68–71 and 93–105. U.S. government disbursements (as a percentage of GDP) were 31.7% in 1980 as against the 43.1% average for the smaller Western European countries in 1980. Japan's 1980 figure was 25.4%. OECD, *Economic Outlook*, December 1982, p. 160. See also U.S. Congress, House of Representatives, Committee on the Budget. *Non-Means-Tested Entitlement Reform Programs.*

74. See the previous discussion on state policies and government choices. Maxcy, *Multinational Motor Industry*, p. 237.

75. The figures were taken from *British Business*, May 13, 1983, p. 284, and OECD, United Kingdom; Economic Survey, 1982–1983, Paris: 1983 p. 64. These figures understate the value of British foreign investment as Britain has historically relied on portfolio, and not direct, investment.

76. The most sophisticated discussion of these issues remains Robert Gilpin's *U.S. Power and the Multinational Corporation: The Political Economy of Foreign Direct Investment*, New York: Basic, 1975, especially chapters 4–7. Another influential understanding of the phenomenon of foreign investment is that of the neo-Marxist "dependencia" literature of which the works of Gunder-Frank, Furtado, Amin, and Dos Santos are the best known.

77. Many multinational corporations in fact raise capital for proposed foreign investment in the targeted market. See Gilpin's discussion of some of the consequences of investment, *U.S. Power and the Multinational Corporation*, ch. 8 and 9. Among the most comprehensive discussion of this issue include a work by Peggy Musgrave published as U.S. Senate, Com-

mittee on Foreign Relations, *Direct Investment Abroad and the Multinationals*; and OECD, International Investment and Multinational Enterprises: Recent International Direct Investment Trends.

78. Among the conditions imposed on Chrysler in return for Federal aid was that Chrysler sell off most of its foreign subsidiaries.

79. John Ruggie. "International Regimes, Transactions, and Change: Embedded Liberalism in the Postwar Economic Order," pp. 379–415.

80. Ford and General Motors risk bearing "legitimacy" costs if they fail to allocate a "fair" market share to, say, Britain. Both Ford and GM were prevented in 1986 from acquiring parts of BL—Austin-Morris and Leyland Truck-Rover, respectively. The opposition to the sale did not come from the British government (at least, that part of it run by Margaret Thatcher). Commons opposition, and controversy in the country as a whole over Westland, ended the takeover bids. In both cases, the substantial "captive imports" of GM and Ford were cited as evidence of the unreliability of these firms in terms of defending British national interests.

81. Several sources report that Nissan will receive up to £110 million in regional and industrial grants from the British government for its assembly plant in Northeast England.

82. A number of writers have developed schema for understanding the domain of state capacity. Among these are Stephen Krasner, "United States Commercial and Monetary Policy: Unraveling the Paradox of External Strength and Internal Weakness," pp. 635–72.; P. J. Katzenstein, "Conclusion: Domestic Structures and Strategies of Foreign Economic Policy," pp. 879–919; and John Zysman, *Governments, Markets, and Growth*, esp, pp. 295–99 and 347–49.

83. Zysman; see also James Womack, *The Competitive Significance of National Financial Systems in the Auto Sector*.

84. The difficulty of the rescue meant that the government as a whole, if not the executive branch, was able to impose unpalatable requirements on both Chrysler and the UAW.

85. *The New York Times*, February 1, 1984, p. D16.

3. The American and British Auto Industries

1. The total was 8.76 million in 1980. *Ward's Automotive Yearbook*, 1982, p. 112.

2. Central Policy Review Staff (CPRS), *The Future of the British Car Industry*, pp. viii, xiii.

3. Krish Bhaskar, *The Future of the UK Motor Industry*, p. 389.

4. *Ward's Automotive Yearbook*, 1973, p. 175.

5. Organization for Economic Cooperation and Development (OECD) countries. These countries included the members of the EC, U.S., Canada, Japan, Australia, New Zealand, and 11 other western countries.

6. *British Business*, August 6, 1982, p. 599. Quoted in answer to a Parliamentary Question by Austin Mitchell on July 29, 1982.

7. In his *Modern Capitalism*, Shonfield accepts the argument of American "exceptionalism." In comparing U.S. and British business behavior, he uses phrases like "by way of contrast" and "in sharp contrast" (see chapter 13).

David Vogel, in his *National Styles of Regulation*, tries to make the case that we should be surprised that the British and the American styles of regulation differ so substantially. He wrote, "It is not only the direction of the differences in government regulation between Great Britain and the United States that is surprising, but their magnitude. Virtually every comparative study of business–government relations has stressed the similarities between the political economies of Great Britain and the United States" (p. 30). He cites Shonfield, among others, as supporting this position. Hence, his own conclusion, the U.S. and Britain have differing styles of national regulation, he regards as challenging conventional wisdom. I, on the other hand, take the differing forms of government intervention as the starting premise of my analysis.

A passage, in chapter 14, does seem to lend a little support to Vogel's reading of Shonfield. Shonfield writes, "In this matter American political assumptions about the relationship between public and private power are closer to British traditional practice, whose remarkable staying power was described in Chapter 6, than to anything in Germany." One sentence later, however, Shonfield sharply qualifies this point. "However, the British are equipped, unlike the Americans, with a unitary and hierarchical form of executive government, which is fully capable of projecting a single set of centrally determined policies to cover the whole national economy. The basic prerequisites for planning therefore exist in Britain—even though the administrative habits required to make a success of the planner's task have not yet been much cultivated. In America, there is no reason why the competing centres of power concerned with different aspects of economic policy should ever agree," p. 330.

8. Dunnett, *Decline of British Motor Industry* pp. 31–42 (hereafter cited as Dunnett, *Decline*).

9. In 1973, the percentage of the total value of components purchased from other firms ranged from 65% to 85% for British firms. GM's (U.S.) figure was 46%. The top three British component makers had a combined automotive sales value in 1979 of over £2.5 billion. J. Scott Ward, *The Changing Face of the UK Component Industry*, p. 19.

10. The OECD in its 1983 survey of Great Britain (pp. 40–51) argues that this characterizes British industry in general. British industrial restructuring was delayed by several factors unique to the postwar world: a dominance of world markets by sellers, including Britain, in the 25 years following the war; Commonwealth trading relations; and "from the mid-1960s up to the early 1970s, the gradual build-up of worldwide inflationary pressures [which] concealed the deterioration in the competitiveness of British manufacturing," p. 43.

11. SMMT, various years.

12. Dunnett, *Decline*, p. 100.

13. Dunnett, p. 39; *Motor Report International*, various issues; *Financial Times*, November 9, 1982; Peugeot Talbot, *Annual Report, 1985*.

14. CPRS, p. 63.

15. Department of Industry study, quoted in the *Financial Times*, March 11, 1983, p. 7.

16. *British Business*, February 19, 1982, p. 360. Answer to a Parliamentary Question by Mr. Teddy Taylor.

17. One political issue was GM's sale in Britain of Spanish produced autos under the Vauxhall name. The TWGU threatened to block imports of the cars, and the British government threatened countervailing duties in order to induce Spain to reduce its tariffs on British and E.C. imports. Beginning in 1983, cars built in Spain were allowed to enter the E.C. by paying a 4.4% tariff. E.C.-built cars pay 36.7% in Spain. (Financial Times, January 11, 1983, p. 7.) Ford and GM have been attacked by members of both parties for their policies regarding "captive imports."

18. Quoted in Maxcy, *Multinational Motor Industry*, p. 227.

19. CPRS, p. 129.

20. Chandler, *Giant Enterprise*, p. 3.

21. The major companies do not wish to become completely integrated. The auto industry is a cyclical industry. By not producing all a car's components, the auto companies transfer the risk of the downturns to the supplier companies. The auto companies can therefore buy components during good years without incurring the costs of excess capacity during lean years. Both Dunnett and Bhaskar discuss this phenomenon.

22. For the first half of 1982, Ford had 11.9% of the E.C. market, and GM had 10%. Renault led all producers with 14.5%. In 1985, Ford took 11.9% of the European market, and GM's market share rose to 11.4%. VW lead all producers with 12.9%. *Financial Times*, September 28, 1982, p. 16.: and February 4, 1986.

23. SMMT, various years.

24. SMMT quoted in the *Financial Times*, March 4, 1983; and March 25, 1986.

25. The exporters, in order, were BL, Ford, Rolls-Royce, Vauxhall and Talbot. *Financial Times*, September 20, 1982, p. 4.

26. A good discussion of organizational forms and ideology in the Western working class is to be found in Michael Mann's *Consciousness and Action Among the Western Working Class.*, 1973.

27. Frederick M. Taylor, *Scientific Management* (1911) is, of course, famous for his time-motion studies of efficiency in manual labor. The classic discussions of this are to be found in E. Chinoy, *Automobile Workers and the American Dream*; Robert Blauner, *Alienation and Freedom*; and Stanley Aronowitz, *False Promises*. Some documentary evidence, with commentary, of the unionization process in the U.S. is available in Chandler, *Giant Enterprise* pp. 179–229. For the British process, see Dunnett, *Decline*; CPRS; and IWC Motors Group, *A Workers' Enquiry Into the Motor Industry*. Maxcy has a short chapter on labor and transnational corporations; *Multinational Motor Industry*, pp. 179–188.

As Japanese firms invest in manufacturing plants in the United States and Great Britain, they are confronted with working class cultures very different from their own. Nissan and Honda, whose labor organizations differ substantially from the Anglo-American model of Taylorism, sought to avoid both the usual American and British union organizations, and locations with traditions of worker–management hostility. Each located plants in regions outside of the auto manufacturing belt (Honda, Southern Ohio; Nissan, Tennessee and Northeastern England), and each sought to avoid national union and work practices. Nissan, for example, negotiated an agreement with only one British union (the Amalgamated Union of Engineering Workers), established only two types of workers (technicians and manufacturers), and hired workers on salary, not on hourly wage. (See Philip Bassett, "Nissan Deal Breaks Motor Sector Mould." *Financial Times*, April 23, 1985.) Nissan was also able to choose 250 workers from an applicant pool of over 11,000. Mazda has opted to locate production in Michigan, and to negotiate directly with the UAW, though the UAW has agreed in advance of the plant's opening to many of Mazda's requests for a more flexible, less confrontational form of work organization.

GM is attempting to break away from the American tradition of confrontation. GM has located its new Saturn project in Tennessee, and has, like Mazda, negotiated a "flexible" contract with the UAW for its Tennessee plant.

28. Michael Burawoy, *The Politics of Production*, (Verso, 1985) argues

that the American and British factory regimes exhibit important differences stemming from the role of the state in regulating factory organization. See chapter 3. For an overview of the British labor movement, see Ben Hooberman, *An Introduction to British Trade Unions*.

29. Thatcher's Government has introduced a series of labor "reforms" aimed at making unions more "responsible." These reforms include provisions aimed at forcing balloting, and at penalizing unions for unauthorized strikes. The issues are more serious than are the catalytic events. At the root of these issues is the tradeoff between worker autonomy and increased efficiency, and, by implication, the weakening of work rules and job divisions by the companies. *The Financial Times* gave full coverage to these events during the fall of 1982 and winter and spring of 1983.

30. IWC, p. 14.

31. Dunnett, *Decline*, p. 112; see also James O'Connor's discussion of wage and price controls in a capitalist economy in *The Fiscal Crisis of the State*, p. 50.

32. The Central Statistical Office (U.K.) publishes the *Monthly Digest of Statistics* (London: HMSO, 1982), in which appears a table (3.15) of industrial stoppages. From 1976 to 1980, the heavy industry, nationalized sector accounted for anywhere between 50% and 90% of the total working days lost in the economy as a whole. Strike activity varied enormously, from just under 2 million days lost in the heavy industry sector in 1976 to 20 million days lost in 1979.

Aside from the long and bitter miners' strike of 1984–85, strike activity in Britain's industries has decreased—an unsurprising outcome given an unemployment rate of 13%. In 1983, 177 days per 100,000 employees were "lost" due to industrial disputes, a figure 18 times higher than that of Japan, but still very much lower than those of Britain in the early 1970s—see my table 3.5. *Financial Times*, January 8, 1986.

33. S. J. Prais et al., *Productivity and Industrial Structure*. In a footnote on page 145, Prais refers to a previous article on the automobile industry that he published with Daniel T. Jones in the *Oxford Bulletin of Economics and Statistics* (May 1978).

34. See, for instance, Department of Industry (U.K.), *British Leyland: The Next Decade* (Ryder Report), London: HMSO, 1975; Department of Industry (U.K.), *The British Motor Vehicle Industry*; Cmnd, 6377, London: HMSO, 1976; CPRS; Dunnett, *Decline* pp. 181–83; and Bhaskar, *U.K. Auto Industry*. Bhaskar and Dunnett see U.K. government policies generally at the root of the industry's troubles.

Williams raises the interesting point that labor troubles might not have had the impact that the "numbers of cars lost to disputes" figure would have us believe. He point out the BL was unable to sell many of the cars it manufactured, even when all was well.

35. Some analysts, most notably Dunnett and Maxcy, have linked Britain's greater industrial turmoil in the auto industry to the longevity of community and worker involvement in the industry. The German, Italian, French, and American auto work forces have a substantial rural migrant base, and the thesis has been advanced that recent migrants are closer to the experiences of poverty, have lower group solidarity, and are hence more cautious and less troublesome. The British work force has been industrial for over a century, hence more confident and troublesome. This thesis is plausible for Britain only if the enormous historical evidence of popular resistance in Britain (from the early 1800s) to the institutionalization of the capitalist market economy is ignored. cf. E. J. Hobsbawm, *Industry and Empire*, and E. P. Thompson, *The Making of the English Working Class*. Thompson and Hobsbawm disagree on much, but agree that the ethos ("moral economy") of the British underclass has always been hostile to a market economy.

36. The 1970 strike was prolonged by several weeks by "local issues," but all locals went back at roughly the same time.

37. *Ward's Automotive Reports*, September 16, 1970, p. 363. This does not mean that plants and men were idle for only 0.95% of the total possible work week on average per year. Almost all assembly line workers are laid off during the model "change over." This period is usually in the late summer and usually lasts between 3 and 30 days, depending on the plant changes. Workers continue to draw 95% of their base pay through unemployment insurance and the SUB plan.

38. *Ryder Report*, pp. 31–2.

39. *Solidarity*, August 1982, p. 15.

40. *Wall Street Journal*, March 23, 1983, p. 33. GM's initial position in the 1982 wage talks was for a $8 per hour wage and benefit cut. *Ward's Automotive Reports*, October 26, 1981.

41. All figures are from Ward's Automotive Yearbook, 1982, p. 28.

42. British industry as a whole is actually less "strike prone" than is the American, and much less so that some others (e.g., Italy). See David Smith's essay in Richard Caves and Lawrence Krause, eds., *Britain's Economic Performance*, esp. pp. 110–18.

43. The assumption in the American auto industry is that the demand elasticity for automobiles is small. That is, a small increase in price produces little falloff in demand. The auto companies also assume a high income elasticity of demand, so that a rise in income will produce a proportionally

greater rise in auto demand. This last consideration helps explain why the multinational firms are willing to invest in comparatively poor countries like Mexico and Brazil. As they grow, the auto industry should grow faster.

44. Dunnett, *Decline*, p. 51.

45. Ibid., p. 52.

46. DOT, 1980, p. 51; SMMT.

47. SMMT, 1971.

48. DOT, 1980, p. 51.

49. DOT, 1980, p. 24. Until recently, product innovation was fairly risky for a motor vehicle manufacturer. Auto buyers tend to be technically unsophisticated; purchases are usually replacement purchases, and brand loyalty, not product quality, seems to be the central influence on purchases. As a result, high-priced quality innovations frequently do not translate into new sales. Styling changes are less expensive, and therefore carry a lower cost in case of failure. Lawrence White, "The Motor Vehicle Industry," pp. 411–450.

50. After imports reached 10% of the domestic market (in 1958), the auto makers did each produce an economy car (e.g., GM's infamous Corvair), but these cars were still larger and less fuel efficient than were European and Japanese compact and subcompact cars.

51. DOT, p. 69.

52. *Ward's Automotive Yearbook*, 1972, p. 32; 1973, p. 28. GM has expressed interest in importing cars from Isuzu and Suzuki, companies in which GM has an equity stake. The "voluntary" quotas at the moment preclude this.

53. *Ward's Automotive Yearbook*

54. The phrase "industrial policy" means different things to different people. An argument can be made that any government action which affects industry is policy. Hence, the Wagner Act (1935) might be considered as an industrial policy by that definition. I mean here only government strategy to promote manufactures.

55. John Stuart Mill, *Principles of Political Economy*, Book 5, Chapter 11, Sections 5 and 7.

56. The ideological justifications of unimpeded capitalism shifted substantially during the nineteenth century. In the early 1800s, the Smithian justification was that of a general prosperity, a "universal opulence" rooted in the essential harmony of interests among all sectors of society, and indeed nations. (Adam Smith, *An Inquiry Into the Nature and Causes of the Wealth of Nations*, Book I, chapter 1; Book III, chapter 1; Book IV, chapters 1 and 2.) By the end of the nineteenth century, the justification for capitalism had lost its Deistic roots, and instead was based on the themes of efficiency,

social evolution, and a vulgar "survival of the fittest." See Richard Hofstader, *Social Darwinism in American Thought*, especially "The Vogue of Spencer."

57. Andrew Shonfield, *Modern Capitalism*, p. 301. See also David Vogel, "Why Businessmen Mistrust Their State," pp. 45–78.

58. See David Vogel, *National Styles of Regulation*, for a detailed description of the differences in regulatory politics between the United States and Great Britain. Vogel's conclusions about policy dissimilarities are somewhat at odds with the conclusions of this book, though Vogel analyzes social regulation (i.e., environmental policies) not economic regulation.

59. Michael Polanyi (The Great Transformation) was among the first to note that in Europe both the Labour and the (European) Conservative political movements arose in response to the spread of market society, and that both contained an organic vision of society threatened by the market order.

Foremost among the numerous excellent discussions of the phenomenon of Tory collectivism, is Samuel Beer's *British Politics in the Collectivist Age*, (published as *Modern British Politics* in the U.K.), especially chapters 1 and 3. See also the section on Britain in G. C. Lodge's *The American Disease*. Good discussions of the National government and interwar period are in Hobsbawm, *Industry and Empire* ch. 12 and Beer, ch. 10.

60. Shonfield, *Modern Capitalism*. pp. 88–89.

61. Ibid., p. 88. Shonfield argued that, even though Britain had the institutional capacity to engage in long-term planning, the political culture was not conducive to this. He cites the traditions of a nondiscretionary civil service, of "arm's length" relations between firms and governments, a preference for macropolicies, and the short-term political horizons of governments. Ibid., ch. 6.

62. See Susan Strange's *Sterling and British Policy*, and Hobsbawm, *Industry and Empire*, chs. 12 and 13. Sterling crises were fairly common: 1947, 1949, 1951, 1955–56, 1960–61, 1964–66, 1967, and 1975–76.

63. Shonfield, *Modern Capitalism*, p. 164. Mikkel Herberg has argued ("Politics, Planning, and Governments," pp. 497–516) that much of the French success has stemmed from the relative weakness of French labor in defending its interest (wage gains), and that the key to "capitalist planning in competitive societies' is squeezing wage costs, a solution made more difficult in Britain by organized labor's greater political strength.

64. Holland, passim. A number of interesting studies of Labour's 1964–1970 period in power are available. Among these are Steven Young (with A. Lowe), *Intervention in a Mixed Economy*; Stuart Holland, *The Socialist Challenge*; Michael Shanks, *Politics and Planning*; and David Coates, *The Labour in Power?*.

65. Young with Lowe, p. 208.

66. For a discussion of the "principles" of a social market industrial strategy, and other contrasting models, see Wyn Grant's *The Political Economy of Industrial Policy*, chs. 1 and 4. The ideological debates within the Conservative Party are well covered in Nigel Harris's *Competition and the Corporate State*; and Andrew Gamble, *Britain in Decline*, pp. 128–58. For a discussion of the tensions between collectivism and individualism, see Lodge, *The American Disease*.

Many of the law and order themes, especially on immigration, were first given public voice in the 1960s by Enoch Powell. Though Powell was effectively exiled from the Conservative Party (he represents Upper Down as a quasi-unionist in Northern Ireland), his "rational populism" has become an important ideological plank for the new right.

Grant notes that the current Thatcher government has been strongly influenced by the Heath experience: "this lady is not for turning." Her steadfast public commitment to a social market strategy is apparently based on the belief that Heath yielded too easily. Grant, pp. 77–78.

67. Parliament (U.K.), Industry Act 1972, pp. 8–10. Note should be taken that Part I of the act has been the section under which regional development grants are paid. From 1972 until the end of Summer 1981, nearly £3 billion were paid out under this section. Somewhat less than half of this amount was paid out under sections 7 and 8 for this same period. Quoted in response to a Parliamentary Question by Chris Patten in British Business of October 30, 1981.

68. Much of the material from this section is drawn from Grant, *Political Economy*, chs. 3 and 5; and David Coates, *Labour in Power*. Grant notes that half of Section 8 money was directed at rescue operations.

69. Grant, p. 51. The 1980 Industry Act repealed most of the provisions of the 1975 Industry Act.

70. The "NEDDY" process has continued under Thatcher, though many observers doubt that it has accomplished much in recent years. A review of its annual report for 1981–82 indicates that the division between the Trade Unions and the Thatcher Government is so deep as to preclude much of value from emerging from the consultation process. See especially pp. 5–10. Perhaps the problem is after all not too little communication.

71. Coates *Labour in Power?*; Grant, *Political Economy* ch. 5.

72. An illustration of the enthusiasm felt for microeconomic intervention as a key to economic growth is to be found in a series of articles published by *The Economist* during the fall of 1976. (Reprinted as *The Uncommon Market*, London: Economist, 1977.) The Economist wrote: "Since the 1939–45 war, the Keynesean revolution in economic theory, successive British

governments have tried to solve the nation's problems by pulling a few large macroeconomic levers: eg, manipulating the size of the public sector's deficit by control of public spending and tax revenue. . . . these have failed to steer the economy. So the emphasis has been shifting towards more microeconomic intervention by government: i.e., pushing hundreds of little buttons in the hope that the aggregate effect will be significant" (p. 2).

73. One major exception was in the NEDC process: no motor industry working party. Dunnett, after all, entitled his book, *The Decline of the British Motor Industry: The Effects of Government Policy,* 1945–79. Bhaskar is no less blunt: "it has been successive and consistent Government action which is primarily to blame for the poor state of the industry as a whole," *Future of U.K. Motor Industry,* p. 15.

74. Dunnett, *Decline,* p. 14.

75. Maxcy, *Multinational Motor Industry,* pp. 227–31.

76. Manpower Services Commission Office for Wales, The Ford Bridgend Report, Cardiff: Manpower Intelligence Unit, 1981, p. 1.1. The study measured the job creation impact and concluded: "About 20% of recruits had been unemployed beforehand. The majority were attracted from other employers. However, their loss caused few difficulties to these employers: on the contrary, most of the employers questioned asserted that Ford's recruitment had eased their own labour force reductions. From December 1979 to February 1980, only one third of the employees lost were replaced, and this proportion fell to 7% for the period May–August 1980." In short, few new jobs were created.

77. Thomas Reynolds Stauffer, *The Measurement of Corporate Rates of Return,* v–12 to v–21; Dunnett, *Decline,* p. 93. Prais et al. claim the "the German and American car industries have shown much the same relative variability about a trend as has the British car industry over the past twenty years" (*Productivity and Industrial Structure,* p. 160). Perhaps so, but, as we know from Chandler, smaller mass producers—e.g., British Leyland— are less able to sustain comparable variability in demand than are larger firms. Hence, even if government induced variability in Britain was not much different from that in the U.S. and Germany, the claim that government policies hurt the industry is not refuted.

78. Great Britain, House of Commons, Third Report from the Industry and Trade Committee, 1981–82, BL Limited. See the testimony of Sir Michael Edwardes, p. 31.

79. Maxcy, *Multinational Motor Industry,* pp. 227–31; Young and Hood, *Chrysler, U.K.* For details of the Chrysler bailout, see Parliament (U.K.), Eighth Report from the Expenditure Committee (1975–1976), Public Expenditure on Chrysler, UK; HC–596–1; and the Government's reply, Public

Expenditure on Chrysler, UK (Command 6745), 1977. For a discussion of the Planning Agreement, see Stephen Wilks, "Planning Agreements," pp. 399–419.

Wilks's book, *Industrial Policy and the Motor Industry* is an excellent study of the British government's motor industry policies. I learned much from his description of the Chrysler "bailout," (particularly with regard to what might be referred to as "pluralist politics") in his discussion and analysis of the bargaining that took place in Cabinet. Wilks's book is not, to my knowledge, available in the States.

80. The actual title was Ministry of Industry (U.K.), British Leyland: The Next Decade, London: HMSO, 1975. Not all the report was made public.

81. Apart from those works already cited, some important discussions of the evolution of this sort of intervention include John Burton, *The Job Support Machine*; Burton, *Picking Losers?*; Michael Parr, "The National Enterprise Board," pp. 51–62; Richard Pryke, *The Nationalized Industries*, especially ch. 12; and Daniel T. Jones, "Technology and the UK Automobile Industry," pp. 14–27.

82. Pryke, pp. 214–216, 224–230; and Dunnett, *Decline*, p. 134. Young and Hood, *Chrysler U.K.* ch. 10, p. 373.

83. Shonfield, *Modern Capitalism*, p. 322.

84. The most recent "bailouts" were those of Lockheed, the Hunt Brothers, New York City, and Chrysler. The financial sector is one where the Federal Government, through the Federal Deposit Insurance Corporation and the Federal Reserve System, does have extensive ability to intervene. For instance, the Continental Illinois rescue was effected quickly and with relatively little political opposition.

85. On the American capacity to plan, cf. Theodore J. Lowi, *The End of Liberalism*, part 11; and Steven D. Krasner, "U.S. Commercial and Monetary Policy."

On business and veto power, see Charles E. Lindblom, "Still Muddling—Not Through," pp. 517–26. A recent study which evaluated McConnell's "capture" hypothesis, and concluded that "this research cannot be considered to provide an explanation of any overwhelming pro-industry bias often attributed to regulatory agencies," is by Paul Quirk, *Industry Influence in Federal Regulatory Agencies*, p. 177.

86. Shonfield, *Modern Capitalism*, p. 330.

87. Among the more elegant discussions of this are Charles E. Schultze, *The Public Use of Private Interest*; and Arthur Okun, *Equality and Efficiency*.

88. Robert Gilpin, *U.S. Power and the Multinational Corporation*. Gilpin has linked these policies (the absence of restraints) to a conscious public

choice that American overseas investments advance American hegemony, and were therefore not impeded.

89. Ira Katznelson and Mark Kesselman, *The Politics of Power*, pp. 98–105.

90. Quoted in Karl Deutsch, *Politics and Government*, pp. 126–127. The Gini index is "a measure of the extent of social or economic inequality prevailing in a country" (p. 125), and is calculated from the Lorenz curve. See Deutsch, pp. 124–29. The British figures are 24% and 2.3%.

91. A careful discussion of this subject is not possible here. Competing discussions of this issue are to be found in Milton Friedman, *Capitalism and Freedom*, chs. 10 and 12; Okun, chs. 3 and 4; Lester Thurow, *The Zero-sum Society*, ch. 7; Katznelson and Kesselman, *Politics and Government*, ch. 7; and Michael Best and William Connolly, *The Politicized Economy*, chs. 3, 5, and 6. A sensitive discussion of the "moral economy" and the consequences of the American political economy is available in Richard Sennett and Jonathan Cobb, *The Hidden Injuries of Class*.

92. Graham Bannock et al, *The Penguin Dictionary of Economics*, p. 174. For a discussion of the "logic" of government intervention and externalities, see Garrett Hardin, "The Tragedy of the Commons," pp. 1243–48; Larry Ruff, "The Economic Common Sense of Pollution," pp. 69–85; and George Stigler, "The Theory of Economic Regulation," pp. 3–21.

93. See, for example, James Q. Wilson, "The Dead Hand of Regulation," pp. 39–58; and Murray Weidenbaum, "The High Cost of Government Regulation," pp. 32–39.

94. Murray Weidenbaum, *Business, Government, and the Public*, p. 374.

95. Joseph A. Schumpeter is the major exception. See *Capitalism, Socialism and Democracy*, part II.

96. On this last point, see Raymond Vernon, ed., *Big Business and the State*. Vernon has advanced a "convergence" argument concerning the European use of "national champions" in Europe, or the use of large firms to advance public interests. European governments have sought to concentrate and rationalize their industries, though I suspect that intra-European competition through the EEC is more at the root of this process than is American or Japanese competition.

97. Richard Hofstader, *The Age of Reform*, 1955, p. 227. See also part IV, ch. 2, and his "Whatever Happen to the Anti-trust Movement?" Apart from Marx, who saw monopolization as an inevitable outcome of capitalism, economists have tended to see monopoly as an avoidable wrong. Smith, for instance, saw monopolies as the "engine of mercantilism" and the "enemy of good management." pp. 145, 165. Schumpeter's view, that the process of

"creative destruction" obviated the need for anti-trust legislation, is still a minority one.

98. Firms do implicitly cooperate. The phenomenon of the "price leader," where a firm like U.S. Steel (now USX) will raise its prices, and other firms will follow suit, is a well-known occurrence in many industries.

99. Alan F. Westin, *The Anatomy of a Constitutional Law Case*. For an extended discussion of judicial influence, see Howard Ball, *Courts and Politics: The Federal Judicial System*.

Some auto industry analysts were fearful that the courts would block the "voluntary" quotas on Japanese cars on restraint of trade grounds.

100. For a discussion of the consumer movement, its origins and its tactics, see Michael Pertschuck, *Revolt Against Regulation*.

101. A study by Robert W. Crandall, et al., *Regulating the Automobile*, in addition to providing a useful summary of U.S. government regulations toward the automobile industry's product, assesses the combined effects of these three types of regulation through the use of econometric models. They conclude that the various regulations conflict with each other while adding between $1300 and $2200 to the price of cars (by 1981). (See their Appendix A for a description of the model.) They do concede—especially with regard to regulation and automobile safety—that "Capturing the precise effect of regulation, however, remains a difficult and elusive problem" (p. 74). some analysts may quarrel with their findings on the grounds that Crandall et al. measure costs in terms of direct costs to car owners. Social costs (insurance and medical payments saved, for instance) and individual costs not directly associated with car operations (e.g., personal unreimbursed hospitalization costs saved) are not factored into their model.

Another issue, which they admittedly do not seek to address, concerns the success of Japanese auto manufacturers in meeting U.S. government standards at a time when U.S. automakers lagged behind. My answer is that Japanese manufacturers did not seek to challenge regulatory standards in court or Congress, but directed their energies to solving the technical problems they confronted, especially in the area of safety standards. American manufacturers, on the other hand, strongly resisted the enforcement of regulatory standards. This strategy paid off for Ford and GM when they failed to meet the CAFE standards in 1985, but the penalties were suspended anyway. Lee Iaccoca is (perhaps apocryphally) quoted as having said "We [Chrysler] got took!" Chrysler, at substantial expense, did meet the standards.

102. White, "Automobile Emissions," p. 434.

103. White, p. 432.

104. Hunker, *Structural Change*, p. 19. Hydrocarbon and Carbon Monoxide levels are to be reduced by 95%, and the various Nitrogen Oxides are to be

reduced by 90%. In fact, the target date for these standards to be met has been pushed back repeatedly. White, p. 432–34; and Lawrence White, "Automobile Emissions Control Policy," pp. 401–20.

105. Estimates have been made that a 50% saving in fuel consumption for automobiles was possible through replacing older cars by new, more fuel efficient cars. These figures were drawn from House of Representatives (U.S.), Committee on Science and Technology, *Federal Role in Developing Automotive Technology*, pp. 17, 56.

For an analysis of "The Future of the Automobile in an Oil-Short World," see a pamphlet by that name by Lester Brown, Christopher Flavin, and Colin Norman.

The breakup of the oil cartel and the cheaper gasoline prices have confounded much of the analysis, at least in the short-term.

106. *Ward's Automotive Yearbook*, 1978. p. 19. The industry-wide average ranged between 15 and 18 when the standards were finally issued in 1977. Thanks to lobbying by the UAW, the domestic producers could not increase their CAFE by importing cars from their European or Japanese allied companies.

107. *Ward's*, 1978, p. 19.

108. *Ward's*, 1974. p. 16. Ward's neglected to mention that the auto industry won quick exemption from wage and price controls.

109. Weidenbaum, p. 41.

110. Lawrence White, "Emissions Control Policy," pp. 405–420. White advocates an effluent fee approach toward auto pollution instead of mandatory standards.

4. Policy Similarity

1. A particularly vexing issue are the methods to employ in comparative politics. The root of the problem is simple—too many variables relative to the number of cases. In our age, the standards of scientific rigor include the testing of hypotheses for confirmation or disconfirmation at the .95 confidence interval; in how many comparative studies of governments or societies are such standards attainable?

One strategy has been to retreat to the inductive methods employed in the nineteenth century. Theda Skocpol (*States and Social Revolutions*) recalls John Stuart Mill's "Joint Method of Agreement and Difference" and proposes its use. This approach has not met with universal approval. Mill's defense of inductionism was fervently attacked even in the nineteenth century. William Stanley Jevons, in his *Principles of Science: A Treatise on Logic and Scientific Method* devoted many pages to Mill's work (though none to economics per se, Jevons' field of primary expertise). The flavor of the discussion may be seen from this next passage, which had followed an extended discussion of induction and Mill: "It seems to me undesirable in a systematic work like this to enter into controversy at any length, or to attempt to refute the views of other logicians. But I shall feel bound to state, in a separate publication, my very deliberate opinion that many of Mill's innovations in logical science, and especially his doctrine of reasoning from particulars to particulars, are entirely groundless and false" (p. 228).

Economists of the twentieth century have not been much kinder. See Blaug, The Methodology..., pp. 59–77, for a discussion of Mill's work, and pp. 69–73 in particular for an analysis of Systems of Logic. Mill does have his defenders among logicians and social scientists. Irving Copi, for instance, in his text, Introduction to Logic, 7th ed. (New York: Macmillan, 1986), pp. 434–78, discusses Mill's "method of inductive inference." The other four "canons" of induction were the Method of Agreement, the Method of Difference, the Method of Residues, and the Method of Concomitant Variation.

The most commonly used approach in comparative politics remains "controlled comparison." See Elliot Feldman's Concorde and Dissent, especially his methodological appendix.

2. Clifford Geertz's Negara is an illustration of a "most different" single country study from which other writers may draw generalizations regarding the nature of the state. In this case, Steven Krasner ("Approaches to the State") reviewed Geertz's work and that of five other authors (or editors) in the context of a review essay.

3. See Elliot Feldman's comments on this in his "Comparative Public Policy: Field or Method?" We do, of course, find exceptions to this. For instance, Douglas Ashford has undertaken comparative policy analysis involving a comparison of Tunisia and Morocco.

4. Adam Przeworski and Henry Teune, The Logic of Comparative Social Inquiry (New York: Wiley, 1973). Teune does defend the utility of the "most similar systems design" in making predictions and gathering "useful" (as opposed to general) knowledge. Henry Teune, "A Logic of Comparative Policy Analysis."

5. James Alt and K. Alec Chrystal's Political Economics (Berkeley: California, 1983) provides a good introduction to the subject, though some of their discussions (e.g., reaction functions) are sophisticated to the point of eluding most of us in the field. See also Murray Weidenbaum's Business, Government and the Public, and Gregory Grossman Economic Systems for introductions to business and public policy studies. Andrew Shonfield's Modern Capitalism remains the benchmark work in the field.

6. The literature is reviewed in Dennis P. Quinn and Robert Jacobson, "Industrial Policy Through the Restriction of Capital Flows."

7. Lindblom's *Politics and Markets* is the focal point of much of the debate.

8. Bachrach and Baratz's distinction between structural power and instrumental power ("Two Faces of Power") is useful here. Those for whom business's influence is decisive are usually examining the broadest of issues (employment, investment) and asking why do we find common patterns among disparate countries. Those for whom business interests are not decisive (Vogel suggests that American firms are subject to a form of interest group coercion) usually examine mid-range issues, where other interest groups are organized. Environmental issues, Vogel's case, is perhaps the issue in Western politics in which business's influence is most heatedly contested. Investment decisions, on the other hand, are left to the firm— ergo, decisive influence.

9. For Marx, nations are forced, on "pain of extinction," to adopt capitalist methods of production and organization. Technology and the resulting economic organizations form a "structural imperative" such that national differences in culture and economy are ultimately overridden. For Weber, the ongoing progressive rationality of modern life, of which capitalism was just one (albeit an important one) of its manifestations, was crucial. Rational standards of behavior culminate in bureaucratic/legal standards of legitimate authority. Bureaucratic organization, with its standards of rationalism and expertise, dominate the modern world, market or nonmarket. From Weber, we would expect some convergence among all industrial societies in form and function of its institutions owing to "bureaucratic imperatives." From Marx, we would expect convergence only among market societies—socialism, we might recall, is said to abolish authority relations.

10. The work of James Burnham (*The Managerial Revolution*), Langdon Winner (*Autonomous Technology*), and John K. Galbraith (*The New Industrial State*) come to mind as examples of work advancing forms of convergence arguments. In the field of Soviet studies, arguments were made that the development of the *aparat* implied a growing specialization and professionalization in Soviet society. Jerry Hough and Skillings & Griffith both advanced arguments understanding Soviet society through the lenses of a form of "elite-pluralist" analysis.

11. Lindblom's argument is a subtle one in that he argues that it is the incentives politicians face, more than any overt organized activity by businessmen, which results in this common pattern. His method is a modified version of the "method of difference."

12. Williams, et al. *Why Are the British So Bad at Manufacturing?* (hereafter Williams et al.) published a table showing that in the late 1960s, 55% to 60% of the British new car market was held by cars with engine capacities at or below 1300cc. (pp. 278–279) Dunnett, *Decline*, attributes much of the differences in engine capacity in British cars to British government policies that taxed cars by the size of the engine bore, and later, the size of the engine itself. American figures are taken from William Abernathy, *The Productivity Dilemma* Appendix 2. Abernathy notes that the 1971 Ford Pinto's engine was the first American produced four stroke engine below 100 cubic inches since the 1930s.

13. The multinational producers, especially Ford, did produce cars in the 1970s that sold reasonably well in European markets and in a few third world markets—Iran and the old Commonwealth area.

14. CBO, p. 11

15. *Ward's Automotive Yearbook*, 1974, p. 36.

16. Ibid., 1977, p. 19

17. Ibid., 1982, p. 111

18. DOT, pp. 40–44; CBO, p. 16. They quote several *Consumer Reports* evaluations of American and Japanese products that were critical of the American products. *Consumer Reports* in 1986 continued to rate Japanese cars as being of superior quality to their American counterparts.

19. As Stefanie Lenway notes in her *The Politics of International Trade*, the UAW was successful in having only American produced automobiles count toward the CAFE requirements. In 1985, the Reagan administration proposed in effect not to enforce these standards. Neither Ford nor General Motors achieved 1985 CAFE targets, and both have threatened to relocate some of their engine production outside the U.S. as a strategy for avoiding the fines unless the CAFE requirements are waived. The issue is currently before the courts.

20. *Ward's Automotive Yearbook*, 1982, p. 111.

21. *Financial Times*, February 5, 1986.

22. Even should the pound have fully depreciated, Britain's manufacturing cost per unit would still have risen in real terms as Britain imports much of its raw materials—iron ore, for example. Britain's effective exchange rate, measured against the basket of OECD currencies each equaling 100 (the benchmark value assigned to all currencies during the first quarter of 1970), has declined to 72.2 (1981) with a low of 61.3 in 1977. The German and French figures in 1981 were 142.8 and 82.2, respectively. All figures are from OECD, *Economic Observer*, December 1982, p. 167, Table R16. Williams, et al. have argued that, in real terms, wage costs in Britain have fallen and that this cannot account for the relative decline of Britain's auto sector.

23. See, for example, F. E. Jones, "Our Manufacturing Industry," pp. 8–17. The relatively low rates of investment suggest that would-be investors believed (generally with some degree of accuracy) that higher rates of return were available through other investment instruments.

24. Williams *et al* dissent, in part, from this analysis. They argue that, among other things, non-price factors (e.g. poor quality of products, marketing failures) account for much of Britain's decline, and these non-price factors they largely attribute to the failure of British management. Their analysis is clearly correct for some industrial sectors, but at least in the auto sector, the three MNC auto producers presumably maintain similar standards of production, marketing, and product development in Britain as elsewhere.

25. Williams, et al., p. 233

26. The *Financial Times* published a survey of "Vehicle Fleet Management" on February 10, 1986, from which much of this discussion is drawn. In explaining why the estimates of the vehicle fleet market vary by 20 points, John Griffiths wrote "that there is such a wide band in the estimate of business car purchases reflects the fact that a great many vehicles are bought with company, partnership or one-man business cash, yet [are] registered in an individual's name."

27. George Graham, "Tax Benefits: Perk Incentive still worthwhile." *FT* survey. The Conservative Government, in addition to reducing marginal tax rates on income, increased taxes on company cars. "But the Chancellor has still not removed the incentive for employers to given their employees cars rather than cash. Company cars are still tax-efficient [for the employees] in most cases."

28. Karel Williams' "BMC/BLMC/BL—A misunderstood failure" (in Williams, et al., pp. 217–81) provides a "market-specific" analysis of British Leyland's failure, the first analysis (to my knowledge) to do so. All figures in this paragraph, unless noted otherwise, are taken from Williams.

29. We do have measures of productivity that are not calibrated in costs per unit. "Man hours per car" is one such measure.

30. William J. Abernathy, et al., *Industrial Renaissance*, p. 107.

31. "Technology affects competition only to the extent that it—and the way that it—supports or threatens existing commitments: to production systems, to tactical plans and strategic goals, and to the use of resources." Abernathy et al., p. 109. The shift to front wheel drive was seen as being "as destructive to entrenched competence as any tornado on the Kansas plains."

32. DOT, p. 62. The estimate was based on "normal" shifts. Overtime work was not included. The report noted that actual production levels during

1980 had (when annualized) exceeded 12 million units (vs. a capacity estimate of 9.4 million units in 1980).

33. See most recently Robert Reich, *The Next American Frontier*. An important note of caution about the applicability of these Japanese methods, especially "Kanban," to other countries has been issued by Thomas Roehl and Thomas Schmitt, "The Kanban Inventory Control System." Specifically, they warn about the difficulties of establishing close interfirm relationships absent several features unique to Japan.

34. Abernathy *et al.*, *Industrial Renaissance*, also provide comparative cost estimates, and these are firm specific. See p. 61. The Japanese cost advantage in 1981 for producing small cars they estimate to be between $1285–1670.

35. The evidence "refutes the argument that Japan has achieved its edge in labor productivity by the simple substitution of capital for labor. The unpleasant truth is that Japanese producers use less capital to produce a vehicle than do their U.S. competitors and can sustain a given volume of production with much lower levels of investment." Abernathy et al., p. 62. The American producers are attempting to increase the capital intensity of production so as to offset the Japanese cost advantage.

36. See the chapter on quality control in the Japanese automotive industry in Cusumano, *Japanese Automobile Industry*, pp. 320–373.

37. Commission of the European Community, The European Automobile Industry (Luxembourg, 1981), p. 30. These figures are valuable in that they indicate a magnitude of difference between the Japanese industry and their competitors, but the figures should not be taken too literally. The size of the car (hence the labor required) and the amount of work done by outside contractors are relevant to productivity comparisons, but are not reflected in these figures.

38. This section is drawn in part from C. S. Chang, *The Japanese Auto Industry and the U.S. Market*; William C. Duncan, *U.S.–Japan Automobile Diplomacy*; and Maxcy, *Multinational Motor Industry*. See also Ira C. Magaziner, "Japanese Industrial Policy."

39. Chalmers Johnson, "MITI and the Japanese Miracle," pp. 286–89.

40. Hunker, *Structural Change*, p. 73.

41. Duncan, *U.S.–Japan*, chs. 3, 4.

42. See John Zysman, *Governments, Markets, and Growth*, chs. 5, 6. Toyota, for instance, owes debts only to shareholders. Toyota Motor Company, Annual Report, 1981, p. 17.

With regard to the decline in the value of the yen and its effects on Japanese car sales, we should note that product price is crucial in auto sales only in the "lower end" of the market. Because the Japanese companies have a reputation for quality, and because they have successfully produced many different types of motor vehicles each with its own market, an increase in the value of the yen might not reduce Japanese car sales in the U.S.. In 1985 and 1986 Honda Accords, for instance, were sold in the Northeastern U.S. for two or three thousand dollars above the suggested retail price, and were often in scarce supply. This markup was added by Honda's dealers; Honda could well have pocketed the price increase itself.

43. OECD, *Historical Statistics*, Table D.

44. *The Economist*, September 27, 1986.

45. OECD, *Economic Outlook*, December 1982, p. 166.; U.S., Department of Commerce, International Economic Indicators, March 1983, p. 58. Index based on exchange value of the U.S. dollar.

46. *The Economist*, December 25, 1982, p. 74; March 1976, pp. 54–55. The mechanism(s) through which these restrictions are applied is not clear, but the evidence for the presence of these restrictions is. For instance, during the last week of 1982, Prime lending rates in the United States, Great Britain, Germany and Japan were 11.50%, 11.00%, 9.00%, and 6.00% respectively. For the same period, the Day-to-day money market rates for each country were 8.63%, 10.63%, 6.05%, and 6.81%, respectively. In other words, in Japan one could in theory borrow money at 6% and lend it back at 6.81%, and profit from the arbitrage. A "free" market would quickly restore equilibrium, so we can only assume that a credit rationing system is in operation. (Similar results are to be found in the French data.)

The government has succeeded so well in this regard that Japanese companies do not usually use yen in their overseas dealings. The *Financial Times* reported that, in 1984, 40% of Japanese exports were invoiced in yen, as were 3% of Japanese imports. By way of contrast, the American (dollar denominated) figures for 1984 were 90% and 70–85%, respectively. *Financial Times*, April 17, 1985.

47. See, for instance, Robert Hershey's account published in *The New York Times*, May 30, 1984; *Financial Times*, April 17, 1985.

48. The Japanese firms are attempting to move "upmarket." Each of the major firms has established a luxury line of cars. Given the price competition from Korean imports, the Japanese move away from the bottom end of the mass market is a necessary strategic choice. Ironically, the system of "voluntary" quotas allowed the Japanese to introduce "upscale" models while disassociating themselves from the very cheapest product lines. The inadvertent consequence of the quota system is the penetration of the Japanese firms into a once exclusively American sector of the market.

49. Dunnett (*Decline*) reprints a table from the *Fourteenth Report* that shows Volvo, Saab, and Daimler with a higher "fixed assets per man, 1974"

than for any of the British car makers, but the "assets per man" ratio was highest of all for Ford, while GM, VW, and Fiat had higher ratios than either Daimler or Saab (p. 126).

50. See the section on the "Competitiveness of Western European Manufacturers" in Altschuler et al., *Future of Automobile*, pp. 164–171. See also the discussion on specialist manufacturers in OECD, *Long-Term*....

51. *Financial Times*, March 26, 1986.

52. Society for Motor Manufacturers and Traders; *Long- Term*....

53. Figures calculated from Williams, *Why*..., and SMMT, various years.

54. Phillips, et al, *Auto Industries of Europe, U.S., and Japan; Financial Times*, March 18, 1986.

55. *Financial Times*, February 10, 1986. The *New York Times* reported that the Congressional Research Service showed that the proportion of income (not wealth) going to the middle 60% of American families decreased from 53.8% in 1967 to 52.4% in 1983. The income going to the upper 20% rose from 40.4% to 42.9% for the same period. While the absolute magnitude of income changes might be small, it is the (expected) *marginal* change in income that influences sales in consumer durables like cars. Robert Z. Lawrence (*Can America Compete?*; "The Middle Class Is Alive and Well," *The New York Times*, June 23, 1985) has analyzed changing income patterns in the U.S. His findings seem to be broadly in line with the CSR's findings, even allowing for category differences; Lawrence divides the work force into thirds, and focuses on individuals, not households.

56. Figures taken from *Financial Times*, August 30, 1985 and SMMT; *Financial Times*, March 18, 1986.

57. OECD, *Long-Term*, p. 115; *Financial Times*, February 5, 1986. (Jaguar exports 80% of its production, much of it to the United States, and is in consequence, one of Britain's leading exporters.) SMMT, *Financial Times*, November 28, 1985. (Rolls-Royce exports 70% of its production.) *Financial Times* February 5, 1986 and January 29, 1985.

58. The references are to Weber and to Robert Bellah, *Tokugawa Religion* (Boston: Beacon, 1957).

59. Dunnett suggests such an explanation: "Perhaps Britain, quite simply, was an unsuitable place to produce cars. In Japan, Brazil and Spain the recent memory of poverty was sufficient to outweigh the tedium of work on the production lines.... the labor force in Germany, France, Italy and the USA had similar characteristics. All the European car factories employed many guest workers from Southern Europe and North Africa, whilst much of the labor on Detroit's production lines were first-generation black immigrants from the South. Therefore they too had often had a first-hand experience of real poverty" (*Decline*, p. 144).

Sabel's argument is less that the guest workers were poor, but that they were peasants with attitudes towards work that militated against industrial militancy. *Work and Politics*, pp. 101–9.

60. The phrases are taken from Ronald Dore's *British Factory, Japanese Factory*. On labor relations in Germany, see Wolfgang Streeck, *Industrial Relations in West Germany: A Case Study of the Car Industry* (New York: St. Martin's Press, 1984).

61. See Lincoln and Kallenberg, "Work Organization"; Michael Burawoy, in *The Politics of Production* extends the notion of hegemony to include the organization of workers into corporatism. Of the Japanese, he writes, "It is difficult to penetrate the mythologies of harmony and integration associated with the Japanese hegemonic regime, but for that very reason the task is all the more necessary. It is easy to miss the coercive face of paternalism" (p. 143).

Claus Offe (*Contradictions of the Welfare State*) argues that corporatism is limited by two factors. First, nonincorporated groups (consumers) are exploited by agreements among producer groups. Second, even in the German case, the labor movement suffers from an asymmetry in terms of responsibility. Unions are responsible for their members' actions in a bargained situation, though the umbrella groups of the employers are not so restrained (pp. 290–292).

62. Grant, *The Political Economy of Industrial Policy*; Offe, *Contradictions*. Offe notes that the incorporation of the German unions in the decision-making apparatus of the state delegitimates the union hierarchy. With corporatist arrangements, the unions became responsible in part for layoffs and other wage and benefit reductions.

The union hierarchy in Germany has had its own management troubles. *Neue Heimat*'s bankruptcy highlighted the problems in the DGB. Some observers saw the 1984 "35-hour workweek" strike as an effect by parts of the union hierarchy to reestablish the union's militancy credentials.

63. This is at least the portrait of modern Japan found in William Ouchi's *Theory Z*, and, to a lesser extent, in Dore.

64. For instance, Nissan's workers won from management the right to be consulted prior to the introduction of labor-saving technological innovations. *The New York Times*, March 30, 1983.

65. In the immediate postwar era, the workers in the automobile industry were organized by an industry-wide union, but the union collapsed after a 1953 strike. See Cusumano, *Japanese Automobile Industry*, pp. 143–146; 160–85.

66. See, however, Satoshi Kamata, *Japan in the Passing Lane*, in which he recounts his experiences working in a Toyota factory. The Japanese title

was "Automobile Factory of Despair." Ronald Dore, in the introduction to Kamata's book, puts a rather different face on Kamata's work, noting that, by British standards, the workers were far from disaffected. Dore wryly comments on Kamata's high standing among his superiors.

67. The Japanese have a high "marginal propensity" to save, which is then translated by Japanese financial institutions into pools of "cheap" capital for firm investment. (See Quinn and Jacobson, "Industrial Policy" for a discussion of the literature and evidence on Japanese saving behavior.) The question of why the Japanese should have such a high saving rate has produced several proposed answers. These include limited government funding of social welfare programs, a conscious policy by government to force consumers to subsidize firm investment by restricting home buying and other consumer consumption, and the non-Western "social rate of time preference" found in Japanese society. See Manfred Neuman, "Long Swings in Economic Development" for a review of the social rate of time discussion.

68. Perhaps the most famous of these articles is Robert Hayes and William Abernathy, "Managing Our Way to Economic Decline." For an analysis of the role of management education, see Robert Harris, "The Value of Economic Theory in Management Education." The short-term orientation thesis has not been universally accepted. See, for instance, "The False Doctrines of Productivity" by Richard R. West and Dennis E. Logue in *The New York Times* of January 9, 1983.

69. For a discussion of the various techniques of capital budgeting, please see Thomas E. Copeland and J. Fred Weston, *Financial Theory and Corporate Policy*, chs. 2 and 3. See also their discussion of the Capital Asset Pricing Model (CAPM) in chapters 7 and 8. The CAPM allows one to adjust the value of investments for risk.

70. The formula for calculating NPV is $NPV = \Sigma(n, t = 1)\ C_t/(1 + r)^t - I$ where C = cash flow, r = rate of interest (or the firm's capital cost), and I = initial investment.

71. Treasury bills, for instance, are thought to have little risk associated with their purchase, hence are one of the benchmarks against which other investments are measured. The treasury yields are therefore the minimum acceptable yields other investments need to achieve.

72. Richard Brealey and Stewart Meyers, *Principles of Corporate Finance*, esp. parts 3 and 11.

73. One mechanism of "market discipline" is the price/earnings ratio of a firm, which measures the value of a company's stock against dividends. Though in practice the market "accepts" a wide range of P/E's. The closer a firm's p/e approximates the market average, the less vulnerable the firm's management will be to takeover bids or other threats to their autonomy.

Puzzling anomalies to these axioms exist. For instance, the p/e ratios for Ford and Chrysler were approximately 5 and 3 respectively during in Summer 1985. Further, no clear pattern seems to exist with regard to p/e values of those stocks targeted for hostile takeover bids.

74. Copeland and Weston, p. 44.

75. Copeland and Weston write "On the average the market values of nonfinancial corporations are 70% to 80% of the current replacement values of their assets. Often firms can buy other companies below replacement values while new investments in their own line of business do not offer prospects of NPV's that would be positive. This is one of the reasons why new investments in the economy as a whole have lagged" (p. 267).

76. Among the useful secondary sources on the Japanese financial system are: Yoshio Suzuki, *Money and Banking in Japan*; J. Andrew Spindler, *The Politics of International Credit*; Zysman, *Governments, Markets*; Charles Pigott, "Financial Reform in Japan"; Gary R. Saxonhouse, "The Micro- and Macroeconomics of Foreign Sales to Japan"; Jeffrey A. Frankel, *The Yen/Dollar Agreement*; Morgan Guaranty Trust Company (MG), *World Financial Markets*, June 1984. The *Financial Times* published an extremely useful survey on "Japan: Banking, Finance, Investment" on February 17, 1986.

Saxonhouse has argued that Japanese financial and policy institutions, which he terms "illiberal," serve as surrogates for open market institutions. He concludes that Japanese financial and industrial policies and institutions are substitutes for, not complements to, American financial institutions.

Japanese banking consumers are forced to save at very high rates (limited social security and pension plans; extremely restricted housing credits; high educational costs) while their savings earn much less than would be the case in a less regulated market. See Pigott and Morgan Guarantee.

The capital cost advantage enjoyed by Japanese firms in comparison to U.S. firms is well documented. George Hatsopoulos ("High cost of Capital: Handicap of American Industry") estimated that the real cost of capital to American firms in 1981 was 18.8% as opposed to 5.8% for Japanese firms. (Numbers derived from the *Economist's* report of Hatsopoulos' findings, April 30, 1983.)

77. Pigott, p. 27.

78. *The Economist* of June 21, 1986 reported that the debt to equity ratio for Japanese firms is now below 2. For most of the 1960s and the 1960s and 1970s, the figure was above 3. American and British firms, by way of contrast, average debt to equity ratios of below 1. The decreasing debt to equity ratio is an indication of a more developed equity market. *The Economist* (December 8, 1984) also reported that the capital raised by Japanese firms from

Japanese banks fell to 14% of total external capital in 1984, a figure which contrasted to 56% in the previous five years and over 80% in the 1960s. The financing of Japanese corporations more closely resembles the financing of US and UK companies than in any time previously.

79. Corporations placed 59% of increases in financial assets in yen denominated demand and time deposits in the period from 1970–1974. Only 7.8% of these assets were placed in these instruments during the 1980–1982 period. 16.6% were placed in the newly created CD instruments, 26.7% were in various foreign currency denominated assets (as opposed to 2.2% in the 1970–1974 period), and 36.5% were placed in equity holdings (vs. 28.9%). Consumers, on the other hand, placed 53.% of their increases in personal financial assets in times and savings deposits in 1970–1974, and 56.4% in 1980–1982. Equity placements increased from 0.5% to 0.6% for these periods. No figures for CDs or other money market instruments were reported. MG, p. 6.

Takatoshi Ito has examined the interest rate differentials between the Euromarket and Japanese domestic markets, and has concluded that the interbank rate prevailing in Europe and the "Gensaki" (secondary market for 3 month bills) market in Tokyo reveal no "uncovered interest parity" after 1981. Simply put, no arbitrage possibilities exist. Takatoshi Ito, "Use of (time-Domain) Vector Autoregressions." These instruments are not available to consumers. See also Ichiro Otani and Siddharth Tiwari, "Capital Controls and Interest Rate Parity: The Japanese Experience, 1978–1981," *IMF Staff Paper*, December 1981. They note that, even after the lifting of formal regulatory controls, the Japanese government was able to use "moral suasion . . . to encourage Japanese residents to bring in funds from abroad" (p. 811).

The regulation of Japan's financial industry became an issue of negotiation between the U.S. and Japan in 1983–1984. The two governments negotiated a series of agreements (Spring 1984) aimed at reducing Japanese government restrictions on the domestic and international (yen) financial markets. Interest-withholding penalties and other disincentives against borrowing by Japanese citizens on the Euroyen market were to be lifted eventually, a Euroyen Certificate of Deposit (CD) market would be opened in December of 1984, and the Euroyen market would be opened to corporate (Japanese) borrowers.

80. The standard reference in English on the West German banking system and the political environment of banking remains Andrew Shonfield's *Modern Capitalism*, chs. 11 and 12. Charles Kindleberger's *A Financial History of Western Europe* contains a very concise history of German banking and government regulation (see chs. 7, 9, 17, 22, and 24). Spindler, though pri-

marily concerned with the foreign policy implications of bank-government relations, provides a useful overview of the current German banking system in *Politics of International Credit*, ch. 2. See also Richard Medley, "Monetary Stability and Industrial Adaptation in West Germany"; Zysman, *Governments, Markets* ch. 5; and Brian S. Quinn, *The New Euromarkets*.

81. This figure is calculated from the *Economist* of June 21, 1986. The German average figure in 1985 was 2.4. Medley notes that owning or controlling 25% plus one of the stock of a company gives someone a "blocking" or veto interest in the firm's decisions. "Monetary Stability," p. 118.

82. The sources from which this discussion is drawn are primarily Shonfield, *Modern Capitalism* and *In Defense*; Medley, "Monetary Stability," Spindler, *Politics of International Credit*. Zysman, speaking directly to the issue of government-set interest rates, says that the German government "does not intervene in a detailed way to affect the allocation of credit, either by quantitative intervention or by manipulating the relative prices in the various financial markets.... in Germany... resources are allocated in the markets by freely moving prices" (*Governments, Markets* p. 260). Ellsworth appears to disagree.

83. OECD, *Historical Statistics, 1960-1982*. The EC average for the period (including Germany) was 6.9%.

84. In addition to the aforementioned subcommittee of the Central Capital Markets Committee, the government has in the past required German firms that acquired overseas loans to place 50% of the amount of the loan in a non-interest-bearing account with the Bundesbank. The government may also suspend interest payments on the accounts of "non-residents" (Medley, p. 108). The *Financial Times* commented that "Unlike many other currency sectors of the Eurobond market, Deutschemark-denominated Eurobonds are still fairly tightly controlled by the financial authorities of the currency's home country." March 18, 1985.

85. Trade in Euromarks began in the early 1960s, though the market was "relatively insignificant" prior to 1968. Quinn, *New Euromarket*, p. 123. 11.48% of Eurocurrency transactions were DM denominated in 1984. *Financial Times*, April 17, 1985.

86. See Wyn Grant, *The Political Economy of Industrial Policy*, especially pp. 74-77. Grant does note that "selective intervention" aid to firms has substantially increased in Germany in recent years. Agriculture has been the main beneficiary of German subsidies.

87. The sources used in writing this section include: Michael Moran, *The Politics of Banking* and "Politics, Banks and Markets;" Catharine Hill, "Monetarism and Supply-Side Economics in the United Kingdom," JEC,; Williams et al.; John Carrington and George Edwards, *Financing Industrial Investment*;

Kindleberger, *Financial History*; Shonfield, *Modern Capitalism* and *In Defense*; Zysman, *Government, Markets*, and numerous articles from the *Economist*, the *Financial Times*, and the *New York Times*.

88. Zysman compares merchant banks to *banques d'affaires* and American investment banks (pp. 190–201), but the differences between U.S. investment banks and UK merchant banks have substantially eroded. Public regulations of the financial industry has been (comparatively) minimal. Moran and Kindleberger each argue that the "industry profile" of the financial industry was the result of market forces and competition.

89. The tradeoff between finance and industry is usually seen as being fought out over two issues, the value of sterling and the absence of loans to industry.

The finance-manufacturing "split" is usually seen in one of two lights. For economists, the question is whether or not the British financial markets are "efficient," by which is meant, did British finance ignore profit-making opportunities in Britain in preference to more risky or less lucrative overseas investments? A few economists have answered yes (Sir Arthur Lewis), but most regard this question as a "theoretical" impossibility. Williams et al. dissent, providing instead a highly original, institutional analysis of British financial practices.

For neo-Marxists, the issue revolves around "factions" of capital— finance vs. manufacturing—and the relative political influence of each faction. Neither the economists nor the neo-Marxists footnote each other's work.

The debt to equity ratio for British firms has generally averaged below 1 for the past 20 years. *Economist*, June 21, 1986.

90. Hill reprints an interesting Bank of England notice (April 11, 1978), which reads in part, "Banks and finance houses are asked: (i) to provide, within the bounds of banking prudence, finance required for both working capital and fixed investment by manufacturing industry and for the expansion of exports and the saving of imports; (ii) in order to insure the future ability to meet the requirements in (i) above, to exercise strict restraint on lending or provisions of facilities for other purposes including...those... for purely financial transactions" (p. 50). She does not say what effect this missive had.

91. Partly in consequence of uncoordinated public policy, these regulatory boundaries are breaking down, though often to be replaced with a different set. Michael Moran argues that, in this country, "markets [have] dismantle[d] regulation." This claim may be too strong. The Tolchins, Pertschuk, MacAvoy and Weidenbaum have each in their own way demonstrated that the deregulation movement has both powerful interests behind it and a well-articulated and internally consistent ideology leading it. But, Moran's central

claim, that competitive pressure within the banking community and among state governments led to deregulation, is consistent with the evidence. The deregulation process at the Federal level, while also influenced by the more "competitive" (i.e. internationalized) environment of the nation's financial industry, is characterized by legislative, bureaucratic, and legal confusion. The domain and range of financial regulation is being determined now by the courts and by Congress.

92. The standard justification for relying on equity rather than bank debt is that, even though equity-financed debt is more expensive than is banking debt, equity debt is not fixed-cost. In times of financial trouble, a common occurrence in America's volatile economy, the corporation's managers may simply reduce or omit the shareholder's dividend. This may not please the shareholders much, but they have little practical recourse but to sell the stock or accept the dividend reduction. A bank denied its interest payments has many legal avenues open to it.

93. *The New York Times*, July 13, 1985.

94. See the *Financial Times* survey of "Venture Capital" of December 3, 1985.

95. *The New York Times*, "How the Institutions Rule the Market," November 25, 1984.

96. U.S., Congress, Senate, Committee on Banking, Housing and Urban Affairs, *The Automobile and the World Economy*, p. 26, testimony of Maryann Keller.

97. OECD, *Financial Accounts of OECD Countries*, part 3, (1983), p. 93.

98. BL Limited, p. 11.; OECD, Financial Accounts, p. 177.

99. The Automobile Industry and the World Economy, pp. 25–7.

100. Ibid., pp. 29–30. The debt to equity ratio is a measurement of long-term debt to shareholders capital plus debt. The normal "gearing" or ratio is approximately 1 to 3, though for a mature industry like autos, this figure is too high.

101. BL's debt to equity ratio was calculated from figures given in the Ryder Report, pp. 22–23. Chrysler's ratio was more difficult to calculate since Chrysler's Annual Reports did not contain such standard information as equity figures. Figures were derived from U.S., Congress, House of Representatives, Report of the Chrysler Corporation Loan Guarantee Board, pp. 65, 318, 319, 322.; Chrysler's improved prospects allowed it to raise several hundred million dollars in new equity funds in 1983. Chrysler Corporation Annual Report, 1982, p. 15.

102. See Young & Hood, *Chrysler, U.K.*, pp. 330–33. The British government did have veto power over the Peugeot deal, but given Chrysler's impending world collapse, the government was in no position to veto. For

details of the commitment, see Great Britain, Department of Industry, Public Expenditures on Chrysler U.K. Ltd., Command Paper 6745 (London: HMSO, 1977). For details of Chrysler's financial troubles, see *Ward's Automotive Yearbook*, 1982, p. 177. The U.S. has turned a profit on its Chrysler deals. The Treasury exercised Chrysler share warrants thereby bringing several hundred million dollars to the state.

103. Figures derived from Answer to Parliamentary Questions on October 23, 1981 and April 19, 1983, and from House of Commons, Industry and Trade Committee, 1982–83, BL, PLC, p. 7.

104. CBO. Current Problems of the U.S. Automobile Industry and Policies to Address Them. (Washington, 1980), p. 25.

105. Trade Union Congress. The Battle for Jobs: *TUC Economic Review* (1983), p. 12.

106. Arthur Okun "Potential GNP." This issue is also discussed in Robert J. Gordon, *Macroeconomics*, p. 292.

107. McConnell, *Private Power*, p. 283.

108. Employment and the American Auto Industry, p. 47. Testimony of Sheldon Friedman.

109. A casual look at the graph might lead one to suggest that the American and Japanese accounts correspond inversely. They do not. Japan has run a multibillion dollar trade surplus with the U.S. since the 1960s.

110. That is so unless exchange rates are fixed through some transnational agreement or a nation is willing to use its foreign reserves to defend the value of its currency, as the U.S. did in the 1960s.

111. For an interesting discussion of the issues raised in this section, see Edward Chambers et al, *National Income Analysis and Forecasting*, Glenview, Ill.: Scott, Foreman, 1975, chapter 15; and Ott and Ott, op. cit.

112. *Unemployment and the American Automobile Industry*, 1982, p. 47.

113. Economist Intelligence Unit. Quarterly Economic Review of Japan and South Korea: Annual Supplement, 1981 (London, 1982), p. 17. Japan's auto imports are statistically insignificant. During the same five-year period, Japan's oil imports cost over $154 billion, mostly to Saudi Arabia and Indonesia.

114. *The Future of the British Car Industry*, p. viii.

115. In the case of BL, redundancy payments cost the company £98 million in 1981 and £30 million in 1982. BL: Reports & Accounts (1982), p. 20.

116. OECD, UK: Economic Survey, pp. 12, 26; TUC, p. 12. British unemployment averaged 2.4% of the workforce between 1963 and 1975. Thereafter, unemployment rose from 5.3% in 1976 to 5.4% in 1979. During the Thatcher administration, unemployment rose to 6.8% in 1980, 10.6% in 1981, and nearly 13% in 1982 (with 3 million people registered as being

unemployed.) Britain's unemployment rate is 50% above the OECD average (including the UK.) In May of 1982, a House of Lords Select Committee estimated that each unemployed person cost the British Treasury £5000 per year in transfer payments and lost tax income.

117. Institute of Fiscal Studies quoted in *Financial Times* October 2, 1982, p. 3.

118. The bulk of the price difference is accountable to government policies to maintain BL's price margins and to company (and government) restriction on personal imports, and not to the added expense of manufacturing right-hand-drive vehicles. See the series of articles in *The Economist* Sept. 19, Oct. 3, Nov. 14, Dec. 12, 1981.

119. *The Economist*, November 28, 1981, p. 103.

120. Britain's initial postwar wave of nationalizations of steel, coal, and several other industries was ideologically motivated. More recent nationalizations (more correctly, public takeovers) have been undertaken to prevent firm bankruptcies. BL is such an instance.

121. *The Economist*, November 21, 1981; December 12, 1981, letter of Mr. B. A. Walker; TUC, 1982, p. 8. The nationalized industries contribute to over 10% of British GNP.

122. *Congressional Quarterly Weekly*, September 19, 1982 and November 19, 1983. The EDA has granted some $11 billion since its creation in 1965, but has done so in uneven blocks; $6 billion of its funds were distributed in 1976 and 1977. SBA appropriations have hovered around $500 million since 1980. Among the projects funded by the EDA is the Indiana pyramid; the Reagan administration has, so far without success, attempted to eliminate the EDA and the SBA. These agencies survived the first round of mandatory Gramm-Rudman cuts.

A number of recent articles have included America's defense policies in the category of industrial policy. As industrial policy goes, defense expenditures are a poor mechanism of industrial growth. For a discussion of this, see Robert W. DeGrasse, Jr. "Military Buildup Exacts Toll on Economy."

123. The theory behind this decrease in corporate taxation was that the newly available funds would then be reinvested in productive enterprise (the supply side of the economy.) As of yet, this boom in nonresidential fixed investment (NRFI) has not materialized. NRFI did rise from $309 billion in 1980 to $352 billion in 1981. But, in 1982, the figure was $348 billion and the annualized figures for the 1st and 2nd Quarters of 1983 were $332 and $336 billion respectively. *Economic Indicators*, p. 9).

124. This section is substantially drawn from C. E. Ferguson and J. P. Gould, *Microeconomic Theory*, and Edwin Mansfield, *Microeconomics*. For a more empirically grounded discussion of the price structures (and their

origins) of American industry, see F. M. Scherer, *Industrial Market Structure*, chs. 5–12. He describes himself as an agnostic with regard to neoclassical microeconomic theory.

125. The alternative to "floor" pricing is state subsidy of the prices, a cost ultimately borne by the taxpayers. Japanese corporate profitability has benefited from floor pricing and other restrictions on their products. Japanese export prices have risen on average an estimated 5.5% more than they would have done without quotas and other restrictions. In consequence, to quote *The Economist*, December 17, 1983, p. 63. "Japan's share of world exports of manufactured goods has stayed stable (since 1980) at 13 to 13 ½%, after having trebled in the previous quarter century . . . Japan's trade surplus has soared from $2 billion in 1980 to a likely $30 billion in 1983. And the yen's value has stayed low while Japan's internal wholesale prices of manufactures dropped slightly between 1981 and last month. In the same period, the internal prices of manufactures in other industrial countries rose by over 13%."

126. CBO, p. 61. Among the options considered by the CBO were new-car subsidies, quotas, changes in depreciation allowances, refundable tax credits, relaxation of environmental and safety standards, and loan guarantees.

127. Denison writes, "Government probably influences private productivity for either good or ill less than public discussions would suggest. The extent to which it succeeds in the provision of education . . . has the greatest impact in the long run. But government cannot have had very much to do with the recent slowdown in the growth rate of productivity computed on a potential basis" Edward F. Denison, *Trends in American Economic Growth, 1929–1982*, p. 61.

128. In 1979, the Government Statistical Service (GSS) of Great Britain listed the working population as 26.5 million, of whom 13.5 million were members of a trade union. I have seen more recent figures from other sources (TUC, CSO), but these figures do not agree.

129. Congress, U.S., Joint Economic Committee, U.S. International Economic Policy in the 1980s, p. 45.

130. For a summary of industrial policies in each of the major European countries, see National Economics Development Council (NEDC), *Industrial Policies in Europe* (London: NEDO, 1981). About an EC-wide industrial policy, the NEDC report said "Priority in the EEC throughout its 20 years history has been given to the creation of the common market, and industrial policy has primarily involved the establishment of the ground rules for trading within that market. The role of the Commission has therefore es-

sentially been one of regulation, control and co-ordination. . . . [furthermore] given current nationalist attitudes towards advanced technologies, it is uncertain whether any initiative other than the relatively limited co-ordination procedures currently proposed would be likely to receive backing from member states. It is futile to imposed upon the Commission a role which it is incapable of fulfilling" (p. 11).

131. OECD. United Kingdom; Economic Survey, 1983, p. 21.

132. See, for example, the TUC's Economic Review for 1982 and 1983, pp. 36–37, 44–45, (London: 1982, 1983). See also Grant, *Political Economy* pp. 130–35. Britain's membership in a European Community has been a major issue in British politics since the formation of the European Coal and Steel Community (1951) and the EC itself (1957). Britain was invited to join both groups, but it refused. When Britain finally did apply to join, Charles de Gaulle twice vetoed the application (1963 and 1967). Britain finally did vote to join (1971) with membership effective in 1972 and complete entry by 1975. The Labour Party, however, opposed membership, and pledged to either withdraw or renegotiate the membership terms and hold a referendum on the results. Minor changes were made by Labour, and two thirds of the electorate voted to remain in the EC (1975.) Popular disaffection with the EC has risen in recent years, and in election of 1983, the Labour Party, led by Michael Foot, had promised a withdrawal were it to have won. Interestingly, only in recent years has the economic cost of membership become a substantial issue in Britain, and then largely over budgetary issues.

133. The proposition that free trade is universally beneficial is widely accepted in neoclassical economics. The association of the expansion of world trade and of world economic growth is often held to demonstrate this proposition. The figures are: between 1953 and 1960, a 7.6% annual increase in world export volume and a 5.2% annual increase in world production; for 1960–1973, the figures were 8.5% and 6%; for 1973–78, 4% and 3.5%, respectively. *U.S. International Economic Policy*, pp. 46–47.

Some new models of trade suggest that, although cumulative global welfare might not be advanced by forms of protectionism, the welfare of individual nations might be. These recent models of intraindustry trade and technological competition suggest that the incentives for governments to provide protection for some industries, particularly "high-tech" industries, might be very strong. See Paul Krugman, "New Theories of Trade Among Industrial Countries," pp. 343–347.

134. Pareto is reputed to have once claimed that, in any given democracy, a bill which gave large sums to a few men from the general till (i.e. all of us) was sure to pass due to the intensity of the small group's labors and the

general corruption of democratic life. Mancur Olson, in his *The Logic of Collective Action*, gives a formalization of the logic behind Pareto's comment. See also his *Rise and Decline of Nations*.

135. Much of the material in this section is drawn from Fred Lazar, *The New Protectionism*; John Volpe, *Industrial Incentive Policies and Programs in the Canadian–American Context*. Congress (U.S.), Joint Economic Committee, Monetary Policy, Selective Credit Policy, and Industrial Policy in France, Britain, West Germany, and Sweden; U.S. International Economic Policy; and Victoria Curzon-Price, *Industrial Policies in the European Community*. For a discussion of American trade policy with regard to several industries, including autos, see Stefanie Ann Lenway's *The Politics of International Trade*.

136. In addition to these barriers, Japan in particular has evolved several "cultural" impediments to trade, though their significance is hard to assess given the poor information available on the Japanese elite. These practices, administrative guidance, and the distribution system, make importing consumer products difficult. *U.S. International Economic Policy*, pp. 48–49. For a discussion of the Japanese distribution system, see Tom Roehl, "The General Trading Company."

137. Curzon-Price, *Industrial Policies*, pp. 36–37. For instance, the U.S. Government has been providing export credits to help Boeing in its battle for overseas markets with the Airbus consortium.

138. I understood the full effect of this for the first time as I was examining glassware in a Sunday market in Northern Italy. The set had printed on it, in English, "Made in Italy," in conformance with U.S. Law.

139. Curzon-Price, *Industrial Policies*, pp. 36–37. She writes, "Before the Trade Agreements Act of 1979, implementing the Tokyo round agreements, the United States applied its own domestic trade law to other countries' subsidies and it was much stricter than any found in the GATT; it provided for the mandatory application of countervailing duties to any product bearing any subsidy, whether or not it caused damage to an American producer. In the GATT, countervailing duties may only be applied against imports assisted by subsidies if they cause 'material' injury to local firms. Had it not been, then, for the deterrent effect of American law, the spread and growth of subsidization might have been even greater than it anyway has been. In fact, private parties may still (and often do) bring action."

140. Lazar, *New Protectionism*, pp. 27–45, has a good discussion of this. He agrees with Curzon-Price that the 1979 Act is a break with the past, though he disagrees with the normative value of this.

141. Ibid., p. 36. The issue of whether or not the United States subsidizes its industries, and thus violates its own free-trade principles, is one that

separates the U.S. from its allies (though not as much as American claims of extraterritoriality). The presumption in the field of comparative and international political economy is that the U.S. has been committed in practice as well as in theory to a liberal, free-trade regime. Many analysts, however, have noted that protection was a growing phenomenon of the late 1970s and early 1980s in many Western countries, the U.S. included (see for instance, Susan Strange, "The Management of Surplus Capacity"). American claims of European and Japanese fudging on free trade is met by similar counterclaims. The Federal government does heavily support industrial R & D, having accounted for 40% of it in 1973 (Volpe, *Industrial Incentive Policies*, p. 34). The U.S. also subsidizes exports through the Domestic International Sales Corporation (DISC), which grants tax deferrals, and the Export-Import Bank, which helps finance exports. DISC has been particularly controversial, as many corporations have established DISCs. Approximately two thirds of American manufactured exports are exported through DISCs (*U.S. International Economic Policy*, p. 61). For some corporations, the tax deferrals have become outright grants. *Fortune* reported (November 26, 1984) that "In the 1984 tax act, Congress forgave about $11 billion in deferred taxes accumulated through [DISCs] by Boeing, General Electric, and thousands of other U.S. exporters" (p. 33). In addition, the Buy American Act of 1933 has resulted in Government procurements, a large market which constitutes almost 10% of U.S. GNP (1973), being 99% of American origin (Volpe, pp. 35–38). A reasonable person would, I think conclude that the U.S. does indeed sin.

142. Several recent works on this include David Yoffie, "Orderly Marketing Agreements as Industrial Policy" and the essays in Susan Strange and Roger Tooze, eds., *The International Politics of Surplus Capacity*.

143. The ITC found the general economic downturn to be of greater significance. See Gilbert Winhan, *The Automobile Trade Crisis of 1980*, pp. 36–44; and *U.S. International Economic Policy*, pp. 99–102.

144. *Solidarity*, April 1982, p. 13.

145. All facts in this section are drawn from various issues of *Ward's Automotive Reports*. The 1980 total sales for Japanese cars was 1.8 million.

146. The quotas have been in place for three years, and some of the consequences are already clear. For instance, the total value of Japanese cars sold in the United States has risen from $8.4 billion in 1980 to $10.3 billion in 1982 (*Congressional Quarterly Weekly*, July 9, 1983, p. 1396.) This implies an upmarket shift in the product mix.

147. Answer in response to a Parliamentary Question by Tony Marlow, 1 May 1981. Quoted in *British Business*, May 8, 1981.

148. Dunnett, *Decline*, p. 167.

149. *The Economist*, February 6, 1982, p. 47. Higher prices are essential to BL's survival. Had BL been forced to sell cars at Continental prices, its losses would have been much deeper.

150. Other methods through which governments can block markets include the use of state buying policies. For instance, the U.S. government purchases only American cars. Governments can also limit access to private markets. The British Government permits British companies to give access to company cars to executives as part of the fringe benefits package. British company fleets are overwhelmingly composed of British manufactured cars; this market is usually 40% of the total U.K. car market in 1982 (CPRS, p. 60). The *Financial Times* estimates that this market could be as large as 60% of total U.K. sales, February 10, 1986, p. I. As the government's taxation policies have created the size of this market, the state could—and in effect did—require the cars to be British.

151. *Ward's Automotive Reports*, 1982.

152. The $200 billion figure was calculated from Joint Economic Committee, *Economic Indicators*, September 1983, p. 3. Under the current law, firms get both an investment credit and depreciate 100% of capital goods purchases. This law has been modified for the 1984 tax year. See *Congressional Quarterly Weekly* (CQW), August 28, 1982, pp. 2119–20, for details. See also George Yost, "Safe Harbor Leasing," pp. 85–101; Edward A. Dahlka, "TBTs—A Potential Audit Time Bomb," pp. 55–63. The "tax swap" scheme was repealed by Congress for the 1984 tax year after profitable companies like General Electric were able to gain up to $100 million from the treasury, CQW, January 16, 1982, pp. 89–90.

153. The details of these deals have been difficult to obtain. Firms are to report them, but the data are not reported in any obvious place. These figures are from Ford's and Chrysler's 1982 Annual Reports. I doubt their accuracy.

154. Cited in *Fortune*, November 24, 1984. G.E.'s tax rate was −4.3% ($283.3 million), Boeing's −17.5% ($267.0 million), General Dynamic's −7.6% ($70.6 million), and Dow's −28.7% ($223.0 million).

155. Grant, *Political Economy*, p. 53.

156. Ford, U.K., Annual Report, 1982; British Business, various issues.

157. One measure of the capital intensity of production (that is, the relative mix of capital and labor) is the capital/labor ratio—K/L. From aggregated corporate tax returns published by the OECD, I have calculated the depreciation allowance–investment tax credit to wage costs ratio for firms in the United States from .129 in 1969 to .166 in 1983, and from .167 in 1969 to .209 in 1983 for Great Britain.

158. House of Commons (U.K.), Industry and Trade Committee, BL Plc, 1982–83, p. 12. This figure does not include depreciation/amortization al-

lowances, which came to over £275 million for 1982 and 1981 combined. BL Plc: Report and Accounts, 1982. Wilks estimated BL's total subsidy at £2.4 billion.

159. BL's productivity, as expressed by vehicles per man per year, rose 45% between 1980 and 1982; 5.06 cars per man per year vs. 8.83 cars per man per year. BL Plc, pp. 6, 22. The New York Times (July 24, 1983) reported that, over the same period, Chrysler's productivity rose 18%; 13.23 vs. 16.03. The "break-even" point of the U.S. industry as a whole fell from 11.2 million cars a year in 1980 to 8.1 million units in 1982. This is a good thing given that the annual sale of U.S.-made cars averaged just over 6 million units in 1980–82.

160. Douglas Fraser had been invited to sit on the Board of Directors of Chrysler, although his successor, Owen Bieber, was not (until recently) so invited. In a sense, this development to give Chrysler workers "voice" was an outgrowth of the movement to a form of tripartism (e.g. sectoral committees of labor, business, and government) begun under the 1974 Trade Act, which attempted to induce a negotiated trade and production regime in the United States to match perceived developments in Japan and Western Europe.

161. Ben Hooberman, An Introduction to British Trade Unions, pp. 87–102.

162. See, for instance, BVMI, p. 2; CPRS, pp. v, xiii-xiv, 101–3, 121, 132. The CPRS called for both management and labor to work to "combat the influence of politically-motivated extremists out to wreck the industry" (p. 132).

163. The Thatcher government has had some success in confronting the trade unions, most notably over the miners' strike in 1984–5. Apart from the well-publicized split in the miners' ranks, many unions in related industries provided no real support for the miners. Some analysts have cited the steelworkers' lack of support for the mine strike as being behind the Tories' reluctance to close the steel plant at Ravenscraig.

164. The auto industry in the U.S. is a good example of this. Every summer, most of the American industry's workers are laid off while the factories are retooled to produce the new model year's cars. Workers are eligible for unemployment benefits, thereby reducing the wage demands on the industry and lessening the chance that members of the work force will seek more steady employment.

165. CBO, p. 23.

166. Unemployment and the American Automobile Industry, 1982, p. 47.

167. TUC, p. 12.

168. UK: Economic Survey, p. 26.

169. By 1975, BL stock was selling at 8p though the government took equity at 50p per share. Some private stockholders remain. British Leyland, Annual Report, 1976, p. 28; Ryder Report, pp. 22–3. The supplier industries have also absorbed some of the costs (Chrysler's suppliers provided $180 million in aid as part of the overall package), and banks that had extended credit to Chrysler and BL before their financial troubles have had both the principal and interest on loans extended beyond their original terms.

170. The words "commercial viability" are not my own. They appeared first (as near as I can tell) in British Government documents of the early 1970s regarding the nationalized industries. As one reviewer has pointed out to me, in and of itself, this phrase is rather meaningless—IBM and the flourishing local grocery store are equally "viable" in some sense. What this phrase came to mean in policy terms was the provision of a type of aid such that the firm would no longer need public assistance. Such a firm would be capable of independent existence. Governments would not specify employment, production, or location targets for the aided firms. Nor did governments particularly care about the levels of firm profitability per se. Rather, reducing costs to the national economies became the public aim, and commercial viability was the code phrase for this policy.

171. See Joseph Schumpeter's discussion of this in his Capitalism, Socialism, and Democracy, part II.

172. The languages of description and the motivations ascribed to the state with regard to this sector vary greatly among analysts. Neoclassical economists have seen these nonmarket sectors as inherently inefficient and illegitimate. (Milton Friedman is in some ways the ideal neoclassical economist. For him, not even education ought to remain in the public domain.) Many pluralists have seen the state as "capturable" by private interests, and the nonmarket sector is part of the prize of political victory, though most also see this as illegitimate (Lowi, End of Liberalism; Samuel Brittan, The Economic Consequences of Democracy, London: Temple Smith, 1977). Neo-Marxists—Claus Offe and Jurgen Habermas (more or less) among them—see these nonmarket sectors as essential parts of the capitalist state. These sectors act to legitimate bourgeois class rule, by mitigating some of the consequences of capitalism, and also by reserving to the state only the least profitable activities, thus "proving" the incompetence of the state in other areas of economic life. (Jürgen Habermas, Legitimation Crisis; Claus Offe and Volker Ronge, "Theses on the Theory of the State.")

173. Department of Industry, (U.K.), An Approach to Industrial Strategy, (London: HMSO, 1975).

174. See Michael Pertschuk, Revolt Against Regulation; also, Susan Tolchin and Martin Tolchin, Dismantling America.

175. In a previous section, I argued that, although subsidies prevented high short-term social costs, we should assume (following micro-economic theory on this matter) that subsidies incur long-term opportunity costs.

176. Department of Industry (UK), *Public Expenditure on Chrysler*, UK. Command 6745. (London: HMSO, 1977), p. 3. See also House of Commons (UK). *Eighth Report from the Expenditure Committee. Session 1975–6. HC–651–1.*

177. *Public Expenditure*, p. 3.

178. Ibid. p. 6.

179. Ibid. p. 10–11.

180. For a discussion of Chrysler, UK, see Young and Hood, *Chrysler, U.K.*; Dunnett, *Decline*; and, on the planning agreement, Stephen Wilks, "Planning Agreements," pp. 399–420.

181. After the closure of the Linwood plant in Scotland, Talbot was forced to repay some of the grants made it to the Exchequer. Answer to a Parliamentary Question, reported in *British Business*, December 18, 1981. Peugeot lost substantial sums of money in 1982 and 1983, in part owing to Peugeot's purchase of Chrysler, Europe.

182. CBO, p. 50.

183. The one exception to this is to be found in the CAFE (fuel economy) rules. Foreign-built cars sold under an American company's name do not count toward the fleet fuel average. As the Reagan administration decided not to enforce the penalties on GM and Ford for having violated the CAFE rules for 1984, this exception makes little practical difference.

184. Chrysler has succeeded in meeting the CAFE standards. The Department of Transportation waived the penalties and relaxed the CAFE standards, however. This action saved GM $385 million in fines for the 1985 model year. *The New York Times*, September 29, 1986.

185. For instance, see the exchange between BL's former chairman, Sir Michael Edwardes, and members of Parliament over BL's past and future layoffs. BL, 1981–2, pp. 28, 55. Sir Michael, interestingly, did not feel that BL needed to achieve Japanese productivity levels as a result of the EC's "political position" (p. 28).

186. *The Economist*, December 3, 1983. *The Guardian* reported on April 13, 1983, that Nissan had been negotiating for the purchase of BL. These talks apparently were for naught as Nissan began to assemble its own cars in Britain in 1987.

187. These are the end of market isolation and efficient foreign competitors; a number of U.S. and British industries face the same.

188. These are the access of firms to finance and the welfare costs of large firms failure.

189. The business cycle, sometimes referred to as the trade cycle, is a recurring fluctuation endemic to capitalist economies. For instance, The Economist ("World Business Cycles," London, 1982) reports 16 downturns and 17 upturns in the rate of change in U.S. gross domestic product between 1860 and 1980, and 20 upturns and 21 downturns for Great Britain over the same period. The root of the business cycle is usually seen as being in either changes in the inventories held by firms (one or two years in duration), changes in the national levels of utilization of existing stock of material goods (three to six years), or changes in the capacity to produce goods (eight to ten years). Here, I am concerned only with changes in the rate of growth of gross domestic product—that is, in second difference data $- D^1_t - D^1_{t-1} = D^2_t = X$.

190. See Robert Hall and Dale Jorgenson, "Tax Policy and Investment Behavior." and David G. Davies, United States Taxes and Tax Policy, pp. 138–149. Further references to these volumes will appear in the text.

Not everyone agrees that tax incentives have promoted higher rates of firm investment. See Robert S. McIntyre, "The Failure of Corporate Tax Incentives." McIntyre presents evidence, derived from corporate tax returns, that little association exists either between firms with low tax rates and higher investment or between firms with high tax rates and lower investment. McIntyre does not present econometric evidence for his claim, so his argument and that of Hall and Jorgenson are difficult to reconcile on the basis of the evidence presented in the articles. Hall and Jorgenson might respond to McIntyre by noting that the question of incentives has little to do with the overall tax rates but with the marginal rate of investment. Hence, the relevant point is not that Whirlpool invested heavily despite being taxed heavily; the question is rather what added investment did Whirlpool undertake because of its lowered capital costs?

191. Currently, three methods of depreciation accounting are in use, though not among all Western countries; the straight line (or historic cost) method, the declining balance (DB) method, and the sum of the years' digits (SYD) methods. Unlike the straight line method of depreciation, in which a firm depreciates a constant percentage of its investment per year, DB and SYD accelerate the depreciation schedules, thereby reducing the impact of inflation on the firm's investment capital. The Accelerated Depreciation Allowances and the Investment Tax Credits allow for even more rapid depreciation of investments than either the DB or the SYD methods. For a discussion of the consequences of different depreciation schedules, see Mack Ott, "Depreciation, Inflation and Investment Incentives."

192. I am following the notation conventions used by Hall and Jorgenson in Tax Incentives and Capital Spending, (Gary Fromm, editor, Washington:

Brookings, 1971) when their notations differ from those of Przeworski and Wallerstein. (See Bibliography for publication information on this title, as well as Auerbach's.)

193. Przeworski and Wallerstein were interested in demonstrating that fiscal policy and investment policy were potentially separable, and that the many tax rates that satisfy the condition, $\mu = k + \mu z$, would promote the same level of firm investment. This would mean, in effect, that taxes would be levied only on uninvested profits. While no country's corporate tax code has this feature, the high levels of Japanese firm investment despite the high levels of corporate taxation in Japan indicate that fiscal and investment policies can be separated.

194. See Franklin Fisher and John McGowan, "On the Misuse of Accounting Rates of Return to Infer Monopoly Profits," and the follow on comments. Fisher and McGowan write, "Unless depreciation schedules are chosen in a particular way, so that the value of the investment is calculated as the present value at the economic rate of return of the stream of benefits remaining in it—a choice which is exceptionally unlikely to be made—the accounting rate of return on a particular investment will differ from year to year, and will not in general equal the economic rate of return on that investment in any year" (p. 84).

195. Depreciation charges will not equal total firm investment. In the fifteen year period, 1970–1984 inclusive, gross physical investment by American nonfinancial enterprises totaled $3.8 trillion. For the same period, depreciation charges for these firms against taxation totaled $1.9 trillion: 50.5% of total investment to be exact. For German firms, for the same period, 2.2 trillion DM were invested, and 1.2 trillion DM were charged against taxes: 55.3% of total investment. (The OECD does not report total firm investment for Japan, and the data are not yet available for Great Britain.) Non-Financial ...; and OECD Financial Statistics, Part 2. Financial Accounts of OECD Countries, (Paris, 1986) Table 33.F.

196. See Hywel Jones, An Introduction to Modern Theories of Economic Growth, for a well written and (comparatively) simple discussion of capital and its relation to growth.

197. Another influence has been the demonstration effect from the (postwar) high rates of economic growth of East Asian societies, especially Japan. The saving and investment rates are much higher in Japan than in other capitalist nations, as are rates of economic growth. (The OECD, in its Historical Statistics, 1960–1983, gives the following figures for Net Savings as a percentage of GDP for 1960–1983: U.S., 7.7; Japan, 20.8; West Germany, 14.7; and Great Britain, 8.9. Table 6.16) Whether this (apparently) cause and effect relationship between saving and growth in Japan can be translated

into other political-economic situations is a point of much ideological contention and little firm evidence. But, the evidence would seem to demonstrate that traditional Keynesean models of the economy, which treat savings as a drain on aggregate demand—and therefore, economic growth and investment—are in need of some revision, at least regarding the relationship among saving, investment, and taxation.

198. J. R. Sargent and M. F. G. Scott, in their "Investment and the Tax System in the UK," pp. 10–11, raise another objection to accelerated allowances. They propose that accelerated investment may result in decreasing efficiency of investment—the declining productivity of fixed capital. The argument is that, because of lower "hurdle rates" for investment, lower profitability projects will be undertaken than would otherwise be the case, and the rate of profitability will decrease. Some economic growth will nevertheless result, but this will be offset by increasing wage expectations by employees and by the increasing taxation expectations of governments.

199. For a discussion of types of depreciation and the general rules governing the allowances in the OECD and various Third World countries, see Price-Waterhouse Capital Formation: International Survey and Analysis.

200. Figures drawn from British Business, October 30, 1981, and OECD, Non-Financial . . . , various.

201. Non-Financial . . . , 1985; OECD. Economic Surveys, 1985/1986: United States, (Paris, 1985) p. 118. The OECD writes, "According to flow of funds statistics, the depreciation allowances given by the tax system now exceed true ('economic') depreciation. The difference between tax allowances and true depreciation (known as the "capital consumption adjustment") increased significantly between 1980 and 1984. For nonfinancial corporate businesses there was a shift from a negative $14.25 billion (the tax system inadequately allowing for true depreciation) to a positive $54.5 billion."

202. Reported in the New York Times, November 13th, 1984, p. A24.

203. See Martin Feldstein, "Tax Incentives, Corporate Saving, and Capital Accumulation in the United States." (Professor William Vickery of Columbia University made this point rather forcefully during a presentation of a draft of a previous paper.)

Przeworski and Wallerstein concede that "In the initial period [when the corporation tax is imposed] there is always a trade-off between the target level of capital stock, or equivalently, the target level of investment, and the maximum tax receipts from profits" (p. 509).

204. See Davies for a discussion of the history of the corporation tax, the reasons for its continued imposition, and of some the difficulties associated with it; see also chapter 6.

205. Despite the difficulties involved, part of this task, the modeling both of the incentives found in various tax codes and of the real effective rates of taxation, was successfully undertaken by the research team that produced *The Taxation of Income From Capital: A Comparative Study of the U.S., the U.K., Sweden, and West Germany* (Mervyn King and Don Fullerton, eds. Chicago: Chicago, 1984).

206. Mervyn King and Don Fullerton, eds., *The Taxation of Income From Capital*, pp. 268–302. They write, "Another startling result is the ordering of countries according to [the] coefficients of variation [among industries.] Britain has the highest variation of tax rates on different combinations and the lowest growth from 1960 and 1980. Sweden is second for both parameters, and the United States is third. Germany has the lowest coefficient of variation and the highest overall growth."

See J. R. Sargent and M. F. G. Scott, "Investment and the Tax System in the UK," for a discussion of the post–1984 tax reform in Great Britain.

207. Some attempts to model aspects of the tax systems has had some success. For instance, *The Economist* reported in its December 25th, 1982 issue on a study published by the Bulletin for International Fiscal Documentation (BIFD) that attempted to measure the deviation from tax neutrality of various national corporate tax codes. Among the results reported was that, as of 1981, the United States was providing the largest percentage subsidy to investment by firms of any Western government, a result that accords with my findings. The BIFD approach is, however, not useful for measuring change over time, or for capturing any cross-national similarities as it does not capture the discretionary elements of the tax system. Robert Barro, in a working paper (#1309) recently published by the National Bureau of Economic Research (NBER) entitled "The Behavior of U.S. Deficits," also models elements of the tax system, but only for the United States.

208. Przeworski and Wallerstein's article makes this point in criticizing the otherwise fine study on the impact of taxes done by Katz, Mahler, and Franz, who use the percentage of GDP accounted for by the corporate tax in assessing the impact of taxation on investment. In essence, they use "levels of taxation" data. In my study, changes in the rates of depreciation and investment tax credits are more relevant for assessing government policies towards firm investment. See Claudio J. Katz, Vincent A. Mahler, and Michael G. Franz, "The Impact of Taxes on Growth and Distribution in Developed Capitalist Countries: A Cross-National Study," *American Political Science Review* (1983) 77(3):871–886. See also Ronald F. King and Steven I. Jackson, "The Impact of Taxes in Developed Capitalist Countries, *American Political Science Review*; (1983) 80(1):251–255, and Katz et al.'s reponse, immediately following in the same issue.

209. A recent National Bureau of Economic Research study conducted by Robert Lipsey and Irving Kravis indicates that American multinational firms continue to retain export markets even when the total world share of volume of exports accounted for by the United States has decreased. See "Business Holds Its Own as America Slips," *The New York Times*, January 18, 1987.

210. The data are part of the Three Volume *National Accounts of OECD Countries* published annually by the OECD. The data were published in one volume prior to 1981.

211. The American data are drawn from a universal sample of all non-farm, non-financial enterprises. The British figures are drawn from all manufacturing enterprises whose gross capital was over £4 million in 1983— roughly 1200 companies. The Japanese data cover "all privately-owned corporations . . . engaged in non-financial activities." The German sample represents the balance sheets of 74,000 enterprises. The OECD notes that, in the case of the Federal Republic of Germany, "large and sound" enterprises and public limited companies are "over-represented." See the editions of OECD Financial Statistics, *Methodological Supplement*, Paris: various years.

212. The depreciation methods vary somewhat from country and from firm to firm. In Germany, firms may choose between straight line depreciation or the declining balance method, with a 30% maximum first year allowance. Before 1984, British firms were permitted to immediately depreciate investment ("exponential depreciation" in the words of King and Fullerton), though the choice of method was reserved to the firm. American firms also had a range of choices among depreciation methods; these were discussed earlier in the text. Japanese firms usually, but not always, use the straight-line method of depreciation, though Price-Waterhouse notes that, unless specified otherwise, the default system of accounting is the declining-balance method. See *OECD Financial Statistics; Methodological Supplement* (Paris: various years) and Price-Waterhouse, *Capital Formation*.

213. This study, unlike those of Cameron(1978) and Katz, Mahler, and Franz(1983) does not attempt to measure the influence of public policy on economic growth and investment, though other papers I have completed do make such an attempt; Quinn and Jacobson(1986) and Jacobson and Quinn(1987). That is, I am not attempting to estimate the influence on X (rate of economic growth) of Y (increasing investment and income of firms) because of limitations imposed by a small data sample (64) and the complexity of modeling the nonrecursive relationships among these variables. See also David R. Cameron, "On the Limits of Political Economy," in J. Rogers Hollingsworth, ed., *Government and Economic Performance, The Annals of the American Academy of Political and Social Science* (January 1982) 459: 46–62.

214. I used OECD data from the *Historical Statistics: 1960–83;* Paris, 1985.; Table 3.1—"Real Gross Domestic Product: Year to Year Percentage Changes," p. 44. (I used the same table from earlier versions of this series for the data for the 1960s.) Hence, I started with first difference data, and thereafter calculated the second difference.

215. See Peter Kennedy *A Guide to Econometrics,* for a discussion of the use of dummy variables in pooled, cross-sectional data.

216. The use of second difference data does introduce one bias. For instance, it counts as part of an upturn a year like 1975 in Japan where the economy grew at a rate of 2.3%, not such a high figure for Japan, but better than 1974 (-1.0%.) 1982 is accounted as being a downturn year, though the economy grew at a rate of 3.0%; this is less than the previous year's growth of 4.2%. The bias will not be in my favor. For instance, tax reductions precipitated by the 1973 recession but not introduced until 1974 for the 1975 tax year would not much help to produce the hypothesized results in my regression equations: the second difference was positive for Britain and Japan in 1975.

217. It may be argued that part of the results obtained in this investigation are the natural consequences of movements of the business cycle: no changes in tax policy were necessary to bring about these findings. That is, while depreciation allowances are monotonically increasing, the level of firm taxation is cyclical. It follows, therefore, that Y should vary inversely with changes in economic activity: $Y = -X$.

If it were the case that $Y = -X$ is the proper relationship, this would tell us that Western governments do have a common tax policy regarding firms, and this would be that an automatic effect has been built into the structure of the corporate tax code. We, however, have little reason for believing that the value of the depreciation/trading profit ratio will vary more or less than the taxation/trading profit ratio. While it is the case that the value of the depreciation allowance figure does increase for all countries during this period, it does so only in nominal terms. The value of depreciation as a percentage of gross trading profit is cyclical, and therefore moves with changing economic circumstances. That is, both depreciation divided by gross trading profit and taxation divided by gross trading profit vary with the cyclical changes in economic activity. The difference between these two ratios should be stable. Some might further argue that levels of taxation are more influenced perhaps by cyclical movements than are depreciation claims. We do not, however, find evidence for this claim (that levels of corporate taxation rise as economic activity increases) from the results from the 1978–1984.

218. The "Safe Harbors" and leaseback provisions allowed companies

(e.g. Ford) to sell its tax breaks to other, profitable, companies (e.g. IBM, General Electric). The general theory behind the 1981 tax incentives is under some assault. The *New York Times* has recently (6/19/85, 7/5/85, 7/7/85) run a series of articles in its business pages that have questioned the efficacy of both the 1981 corporate tax incentives and "supply-side" economics.

219. The scoring was more complex, given that governments did not always enact consistent policies. When in doubt, I used 0.

220. Because I am using up to three dummy variables as my independent variables, problems of colinearity prevent me from measuring the interaction effects of X and Z.

221. Because dummy variables that sum to 1 are used, the constant is suppressed (Judge et al., p. 479; Kennedy [1985], pp. 181–182). Suppressing the constant causes the the coefficient of determination (R^2) to be redefined. In this case, the R^2 is correctly calculated using the procedure outlined in Pindyck and Rubinfeld (1981, pp. 78–82).

I did run a series of tests of $\beta_0 = 0$. T-tests on the intercepts were run for each equation by omitting one of the dummy variables of X; each intercept term was insignificant. Using OLS procedures, I also tested $Y = \beta_0 C$ for each equation. The hypothesis, $\beta_0 = 0$, cannot be rejected.

222. If, for instance, the relationship between X and Y were inverse for the United States and West Germany, but were positive for Japan and Great Britain, the regression equations would yield a value for $R -$ Square approaching 0, and the coefficients of X would likely be insignificant.

223. See Roger Friedland and Jimy Sanders, "The Public Economy and Economic Growth in Western Market Economies," pp. 421–437; James A. Stimson, "Regression in Space and Time, pp. 914–947. Stimson points out that the choice of the Best Linear Unbiased Estimator (BLUE) is a difficult one in analyzing pooled data, and the various alternatives need to be evaluated in light of the characteristics of the sample—e.g., cross-sectional dominance, time-serial dominance, and so on. In the case of the data used here, EGLS procedures appear to be appropriate. We have cross-sectional dominance, without serious serial correlation, and with between-unit effects.

224. I used the "pooled cross section—times series" procedure in Shazam. See Kenneth J. White and Nancy G. Horsman, *Shazam: User's Reference Manual*. This procedures appears to be the same one used by Friedland and Sanders. The Kmenta reference is to Jan Kmenta, *Elements of Econometrics* (New York: Macmillan, 1971). The Judge et al. reference is to George G. Judge, R. Carter Hill, William Griffiths, Helmut Lütkepohl, and Tsoung-Chao Lee, *Introduction to the Theory and Practice of Econometrics* (New York: Wiley Sons, 1982). See ch. 16.

225. This may seem counter-intuitive. A regression equation measures the change in the value of Y caused by a change in the value of X. When I dichotomize X into upturn and downturn dummys, each is represented in terms of 0's and 1's. Hence, a negative value of X is scored as 1, a positive number. So when the coefficient of the downturn dummy is positive, this means that the presence of a downturn in the economy had a positive influence of the value of Y. It follows that a negative coefficient of the downturn dummy means that the presence of an economic downturn produced a negative effect on Y.

226. Measuring the interaction effects of Z and upturn/downturn is difficult because all the independent variable are qualitative, and extensive multicollinearity results from $Y = \beta_1(\text{upturn}) + \beta_2(\text{downturn}) + \beta_3 Z + \beta_4[\beta_1(\text{upturn})^*\beta_3 Z] + \beta_5[\beta_2(\text{downturn})^*\beta_3 Z]$. Another problem results from the choice I made regarding the values of Z: -1, 0, 1. Interpreting the meaning of, say, a negative coefficient for $\beta_5[\beta_2(\text{downturn})^*\beta_3 Z]$ would be extremely difficult.

227. The restricted Error Sum of Squares of the overall equation is 49.7; the unrestricted ESS is 13.0 plus 21.048; Q is 3; and k is 3. The F-test is significant at the .01 level.

228. In his *Federal Tax Policy*, 3d ed., Joseph Pechman concluded, "the corporation income tax is not regarded as one of the significant built-in stabilizers, despite its heavy contribution to the large swings in federal surpluses and deficits during business cycles," because to qualify as a built-in stabilizer, "a tax must automatically moderate the changes in consumer disposable income or reduce fluctuations in investment" (Washington: Brookings, 1977, pp. 141–142). The corporate tax does appear to have been somewhat "automatic" in its swings in the 1970s, even if it did not (in the United States) rank as one of the main stabilizers. The overall results seem to suggest that changes in public policy, not just automatic effects, were important in achieving these "swings."

229. To have a (microeconomic) industrial policy is not necessarily to have industrial planning, though the two may overlap. Britain, for instance, has an elaborate industrial policy, but (save for the first Wilson government) not had a (post–1951) plan per se. In 1977, *The Economist* wrote of Britain that, "Since the 1939–45 war, and the Keynesean revolution in economic theory, successive British governments have tried to solve the nation's problems by pulling a few large macro-economic levers: e.g., manipulating the size of the public sector's deficit by control of public spending and tax revenue. . . . these have failed to steer the economy. So the emphasis has been shifting toward more microeconomic intervention by government: i.e., push-

ing hundreds of little buttons in the hope that the aggregate effect will be significant. This fashion in policy feeds back into theory, which is stimulated by the new preoccupations of economic management."

230. New York Times (March 20, 1983) reported that the variance in the effective corporate tax rates ranged in 1981 from −14% (paper products) to 48% (motor vehicles).

231. A result that indicates that we cannot reject a given argument (i.e. the null hypothesis, $b = 0$, is within the confidence interval) does not mean that no government's activities can be explained by that argument. Rather, we simply do not find any cross-national pattern explained by the argument.

232. As I argued in a previous note, increasing capital investment does not automatically lead to a proportional increase in economic growth since, as with all factors of production, capital is subject to diminishing marginal returns.

One point of divergence (among business policies, not public policies) should be noted. American and British firms have used their investment strategies to increase their capital/labor ratios (as measured by depreciation divided by wages) over the last decade. These firms will not necessarily be more profitable; firms (and economies) have choices regarding the relative capital/labor mix in the production of products, and the optimal mix depends on many variables: many routes to profitability. The increasing ratio (of depreciation divided by wages) does imply that the position of American and British workers is likely to erode further as Korea, Brazil and other Newly Industrializing Countries penetrate the market for standardized, high-fixed-cost products—after all, given comparable capital equipment, wages become the basis for competition—competition that high-wage countries are likely to lose.

5. Explanations for Similarity

1. International Monetary Fund, International Financial Statistics, pp. 431, 437. While GM was planning on $40 billion expansion, and Ford, $28 billion, Chrysler was capable of raising only $6.5 billion. Source: Economist Intelligence Unit, 3rd Quarter 1982.

2. Andrea Boltho, "Is Western Europe Caught in an Expectations Trap?" On the privileged position of business, see Charles E. Lindblom, Politics and Markets, ch. 13.

3. The experience of the Mitterrand Government in France in 1981–83 is instructive of this limit of state authority. Even though many analysts believe that the French state is "stronger" than either the American or the British state (cf. Krasner and Zysman), the French government's initial eco-

nomic program was reined in following the early 1980s fall of the value of the Franc (from roughly 6 to the dollar to over 9 to the dollar). The Mitterrand Government initially attempted such standbys as exchange controls, but finally opted for "austerity," a code word for a return to economic policies similar to those of other European countries.

4. See Maurice Zeitlin's introduction in Zeitlin, ed., *Classes, Class Conflict, and the State*, pp. 23–25., for a discussion of the role of coercion. British earnings figures derived from International Financial Statistics and *The Economist* of August 6, 1983, p. 63. All figures for credit funds were derived from OECD, Financial Accounts, pp. 93, 177, 149. Numbers were derived by dividing foreign money by total domestic credit. The U.S. figure for 1979 was distorted.

5. Zysman, *Governments, Markets*, ch. 6.

6. Eric Nordlinger, in *On the Autonomy of the Democratic State* identifies four major strands of societal constraint theories and, following accepted conventions, labels these the pluralist, the neopluralist, the social corporatist, and the Marxist variants. See his chapter 2. Though his work was helpful to me in thinking about these problems, the reader will soon see that I have made different divisions in the literature on state-society relations.

7. Anthony Downs. *An Economic Theory of Democracy*. See also Edward Tufte, *Political Control of the Economy* for a more recent statement of the argument.

8. Donald R. Kinder. "Presidents, Prosperity, and Public Opinion (hereafter Kinder, POQ)" See also Kinder and D. Roderick Kiewiet. "Economic Grievances and Political Behavior."

9. Kinder, *POQ*. See also Robert Y. Shapiro and Bruce M. Conforto. "Presidential Performance, the Economy, and the Public's Evaluation of Economic Conditions." Bob Shapiro was very helpful in thinking through these issues.

10. A related area of research, though not of relevance for this study, is that of the political business cycle. Many of the important works in the field are to be found in a volume edited by Douglas A. Hibbs and Heino Fassbender entitled *Contemporary Political Economy*. See the essay by Frey and Schneider. Alt and Chrystal review much of this literature in ch. 5 of their *Political Economics*. They conclude, "No one could read the political business cycle literature without being struck by the lack of supporting evidence" (p. 125).

11. The data were calculated from the *Financial Statements of Non-Financial Enterprises* (various years) published by the OECD. This is the same data used in the econometric model at the end of ch. 3. The data for West Germany and Japan do not show the same pattern: divergence. The

value of the ratio has fallen for Germany from .217 in 1968 to .167 in 1982. The figures for Japan are .238 in 1970 and .162 in 1981.

12. James E. Alt, *The Politics of Economic Decline.*

13. See Robert Alford's essay in Leon Lindberg, et al, *Stress and Contradiction in Modern Capitalism* (Lexington, Mass.: D.C. Heath, 1975).

14. Peter Bachrach and Morton Baratz. "Two Faces of Power."

15. Robert Dahl. *A Preface to Democratic Theory.* Dahl turns this vision of political practice into a normative description of representative democracy.

16. Perhaps the central work in Neopluralism is Charles Lindblom's *Politics and Markets.* Lindblom is one of the early advocates in American political science of the Schumpeterian notion of democracy as competition among elites. His *Politics and Markets* provoked something akin to hysteria among conservative academicians and politicians. See, for instance, the essays by Bardach, Brandis and Brown in Robert Hessen, ed., *Does Big Business Rule America?* (Washington D.C.: Ethics and Public Policy Center, 1981). For a more recent discussion of Neopluralist analysis, called there Pluralism II, see John Manley, "Neopluralism," and Robert Dahl's and Charles Lindblom's following comments. In the British context, see *West European Politics* (April 1983), vol. 6(2), which has a number of articles of concern for students of Pluralist and Neopluralist analysis. See the articles by David Marsh, Gareth Locksley, and Bob Jessop.

17. One alternative is for the government to compensate by engaging in public sector investment. At least in Britain, this strategy has withered, even under Labour, as public sector investment (as a % of GDP) has fallen steadily from 1973 (5.9%) to 1982 (1.4%) UK: Economic Survey.

18. Kinder, *POQ*, pp. 5, 8–10.

19. For a discussion of instrumental linkages, see David Marsh and Wyn Grant, *The Confederation of British Industry* (London: Hodder and Stoughton, 1977). They concluded that "our study is a reaffirmation of the autonomy of the political sphere over the economic" (p. 187). See also Bob Jessop, "The Capitalist State and the Rule of Capital." He argues there that capitalist associations have no particular bearing on the success of capital in general. For a discussion of the relative capacities of interest group influence, see Grant McConnell, *Private Power and American Democracy*, chs. 4 and 8, for discussion of influence within existing institutions. Paul Quirk's findings in *Industry Influence in Regulatory Agencies* led him to question much of the thesis of capture.

20. Stephen Krasner. "United States Commercial and Monetary Policy."

21. The more important readings in the field have been compiled in edited volumes like Frederick B. Pike and Thomas Stritch, eds., *The New Corpo-*

ratism; P. Schmitter and G. Lehmbruch, eds. *Trends Toward Corporatist Intermediation*; Suzanne Berger, ed. *Organizing Interests in Western Europe.* New York: Cambridge, 1981.; and Schmitter and Lehmbruch, eds. *Patterns of Corporatist Policy Making.* (Beverly Hills: Sage, 1982.

22. Philippe C. Schmitter, "Still the Century of Corporatism?" p. 13.

23. Reinhard Bendix. *Citizenship and Nation-Building.*

24. Claus Offe, "The Attribution of Public Status to Interest Groups."

25. See Andrew Cox and Jack Hayward. "The Inapplicability of the Corporatist Model in Britain and France."

26. Arthur Stinchcombe, *Constructing Social Theory.* In recognition of the tremendous diversity in Marxist and neo-Marxist analyses, I have discussions of neo-Marxist writers in various places in this work. The "functional needs of capitalism," "a crisis in the production process," and "the tendency of the rate of profit to fall" are each potentially causal explanations for congruence, but these each specify a "central problem" different from the others.

The full range of diversity of Marxist or class perspectives can be sampled in several excellent secondary sources. Alford and Friedland, *Capitalism . . .* devoted a quarter of their book to class theorists. Martin Carnoy's *The State and Political Theory* provides perhaps the most through review of the various neoMarxist theories of the state. Bob Jessop's *The Capitalist State* was also very useful, though the text would be a difficult read for those not already familiar with the neoMarxist language of description.

There are many forms of Marxist analysis, some of which are incompatible with others. This particular variant, usually called structural or form-centered Marxism, is probably the dominant strand in Western academic Marxism. The bibliographical list of important works in the field fills a score of pages; I can not do it justice in the space allotted. Among the more important works are those by Louis Althusser, Antonio Gramsci, Nico Poulantzas, Ernesto Laclau, J. O'Conner, Claus Offe and Jürgen Habermas. (Though neither Offe nor Habermas are Marxists, they have been major contributors to the debate concerning State-Society relations.) See especially Habermas's *Legitimation Crisis*; Offe, "The Theory of the Capitalist State and the Problems of Policy Formation," and Offe and Volker Ronge, "Theses on the Theory of the State." For recent reviews of some of this literature see Jessop, *Capitalist State* and Mark Kesselman, "The State and Class Struggles in Advanced Capitalism."

27. James O'Conner in his *Fiscal Crisis of the State* is generally credited with introducing into the American neo-Marxist debate Schumpeter's notion of a public-spending induced tax crisis with the attending crisis of political legitimation.

Anthony Giddens has compared the difference between structures and functions as analogous to that between a code and its message. He says "Structure is understood as referring to a 'pattern' of social relationships; function, to how such patterns actually operate as a system." See Giddens, *Central Problems in Social Theory*, p. 60. See especially ch. 3 for his discussion of (and attack on) Marxist functionalism.

28. The early work of the late Nicos Poulantzas, especially *Political Power and Social Classes* was the influential source of much of this analysis. Fred Block in "The Ruling Class Does Not Rule," has taken this argument to its logical extension by arguing that the state, if necessary, will be autonomous from all of the capitalist class.

29. The starting point for Marxist analysis of the consequences of this contradiction is Karl Marx's *The Eighteenth Brumaire of Louis Bonaparte*. Following Antonio Gramsci, Nicos Poulantzas, *Fascism and Dictatorship*, has argued that fascism is the extreme consequence of a contradiction between the profitability of capitalism and popular legitimacy. In the context of Latin America, Guillermo O'Donnell, *Modernization and Bureaucratic Authoritarianism*, though not himself a Marxist, has used this form of analysis by writing about the "tradeoff" between popular support and capital accumulation in a situation of a shift from Import Substitution Industrialization to a more "capital intensive" industrialization.

Mark Kesselman has pointed out to me that, since 1981, several scholars who work within the neo-Marxist framework have broken with functional Marxism, and instead talk about the historical specificity of state actions. Samuel Bowles and Herbert Gintis, in "The Crisis of Liberal Democratic Capitalism," break with much traditional Marxist analysis (especially those who see democratic government as necessarily only a façade of bourgeois class rule) and argue that the bases of capitalism and liberal democracy are in essential contradiction, and that the state does not necessarily act for anyone. Fred Block, in "Beyond Relative Autonomy" advances an argument in which he sees "a sharpening contradiction between the interests of capital and the fundamental interests of state managers," though, unlike the analysis I advance here, Block locates these points of contradiction in periods of extreme crisis— "tipping points" such as Germany post–1936. Gosta Epsing-Andersen and Roger Friedland, in their "Class Coalitions in the Making of West European Economies," in Maurice Zeitlin, ed. *Political Power and Social Theory*, vol. 3 (Greenwich: JAI, 1982), in a style of analysis reminiscent of Barrington Moore, argue for the historical specificity of political outcomes in each of four European nations on the basis of shifting class power and alignments. These arguments represent a major advance in Marxist theory away from both economic determinism and structural-functional analysis. Where they will lead is not yet clear. Friedland, and his coauthor, Jimy Sanders, in "The Public Economy and Economic Growth in Western Market Economies" continue the development of a nondeterminist, empirically based research agenda while employing Marxist categories.

30. Offe and Ronge, "Theses on the Theory of State." Offe contrasts "two modes of political rationality," one for "conjunctural" policies, the other for "structural" policies which are relevant under (respectively) "normal" and "crisis" conditions. The difference ("shift" as he says) is between "policy output and economic demand management to the shaping of political input and economic supply." (In "Attribution of Public Status to Interest Groups," pp. 125–28).

31. Stinchcombe describes functional analysis as being on the level of general causal imagery, which he describes as being on his second level of propositions. I am seeking to isolate a variable that explains policy congruence, a lower order task.

32. Giddens, Central Problems, pp. 110–115. See also Alvin Gouldner's The Coming Crisis of Western Sociology. Several of the neo-Marxist writers deny that their schema are functional. Both Poulantzas and Louis Althusser deny functionalism in their work while continuing to speak of the "needs" of capitalism. Jessop has argued that Poulantzas's last work, State, Power and Socialism, is "neo-Gramscian" rather than "structuralist." Jessop, Capitalist State, pp. 153–80.

33. Percy S. Cohen, Modern Social Theory. Chapter 3 is devoted to a discussion of functionalism and its logical, substantive, and methodological critiques.

34. Miliband's argument about a capitalist elite as a governing elite, is often true. As Poulantzas has pointed out, even a governing party hostile to the capitalist class is still constrained by the structure of the capitalist state. Miliband, The State in Capitalist Society. Miliband has himself given up the ghost of instrumentalism in his more recent Marxism and Politics.

35. "Preface to A Contribution to the Critique of Political Economy," p. 5. One plausible mechanism for a state's acting for capital's interest would probably require a state planning elite, insulated from political pressure, able and willing to act for capitalism's (and the state's) interests. Such claims are possible for Japan and France, if Zysman's accounting of political processes in these countries is correct. Interestingly, many of the "functional" Marxists, like Poulantzas, were French nationals or residents.

36. See articles in The Public Interest (special issue, 1980: The Crisis in

Economic Theory) by James Dean, "The Dissolution of the Keynesean Consensus," and Alan Meltzer, "Monetarism and the Crisis in Economics."

37. Some Republican demonologists blame government regulation for the industry's problems, and some also add that the Japanese government's direction of their economy constitutes an unfair practice. This revisionism argues that the firms did not fail; state intervention failed. Though some evidence exists for such a claim in Britain (see Dunnett, *Decline*), government intervention is not the root cause of the Big Three's problems. In fact, the government's mileage requirements may have saved Detroit.

Relatively few social scientists have seen ideology, or the formally organized, hierarchically ordered, political values of decisionmakers, as a major driving force in policy outcomes. If analysts have seen the ideas of policymakers as being important, it is because the belief structures and cultural assumptions of these actors color their perceptions of, and the meanings they give to, events. It is in the context of perception and meaning that "ideas" have force. In the social science, writers in International Relations/Decision Theory and in Phenomenological Sociology/Cultural Anthropology are particularly concerned with this issue. In the first area, see John Steinbruner, *The Cybernetic Theory of Decision*, ch. 4; Graham Allison, *The Essence of Decision*; Robert Jervis, *Perception and Misperception in International Politics*, and Jeffrey A. Hart, "Cognitive Mapping" *World Politics* 1977. In the second, see Clifford Geertz's "Ideology as a Cultural System"; Peter Berger and Thomas Luckmann, *The Social Construction of Reality*; and Alfred Schutz, *Collected Papers*, vol. 1.

A few other writers have focused on the social consequences (the "latent functions" or the objective consequences) of belief structures in producing political and social outcomes, but these analysts rarely treat as a serious subject of study the conscious motivations of actors. Even Max Weber, *verstehen* not-withstanding, is ultimately concerned with social consequences in his *The Protestant Ethic and the Spirit of Capitalism*.

38. Marx's most comprehensive statement of this problem in to be found in *Capital*, vol. 3, part 3, chs. 13–15. He also discussed this in his notes that were published as *Grundrisse*, section 3, "Capital as Fructiferous." Some recent discussions of this debate include Erik Olin Wright, "Alternative Perspectives in Marxist Theory of Accumulation," and Thomas Weisskopf, "Marxist perspectives on Cyclical Crises." For a more theoretical discussion on this issue see Joachim Hirsch's essay "The State Apparatus and Social Reproduction," and Bob Jessop, *The Capitalist State*.

One difficulty in evaluating this argument is that much of Marx's argument is incommensurable with modern economics. For instance, his expression for the rate of profit is surplus value/capital equals profit; this has no counterpart in "bourgeois" economics. I have taken standard OECD profit figures as the best measure of this argument, but many orthodox Marxists do not accept these measures of profitability as valid, and would, hence, reject my argument.

39. Wright, "Alternative Perspectives," p. 200.

40. *Capital*, vol. 3, chs. 9 and 10.

41. For a mathematical expression of the logic of this process, see Weisskopf, "Marxist Perspectives," pp. 242–50.

42. This interest has not been confined to the Western nations. Jessop analyses State Monopoly Capitalism theses, both Leninist and "form centered," East and West European, in *Capitalist State*, ch. 3 of his recent book.

43. This analysis is probably the one Marx most relied upon for his argument. See Weisskopf, "Marxist Perspectives," pp. 242–246. In recent years, only David Yaffie, in "The Crisis of Profitability," and Ernst Mandel in *Late Capitalism*, seem to accept this mechanism.

44. Paul Baran and Paul Sweezy, *Monopoly Capital*.

45. p. 243. See also Wright, "Alternative Perspectives," pp. 210–216.

46. Wright, pp. 216, 222. Among those who have accepted this argument are Andrew Glyn and Bob Subcliffe, *Capitalism in Crisis* and Raford Body and James Crotty, "Class Conflict and Macro-Policy."

47. See Joseph Pechman, "Taxation"; Richard Jankowski, "The Profit-Squeeze and Tax Policy."

48. Jankowski, pp. 19–28. Quote is on p. 28. Capital stock is in practice a problematic concept. Some countries calculate it in terms of the present value of the corporate sector's income stream, others by the valuations of corporate assets, or by the collective insurance valuations.

49. Jankowski, p. 35.

50. Jankowski, p. 40. His assumption that we should find immediate results does not appear to me to be sound. Firms in the "capital goods" sector usually have a 12- to 15-month lag between planning and investing.

51. Jankowski, p. 43. The results would be quite different if he were to test the consequences of the 1981 Economic Recovery Act, as the graphs in chapter 4 show.

52. This issue of taxing corporate profits as both earnings and dividends (or capital gains) produces a degree of froth among businessmen akin to that found among environmentalists over strip mining in national forests. For a reasonably calm discussion of this issue, see Martin Feldstein and Joel Slemrod, "How Inflation Distorts the Taxation of Capital Gains."

53. In the research that I undertook on corporate taxation, I was careful to exclude dividends and interest payments from the measure of corporate taxation I derived.

54. OECD. U.S., p. 40.

55. Among the recent books published about the U.S. problems include Barry Bluestone and Bennett Harrison, The *Deindustrialization of America*; David Calleo, *The Impervious Economy*; Robert Reich,*The Next American Frontier*; Lester C. Thurow, *The Zero-Sum Society*, Alan Wolfe; *America's Impasse*; and Samuel Bowles, et al., *Beyond the Wasteland*.

The literature on the facets of the British industrial crisis is impressive in volume if not always in perspicuity. Among the most interesting analyses are Stephen Blank, "Britain: The Politics of Foreign Economic Policy and the Problem of Pluralist Stagnation"; E. J. Hobsbawm, *Industry and Empire*; Susan Strange, *Sterling and British Policy*; Karel Williams et al., *Why Are the British So Bad at Manufacturing?* Wyn Grant, *Political Economy of Industrial Policy*; Andrew Gamble, *Britain in Decline* London; R. Bacon and W. Eltis, *Britain's Economic Problem*; Sidney Pollard, *The Wasting of the British Economy*; and James Alt, *The Politics of Economic Decline*.

There have been a number of cultural explanations for Britain's problems. These include J. H. McEnery, *Manufacturing Two Nations*; and two by Roderick Gordon and Michael Stephens. One is an edited volume entitled *Where Did We Go Wrong?* the other is *The British Malaise*. Mancur Olson correctly (I think) rebuts this type of analysis in *The Rise and Decline of Nations*, pp. 77 ff.

56. See Alfred P. Chandler, Jr. *The Visible Hand*, (Cambridge: Harvard, 1977.) and Hobsbawm, chs. 6, 7, 9, 12.

57. Robert Reich, *The Next American Frontier* (N.Y.: Times Books, 1983.) See also Reich's articles in *The Atlantic Monthly* of March and April of 1983 (hereafter, Reich *AM*).

58. Reich, *AM*, April 1983, p. 44.

59. *The Next American Frontier*, pp. 128–139. The popular press in America has devoted much attention to the Japanese "model," much as the British press did in the 1960s to the French "model" of indicative planning.

60. Reich, *AM*, April 1983, pp. 50–58.

61. Raymond Vernon, "International Investment and International Trade in the Product Cycle"; Vernon, *Economic Environment of International Business*.

62. Vernon, *Economic*, p. 184.

63. See George Maxcy's discussion of the applicability of product cycle theory to the world auto industry in his *The Multinational Motor Industry*, pp. 23–31 and 270–274. See also Louis T. Wells. "The International Product Life Cycle." in Ginsburg and Abernathy.

64. Vernon does advance a convergence argument in his essay in his edited volume, *Big Business and the State*. His convergence among Western Eu-

ropean states is generated from the external threats to domestic industries from foreign (American) subsidiaries of multinational firms that are producing in Europe. Convergence takes the form of state-sponsored national champions. This European convergence was always in form, though not in substance, and is not the issue here.)

65. A useful introduction to public choice economics is to be found in Dennis C. Mueller, *Public Choice*.

66. Olson, p. 235. Subsequent page references will be found in the text. His work has produced much debate. For instance, those inclined to accept Professor Olson's arguments should read David Cameron's paper presented at the 1983 APSA Chicago convention. "Creating Theory in Comparative Political Economy: On Mancur Olson's Explanation of Growth." See also the companion volume to Olson's book, *The Political Economy of Growth*, edited by Dennis Mueller (New Haven: Yale, 1982), and the articles in *International Studies Quarterly* (March 1983), vol. 27(1) by Kindleberger, de Vries, and Barry, and Olson's response to them.

One innovative, alternative explanation for differing rates of economic growth among Western nations has been proposed by Manfred Neumann in "Long Swings in Economic Development." Neuman argues that change in the Social Rate of Time Preference (the tradeoff between consumption at different points in time) accounts for changes in saving and discount rates, and, thereby, growth rates. My thanks to an anonymous referee for this citation.

67. Olson, unlike most "rational expectation" or public choice economists, doesn't accept the premise that unemployment is largely voluntary.

68. Johnson, *MITI*.

69. Chang, *The Japanese* ...

70. For example, see Graham Allison's discussion of what he terms decision models 2 & 3 in his *Essence of Decision*. See also Charles Anderson's article in Douglas Ashford, ed. *Comparing Public Policies* (Beverly Hills: Sage, 1978).

71. The realist tradition in international politics, personified by people like Waltz, Knorr, Carr, and Morganthau, sees power as the "utility" that states seek to maximize. For instance, some "realists" have argued that there exists an essential continuity of Soviet foreign policy from its Czarist predecessors on the grounds that the Russian national interest of increasing Russian power vis-à-vis its neighbors remains constant.

72. Stephen D. Krasner, *Defending the National Interest*. Robert Gilpin, *U.S. Power and the Multinational Corporation*.

73. Weber's notion of the bureaucratic-rational state can be found in his essays on "Legal Authority," "Sociology of Law," and "Bureaucracy" in

Economy and Society. See also "Politics as a Vocation," in Gerth and Mills, eds. *From Max Weber* (New York: Oxford, 1946), pp. 77–128.

74. Krasner recently published a review essay entitled "Approaches to the State." In this essay, he advances a concept borrowed from evolutionary biology, that of punctuated equilibrium, as being one useful for an understanding of states. See also Howard Lentner's reply in the April 1984 issue of *Comparative Politics.*

75. Andrew Shonfield, *Modern Capitalism*, chs. 5–9; Michael Crozier, *The Bureaucratic Phenomenon*; Steven Blank, "Britain: The Politics of Foreign Economic Policy Making"; Ezra Suleiman, *Elites in French Society*; Robert Solo, "The Economist and Economic Roles of the Political Authority in Advanced Industrial Societies"; Theda Skocpol, *States and Social Revolutions*, and Charles Tilly, *The Formation of the National State in Europe.*

76. In addition to advancing an interesting thesis about the development of the postwar welfare state, John Dryzek and Robert E. Goodin provide a useful review of the literature. John Dryzek and Robert E. Goodin, "Risk-Sharing and Social Justice: The Motivational Foundations of the Post-War Welfare State." *British Journal of Political Science* (January 1986) 16: 1–34.

The proposition that, through the activity of individuals pursuing their self-interests, some markets will produce nonoptimal results is something of a truism. Situations resembling the "prisoners' dilemma" and the "tragedy of the commons" are such recurrent features of the real world that even microeconomic textbooks now routinely discuss them. The question economists tend to ask about markets is not "do they fail?" but "under what circumstances do they fail?" See Kenneth Arrow, "Two Cheers for Regulation," *Harpers*, March 1981. The central "failure" of concern here is the business cycle. (See note 189 in chapter 4 for a discussion of the business cycle.) Shonfield argued that, whatever its other limitations, Keyneseanism greatest success was in taming the business cycle (*Modern Capitalism*, pp. 63–65). The debate about the modern business cycle (does it exist? with what intensity?) was discussed in a *New York Times* article by Nicholas Kristoff on April 21, 1985.

I think Irving Kristol's best writing is his "When Virtue Loses All Her Loveliness," in which he discusses the legitimating foundations of capitalism. He concludes, rightly, that the "technocratic ethic" is the most widespread justification for welfare capitalism. Capitalist civilization itself is "spiritually impoverished." This is roughly Schumpeter's point in his chapter on "The Civilization of Capitalism" in *Capitalism . . .*, and Weber's in the second chapter of *The Protestant Ethic and the Spirit of Capitalism.*

77. Keynes's critics, Shonfield among them, shared his views here. Shonfield argued that management of macroeconomic aggregates was insufficient

to ensure economic prosperity. Indicative planning, which Shonfield defended, presumes that states have discretionary authority. The "independent official," not the politician, was the preferred instrument of discretionary authority for Shonfield, pp. 404–8.

78. The general theory was (and is) that, as the economy entered a recession, people who lost their jobs or otherwise suffered from a market failure (e.g. bank closure) would receive benefits that would reduce both their suffering and the multiplier consequences of economic downturn. In conjunction with other fiscal policies, the government would be able to maintain aggregate demand. See Joseph A. Pechman's 1971 edition of *Federal Tax Policy* (Washington: Brookings), ch. 2, for a discussion of automatic stabilizers and economic policy. See also Richard A. Musgrave and Peggy Musgrave, *The Theory of Public Finance*, (New York: McGraw-Hill, 1980).

79. A description of the growth of the welfare state is to be found in a publication by the OECD entitled *Public Expenditure Trends* (Paris, 1978). The Chapter on "Demands for Public Expenditure" is useful in demonstrating the magnitude of the growth of expenditures. The publication's focus on the "demand" side of public expenditures among OECD countries is also useful.

80. For some recent discussions of these cases, see Shonfield, *In Defense of the Mixed Economy*; James K. Galbraith, "A Comparison of Economic Policies and Doctrines in the Major Industrial Countries"; Zysman, *Governments, Markets*, and Andrew Spindler, *The Politics of International Credit*.

81. *Public Expenditure Trends*, pp. 24–30. The literature on the welfare state is voluminous. Two standard works are Harold Wilensky, *The Welfare State and Equality*, and Aaron Wildavsky, *Budgeting: A Comparative Theory of Budgetary Process*. Two more recent discussions are essays by B. Guy Peters ("The Limits of the Welfare State") and by Duane Swank and Alexander Hicks ("The Determinants and Redistributive Impacts of State Welfare Spending in the Advanced Capitalist Democracies, 1960–1980") in Vig and Schier, eds., *Political Economy in Western Democracies*. A discussion of some of the differences among capitalist nations is to be found in David Cameron's "The Expansion of the Public Economy," *American Political Science Review* (December 1978), vol. 72(4). See also the OECD symposium on the entitled *Prospects for the Welfare State in the 1980s*.

82. The post-Keynesean theories enjoyed something of a resurgence in 1985, what with the huge American budget deficit fueling America's economic recovery, a recovery more or less consistent with Keynesean expectations.

Daniel Bell and Irving Kristol edited an interesting collection of essays under the title "The Crisis in Economic Theory," published as a special issue of *The Public Interest* in 1980. The primary theme was the collapse of the Keynesean consensus.

83. OECD. *Social Expenditure, 1960–1990*, p. 14.

84. See James Buchanan, et al., eds. *Towards a Theory of the Rent-Seeking Society.*

85. Richard Posner reviews this literature in his essay, "Theories of Economic Regulation." His discussion of Stigler's argument involves a good summary of much of it.

86. See the article in the December 1984 edition of the *American Economic Review* by Bruno Frey et al. The investigators found a surprising degree of dissension, even on presumably basic points.

87. OECD, *Social Expenditures, 1985*, p. 15.

88. West European governments have traditionally sought to promote full employment where possible, unlike the American state. These governments have surrendered full employment as a viable public policy goal (assuming that it was ever viable). The concern for labor policy remains, however, in the form of "manpower" training policies—policies that governments hope will insulate them from lower-wage though capital-intensive overseas competitors. For a discussion of American Manpower policies (or the lack thereof) see, Joint Economic Committee, *Industrial Policy: the Retraining Needs of the Nation's Long-Term Structurally Unemployed Workers*, Hearings September 16, 23, 26, October 26, 1983 (Washington: GPO, 1984).

89. I do not, however, believe that this congruence is the result of interest group politics. As I have argued earlier in this chapter, the policies of governments in the 1960s and early 1970s may well be understandable in terms of interest-group pluralism. The politics of industrial restructuring, however, have followed a different pattern. The maintenance of full employment is no longer the sine qua non of Western politics.

90. A number of writers, especially Hayes and Abernathy ("Managing Our Way to Economic Decline"), have attributed part of this decline to short-term orientation by managers to profits. This is probably true, but misses the point that American and British managers are themselves responding to the structure of incentives (in this case, the prevailing rate of return) they find in their environment. See also the article by Neuman in the *Zeitscrift* . . . .

91. Despite their obvious differences, I find some striking areas of agreement between "orthodox Marxism" and "public choice" economics. Both, in a sense, presume a game theoretical perspective as their starting positions. Actors are rational, seek to satisfy self-interest, and could be expected to change strategies if their "positions" were to change. In a phrase, economic determinism.

92. Social scientists remain divided as to the appropriate relationship between theory and research, the appropriate methods to be employed in research, and the standards for assessing the adequacy of theories. The 1985 denial of tenure at Harvard to Paul Starr precipitated a number of articles on the *methodenstreit* in the social sciences. Although I have nothing original to add to this discussion, I would like to point to the dangers of a reliance on avowedly "paradigmatic" thought, both in the insistence upon a set of methodological prescriptions and in the exclusive use of a given language of description. These and other dangers are described in the work of Thomas Kuhn (*The Structure of Scientific Revolutions*) and Albert O. Hirschman ("Paradigmatic Thought at a Hindrance to Understanding" in *A Bias for Hope*, and "Against Parsimony"). Of course, we cannot help but think metaphorically. Hence, elements of reality will inevitably be screened from us—readers of Hume, Kant, and Wittgenstein will not be surprised by this claim. But, the enthusiasm with which some positivistic social scientists dismiss "nonscientific" approaches to problems is evidence of narrow-mindedness, a narrow-mindedness not unlike that of those who insist on the veracity of only one language of description, be it, for example, Marxism or neo-Classical microeconomics.

6. Conclusion

1. See Jacques Mistral, "Competitiveness of the Productive System and International Specialization." Also his "Economic Growth of Nations and International Competitiveness," a talk presented at Columbia University, September 13, 1984.

2. See Strange and Tooze, eds. *International Politics*; Mistral, "Competitiveness," chapter 2 of this work.

3. Bluestone and Bennett, *The Deindustrialization*.... Some economists, Robert Z. Lawrence among them, have challenged this argument, claiming that this shift is at most a short term consequence of recession. This debate was reviewed in chapter 3.

4. See Charles P. Kindleberger and Bruce Herrick, *Economic Development*, ch. 3. See also Herberg, "Politics, Planning." The evidence for the Two Class Model of growth is not as clear as the more evangelical "supply-siders" believe. Many economists, Roger Lekachman among them, argue that the recent American economic recovery is Keynesean (i.e. deficit induced) in nature.

5. By community, I mean here only a set of social and exchange relationships based within a locality that itself is founded on an industry. I do not mean to evoke the image of a traditional rural *Gemeinschaft*. I mean com-

munity as a focal point in reference to which people understand their actions and organize social meaning. Community in this sense can often be repressive and tyrannical, but that is a problem of social repression rather than a problem of expenses to the state.

6. Efficiency means here the amount of "good" or "utility" an organization produces from some output. As such, it is a measure of "utility." In turn, efficiency is itself measurable. Hence, efficiency is both a measure and an object to be measured. In the administrative organization literature in business schools, efficiency is taken to mean a measure of the success with which an organization undertakes a particular task. Effectiveness is taken to mean the overall adaptability of an organization to its environment. I have followed this convention even though most economists and industrial organization specialists do not use efficiency in this way. However, my interests are in discussing the implications of technocratic politics.

7. "Efficiency," *Encyclopaedia of the Social Sciences* (New York: MacMillan, 1931), pp. 437–39.

8. Max Weber, *The Protestant Ethic and the Spirit of Capitalism*, p. 26.

9. Ibid., p. 68. In this, as in much else, Weber follows Marx. "[Capitalism] compels all nations, on pain of extinction, to adopt the bourgeois mode of production; it compels them to introduce what it calls civilization into their midst, i.e., to become bourgeois themselves. In one word, it creates a world after its own image."

10. Max Weber, *Economy and Society*, edited by Guenther Roth and Claus Wittich, pp. 998, 1002. All quotation marks are in the original. Weber's sentence structures are complex even by the standards of the German academy of the nineteenth century. After looking at several translations of this passage, and the original German, I slightly rearranged the first passage from the order of Roth and Wittich.

11. Even here, there are problems. For instance, we would say that, using price as the measure of utility, the utility of rice is very low even when the rich in the community had enough but the starving had nothing to exchange for it.

I should note here that the notion and measurement of utility has changed since Marshall and the "marginalists." John Hicks and other "Ordinalists" rejected the idea that utility was comparable among people, and focused instead on indifference analysis. For a discussion of this this, see Robert Cooter and Peter Rappoport, "Were the Ordinalists Wrong About Welfare Economics."

12. See Stephen Kelman's discussion of these biases in "Cost-Benefit Analysis."

13. There is an additional problem, and it is that, in any given situation,

there may be many (Pareto-) efficient outcomes. If intervention is required to lead to an outcome that is Pareto-superior to the status quo, then the whole enterprise is biased towards the existing distribution. My thanks to Thomas Pogge for this insight.

14. Adam Smith, *Wealth of Nations*, 2:231–32, 236.

15. Richard Hofstadter, *Social Darwinism*, p. 144.

16. "I hold that the real tragedy [of unemployment] is not unemployment per se, but unemployment plus the impossibility of providing adequately for the unemployed *without impairing the conditions of further economic development.*" (italics in the original) p. 71.

17. See Jonathan Alter, "Harvard vs. Democracy" for an interesting view of this process of professionalizing public policy.

18. Daniel Bell, *The End of Ideology*. Alford and Friedland discuss Bell's work in the second part of their book, *Capitalism....*

19. Some of the more interesting formulations of this argument are to be found in essays by Samuel P. Huntington and Michael Crozier in Crozier, et al, *The Crisis of Democracy*. The overload thesis has been advanced a number of times for Britain. See James Douglas, "Overloaded Crown," and Anthony King, ed. *Why is Britain Becoming Harder to Govern*.

20. Weber, in commenting on the limits of bureaucracies, stressed the incompatibility of political and bureaucratic logic. He wrote:

"Our [German] officialdom has been brilliant wherever it had to prove its sense of duty, its impartiality and mastery of organizational problems in the face of official, clearly formulated tasks of a specialized nature.... But here we are concerned with political, not bureaucratic achievements, and the facts themselves provoke the recognition which nobody can truthfully deny: that bureaucracy failed completely whenever it was expected to deal with political problems. This is not an accident; rather, it would be astonishing if capabilities inherently so alien to one another would emerge within the same political structure." (*Economy and Society* p. 1417. I first saw reference to this passage in Joel Krieger's *Undermining Capitalism*.) The problem seems to me to be less the political incompetence of bureaucrats than the limits of bureaucratic legitimacy. People seem to agree only to the limits of "impartiality," and resist thereafter.

21. Claus Offe, *Contradictions of the Welfare State*, p. 132. See also Jürgen Habermas, *Legitimation Crisis*. Chapter 5 of Offe's book is an interesting essay, slightly revised from the *Stress and Contradiction* volume, entitled "Legitimacy vs. Efficiency." Though I found this essay to be very thought-provoking and helpful, I have not followed several of Offe's conventions. He defines state efficiency "not by its own criteria, but to the extent that it succeeds in the universalization of the commodity form" (p. 137–38). I mean

efficiency in terms of social accounting, a justification for action. His concept, I think, assumes some final "end" rationality of the state; mine, only instrumental rationality. I also use the term contradiction in a looser sense than he does. In order to avoid the historicist's error, we need to remember that we only truly know a contradictory situation post mortem; I prefer to speak here only of potential contradictions and dilemmas.

22. Those familiar with Offe and Habermas will forgive, I hope, my translation of these extremely complex arguments into simpler language. I believe that I have preserved the essential points. Offe, pp. 139–145.

23. Several caveats to this argument should be noted. First, this "language of description" does not tell us much about how state policies are likely to evolve in the face of this contradiction. Secondly, James Alt has shown that, as expectations can be learned, so they can be "unlearned." See his *Politics of Economic Decline*.

24. Max Weber, *The Protestant Ethic*, pp. 181–82.

25. Daniel Bell, "The Cultural Contradictions of Capitalism" and Irving Kristol, "When Virtue Loses All Her Loveliness," both in *The Public Interest*, Fall 1970.

26. E. P. Thompson, of course, is concerned with the legitimacy of the predecessor to market economy, moral economy. But, even he would concede that, despite initial resistance, the market economy has had some of its features legitimated as a result of growth.

27. I have been careful to avoid raising the issue of markets per se, and the relative justice and efficiency of markets. Given that all societies have some mixture of market and nonmarket methods of resource allocation, the question becomes really what types of markets and with what constraints? rather than, markets—yes or no?

See Amartya Sen, "The Moral Standing of the Market."

28. The remarkable success of Robert Nozick's *Anarchy, State, and Utopia* (New York: Basic Books, 1974), in conjunction with the work of Milton Friedman and Friedrich von Hayek, has resurrected the libertarian cause.

29. Friedrich Hayek, *Law, Legislation, and Liberty*, p. 63. Thomas Pogge has pointed out that utilitarianism still appears implicitly in Hayek's work.

30. Note should be made here that Rawls intends his work to be read as a treatise of sorts about the formation of institutions and general practices, and not about the justice of particular policies. I think the line between practices and policies is a thin one at best, at least in terms of economic policy-making. That is, whether the state ought to do something is usually thought of in terms of the likely consequences and content of the proposed policies. Even though I try to work within the limits he prescribes for his

theory, I think his work has broader application. My thanks to Thomas Pogge and Bob Amdur for their comments on this section.

31. Rawls, "Justice as Fairness." In TJ, Rawls changes "everyone" to the least well off, a subtle but important difference.

32. Many economists argue that, "trickle-down" economics will make us, on average, better off, though they concede that "pockets of poverty" will remain. This is not just in a Rawlsean sense. The least well off would have to benefit. Some economists, Thomas Sowell and Milton Friedman among them, make arguments that, if true, would be consistent with the difference principle and would still presume "trickle-down."

33. "Fairness to Goodness."

34. We might also note that, owing to "Fordism" and economies of scale, large factories were established in the automobile industry, as well in other industries. Communities necessarily sprang up near the factories. The communities then are the creations of the factory system, but they also made the factory system possible. Communities created the private conditions that made possible the "working-lives" of the employees of Chrysler, GM, and Ford. While the firms did not always have a direct interest in "community" per se, firms benefited from the positive externalities created by social organization.

35. Lodge, however, notes in *The American Disease* that Britain exhibits a "wasteful" tension between communitarianism and individualism, pp. 240–246.

36. The social and psychological costs of modern American individualism are explored in Robert Bellah et al., *Habits of the Heart*. Berkeley: University of California Press, 1985.

BIBLIOGRAPHY

Abernathy, William J. *The Productivity Dilemma: Roadblock to In-novation in the Automobile Industry.* Baltimore: Johns Hopkins, 1978.

Abernathy, William J., Kim B. Clark, and Alan M. Kantrow. *Industrial Renaissance: Producing a Competitive Future for America.* New York: Basic Books, 1983.

Abernathy, William J., et al. "The New Industrial Competition." *Harvard Business Review.* September–October 1981. 59(4):68–81.

Alford, Robert R. and Roger Friedland. *Powers of Theory: Capitalism, the State, and Democracy.* New York: Cambridge University Press, 1985.

Alperovitz, Gar and Jeff Faux. *Rebuilding America.* New York: Random House, 1984.

Allison, Graham. *The Essence of Decision.* Boston: Little Brown, 1971.

Alt, James E. *The Politics of Economic Decline: Economic Management and Behavior in Britain since 1964.* Cambridge, U.K.: Cambridge University Press 1979.

Alt, James E. and K. Alec Chrystal. *Political Economics.* Berkeley: University of California Press, 1983.

Alter, Jonathan, "Harvard v. Democracy." *Washington Monthly.* March 1983, pp. 32–39.

Altschuler, Alan, et al. *The Future of the Automobile.* Cambridge: MIT, 1984.

Anderson, Martin. *Financial Restructuring of the World Auto Industry.* Cambridge: Future of the Automobile Program, 1982.

Aronowitz, Stanley. *False Promises: The Shaping of American Working Class Consciousness.* New York: McGraw-Hill, 1973.

Auerbach, Alan J. "Taxation, Corporate Financial Policy and the Cost of Capital." *Journal of Economic Literature.* (September 1983) 21:905–940.

Bachrach, Peter and Morton Baratz. "Two Faces of Power." *American Political Science Review* (1962) 56(4):947–52.

Bacon, R. and W. Eltis. *Britain's Economic Problem,* 2d ed. London: Macmillan, 1978.

Ball, Howard. *Courts and Politics: The Federal Judicial System.* Englewood Cliffs: Prentice-Hall, 1980.

Bannock, Graham, R. E. Baxter, and Ray Rees. *The Peguin Dictionary of Economics.* Harmondsworth: Penguin, 1978.

Baran, Paul and Paul Sweezy. *Monopoly Capital.* New York: Monthly Review, 1966.

Beer, Samuel. *Modern British Politics. [British Politics in the Collectivist Age]* London: Farber, 1965. [New York: Vintage, 1965]

Bell, Daniel. "The Cultural Contradictions of Capitalism." *The Public Interest.* Fall 1970. 21:16–43.

Bell, Daniel. *The End of Ideology: On the Exhaustion of Political Ideas in the 1950s.* Glencoe, Ill.: Free Press, 1966.

Bendix, Reinhard. *Citizenship and Nation-Building: Studies of Our Changing Social Order.* Berkeley: University of California Press, 1964.

Bennett, Douglas C. and Kenneth E. Sharpe. *Transnational Corporations Versus the State: the Political Economy of the Mexican Auto Industry.* Princeton: Princeton University Press, 1985.

Berger, Suzanne, ed. *Organizing Interests in Western Europe.* New York: Cambridge, 1981.

Berger, Peter and Thomas Luckmann. *The Social Construction of Reality.* New York: Doubleday, 1966.

Best, Michael and William Connolly. *The Politicized Economy,* 2d ed. Lexington: D.C. Heath, 1982.

Bhaskar, Krish. *The Future of the United Kingdom Motor Industry.* London: Kogan, Page, 1976.

Bhaskar, Krish. *The Future of the World Motor Industry.* London: Kogan, Page, 1980.

Blank, Steven. "Britain: The Politics of Foreign Economic Policy and the Problem of Pluralist Stagnation." *International Organization* (Autumn 1977) 31(4):673–722.

Blaug, Mark. *The Methodology of Economics: or How Economists Explain.* Cambridge: Cambridge University Press, 1980.

Blauner, Robert. *Alienation and Freedom.* Chicago: University of Chicago Press, 1966.

Block, Fred. "Beyond Relative Autonomy." *New Political Science.* (Fall 1981) 7:33–50.

Block, Fred. "The Ruling Class Does Not Rule." *Socialist Revolution.* (May-June 1977) 33:6–28.

Bluestone, Barry and Bennett Harrison. *The Deindustrialization of America: Plant Closings, Community Abandonment, and the Dismantling of Basic Industry.* New York: Basic Books, 1983.

Body, Raford and James Cotty. "Class Conflict and Macro-Policy." *Review of Radical Political Economics* (1975), vol. 7(1).

Boltho, Andrea. "Is Western Europe Caught in an Expectations Trap?" *Lloyd's Bank Review.* April 1983, pp. 1–13.

Bowles, Samuel, David M. Gordon, and Thomas E. Weisskopf. *Beyond the Wasteland: A Democratic Alternative to Economic Decline.* New York: Doubleday, 1983.

Bowles, Samuel and Herbert Gintis. "The Crisis of Liberal Democratic Capitalism." *Politics & Society* (1982) 11(1):51–93.

Breley, Richard and Stewart Meyers. *Principles of Corporate Finance,* 2d ed. New York: McGraw-Hill, 1985.

British Business. [formerly Trade and Industry.] various issues.

British Leyland, Limited [BL, Limited] [BL, Public Limited Company]. Annual Report. [Reports and Accounts.] various years.

Brittan, Samuel. *The Economic Consequences of Democracy.* London: Temple Smith, 1977.

Brown, Lester, Christopher Flavin, and Colin Norman. "The Future of the Automobile in an Oil-Short World." Worldwatch Institute, 1979.

Buchanan, James, Robert Tollison and Gordon Tullock, eds. *Towards a Theory of the Rent-Seeking Society*. College Station: Texas A & M University Press, 1980.

Burawoy, Michael. *Manufacturing Consent: Changes in the Labor Process Under Monopoly Capitalism*. Chicago: Chicago, 1979.

Burawoy, Michael. *The Politics of Production*. London: Verso, 1985.

Burton, John. *The Job Support Machine*. London: CPS, 1979.

Burton, John. *Picking Losers?* London: IEA, 1983.

Calleo, David. *The Impervious Economy*. Cambridge: Harvard University Press, 1982.

Cameron, David. "Creating Theory in Comparative Political Economy: On Mancur Olson's Explanation of Growth." Paper Presented at the 1983 American Political Science Association Convention.

Cameron, David. "On the Limits of the Public Economy." *American Political Science Review* (1978) 78,1243–61.

Carnoy, Martin. *The State and Political Theory*. Princeton: Princeton, 1984.

Carrington, John and George Edwards. *Financing Industrial Investment*. London: Macmillan, 1979.

Caves, Richard and Lawrence Krause, eds. *Britain's Economic Performance*. Washington: Brookings, 1980.

Center for Studies in Social Policy. *Corporate State—Reality or Myth?* London: Center for Studies in Social Policy, 1977.

Chambers, Edward et al. *National Income Analysis and Forecasting*. Glenview, Ill.: Scott, Foresman, 1975.

Chandler, Alfred D., Jr. *The Visible Hand: the Managerial Revolution in American Business*. Cambridge: Harvard University Press, 1977.

Chandler, Alfred D., Jr., ed. *Giant Enterprise*. New York: Harcourt, Brace, 1964.

Chang, C. S. *The Japanese Auto Industry and the U.S. Market*. New York: Praeger, 1981.

Chilton's Automotive Industries. various issues.

Chinoy, E. *Automobile Workers and the American Dream.* New York: Doubleday, 1955.

Chrysler Corporation. Annual Report. various years.

Coates, David. *Labour in Power? A Study of the Labor Government 1974–1979.* London: Longman, 1980.

Cohen, Percy S. *Modern Social Theory.* London: Heineman, 1968.

Cole, Robert E. and Taizo Yajusiji, eds. *The American and Japanese Auto Industries in Transition.* Ann Arbor: Center for Japanese Studies, 1984.

Congressional Quarterly Weekly. various issues.

Cooter, Robert and Peter Rappoport. "Were the Ordinalists Wrong About Welfare Economics?" *Journal of Economic Literature* June 1984. 22(2):507–530.

Copeland, Thomas E. and J. Fred Weston. *Financial Theory and Corporate Policy,* 2d ed. Reading, Mass.: Addison-Wesley, 1984.

Cowhey, Peter F. and Edward Long. "Testing Theories of Regime Change." *International Organization* (Winter 1983) 37(1):157–188.

Cox, Andrew and Jack Hayward. "The Inapplicability of the Corporatist Model in Britain and France." *International Political Science Review* (1983.) 4(2):217–240.

Crandall, Robert W. et al. *Regulating the Automobile.* Washington: Brookings, 1986.

Crouch, Colin, ed. *State and Economy in Contemporary Capitalism.* London: Croom Helm, 1979.

Crozier, Michel. *The Bureaucratic Phenomenon.* Chicago: University of Chicago Press, 1964.

Crozier, Michel and Samuel P. Huntington. *The Crisis of Democracy.* New York: NYU Press, 1975.

Curzon-Price, Victoria. *Industrial Policies in the European Community.* New York: St. Martin's, 1981.

Cusumano, Michael A. *The Japanese Automobile Industry: Technology and Management at Nissan and Toyota.* Cambridge: Harvard University Press, 1985.

Davies, David G. *United States Taxes and Tax Policy.* New York: Cambridge University Press, 1986.

Dahlka, Edward A. "TBTs—A Potential Audit Time Bomb." *The Journal of Commercial Banking.* February 1983, pp. 55–63.

Dahl, Robert. *A Preface to Democratic Theory.* Chicago: University of Chicago Press, 1957.

DeGrasse, Robert W., Jr. "Military Buildup Exacts Toll on Economy." Council on Economic Priorities Newsletter. May 1983.

Denison, Edward F. *Trends in American Economic Growth, 1929– 1982.* Washington: Brookings, 1985.

Deutsch, Karl. *Politics and Government.* Boston: Houghton Mifflin, 1980.

Dore, Ronald. *British Factory, Japanese Factory.* Berkeley: University of California Press, 1973.

Douglas, James. "The Overloaded Crown." *British Journal of Political Science* (1976), vol. 6:483–505.

Downs, Anthony. *An Economic Theory of Democracy.* New York: Harper, 1957.

Dryzek, John and Robert E. Goodin, "Risk-Sharing and Social Justice: The Motivational Foundations of the Post-War Welfare State." *British Journal of Political Science.* (January 1986) 16:1–34.

Duncan, William C. *U.S.—Japan Automobile Diplomacy.* Cambridge: Ballinger, 1973.

Dunnett, Peter J. S. *The Decline of the British Motor Industry.* London: Croom Helm, 1980.

Economist Intelligence Unit. *Quarterly Economic Reviews; Japan: Annual Supplement, 1981.* London: EIU, 1981.

Economist Intelligence Unit. *The Motor Business; Quarterly Report.* London: EIU, various issues.

"Efficiency." *Encyclopaedia of the Social Sciences,* pp. 437–39. New York: MacMillan, 1931.

Elsenhaus, Helmut. "Rising Mass Incomes as a Condition of Capitalist Growth." International Organization. (Winter 1983) 37(1). 1–39.

Epsing-Andersen, Gosta and Roger Friedland. "Class Coalitions in the Making of West European Economies." In Maurice Zeitland, ed. *Political Power and Social Theory.* Volume 3. Greenwich: JAI, 1982.

E.C. Commission of the European Communities. *The European Automobile Industry.* Luxembourg: 1981.

Feldman, Elliot. "Comparative Public Policy: Field or Method?" *Comparative Politics* (January 1978), vol. 10(2):287–305.

Feldman, Elliot. *Concorde and Dissent.* Cambridge: Cambridge University Press, 1985.

Feldstein, Martin. "Tax Incentives, Corporate Saving, and Capital Accumulation in the United States." *Journal of Public Economics* (1973) 2(1):159–71.

Feldstein, Martin and Joel Slemrod. "How Inflation Distorts the Taxation of Capital Gains." *Harvard Business Review.* September 1975, vol. 99.

Ferguson, C. E. and J. P. Gould. *Microeconomic Theory.* 4th Edition. Homewood, Ill.: Irwin, 1975.

Financial Times. various issues.

Finer, Steven E. "The Political Power of Private Capital." *Sociological Review.* (1955) 3:279–94.

Finger, J. Michael. "Industrial Country Policy and Adjustment to Imports." World Bank Working Paper, #470. Washington: 1981.

Fisher, Franklin and John McGowan. "On the Misuse of Accounting Rates of Return to Infer Monopoly Profits." *American Economic Review.* (March 1983) 71(1):82–97.

Ford Motor Company (U.K.), Limited. Annual Report, 1982.

Ford Motor Company. Annual Report. various years.

Fox, J. Ronald, ed. *Managing Business–Government Relations.* Homewood, Ill.: Irwin, 1982.

Frankel, Jeffrey A. *The Yen/Dollar Agreement.* Washington: IIE, December 1984.

Freeman, John R. and James Alt. "The Politics of Public and Private Investment in Britain." Paper Presented at the Western Political Science Association Convention, 1986.

Friedland, Roger and Jimy Sanders. "The Public Economy and Economic Growth in Western Market Economies." *American Sociological Review* (August 1985) 50:421–37.

Friedman, David. "Beyond the Age of Ford: The Strategic Basis of the Japanese Success in Automobiles." In John Zysman and Laura Tyson, eds., *American Industry in International Competition: Government Policies and Corporate Strategies.* Ithaca: Cornell University Press, 1983.

Friedman, Milton. *Capitalism and Freedom.* Chicago: Chicago, 1962.

Fromm, Gary, ed. *Tax Incentives and Capital Spending.* Washington, D.C.: Brookings, 1971.

Galbraith, James K. "A Comparison of Economic Policies and Doctrines in the Major Industrial Countries." In Joint Economic Committee, *U.S. International Economic Policy in the 1980s.* Washington: GPO, 1982.

Gamble, Andrew. *Britain in Decline.* London: Macmillan, 1981.

Geertz, Clifford. "Ideology as a Cultural System." In David Apter, ed. *Ideology and Discontent.* Glencoe: Free Press, 1974.

Geertz, Clifford. *Negara: The Theatre State in Nineteenth Century Bali.* Princeton: Princeton University Press, 1981.

General Motors, Inc. Annual Report. Various years.

Giddens, Anthony. *Central Problems in Social Theory.* Berkeley: University of California Press, 1979.

Gilpin, Robert. *U.S. Power and the Multinational Corporation: The Political Economy of Foreign Direct Investment.* New York: Basic, 1975.

Ginsburg, Douglas and William Abernathy, eds. *Government, Technology, and the Future of the Automobile.* New York: McGraw-Hill, 1980.

Glyn, Andrew and Bob Sutcliffe. *Capitalism in Crisis.* New York: Pantheon, 1972.

Goodin, Robert E. *Political Theory and Public Policy.* Chicago: University of Chicago Press, 1982.

Gordon, Robert J. *Macroeconomics.* 2d ed. Boston: Little, Brown, 1981.

Gordon, Roderick and Michael Stevens, eds. *Where Did We Go Wrong?* Barcombe, U.K.: Falmer, 1981.

Gordon, Roderick and Michael Stevens. *The British Malaise.* Barcombe, U.K.: Falmer, 1981.

Gouldner, Alvin. *The Coming Crisis of Western Sociology.* New York: Basic, 1970.

Grant, Wyn. "Business Interests and the Conservative Party." *Government and Opposition.* (1980) 15:143–61.

Grant, Wyn. "Large Firms and Public Policy in Britain." *Journal of Public Policy.* (February 1984), vol. 4, no. 1:1–17.

Grant, Wyn. *The Political Economy of Industrial Policy.* London: Buttersworth, 1982.

Grant, Wyn and David Marsh. *The Confederation of British Industry.* London: Hodder and Stoughton, 1977.

Great Britain. Central Policy Review Staff. *The Future of the British Car Industry.* London: HMSO, 1975.

Great Britain. Department of Industry. *An Approach to Industrial Strategy.* London: HMSO, 1975.

Great Britain. Department of Industry. *British Leyland: The Next Decade.* [Ryder Report]. London: HMSO, 1975.

Great Britain. Department of Industry. *Public Expenditure on Chrysler.* Command 6745. London: HMSO, 1975.

Great Britain. Department of Industry. *The British Motor Vehicle Industry.* Command 6377. London: HMSO, 1976.

Great Britain. Manpower Services Commission for Wales. *The Ford Bridgend Report.* Cardiff: Manpower Intelligence Unit, 1981.

Great Britain. Parliament, Commons. Eighth Report from the Expenditure Committee, 1975–6. *Public Expenditure on Chrysler, UK.* HC- 596–1. London: HMSO, 1976.

Great Britain. Parliament, Commons. Industry and Trade Committee. *BL Limited, 1981–1982 [BL Plc, 1982–1983].* London: HMSO, 1982 [1983].

Great Britain. Parliament. *Industry Act 1972 [1975] [1980].* London: HMSO, 1972 [1975] [1980].

Great Britain. The Central Statistical Office. *Monthly Digest of Statistics.* London: HMSO, various issues.

Grossman, Gregory. *Economic Systems.* Prentice-Hall, 1974.

Habermas, Jürgen. *Legitimation Crisis.* Boston: Beacon, 1975.

Hall, Robert and Dale Jorgenson. "Tax Policy and Investment Behavior." *American Economic Review* (June 1967), vol. 57, no. 3:391–414.

Hardin, Garrett. "The Tragedy of the Commons." *Science,* December 13, 1968, pp. 1243–1248.

Harris, Nigel. *Competition and the Corporate State: British Conservatives, the State and Industry 1945–64.* London: Metheun, 1972.

Harris, Robert. "The Value of Economic Theory in Management Education." *Berkeley Working Papers,* January 1984, pp. 1–12.

Hausman, Daniel, ed. *The Philosophy of Economics.* Cambridge: Cambridge University Press, 1984.

Hayek, Friedrich. *Law, Legislation, and Liberty: The Mirage of Social Justice,* vol. 2. Chicago: Chicago, 1976.

Hayes, Robert and William J. Abernathy. "Managing Our Way to Industrial Decline." *Harvard Business Review.* July-August 1980. 58(4):67–77.

Hayes, Robert and D. Garvin. "Managing As if Tomorrow Mattered." *Harvard Business Review.* (May-June 1982) 60(3):70–79.

Herberg, Mikkel. "Politics, Planning, and Governments." *Political Studies* (1981) 29(4):497–516.

Hibbs, Douglas A. and Heino Fassbender, eds. *Contemporary Political Economy.* Amsterdam: North Holland, 1981.

Hirsch, Joachim. "The State Apparatus and Social Reproduction." In John Holloway and Sol Picciotto, eds. *State and Capital.* Austin: University of Texas Press, 1979.

Hirschman, Albert O. "Against Parsimony" *American Economic Review* (May 1984) 74:89–96.

Hirschman, Albert O. *A Bias for Hope: Essays on Development and Latin America.* New Haven: Yale University Press, 1971.

Hobsbawm, E. J. *Industry and Empire*. Harmondsworth: Penguin, 1969.

Hofstadter, Richard. *The Age of Reform*. New York: Vintage, 1965.

Hofstadter, Richard. *Social Darwinism in American Thought*. Boston: Little, Brown, 1955.

Hofstadter, Richard. "What Happened to the Anti-Trust Movement?" In Earl F. Cheit, ed. *The Business Establishment*. New York: Wiley, 1964.

Holland, Stuart. *The Socialist Challenge*. London: Quartet, 1975.

Hooberman, Ben. *An Introduction to British Trade Unions*. Harmondsworth: Penguin, 1974.

Hunker, Jeffery A. *Structural Change in the U.S. Automobile Industry*. Lexington: D.C. Heath, 1983.

International Herald Tribune. various issues.

International Monetary Fund. *International Financial Statistics*. Washington: June, 1983.

Ito, Takatoshi. "Use of (time-Domain) Vector Autoregressions to Test Uncovered Interest Parity." Unpublished Paper. University of Minnesota, June 1985.

Irwin, Alan. *Risk and the Control of Technology: Public Policies for Road Traffic Safety in Britain and the United States*. Manchester, U.K.: Manchester University Press, 1985.

IWC Motors Group. *A Workers' Enquiry into the Motor Industry*. London: 1979.

Jankowski, Ron. "The Profit-Squeeze and Tax Policy: Has the State Actively Intervened?" University of Iowa Occasional Papers, no. 8. Iowa City: 1983.

Jervis, Robert. *Perception and Misperception in International Politics*. Princeton: Princeton University Press, 1976.

Jessop, Bob. *The Capitalist State*. New York: NYU Press, 1982.

Jessop, Bob. "The Capitalist State and the Rule of Capital: Problems in the Analysis of Business Associations." *West European Politics* (April 1983) 6(2):139–62.

Jevons, William Stanley. *Principles of Science: A Treatise on Logic* and *Scientific Method.* 1873; reprint, New York: Dover Books, 1958.

Johnson, Chalmers. *MITI and the Japanese Miracle.* Stanford: Stanford University Press, 1982.

Jones, Daniel T. "Technology and the U.K. Automotive Industry." *Lloyds Bank Review.* April 1983, pp. 14–27.

Jones, Daniel T. and S. J. Prais. "Plant-size and Productivity in the Motor Industry." *Oxford Bulletin of Economics and Statistics.* May 1978. 40:131–152.

Jones, F. E. "Our Manufacturing Industry: The Missing £100,000 Million." *National Westminster Quarterly Bank Review.* May 1978, pp. 8–17.

Jones, Hywel. *An Introduction to Modern Theories of Economic Growth.* Van Nostrand Reinhold (UK), 1975.

Judge, George G., R. Carter Hill, William Griffiths, Helmut Lütkepohl, and Tsoung-Chao Lee. *Introduction to the Theory and Practice of Econometrics.* New York: Wiley, 1982.

Kamata, Satoshi. *Japan in the Passing Lane.* New York: Pantheon, 1982.

Katz, Harry C. "Collective Bargaining in the U.S. Auto Industry." Cambridge: Future of the Automobile Program, 1982.

Katz, Harry C. *Shifting Gears: Changing Labor Relations in the U.S. Automobile Industry.* Cambridge: MIT Press, 1985.

Katzenstein, Peter J. "Conclusion: Domestic Structures and Strategies of Foreign Economic Policy." In Peter J. Katzenstein, ed. *Between Power and Plenty.* Madison: University of Wisconsin Press, 1978.

Katzenstein, Peter J. *Small States in World Markets: Industrial Policy in Europe.* Ithaca: Cornell University Press, 1985.

Katznelson, Ira and Mark Kesselman. *The Politics of Power.* 2d ed. New York: Harcourt, 1979.

Kay, John A. and Mervyn King. *The British Tax System.* 3d ed. Oxford: Oxford University Press, 1983.

Kelman, Stephen. "Cost-Benefit Analysis: An Ethical Critique." *Regulation.* January/February 1981, pp. 33–40.

Kennedy, Peter. *A Guide to Econometrics*. Cambridge: MIT Press, 1985.

Kesselman, Mark. "The State and Class Struggles in Advanced Capitalism." *New Political Science*. Summer 1982, pp. 113–36.

Kindleberger, Charles P. *A Financial History of Western Europe*. Boston: George Allen & Unwin, 1984.

Kindleberger, Charles P. and Bruce Herrick. *Economic Development*. 3d ed. New York: McGraw-Hill, 1977.

Kinder, Donald R. "Presidents, Prosperity, and Public Opinion." *Public Opinion Quarterly*. (Spring 1981) 45(1):1–21.

Kinder, Donald R. and D. Roderick Kiewiet. "Economic Grievances and Political Behavior." *American Journal of Political Science*. (August 1979) 23(3)495–527.

King, Anthony, ed. *Why is Britain Becoming Harder to Govern?* London: BBC, 1976.

King, Mervyn and Don Fullerton, eds. *The Taxation of Income From Capital: A Comparative Study of the U.S., the U.K., Sweden, and West Germany*. Chicago: University of Chicago Press, 1984.

Kmenta, Jan. *Elements of Econometrics*. New York: Macmillan, 1971.

Krasner, Stephen. "Approaches to the State: Alternative Conceptions and Historical Dynamics." *Comparative Politics* (January 1984) vol. 16(2):223–246.

Krasner, Stephen. *Defending the National Interest: Raw Materials Investment and U.S. Foreign Policy*. Princeton: Princeton University Press, 1978.

Krasner, Stephen. "United States Commercial and Monetary Policy." In Peter J. Katzenstein, ed. *Between Power and Plenty*. Madison: Wisconsin, 1978.

Krasner, Stephen, ed. *International Regimes*. Ithaca: Cornell University Press, 1983.

Krieger, Joel. *Reagan, Thatcher and the Politics of Economic Decline*. New York: Oxford University Press, 1986.

Krieger, Joel. *Undermining Capitalism*. Princeton: Princeton University Press, 1984.

Kristol, Irving. "When Virtue Loses All Her Loveliness—Some Reflections on Capitalism and the Free Society." *The Public Interest*. Fall 1970. 21:3–15.

Kristol, Irving and Daniel Bell, eds. "The Crisis in Economic Theory." Special Issue, 1980, of *The Public Interest*.

Krugman, Paul. "New Theories of Trade Among Industrial Countries." *American Economic Review*. (May 1983) 73(2):343–47.

Lall, Sanjaya. "Prospects for Automotive Transnationals in the Third World." *National Westminister Bank Quarterly Review*. February 1983, pp. 13–20.

Lall, Sanjaya. "The International Automotive Industry and the Developing World." *World Development*. October 1980.

Lakatos, Imre. *The Methodology of Scientific Research Programmes: Philosophical Papers*. Vol. 1. Cambridge: Cambridge University Press, 1978.

Laux, James. "The Genesis of the Automobile Revolution." In J. Bardou et al., eds. *The Automobile Revolution*. Chapel Hill: University of North Carolina Press, 1982.

Lawrence, Paul and David Dyer. *Renewing American Industry*. New York: Free Press, 1983.

Lawrence, Robert Z. *Can America Compete?* Washington: Brookings, 1984.

Lazar, Fred. *The New Protectionism*. Ottawa: CIEP, 1981.

Lenway, Stefanie Ann. *The Politics of International Trade*. Boston: Pitman, 1985.

Lincoln, James R. and Arne L. Kalleberg. "Work Organization and Work Force Commitment." *American Sociological Review* (1985) 50:738–60.

Lindblom, Charles E. *Politics and Markets: The World's Political-Economic System*. New York: Basic Books, 1977.

Lindblom, Charles E. "Still Muddling—Not Through." *Public Administration Review*. November–December 1979, pp. 517–26.

Lodge, George C. *The American Disease*. New York: Knopf, 1984.

Lowi, Theodore J. *The End of Liberalism: The Second Republic of the United States*. 2d ed. New York: Norton, 1979.

Magaziner, Ira C. "Japanese Industrial Policy: Source of Strength for the Automobile Industry." In Robert E. Cole, ed., *The Japanese Automobile Industry*. (Ann Arbor: Michigan Papers in Japanese Studies #3, 1981.

Maitland, Ian. *The Causes of Industrial Disorder: A Comparison of a British and a German Factory*. London: Routledge, Kegan Paul, 1983.

Mandel, Ernst. *Late Capitalism*. New York: Schocken, 1978.

Manley, John. "Neopluralism." *American Political Science Review* (June 1983) 77(2):368–83.

Mann, Michael. *Consciousness and Action Among the Western Working Class*. London: Macmillan, 1973.

Mansfield, Edwin. *Microeconomics*. 2d ed. New York: Norton, 1975.

Marsh, David and Wyn Grant. "Tripartism: Reality or Myth?" *Government and Opposition*. (1977) 12:194–211.

Marsh, David, ed. "Special Issue on Capital and Politics in Western Europe." *West European Politics*. (April 1983), vol. 6(2).

Marx, Karl. *Capital*. Vols 1–3. Moscow: Progress, 1959.

Marx, Karl. *Grundrisse*. New York: Random House, 1973.

Marx, Karl. "Preface to A Contribution to the Critique of Political Economy." In Robert Tucker, ed. *The Marx-Engels Reader*. New York: Norton, 1972.

Marx, Karl. *The Eighteenth Brumaire of Louis Bonaparte*. Moscow: Progress, 1975.

Maxcy, George. *The Multinational Motor Industry*. London: Croom Helm, 1981.

McCloskey, Donald N. *The Rhetoric of Economics*. Madison: Wisconsin, 1985.

McConnell, Grant. *Private Power and American Democracy*. New York: Vintage, 1966.

McEnery, J. H. *Manufacturing Two Nations*. London: IEA, 1981.

McIntyre, Robert S. "The Failure of Corporate Tax Incentives," *Multinational Monitor*. October 1984, pp. 3–10.

Meade, James. *Alternative Systems of Business Organization and Worker's Renumeration*. London: George Allen & Unwin, 1986.

Medley, Richard. "Monetary Stability and Industrial Adaptation in

West Germany." In Joint Economic Committee (Congress). *Monetary Policy, Selective Credit Policy, and Industrial Policy in France, Britain, West Germany, and Sweden.* Washington: GPO, 1981.

Miliband, Ralph. *Marxism and Politics.* New York: Oxford University Press, 1977.

Miliband, Ralph. *The State in Capitalist Society.* New York: Basic Books, 1969.

Mill, John Stuart. *Principles of Political Economy.* Harmondsworth: Penguin, 1970.

Mistral, Jacques. "Competitiveness of the Productive System and International Specialization." OECD. Paris: 1981.

Modigliani, F. and A. Ando. "The Life-Cycle Hypothesis of Saving: Aggregate Implications and Tests." *American Economic Review.* (1963) 53(1):55–84.

Moran, Michael. "Politics, Banks and Markets: An Anglo-American Comparison." *Political Studies.* (June 1984) vol. 32(2):173–189.

Moran, Michael. *The Politics of Banking.* London: Macmillan, 1984.

Morgan Guaranty Trust Company (MG). *World Financial Markets.* June, 1984.

Motor Vehicle Manufacturers Association. World Motor Vehicle Data. (various years)

Mueller, Dennis, ed. *The Political Economy of Growth.* New Haven: Yale University Press, 1982.

Mueller, Dennis C. *Public Choice.* Cambridge: Cambridge University Press, 1979.

Mutti, John. *Taxes, Subsidies and Competitiveness Internationally.* Washington: National Planning Association, 1982.

National Economic Development Council. *Industrial Policies in Europe.* London: NEDO, 1981.

National Economic Development Council. NEDC Annual Report, 1981–82. London: 1982.

Neumann, Manfred. "Long Swings in Economic Development, Social Time Preference and Institutional Change." *Zeitschrift für die gesamte Staatswissenscraft* (March 1985), vol. 141(1):21–35. (The article is in English.)

Noble, David. *America By Design.* New York: Oxford, 1977.

Nordlinger, Eric. *On the Autonomy of the Democratic State.* Cambridge: Harvard, 1982.

O'Connor, James. *The Fiscal Crisis of the State.* New York: St. Martin's, 1973.

Odell, John S. *U.S. International Monetary Policy.* Princeton: Princeton University Press, 1982.

O'Donnell, Guillermo. *Modernization and Bureaucratic Authoritarianism.* Berkeley: California, 1973.

Offe, Claus. "Attribution of Public Status to Interest Groups." In Suzanne Berger, ed. *Organizing Interests in Western Europe.* New York: Cambridge, 1981.

Offe, Claus. *Contradictions of the Welfare State.* Cambridge: MIT, 1984.

Offe, Claus. "The Theory of the Capitalist State and the Problems of Policy Formation." In Lindberg, et al., eds. *Stress and Contradiction in Modern Capitalism.* Lexington: D.C. Heath, 1975.

Offe, Claus and Volker Ronge. "Theses on the Theory of the State." *New German Critique.* (Fall 1975) 6:137–47.

Okun, Arthur. *Equality and Efficiency.* Washington: Brookings, 1975.

Okun, Arthur. "Potential GNP: Its Measures and Significance." In Arthur Okun, ed. *Political Economy and Prosperity.* Washington: Brookings, 1970.

Olson, Mancur. *The Logic of Collective Action.* Cambridge: Harvard, 1965.

Olson, Mancur. *The Rise and Decline of Nations.* New Haven: Yale, 1982.

Organization for Economic Cooperation and Development (OECD). *Competition and Trade Policies: Their Interaction.* Paris, 1984.

OECD. *Economic Outlook,* December 1982. Paris: 1982.

OECD. Economic Surveys: Canada. Paris: October 1985.

OECD. Financial Accounts of OECD Countries, Parts 1, 2, & 3. Paris: various years.

OECD. *Financial Statements of Non-Financial Enterprises.* Paris, various years.

OECD. *Historical Statistics, 1960–1982.* Paris, 1984.

OECD. *International Investment and Multinational Enterprises: Recent International Direct Investment Trends.* Paris: 1981.

OECD. *Long-Term Outlook for the World Automobile Industry.* Paris: 1983.

OECD. *Prospects for the Welfare State in the 1980s.* Paris: 1980.

OECD. *Revenue Statistics, 1965–1984.* Paris: 1986.

OECD. *Social Expenditure, 1960–1990: Problems of Growth and Control.* Paris: 1985.

OECD *Theoretical and Empirical Aspects of Corporate Taxation.* Paris, 1974.

OECD. *United Kingdom: Economic Survey, 1982–1983.* Paris: 1983.

OECD. *United States: Economic Survey, 1985–1986.* Paris: 1986.

Ott, Attiat F. "An Industrial Policy for the United States." In Edward Altman and Ingo Walter, eds., *Forging New Relationships Among Business, Labor and Government.* Contemporary Studies in Economic and Financial Analysis. Volume 56. Greenwich: JAI, 1986.

Ott, David J. and Attiat F. Ott. *Federal Budget Policy,* 3d ed. Washington: Brookings, 1977.

Ott, Mack. "Depreciation, Inflation and Investment Incentives." *Federal Reserve Bank of St. Louis Bulletin.* November 1984, pp. 17–30.

Ouchi, William. *Theory Z.* Lexington: Addison-Wesley, 1981.

Panitch, Leo. *Social Democracy and Industrial Militancy.* Cambridge, U.K.: Cambridge, 1976.

Parr, Michael. "The National Enterprise Board." *National Westminster Bank Quarterly Review.* (February 1979), pp. 51–62.

Pechman, Joseph. "Taxation." In Richard Caves and Lawrence Krause, eds. *Britain's Economic Performance.* Washington: Brookings, 1980.

Pechman, Joseph A., and Keimei Kaizuka. "Taxation." In Hugh Patrick and Henry Rosovsky, eds., *Asia's New Giant*. Washington, D.C.: Brookings, 1976.

Peretz, Paul. *The Political Economy of Inflation in the United States*. Chicago: University of Chicago Press, 1983.

Perry, Ross. *The Future of Canada's Auto Industry*. Toronto: Lorimar, 1982.

Pertschuck, Michael. *Revolt Against Regulation*. Berkeley: California, 1982.

Philips, Richard and Authur Way. *The West European Automotive Industry*. London: EIU, Special Report no. 77, 1980.

Phillips, Richard, et al. *Auto Industries of Europe, U.S., and Japan*. Cambridge: Abt Books, 1982.

Pigott, Charles. "Financial Reform in Japan." *Federal Reserve Bank of San Fransisco Economic Review*. Winter 1983, pp. 25–46.

Pike, Frederick B. and Thomas Stritch, eds. *The New Corporatism*. South Bend: University of Notre Dame Press, 1974.

Pinder, John. "Industrial Policy in Britain and the European Community." *Policy Studies*. (1982) 2:252–66.

Polanyi, Michael. *The Great Transformation*. Boston: Beacon, 1971.

Pollard, Sidney. *The Wasting of the British Economy*. New York: St. Martin's, 1982.

Poulantzas, Nicos. *Fascism and Dictatorship*. London: NLR, 1974.

Poulantzas, Nicos. *Political Power and Social Classes*. London: NLR, 1973.

Prais, S. J. et al. *Productivity and Industrial Structure: A Statistical Study of Manufacturing Industry in Britain, Germany and the United States*. Cambridge: Cambridge University Press, 1982.

Prais, S. J. and Daniel T. Jones "Plant-size and Productivity in the Motor Industry." *Oxford Bulletin of Economics and Statistics*. (May 1978) vol. 40.

Pryke, Richard. *The Nationalized Industries*. Oxford (U.K.): Martin Robertson, 1981.

Przeworski, Adam and Michael Wallerstein. "Comment on Katz, Mahler, and Frank." *American Political Science Review*. 1985(2). 79:508–510.

Quinn, Brian S. *The New Euromarket*. New York: Wiley, 1975.

Quinn, Dennis P. and Robert Jacobson, "Industrial Policy Through the Restriction of Capital Flows." Paper Presented at American Political Science Association convention, 1986.

Quinn, Dennis P. "Policy Congruence Among Market Societies." Paper presented at American Political Science Convention, 1985.

Quirk, Paul. *Industry Influence in Regulatory America*. Princeton: Princeton University Press, 1981.

Rawls, John. *A Theory of Justice*. Cambridge: Harvard University Press, 1971.

Rawls, John. "Fairness to Goodness." *The Philosophical Review*. (1975.) 84:536–554.

Rawls, John. "Justice as Fairness." *The Philosophical Review*. (1958) 67:164–94. (Reprinted in Peter Laslett and W. G. Runciman, eds. *Philosophy, Politics, and Society*, Second Series. Oxford: Basil Blackwell, 1967.)

Reich, Robert B. *The Next American Frontier*. New York: Times Books, 1983.

Reich, Robert B. and John D. Donahue. *New Deals: The Chrysler Revival and the American System*. New York: Times Books, 1985.

Rhys, D. G. *The Motor Industry: An Economic Survey*. London: Butterworths, 1972.

Rhys, D. G. "Economies of Scale in the Motor Industry." *Bulletin of Economic Research*. November 1977.

Roehl, Tom. "The General Trading Company [Japan]." In Michael G. Harvey and Robert Lusch, eds. *Marketing Channels*. Norman, Oklahoma: Center for Economic and Management Research, 1982.

Roehl, Thomas and Thomas Schmitt. "The Kanban Inventory Control System: The Myth of Zero Inventory." *Proceedings of the Academy of International Business*. Honolulu: East-West Center, 1983.

Ruff, Larry. "The Economic Common Sense of Pollution." *The Public Interest* (Spring 1970) 19:69–85.

Ruggie, John. "International Regimes, Transactions, and Change: Embedded Liberalism in the Postwar Economic Order." *International Organization* (Spring 1982) 36(2):379–415.

Sabel, Charles. *Work and Politics: The Division of Labor in Industry.* New York: Cambridge University Press, 1982.

Saxonhouse, Gary. "The Micro- and Macroeconomics of Foreign Sales to Japan." William Cline, ed. *Trade Policies in the 1980s.* Washington: IIE, 1983.

Scherer, F. M. *Industrial Market Structure and Economic Performance.* 2d. ed. Chicago: Rand McNally, 1980.

Schmitter, Philippe C. "Still the Century of Corporatism?" In Schmitter & Lehmbruch, eds. *Trends Toward Corporatist Intermediation.* Beverly Hills: Sage, 1982.

Schmitter, Philippe C. and Gerhard Lehmbruch, eds. *Patterns of Corporatist Policy Making.* Beverly Hills: Sage, 1982.

Schmitter, Philippe C. and Gerhard Lehmbruch, eds. *Trends Toward Corporatist Intermediation.* Beverly Hills: Sage, 1979.

Schultze, Charles E. "Industrial Policy: A Dissent." *The Brookings Review* (Fall 1983), vol. 2:3–12.

Schultze, Charles E. *The Public Use of Private Interest.* Washington: Brookings, 1977.

Schumpeter, Joseph A. *Capitalism, Socialism and Democracy*, 3d ed. New York: Harper & Row, 1950.

Schutz, Alfred. *Collected Papers.* Vol. 1. The Hague: Nijoff, 1962.

Sen, Amartya. "The Moral Standing of the Market." *Social Philosophy and Policy.* (Spring 1985) 2:1–19.

Sennett, Richard and Jonathan Cobb. *The Hidden Injuries of Class.* New York: Vintage, 1972.

Shanks, Michael. *Politics and Planning.* London: Allen and Unwin, 1977.

Shapiro, Robert Y. and Bruce M. Conforto. "Presidential Performance, the Economy, and the Public's Evaluation of Economic Conditions." *Journal of Politics.* (February 1980) 42:49–67.

Shonfield, Sir Andrew. *In Defense of the Mixed Economy*. New York: Oxford University Press, 1984.

Shonfield, Sir Andrew. *Modern Capitalism*. New York: Oxford University Press, 1969.

Skocpol, Theda. *States and Social Revolutions*. New York: Cambridge, 1979.

Smith, Adam. *An Inquiry into the Nature and Causes of the Wealth of Nations*. Chicago: University of Chicago Press, 1976.

Smith, Trevor. *The Politics of the Corporate Economy*. Oxford: Martin Robertson, 1979.

Society of Motor Manufacturers and Traders, (U.K.). *The Motor Industry of Great Britain*. London: various years.

Solidarity. Various issues.

Solo, Robert. "The Economist and Economic Roles of the Political Authority in Advanced Industrial Societies." In Leon Lindberg et al., eds. *Stress and Contradiction in Modern Capitalism*. Lexington, Mass.: D.C. Heath, 1975.

Spindler, J. Andrew. *The Politics of International Credit: Private Finance and Foreign Policy in Germany and Japan*. Washington: Brookings, 1984.

Stauffer, Thomas Reynolds. *The Measurement of Corporate Rates of Return*. New York: Garland, 1980.

Steel, David R. "Review Article: Government and Industry in Great Britain." *British Journal of Political Science* (1981) 12:449–503.

Steinbruner, John. *The Cybernetic Theory of Decision*. Princeton: Princeton University Press, 1974.

Stigler, George. "The Theory of Economic Regulation." *Bell Journal of Economics and Management Science*. (Spring 1971) 2:3–21.

Stimson, James A. "Regression in Space and Time: A Statistical Essay." *American Journal of Political Science*. (November 1985), 29:914–47.

Stinchcombe, Arthur. *Constructing Social Theory*. New York: Harcourt, 1974.

Strange, Susan. *Sterling and British Policy*. New York: Oxford, 1971.

Strange, Susan. "The Management of Surplus Capacity." *International Organization.* (Summer 1979), vol. 33(3):303–339.

Strange, Susan and Roger Tooze, eds. *The International Politics of Surplus Capacity: Competition for Market Shares in the World Recession.* London: George Allen & Unwin, 1981.

Straussmann, W. Paul. "Economic Growth and Income Distribution." *Quarterly Journal of Economics.* (August 1956). 70(3):426–30.

Streeck, Wolfgang. *Industrial Relations in West Germany: a Case Study of the Car Industry.* New York: St. Martin's Press, 1984.

Suleiman, Ezra. *Elites in French Society.* Princeton: Princeton University Press, 1979.

Suzuki, Yoshio. *Money and Banking in Japan.* New Haven: Yale, 1980.

Tanner, J. C. *Saturation Levels in Car Ownership: Some Recent Data.* TRRL Supplementary Report. Crawthorne, U.K.: 1981.

Teece, David J. "Economies of Scope and the Scope of the Enterprise." *Journal of Economic Behavior and Organization.* (1980), vol. 1(2):223–48.

Teune, Henry. "A Logic of Comparative Policy Analysis." In Douglas Ashford, ed. *Comparing Public Policies.* Beverly Hills: Sage, 1978.

Tharakan, P. K. M. ed. *Intra-Industry Trade.* Amsterdam: North Holland, 1983.

The Economist. Various issues.

The New York Times. Various issues.

The Uncommon Market. London: Economist, 1977.

Thompson, E. P. *The Making of the English Working Class.* New York: Vintage, 1963.

Thurow, Lester. *The Zero-Sum Society.* New York: Penguin, 1980.

Tilly, Charles. *The Formation of the National State in Europe.* Princeton: Princeton University Press, 1975.

Tolchin, Susan and Martin Tolchin. *Dismantling America: the Rush to Deregulate.* New York: Oxford, 1983.

Toyota Motor Company. Annual Report, various years.

Trades Union Congress [TUC]. *Economic Review, 1982 [1983].* London: 1982 [1983].

Tufte, Edward. *Political Control of the Economy.* Princeton: Princeton University Press, 1978.

United Nations. Center on Transnational Corporations. *Transnational Corporations in the International Auto Industry.* New York: UN, 1983.

U.S. Congress. Congressional Budget Office. *Current Problems of the U.S. Auto Industry and Policies to Address Them.* Washington: GPO, 1980.

U.S. Congress. Joint Economic Committee. *Economic Indicators.* Washington: GPO, various issues.

U.S. Congress. Joint Economic Committee. *Industrial Policy: the Retraining Needs of the Nation's Long-Term Structurally Unemployed Workers,* Hearings September 16, 23, & 26, October 26, 1983. Washington: GPO, 1984.

U.S. Congress. Joint Economic Committee. *Japanese and American Economic Policies and U.S. Productivity.* Washington: GPO, 1981.

U.S. Congress. Joint Economic Committee. *Monetary Policy, Selective Credit Policy, and Industrial Policy in France, Britain, West Germany, and Sweden.* Washington: GPO, 1981.

U.S. Congress. Joint Economic Committee. *The Corporate Tax Code as Industrial Policy.* Washington, D.C.: GPO, 1984.

U.S. Congress. Joint Economic Committee. *U.S. International Economic Policy in the 1980s.* Washington: GPO, 1982.

U.S. Department of Commerce. *International Economic Indicators.* Washington: GPO, various years.

U.S. Department of Transportation. *The U.S. Automotive Industry, 1980 [& 1981].* Washington: GPO, 1981 [& 1982].

U.S. House of Representatives. *Report of the Chrysler Corporation Loan Guarantee Board, 1980.* Washington: GPO, 1980.

U.S. Congress. House of Representatives. Committee on the Budget. *Non- Means-Tested Entitlement Reform Programs.* Washington: GPO, 1983.

U.S. House of Representatives. Committee on Government Operations. *The Administration's Proposals to Help the U.S. Auto Industry.* Washington: GPO, 1981.

U.S. House of Representatives. Committee on Science and Technology. *Federal Role in Developing Automotive Technology.* Washington: GPO, 1981.

U.S. House of Representatives. Committee on Science and Technology. *Federal Role in Developing Automotive Technology.* Washington: GPO, 1981.

U.S. Senate. Committee on Banking, Housing and Urban Affairs. *The Automobile Industry and the World Economy.* Washington: GPO, 1980.

U.S. Senate. Committee on Commerce, Science, and Transportation. *Government Regulations Affecting the U.S. Automobile Industry.* Washington: GPO, 1981.

U.S. Senate. Committee on Finance. *Issues Relating to the Domestic Auto Industry.* Washington: GPO, 1981.

U.S. Senate. Committee on Foreign Relations. *Direct Investment Abroad and the Multinationals: Effects on the U.S. Economy,* by Peggy Musgrave. Washington: GPO, 1975.

U.S. Senate. Committee on Labor and Human Resources. *Employment and the American Automobile Industry, 1982.* Washington: GPO, 1982.

U.S. Senate. Committee on the Budget. *Industrial Growth and Productivity.* Washington: GPO, 1981.

Vernon, Raymond, ed. *Big Business and the State: Changing Relations in Western Europe.* Cambridge: Harvard University Press, 1974.

Vernon, Raymond and Louis T. Wells Jr. *Economic Environment of International Business.* Englewood Cliffs: Prentice-Hall, 1972.

Vernon, Raymond. "International Investment and International Trade in the Product Cycle." *Quarterly Journal of Economics.* February 1966. Volume 80.

Vig, Norman and Steven Schier. *Political Economy in Western Democracies.* New York: Holmes and Meier, 1985.

Vogel, David. *National Styles of Regulation*. Ithaca: Cornell, 1986.

Vogel, David. "Why Businessmen Mistrust Their State." *British Journal of Political Science*. (January 1978) 8:45–78.

Volpe, John. *Industrial Incentive Policies and Programs in the Canadian- American Context*. Montreal: Howe, 1975.

Whitman, Marina. v.n. *International Trade and Investment*. Princeton: Essays in International Trade and Finance, no. 143, 1981.

Wall Street Journal. Various issues.

Ward's Automotive Yearbook. Various yearly issues.

Ward's Auto Report. Various issues.

Ward, J. Scott. *The Changing Face of the UK Component Industry*. London: EIU Special Report no. 91, 1981.

Watanabe, Susumu. "Labor-Saving Versus Work-Amplifying Effects of Micro- Electronics." *International Labour Review*. (May-June 1986). 125(3):243–59.

Weber, Max. *Economy and Society*. Günther Roth and Claus Wittich, eds. Berkeley: California, 1978.

Weber, Max. *The Methodology of the Social Sciences*. Edward Shils and Henry Finch, trans. Glencoe, Ill.: Free Press, 1949.

Weber, Max. *The Protestant Ethic and the Spirit of Capitalism*. Foreword by Anthony Giddens. New York: Scribner's, 1976.

Weidenbaum, Murray. *Business, Government, and the Public*, 3d ed. Englewood Cliffs: Prentice-Hall, 1986.

Weidenbaum, Murray. "The High Cost of Government Regulation." *Challenge*. November 1979, pp. 32–39.

Weisskopf, Thomas. "Marxist Perspectives on Cyclical Crises." In *U.S. Capitalism in Crisis*, Special Issue of URPE, 1978.

Weitzman, Martin. *The Share Economy*, Cambridge: Harvard, 1984.

Wells, Louis T., Jr. "The International Product Life Cycle." In Douglas Ginsburg and William Abernathy, eds. *Government, Technology, and the Future of the Automobile*. New York: McGraw-Hill, 1980.

Westin, Alan F. *The Anatomy of a Constitutional Law Case*. New York: MacMillan, 1958.

White, Kenneth J. and Nancy G. Horsman. *Shazam: User's Reference Manual.* Vancouver: University of British Columbia, 1985.

White, Lawrence. "Automobile Emissions Control Policy." In Douglas Ginsburg and William Abernathy, eds. *Government, Technology, and the Future of the Automobile.* New York: McGraw-Hill, 1980.

White, Lawrence. "The Motor Vehicle Industry." In Richard Nelson, ed. *Government and Technical Progress.* New York: Pergamon, 1982.

Wildavsky, Aaron. *Budgeting: A Comparative Theory of Budgetary Process.* Boston: Little, Brown, 1975.

Wilensky, Harold. *The Welfare State and Equality.* Berkeley: University of California Press, 1975.

Wilks, Stephen. *Industrial Policy and the Motor Industry.* Manchester, U.K.: Manchester University Press, 1984.

Wilks, Stephen. "Planning Agreements: The Making of a Paper Tiger." *Public Administration.* (Winter 1981) 59:399–420.

Wilks, Stephen. "The Practice of the Theory of Industrial Adaptation." *Government and Opposition.* (Autumn 1984) 19:451–70.

Williams, Karel et al. *Why Are the British So Bad at Manufacturing?* London: Routledge, 1983.

Willman, Paul and Graham Winch. *Innovation and Management Control.* Cambridge: Cambridge University Press, 1985.

Wilson, James Q. "The Dead Hand of Regulation." *The Public Interest.* (Fall 1971) 25:39–58.

Winham, Gilbert R. *The Automobile Trade Crisis of 1980.* Halifax: Dalhousie, 1981.

Wolfe, Alan. *America's Impasse.* New York: Pantheon, 1981.

Woolley, John T. *Monetary Politics.* N. Y.: Cambridge, 1983.

Womack, James. *The Competitive Significance of National Financial Systems in the Auto Sector.* Cambridge: MIT, Future of the Automobile Program, 1982.

Wright, Eric Olin. "Alternative Perspectives in Marxist Theory of Accumulation." In Jesse Schwartz, ed. *The Subtle Anatomy of Capitalism.* Santa Monica: Goodyear, 1977.

Yaffie, David. "The Crisis of Profitability." *New Left Review.* (1973) 80:45–62.

Yago, Glenn. *The Decline of Transit.* New York: Cambridge University Press, 1980.

Yoffie, David. "Orderly Marketing Agreements as Industrial Policy." *Public Policy.* (Winter 1981). 9(29):93–119.

Yost, George. "Safe Harbor Leasing: The New Tax Haven." *The Tax Executive.* January 1983. 85–101.

Young, Steven and Neil Hood. *Chrysler, U.K.: A Corporation in Transition.* London: Praeger, 1977.

Young, Steven and A. Lowe. *Intervention in a Mixed Economy: The Evolution of British Industrial Policy, 1964–1972.* London: Croom Helm, 1974.

Zeitlin, Maurice, ed. *Classes, Class Conflict, and the State.* Cambridge, Mass.: Winthrop, 1980.

Zysman, John. *Governments, Markets, and Growth.* Ithaca: Cornell University Press, 1983.

INDEX